Lecture Notes of the Institute for Computer Sciences, Social Informatics and Telecommunications Engineering 397

More information about this series at http://www.springer.com/series/8197

Xianbin Wang · Kai-Kit Wong · Shanji Chen ·
Mingqian Liu (Eds.)

Artificial Intelligence for Communications and Networks

Third EAI International Conference, AICON 2021
Xining, China, October 23–24, 2021
Proceedings, Part II

Springer

Editors
Xianbin Wang 🄳
The University of Western Ontario
London, ON, Canada

Kai-Kit Wong 🄳
University College London
London, UK

Shanji Chen
Qinghai University for Nationalities
Xining, China

Mingqian Liu 🄳
Xidian University
Xi'an, China

ISSN 1867-8211   ISSN 1867-822X (electronic)
Lecture Notes of the Institute for Computer Sciences, Social Informatics
and Telecommunications Engineering
ISBN 978-3-030-90198-1   ISBN 978-3-030-90199-8 (eBook)
https://doi.org/10.1007/978-3-030-90199-8

This Springer imprint is published by the registered company Springer Nature Switzerland AG
The registered company address is: Gewerbestrasse 11, 6330 Cham, Switzerland

Preface

We are delighted to introduce the proceedings of the second edition of the European Alliance for Innovation (EAI) International Conference on Artificial Intelligence for Communications and Networks (AICON 2021), which was held in Xining, China, October 23–24, 2021. This conference aims to stimulate debate and provide a forum for researchers working on related problems to exchange ideas and recent results (both positive and negative ones) in applying artificial intelligence to communications and networks. The artificial intelligence based approach may offer some new design approaches for traditionally difficult information and signal processing tasks in wireless communication, networking, and computing.

The technical program of AICON 2021consisted of 81 full papers, including the five best papers, in oral presentation sessions at the main conference tracks: Track 1: Deep Learning/Machine Learning on Information and Signal Processing; Track 2: Artificial Intelligence in Wireless Communications and Satellite Communications; Track 3: Artificial Intelligence in Electromagnetic Signal Processing; Track 4: Artificial Intelligence Application in Wireless Caching and Computing; Track 5: Artificial Intelligence Application in Computer Network; and Track 6: Advances in AI and Their Applications in Information, Circuit, Microwave and Control. Aside from the high-quality technical paper presentations, the technical program also featured three keynote speeches given by Nan Zhao from the Dalian University of Technology, China, Yunfei Chen from the University of Warwick, UK, and Jie Tang from the South China University of Technology, China.

Coordination with the steering chairs, Imrich Chlamtac, Xuemai Gu, and Cheng Li, was essential for the success of the conference. We sincerely appreciate their constant support and guidance. It was also a great pleasure to work with such an excellent organizing committee team for their hard work in organizing and supporting the conference. In particular, the Technical Program Committee, who completed the peer-review process for technical papers and put together a high-quality technical program. We are also grateful to Conference Manager Aleksandra Sledziejowska for her support and to all the authors who submitted their papers to the AICON 2021 conference.

We would like to express our thanks to all members of the organizing committee and all the volunteer reviewers who worked so hard, day and night, for this conference. We would like also to express our gratitude for the sponsorship from various sources. Finally, we are grateful to EAI for sponsoring this conference.

October 2021

Xianbin Wang
Kai-Kit Wong

Organization

Steering Committee

Imrich Chlamtac	University of Trento, Italy
Xuemai Gu	Harbin Institute of Technology, China
Cheng Li	Memorial University of Newfoundland, Canada

Organizing Committee

General Chair

Gang Wang — Qinghai Nationalities University, China

General Co-chairs

Xianbin Wang	Western University, Canada
Kai-Kit Wong	University College London, UK
Shanji Chen	Qinghai Nationalities University, China

Technical Program Committee Co-chairs

Mingqian Liu	Xidian University, China
Tiankui Zhang	Beijing University of Posts and Telecommunications, China
Gongliang Liu	Harbin Institute of Technology, China

Sponsorship and Exhibit Chair

Ying Ma — Qinghai Nationalities University, China

Local Chair

Lingfei Zhang — Qinghai Nationalities University, China

Workshops Chair

Bo Li — Harbin Institute of Technology, China

Publicity and Social Media Chair

Guilian Feng — Qinghai Nationalities University, China

Publications Chair

Weidang Lu   Zhejiang University of Technology, China

Web Chair

Zhutian Yang   Harbin Institute of Technology, China

Posters and PhD Track Chair

Qian Lin   Qinghai Nationalities University, China

Tutorials Chair

Tao Wang   Qinghai Nationalities University, China

Technical Program Committee

Jin Li	Xidian University, China
Junlin Zhang	Xidian University, China
Junfang Li	Xi'an Aeronautical University, China
Nan Qu	Xidian University, China
Bodong Shang	Virginia Tech, USA
Fangfang Liu	Beijing University of Posts and Telecommunications, China
Yang Yang	Beijing University of Posts and Telecommunications, China
Yu Xu	Beijing University of Posts and Telecommunications, China
Guangyu Zhu	Beijing University of Posts and Telecommunications, China
Yuanpeng Zheng	Beijing University of Posts and Telecommunications, China
Qihang Cao	Harbin Institute of Technology, China
Yangfei Liu	Harbin Institute of Technology, China
Mingyi Wang	Harbin Institute of Technology, China
Ziqi Sun	Harbin Institute of Technology, China
Jianrui Lu	Harbin Institute of Technology, China
Hang Yuan	Xidian University, China
Ke Yang	Xidian University, China
Lei Jin	Xidian University, China
Jiakui Wang	Xidian University, China
Zhiyang Gao	Xidian University, China
Yaqi Fan	Xidian University, China
Han Zhu	Xidian University, China

Huigui Cheng	Xidian University, China
Sihao Qin	Xidian University, China
Meng Cao	Xidian University, China
Yuanpo Cai	Xidian University, China
Zhenju Zhang	Xidian University, China
Chen Fan	Xidian University, China
Tianming Yang	Xidian University, China
Yifan Zhang	Xidian University, China
Hongyi Zhang	Xidian University, China
Xinge Bao	Xidian University, China
Yi Wang	Xidian University, China

Contents – Part II

Advances in AI and Their Applications in Information, Circuit, Microwave and Control

Contents – Part I

Artificial Intelligence in Electromagnetic Signal Processing

Artificial Intelligence Application in Wireless Caching and Computing

Artificial Intelligence Application in Computer Network

Information Security Defense Evaluation Based on Bayesian Network

Bao-feng Hui[✉] and Yuan-liang Ma

School of Physics and Electronic Information Engineering, Qinghai Minzu University, Xining 810007, China

Abstract. With development of global informatization, increasingly rampant information security event has caused wide attention of people to information security problem. However, current information security technology based on traditional defense technology is hard to deal with it. Therefore, experts of information security start to focus on information security technology research based on active defense thought. At present, research on information security defense technology mainly focuses on active defense for information security relevant to security situation evaluation and security threat prediction. From the perspective of technology, based on Bayes Model, research has been implemented to security situation evaluation method in information security field and attack route prediction method. Put forward a kind of evaluation method for evaluating overall system security and vulnerabilities severity degree, which can effectively evaluate overall system security and vulnerabilities severity degree, firstly, put forward a kind of Cause Result Detection Algorithm (CRDA) to confirm causal relationship; secondly, provide Bayes Attach Diagram and provide generation algorithm BAGA of BAG according to system structure of attack model; finally, it is proved that the method can effectively solve error calculation problem of node confidence coefficient by experiment to accurately predict transmission route of network threat.

Keywords: Bayes · Network security · Defense · Evaluation

1 Introduction

This Paper has put forward network security situation evaluation model based on Bayes Network because traditional network security evaluation model cannot perceive network security situation. The situation evaluation model is divided into 3 layer structure according to function. Node of Bayes Network shall be divided into situation node and event node according to function; take network and information acquisition of host tool as evidence of event node by network reasoning process to update situation node probability and to influence probability of event node in return, so as to confirm network security situation. Network space attack information security defense situation is to establish dynamic Bayes Network to evaluate network space attack situation for evaluation aiming at situation evaluation concept put forward by network center station, which can

X. Wang et al. (Eds.): AICON 2021, LNICST 397, pp. 3–7, 2021.
https://doi.org/10.1007/978-3-030-90199-8_1

feed back information to deciders quickly, effectively and visually and provide a kind of efficient informatization assisting decision and support, so that information security defense system can take effect better and can better promote resistance of information system for development of the new resistance mode. domestic researches in the field are still in starting stage and research methods are not very specific, which aims at implementing static evaluation to information security defense system of war field network and analysis on unknown threat is not thorough, so that situation evaluation is hard to be dynamic, autonomous and controllable and hard to know influence of unknown and uncertain information on information security situation. Fuzzy Dynamic Bayesian Network (Fuzzy Dynamic Bayesian Network) is a development direction in space situation evaluation field method application. When situation information acquired by sensor is fuzzy and uncertain on time sequence, influence caused by middle information change in the whole war field network system can be perceived and evaluated continuously, which can provide a more active and accurate quantitative analysis and assistant decision means for problem solving for grasping and research and judgment of situation during network space information security defense.

2 Information Security Assessment

Characteristics of network war information security defense decide relatively strong timeliness and co-movement of its situation evaluation process; namely, it has realized continuous perception and analysis on security situation of its own network at certain time node and has realized evaluation and warning to future security situation and process includes two parts of situation perception and threat evaluation, which is comprehensive reflection of all situation factors in information security defense and all factors are closely connected and a situation factor usually constrains and influences other factors in defense process; therefore, it shall take dependency, dynamics, uncertainty and continuity among target network situation factors into consideration during dynamic evaluation, so as to analyze its causal association. Therefore, connect all situation factors in information security defense to establish layer relationship and acquire all factors to be considered for threat evaluation by situation perception means; predict potential threat event according to security event probability prediction at known moment and evaluate for monitoring information security defense situation to predict development trend of information security defense.

3 Bayesian Network Derivation and Fuzzy Comprehensive Evaluation

3.1 Cause of Selecting Dynamic Bayes Network

Dynamic Bayes Network (DBN) is time sequence of Bayes Network (BN), which has function characteristics of Static Bayes Network and has embodied influence of sample data on network structure more accurately in time domain and the method is applicable to influence evaluation of situation factor change in information security defense situation of network space war on the whole defense system. Integrate time sequence casual association at adjacent time section with casual association of the same time section and implement dynamic analysis by quantization inference and DBN can be simply defined as $(B_0, B_\rightarrow)$; B_0 is BN at T0 (time section of initial condition) and prior probability P(X0) of hidden node and observation point can be got from BN structure and is diagram formed by BN at all time sections.

DBN has the functions of integrating new knowledge and expressing, interfering and learning matters and has relatively favorable effect during modeling analysis for uncertain problems of radon process nature and network structure of DBN is shown as Fig. 1:

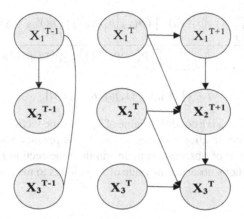

Fig. 1. Dynamic Bayes network structure

3.2 Inference Algorithm of DBN

DBN inference algorithm is inferred from Bayes Formula of Formula (1):

$$p(x|y) = \frac{p(yx)}{p(y)} = \frac{p(yx)}{\sum_x p(yx)} \qquad (1)$$

Its inference process is the same with essence of Static Bayes Network. For disperse Static Bayes Network with n hidden nodes and m observation nodes, according to condition independence characteristics, its inference principle can be reflected into math process of formula (2):

$$p(x_1, x_2, ..., x_n | y1, y2, ..., y_m)$$

$$= \frac{\prod_j p(y_j | p_a(Y_j)) \prod_i p(x_i | p_a(X_i))}{\sum_{x_1, x_2, ..., x_n} \prod_j p(yj | p_a(Yj)) \prod_i p(x_i | p_a(X_i))}$$

$$i \in [1, n], j \in [1, m] \qquad (2)$$

In above formula, x_i is a condition value X_i and $p_a(Y_j)$ shows parent node collection of Y_j.

(3): When hidden nodes and observable nodes are few or coupling of nodes is relatively strong; network structure layers are relatively few and time sections to be considered are few in network, all time sections of DBN can be deemed as a Static Bayes Network; when nodes increase or node coupling performance increases, DBN formed by time sections of the number of T in time domain can be obtained, of which inference process can be reflected in formula (3):

$$p(x_{11}, ..., x_{1n}, ..., x_{T1}, ..., x_{Tn}|Y_{11o}, Y_{12o}, ..., Y_{1mo}, ..., Y_{T1o}, Y_{T2o}, Y_{Tmo})$$

$$= \sum_{y_{11}y_{12}...y_{Tm}} \frac{\prod_{i,j} p(y_{ij}|p_a(Y_{ij})) \prod_{i,k} p(x_{ik}|p_a(X_{ik})) \prod_{i,j} p(Y_{ijo} = y_{ijo})}{\sum_{x_{11},x_{21},...,x_{T1}...x_{Tn}} \prod_{i,j} p(y_{ij}|p_a(Y_{ij})) \prod_{i,k} p(x_{ik}|p_a(X_{ik}))}$$

$$i \in [1, T], j \in [1, m], K \in [1, n] \tag{3}$$

In foresaid formula, x_{ij} is a condition value of X_{ij}; i is time section; j represents hidden nodes; y_{ij} is value of observation variance Y_{ij}; $p_a(Y_{ij})$ is parent node collection y_{ij}; Y_{ijo} is observation condition of observation node j in the time section i and $p(Y_{ijo} = y_{ijo})$ represents that continuous observation value of Y_{ij} belongs to membership of condition y_{ij}.

3.3 Cause of Selecting Fuzzy Comprehensive Evaluation Method

Fuzzy comprehensive evaluation analyzes complex fuzzy system by applying fuzzy conversion principle, which is used to multi-attribute decision-making problems and make comprehensive decision to problems by analysis and fuzzy judgment of quantization and quantification on considerable complex influence factors. Evaluation index set of information security defense situation of network space can be taken as a multi-index evaluation problem and index factor to be established shall be analyzed comprehensively in multi-layer and multi-factor ways and all-layer situation index of evaluation network established and complexity degree is high; therefore, it adapts to such method.

4 Conclusion

It is hard to implement accurate, autonomous and complete controllable evaluation to information security defense situation in network space war; dynamic valuation method based on fuzzy DBN is put forward aiming at such condition so as to implement fuzzy and probability disposal of situation factors in defense system under different time condition and to establish situation perception and situation estimation model Input initial condition probability, condition transfer probability and observation data to model established for simulation experiment and compare simulation result with Static Bayes Network model evaluation result and experiment result shows that evaluation by this methods has integrated feedback relation and observation information among more situation factors and can better reflect objective principle of dynamic change of network space war information security defense situation and can ensure accurate, quick, active and efficient evaluation.

Acknowledgement. This work was supported by the Key R&D and transformation projects of Qinghai (2021-GX-01) and Project of Qinghai Nationalities University (2021XJGH02).

1. References

1. Jia, H., Kikumoto, H.: Source term estimation in complex urban environments based on Bayesian inference and unsteady adjoint equations simulated via large eddy simulation. Build. Environ. **193**, 107669 (2021)
2. Baofeng, H., Guoqing, J., Shanji, C.: Random response privacy data mining based on cloud computing resource association rules. In: Proceedings of 2018 4th International Conference on Education, Management and Information Technology (ICEMIT) (2018)
3. Tian, M., Dong, Z., Wang, X.: Analysis of false data injection attacks in power systems: a dynamic Bayesian game-theoretic approach. ISA Trans. **115**, 108–123 (2021)
4. Zinetullina, A., Yang, M., Khakzad, N., Golman, B., Li, X.: Quantitative resilience assessment of chemical process systems using functional resonance analysis method and dynamic Bayesian network. Reliab. Eng. Syst. Saf. **205**, 107231 (2021)
5. Gomes, I.P., Wolf, D.F.: Health monitoring system for autonomous vehicles using dynamic Bayesian networks for diagnosis and prognosis. J. Intell. Rob. Syst. **101**(1), 1–21 (2020)
6. Machine Learning; New Machine Learning Study Findings Recently Were Reported by Researchers at Nanyang Technological University (Estimating Travel Time Distributions by Bayesian Network Inference). J. Rob. Mach. Learn. (2020)
7. Chen, J., et al.: shinyBN: an online application for interactive Bayesian network inference and visualization. BMC Bioinf. **20**(1), 1–5 (2019)

Time Allocation in Multi-UAV Energy Harvesting Network

Yuchen Li[1], Cong Zhou[1(✉)], Shuo Shi[1,2], and Zhenyu Xu[3]

[1] Harbin Institute of Technology, 150001 Harbin, China
crcss@hit.edu.cn
[2] International Innovation Institute of HIT in Huizhou, 516000 Guangdong, China
[3] Huizhou Engineering Vocational College, 516023 Guangdong, China

Abstract. To handle the problem of energy scarcity and make up for the lack of working ability of single unmanned aerial vehicle (UAV), we studies the time allocation problem in multi-UAV energy harvesting network. In order to get the nodes which each UAV communicates with, we propose a node allocation scheme based on Kuhn-Munkres (KM) algorithm, and give the trajectory of multiple UAVs. Selection weight is designed to make the UAV select next node according to the shortest moving distance. Then we use convex optimization method to get the dual problem of the optimization problem and solve the time allocation problem which maximizes the system throughput. Finally, the simulation results show that our node assignment scheme can achieve better system performance than clustering node assignment scheme.

Keywords: Multi-UAV · Energy harvesting · Convex optimization · Time allocation

1 Introduction

Energy harvesting technology is proposed in order to alleviate energy shortage problem caused by the increase quantity of equipment [1–3]. Devices harvest the surrounding energy through energy harvesting technology, so as to avoid the human and material resources consumption caused by frequent battery replacement. This paper studies the radio frequency (RF) energy harvesting technology. The equipment receives RF signals and converts them into electrical energy through the rectifier circuit, afterwords, energy is stored in the battery or directly used for signal transmission. When device is in weak coverage area, surrounding RF energy is insufficient, thus device is facing the problems of energy consumption and data transmission difficulties. Therefore, in recent years, many scholars combine unmanned aerial vehicle (UAV) with energy harvesting technology [4–7]. UAV is regarded as a mobile base station (BS), which solves the problem of energy shortage in weak coverage area and helps information collection by using the mobility and flexible deployment ability of UAV.

Energy harvesting network with single UAV has become a research hotspot in recent years. [8] studies both one-dimensional and two-dimensional wireless

X. Wang et al. (Eds.): AICON 2021, LNICST 397, pp. 8–19, 2021.
https://doi.org/10.1007/978-3-030-90199-8_2

power transfer model. In order to maximize the harvested energy, the system optimizes the location of UAV and takes the energy consumption of UAV into consideration. W. Feng also aims to find the maximum energy and optimize the three-dimensional coordinates, beam pattern and charging time [9]. S. Cho et al. use UAV to assist remote nodes harvesting energy. Time allocation is optimized to achieve the maximun throughput [10]. The author maximizes the minimum energy received by the node to solve the "far and near problem" in [11]. The successive hover-and-fly trajectory design is proposed in this paper. M. Nguyen et al. studies the model of UAV charging D2D network with wireless signal and optimizes time allocation and the transmission power of D2D to obtain the maximum energy efficiency [12]. Most of the above articles are about the resource allocation optimization of energy harvesting network with single UAV. At the same time, the trajectory of UAV will be optimized when the system performance is optimized.

The combination of multi UAV and communication network has attracted people's attention recently. [13] uses multiple UAV as cooperative relay network to help the communication between transmitters and receivers. The maximum throughput of the receiver is found by optimizing UAV's location, node's powers and bandwidth allocation. D. Liu studies relay selection in multi-channel multi-radio UAV networks based on game model. Channel and radio selection is also studied to optimize the data transmission rate [14]. Two UAV selection strategies is proposed in [15] and the influence of two selection strategies on system performance is compared in simulation. R. Chen maximize the capacity of UAV from the perspective of coverage. Number and location of UAV is optimized [16]. Multi-UAV target assignment and path planning problem is studied in [17] and reinforcement learning method is used to fix the problem. UAV selection or task allocation is one of the research focuses of multi UAV Communication Network. In addition, trajectory planning of multiple UAVs is also a valuable research topic. The current multi UAV network selection strategies are complex, so they are not suitable for large-scale UAV networks.

Considering that UAV is also energy limited devices, the endurance of a single UAV is poor, and it is unable to complete the task of energy transmission and data collection in a large area. Therefore multi UAV energy harvesting network is a valuable research area. At present, there are few researches on multi UAV assisted energy harvesting network. By referring to the relevant literature of multi-UAV in communication network, we established the model of multi-UAV energy harvesting network. We propose a node assignment method suitable for large-scale UAV network and optimize the time allocation strategy.

The main contributions of this paper are as follows:

- We propose a node assignment scheme with KM algorithm. The node assignment algorithm selects the nodes that each UAV is communicate with in multi-UAV energy harvesting network.
- We considering that UAV is an energy limited device, the trajectory of UAV is designed to minimize the flight distance of UAV in multi-UAV energy harvesting network.

– We designed a time allocation scheme in multi-UAV energy harvesting network to handle the tradeoff betweenl energy harvesting and data transmission time.

The rest of the article is arranged as follows. Section II establishes the muiti-UAV energy harvesting network model and the time allocation scheme. Section III gives the nodes assignment scheme based on KM algorithm and performs the multi-UAV trajectory design. Section V gets the optimal time allocation scheme to maximize system throughput. Section VI shows simulation results. Section VII conclude the paper.

2   System Model

2.1   Multi-UAV Energy Harvesting Network

In this Multi-UAV energy harvesting network, M UAVs are acting as aerial BSs in order to provide energy supply for N nodes which have difficulty replacing batteries. After harvesting enough energy, nodes transmit information signal back to their target UAVs. As Fig. 1 shows, we assume that one node communicate with only one UAV but one UAV can charge many nodes one by one.

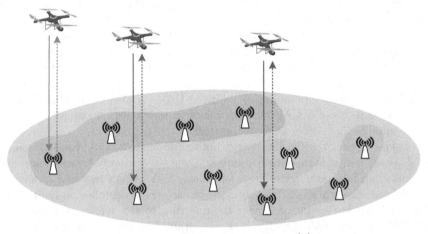

Fig. 1. System model of multi-UAV energy harvesting network with 3 UAVs and 10 nodes.

UAVs follow the successive hover-and-fly trajectory design. Each UAV is responsible for transmitting energy to a series of nodes, and the nodes covered by each UAV are not coincident. After determining the corresponding nodes, UAV traverses these nodes one by one. When flying to the top of the node, the distance between the UAV and the node is the shortest, and the path loss is the smallest, so the channel condition is the best. UAV hovers at this position and performs downlink energy transmission and uplink data collection. Assuming that the total working time T of each UAV is the same, and the time allocation scheme of UAV i is shown as Fig. 2.

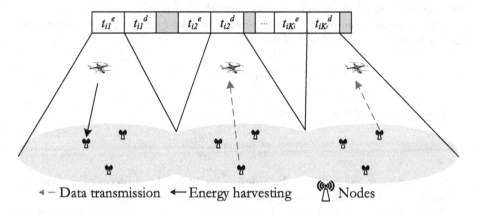

Fig. 2. Time allocation scheme of UAV i with energy harvesting time, data transmission time and flying time.

If the number of nodes communicate with UAV $i(i = 1, 2, ..., M)$ is K_i and we have $\sum_{i=1}^{M} K_i = N$, the time restriction of UAV i is given as

$$\sum_{k=1}^{K_i} t_{ik}^e + \sum_{k=1}^{K_i} t_{ik}^d \leq T - tf_i, \tag{1}$$

where t_{ik}^e refers to the energy harvesting time from UAV i to node k, and t_{ik}^d is the data transmission time from node k to UAV i. tf_i denotes the flight time of UAV i and can be calculated by

$$tf_i = \frac{\sum_{k=1}^{K_i-1} d_{k,k+1}}{v_i} \tag{2}$$

where $d_{k,k+1}$ is the distance between node k and node $k + 1$. v_i is the speed of UAV i.

2.2 Energy Harvesting and Data Transmission Model

UAV transmits energy signal to node during the energy harvesting time and the energy harvested by node k from UAV i can be expressed as

$$E_{ik} = t_{ik}^e Pu_i h d_{ik}^{-\alpha} \tag{3}$$

in which Pu_i is the transmitting power of UAV i, h represents the channel gain and d_{ik} is the distance between UAV i and node k. According to the flight mode of UAV in Sect. 2.1, d_{ik} is the flight altitude of UAV. In this paper, we assume that the flight altitude of UAV is constant. The energy harvesting model follows the path loss model in communication network.

After receiving the energy, node perform wireless information transfer and the transmitting power of node k is

$$Pn_k = \frac{E_{ik}}{t_{ik}^d} \tag{4}$$

Thus the throughput of node k is given as

$$R_k = t_{ik}^d ln(1 + \frac{Pn_k}{\sigma^2}) \tag{5}$$

where σ^2 refers to noise power. In order to facilitate the subsequent derivation calculation, we take nat as the unit of throughput.

We intend to design an optimal time allocation scheme to solve the tradeoff problem between energy harvesting time and data transmission time in order to maximum sum throughput of the system. After confirming the ground nodes that each UAV is connected with, there is no other correlation between each UAV except that the tracks of each other do not collide. Therefore, when optimizing the overall throughput of the multi-UAV energy harvesting network, it is equivalent to optimizing the time allocation scheme of each UAV separately. Thus the optimization problem is designed as maximum the throughput of UAV i:

$$P1 : \max_{t_{ik}^e, t_{ik}^d} \sum_{k=1}^{K_i} R_k$$

$$s.t.C1 : \sum_{k=1}^{K_i} t_{ik}^e + \sum_{k=1}^{K_i} t_{ik}^d \leq T - tf_i \tag{6}$$

$$C2 : t_{ik}^e \geq 0$$

$$C3 : t_{ik}^d \geq 0$$

C1, C2, C3 are three time constraints and considering that each UAV is responsible for different nodes, even if their trajectory has intersection, the probability of two UAVs reaching the same intersection at the same time is very small, so in order to facilitate the subsequent calculation, trajectory collision is not considered in the optimization problem above.

3   Nodes Assignment and Multi-UAV Trajectory Design

3.1   Nodes Assignment Scheme with KM Algorithm

In order to solve the optimization problem P1, first we need to solve a node assignment problem, that is to decide the nodes each UAV communicates with respectively. The result of nodes assignment determines the value of K_i and tf_i in P1 and thus will affect the optimization results. Otherwise, after the nodes covered by UAV are determined, the flying distance of UAV is also determined. UAV is a device with limited energy, so when performing nodes assignment, we want to make path length as the target.

Kuhn-Munkres (KM) algorithm is designed to fix the maximum weight matching problem in bipartite graph. Consider that there are two vertex sets. The left vertex set can match the right vertex set with a certain weight. KM algorithm can get a matching result which maximize the overall weight. Taking UAVs and nodes as two vertex sets, KM algorithm can find the nodes assignment result with the shortest path length.

In KM algorithm, the number of the members in two vertex sets is the same. Every member in left set can match a member in right set and vice versa. However, in our multi-UAV energy harvesting network, the number of UAVs is less than the number of nodes. Thus we sort the nodes according to the distance from the origin, and then each M nodes are divided into a group. The group is denoted as $N_1, N_2,...,N_n$. There is M nodes in the first $n-1$ group. And in N_n, the number of nodes is the remainder M_r of N divided by M. M UAVs fly from the origin to N_1 group and then use KM alorithm to pick next target node in N_2 group. According to the characteristics of KM algorithm to maximize the sum weight, we define the reciprocal of the distance from current position of each UAV to the position of each node in the next node group as the weight to get the shortest path length in each node selection. In order to ensure that the weight is an integer, sometimes the above results need to multiply a certain amplification factor θ. Thus the expression of weight is

$$w_{ij}^{N_m} = \theta \frac{1}{d_{ij}}, i, j = 1, 2, ..., M, m = 1, 2, ..., n-1 \qquad (7)$$

$$w_{ij}^{N_n} = \begin{cases} \theta \frac{1}{d_{ij}}, i = 1, 2, ..., M, j = 1, 2, ..., M_r \\ 0, i = 1, 2, ..., M, j = M_r + 1, M_r + 2, ..., M \end{cases} \qquad (8)$$

We set up $M - M_r$ virtual nodes to ensure the number of menbers in both sets is the same. The weight is 0 means no UAV wants to connect with these virtual nodes. For the UAV which matches with these virtual nodes, the connecting node in group N_{n-1} will be their last visiting node. The nodes assignment algorithm is given in Algorithm 1.

3.2   Multi-UAV Trajectory Design

After the node assignment is completed according to Algorithm 1. Each UAV defines the serving nodes. Based on the successive hover-and-fly trajectory

---

Algorithm 1: Node Assignment for Multi-UAV Energy Harvesting Network

---

Initialize M, N and the node coordinates. Sort the node according to the distance from origin and group the nodes as N_1, N_2,...,N_n

Make the first group of coordinates of UAVs as the coordinates of nodes in N_1.

repeat

    Calculate the distance from the current position of UAVs to each node in the next group.

    Calculate the weight in KM algorithm. If the group number is less than or equal to $n-1$, equation (7) is used. If the group number is n, equation (8) is used.

    Using KM algorithm to get the node assighment result which is also next target location of UAV.

    Update current position of UAV.

until

All nodes have one UAV to communicate with.

---

design, UAV flys from origin and traverse each node. When flying right above the serving node, UAV hovers at this location performing energy transmitting and data collecting. As Fig. 3 shows, the trajectory of UAV can be seen as the line between origin and serving nodes from proximal to distal.

4   Time Allocation Optimization

According to the node assignment result, K_i and tf_i are two constant in P1. Since the Hessian matrix of the objective function in P1 is positive definite, we use convex optimization method to solve the problem in this section. And the lagrangian of P1 is

$$L(t_{ik}^e, t_{ik}^d, \lambda, \boldsymbol{\mu}, \boldsymbol{\nu}) = \sum_{k=1}^{K_i} R_k$$
$$+ \lambda(\sum_{k=1}^{K_i} t_{ik}^e + \sum_{k=1}^{K_i} t_{ik}^d - T + tf_i) - \sum_{k=1}^{K_i} \mu_k t_{ik}^e - \sum_{k=1}^{K_i} \nu_k t_{ik}^d \tag{9}$$

in which λ, $\boldsymbol{\mu}$, $\boldsymbol{\nu}$ are lagrange multipliers. $\boldsymbol{\mu}$ and $\boldsymbol{\nu}$ are vectors and have $\boldsymbol{\mu} = [\mu_1, \mu_2, ..., \mu_{K_i}]$, $\boldsymbol{\nu} = [\nu_1, \nu_2, ..., \nu_{K_i}]$. lagrange dual function is expressed as

$$g(\lambda, \boldsymbol{\mu}, \boldsymbol{\nu}) = \inf L(t_{ik}^e, t_{ik}^d, \lambda, \boldsymbol{\mu}, \boldsymbol{\nu}). \tag{10}$$

To fix the lagrange dual function, we calculate the partial differential of L and the expressions are

$$\frac{\partial L}{\partial t_{ik}^e} = \frac{1}{1 + \frac{E_{ik}}{t_{ik}^d \sigma^2}} \frac{E_{ik}}{t_{ik}^e} + \lambda - \mu_k, \tag{11}$$

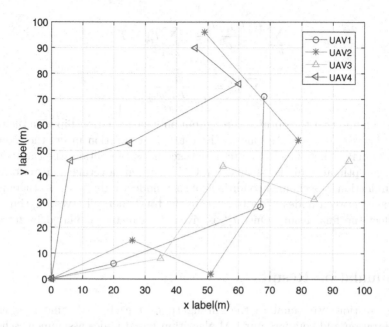

Fig. 3. Trajectory design based on nodes assignment scheme with KM Algorithm for 4 UAVs and 15 nodes.

$$\frac{\partial L}{\partial t_{ik}^d} = ln(1 + \frac{E_{ik}}{t_{ik}^d}) - \frac{1}{1 + \frac{E_{ik}}{t_{ik}^d}} \frac{E_{ik}}{t_{ik}^d} + \lambda - \nu_k. \tag{12}$$

When the optimal solution satisfies KKT condition, we have $\lambda \neq 0, \boldsymbol{\mu} = 0,$ $\boldsymbol{\nu} = 0$. By replacing $\frac{E_{ik}}{t_{ik}^d}$ with x, we have

$$\frac{1}{1 + x} \frac{E_{ik}}{t_{ik}^d} + \lambda = 0, \tag{13}$$

$$ln(1 + x) + \frac{x}{1 + x} + \lambda = 0. \tag{14}$$

Therefore, by solving the following equation, we can get the value of x.

$$ln(1 + x) + \frac{x}{1 + x} = \frac{1}{1 + x} \frac{E_{ik}}{t_{ik}^d} \tag{15}$$

x is the same for all nodes in a group, and we can get the relationship between t_{ik}^e and t_{ik}^d as

$$t_{ik}^d = \frac{t_{ik}^e Pu_i h d_{ik}^{-\alpha}}{x\sigma^2}. \tag{16}$$

According to KKT condition, we have $\sum_{k=1}^{K_i} t_{ik}^e + \sum_{k=1}^{K_i} t_{ik}^d = T - tf_i$. Take formula (16) into the equation, we can get the optimal t_{ik}^e satisfy the following equation:

$$\sum_{k=1}^{K_i} \frac{t_{ik}^{*e} Pu_i hd_{ik}^{-\alpha}}{x\sigma^2} + \sum_{k=1}^{K_i} t_{ik}^e = T, \tag{17}$$

$$\sum_{k=1}^{K_i} t_{ik}^{*e} = \frac{T}{1 + \frac{Pu_i hd_{ik}^{-\alpha}}{x\sigma^2}}. \tag{18}$$

We can find that the optimal throughput only have relationship with the total energy harvesting time. As long as the total time duration meets the requirement, no matter how much time resource each node can obtain, the throughput is always optimal. This is because for UAV i, when hovering and performing communication, the channel conditions of each node are the same, so there is no difference between nodes. How to allocate the total energy harvesting time will not affect the final result. Once t_{ik}^{*} is given, t_{ik}^{*e} can be calculated by formula (16).

5   Simulation Result

In this section, we simulate the throughtput of each UAV under different time duration and compare our KM algorithm based nodes assignment scheme (KMANAS) with clustering nodes assignment scheme (CNAS). The nodes are distributed in the area of $100 * 100$, and 15 nodes' coordinates are randomly generated as (20,6), (26,15), (35,8), (6,46), (51,2), (25,53), (55,44), (67,28), (84,31), (79,54), (60,76), (68,71), (46,90), (95,46) and (49,97). Besides, we set up $Pu_i = 5W$, $d_{ik} = 3m$ and $v_i = 5m/s$.

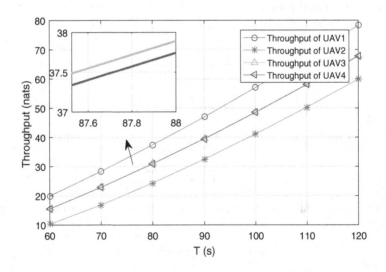

Fig. 4. The throughput of 4 UAVs from $T = 60$ s to $T = 120$ s.

Figure 4 shows the throughput of 4 UAVs with time duration ranging from 60 s to 120 s. The throughput of each UAV is negatively related to its total flight path. The maximum throughput of UAV1 shows that it has the shortest flight path. The close throughput of uav3 and uav4 is due to their close flight path. This is because short flight path means short flight time, thus the time for energy harvesting and data transmitting increase and system can get larger throughput.

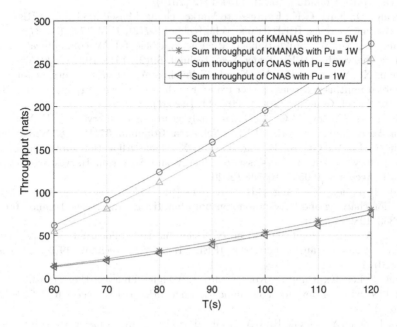

Fig. 5. Sum throughput of KMANAS and CNAS from $T = 60$ s to $T = 120$ s.

Figure 5 shows the sum throughput comparison of our KMANAS and CNAS. Our KMANAS achieves better system performance because it considers the nearest distance of each step, while CNAS only considers the nearest distance of the intermediate nodes, ignoring the path for UAV to take off from the origin.

6   Conclusion

In this paper we optimize the time allocation in multi-UAV energy harvesting network. A node assignment scheme is proposed to help each UAV find its serving nodes based on KM algorithm. UAV selects the next node according to the principle of shortest flight path. The optimal energy harvesting time and data transmission time are obtained based on convex optimization method. The simulation results show the superiority of our node assignment scheme. In the future, we will further refine the grouping method of node selection, so that the node assignment results can improve the system performance.

References

1. Pehlivan, I., Coleri, S.: Joint optimization of energy transfer scheduling and power control in MIMO wireless powered communication networks. IEEE Commun. Lett. **24**(3), 593–597 (2020)
2. Liu, G., Sun, Z., Jiang, T.: Joint time and energy allocation for QoS-aware throughput maximization in mimo-based wireless powered underground sensor networks. IEEE Trans. Commun. **67**(2), 1400–1412 (2019)
3. Altinel, D., Kurt, G.K.: Finite-state Markov channel based modeling of RF energy harvesting systems. IEEE Trans. Veh. Technol. **67**(2), 1713–1725 (2018)
4. Yang, Z., Xu, W., Shikh-Bahaei, M.: Energy efficient UAV communication with energy harvesting. IEEE Trans. Veh. Technol. **69**(2), 1913–1927 (2020)
5. Yuan, X., Yang, T., Hu, Y., Xu, J., Schmeink, A.: Trajectory design for UAV-enabled multiuser wireless power transfer with nonlinear energy harvesting. IEEE Trans. Wirel. Commun. **20**(2), 1105–1121 (2021)
6. Wang, X., Gursoy, M.C.: Coverage analysis for energy-harvesting UAV-assisted mmWave cellular networks. IEEE J. Sel. Areas Commun. **37**(12), 2832–2850 (2019)
7. Shi, S., Li, Y., Gu, S., Huang, T., Gu, X.: Time Allocation Optimization and Trajectory Design in UAV-Assisted Energy and Spectrum Harvesting Network. IEEE Access **8**, 160537–160548 (2020)
8. Yan, H., Chen, Y., Yang, S.H.: UAV-enabled wireless power transfer with base station charging and UAV power consumption. IEEE Trans. Veh. Technol. **69**(11), 12883–12896 (2020)
9. Feng, W., et al.: Joint 3D trajectory design and time allocation for UAV-enabled wireless power transfer networks. IEEE Trans. Veh. Technol. **69**(9), 9265–9278 (2020)
10. Cho, S., Lee, K., Kang, B., Koo, K., Joe, I.: Weighted harvest-then-transmit: UAV-enabled wireless powered communication networks. IEEE Access **6**, 72212–72224 (2018)
11. Xu, J., Zeng, Y., Zhang, R.: UAV-enabled wireless power transfer: trajectory design and energy optimization. IEEE Trans. Wirel. Commun. **17**(8), 5092–5106 (2018)
12. Nguyen, M., Nguyen, L.D., Duong, T.Q., Tuan, H.D.: Real-time optimal resource allocation for embedded UAV communication systems. IEEE Wirel. Commun. Lett. **8**(1), 225–228 (2019)
13. Chen, Q.: Joint position and resource optimization for multi-UAV-aided relaying systems. IEEE Access**8**, 10403–10415 (2020)
14. Liu, D., et al.: Task-driven relay assignment in distributed UAV communication networks. IEEE Trans. Veh. Technol. **68**(11), 11003–11017 (2019)
15. Singh, S.K., Agrawal, K., Singh, K., Li, C.P., Huang, W.J.: On UAV selection and position-based throughput maximization in multi-UAV relaying networks. IEEE Access **8**, 144039–144050 (2020)
16. Chen, R., Li, X., Sun, Y., Li, S., Sun, Z.: Multi-UAV coverage scheme for average capacity maximization. IEEE Commun. Lett. **24**(3), 653–657 (2019)
17. Qie, H., Shi, D., Shen, T., Xu, X., Li, Y., Wang, L.: Joint optimization of multi-UAV target assignment and path planning based on multi-agent reinforcement learning. IEEE Access **7**, 146264–146272 (2019)
18. Arafa, A., Ulukus, S.: Optimal policies for wireless networks with energy harvesting transmitters and receivers: effects of decoding costs. IEEE J. Sel. Areas Commun. **33**(12), 2611–2625 (2015)

19. In, C., Kim, H., Choi, W.: Achievable rate-energy region in two-way decode-and-forward energy harvesting relay systems. IEEE Trans. Commun. **67**(6), 3923–3935 (2019)

20. Rezgui, G., Belmega, E.V., Chorti, A.: Mitigating jamming attacks using energy harvesting. IEEE Wirel. Commun. Lett. **8**(1), 297–300 (2019)

21. Qiu, C., Hu, Y., Chen, Y.: Lyapunov optimized cooperative communications with stochastic energy harvesting relay. IEEE Internet of Things J. **5**(2), 1323–1333 (2018)

22. Deng, F., Yue, X., Fan, X., Guan, S., Xu, Y., Chen, J.: Multisource energy harvesting system for a wireless sensor network node in the field environment. IEEE Internet of Things J. **6**(1), 918–927 (2019)

Positioning Error Modeling with Signal Burst of LEO Constellation

Zhiying Cui[✉], Fuzhan Yue, Run Tian, Shuangna Zhang, and Qijia Dong

Space Star Technology Co., Ltd., Beijing 100095, China

Abstract. In recent years, with the rapid expansion of satellite applications, Global Navigation Satellite System (GNSS) can barely satisfy the increasing demand for precise services. Such that, it becomes a challenge to build a hybrid satellite navigation system to achieve more precise and robust services. With the advantages of less time-delay and less pass-loss, LEO satellite can significantly enhance the accuracy, integrity, availability and anti-interference ability of GNSS, which is expected to break through the bottleneck of global positioning, navigation and timing (PNT) services. Aiming to develop the next generation hybrid satellite navigation system, this paper focuses on the LEO navigation signal's performance analysis. Firstly, we proposes the mathematical model of LEO signal burst, then the estimation error of Doppler and Pseudo-range is derived, and finally, the positioning performance of large-scale LEO constellations is analyzed by STK and MATLAB. The research results of this paper proves the feasibility of LEO satellite navigation and provides a sensible solution for next generation satellite system.

Keywords: LEO navigation · Signal modeling · Doppler error · Pseudo-range error

1 Introduction

GNSS can provide all-weather, continuous navigation services globally, and plays a great role in national security, economic and social fields. However, with the increasing demand for location-based services in complex environment, the "vulnerability" of GNSS reveals gradually. The accuracy, reliability and anti-interference are in urgent need to be improved. To solve the problems of insufficient availability of GNSS, relevant experts and scholars have put forward a variety of navigation augmentation technologies, including Precision Point Positioning (PPP), Real-Time Kinematic (RTK), Satellite Based Augmentation System (SBAS), Ground Based Augmentation System (GBAS) [1]. However, these technologies and systems have the construction problems of "fragmentation" and "patch", which still cannot solve the vulnerability of GNSS fundamentally. Therefore, it is a hot trend to build a new navigation system to provide high-performance navigation services.

Compared with the high orbit of GNSS, LEO satellite has its unique orbital and military advantages. For example, LEO satellite has closer transmission distance than

X. Wang et al. (Eds.): AICON 2021, LNICST 397, pp. 20–32, 2021.
https://doi.org/10.1007/978-3-030-90199-8_3

GNSS, leading to the fact that its signal has much stronger power (the signal intensity is 300–2400 times than GNSS [1, 2]) and not easy to be interfered. Large LEO constellation also has a wide coverage range, and can achieve seamless global coverage [4, 5]. What's more, multiple LEO satellites could be launched with one rocket [6], enabling the rapid deployment of LEO constellation in wartime to satisfy the special operational requirements [7]. Based on the above advantages, relevant organizations and institutions have successively started the construction of LEO satellite system. According to the survey, there are up to 30 companies that have released the LEO constellation construction plan, with the number of satellites as high as tens of thousands. China's LEO satellite planning is still in the research and demonstration stage [8, 9], and the subsequent launch tasks are in full swing.

To realize navigation and positioning function by LEO satellite and solve the bottleneck of GNSS, the research on navigation signal of LEO satellite is becoming a hot spot. This paper focuses on the LEO navigation signal, and further analyzes the influence of LEO signal characteristics on the positioning performance. Firstly, the mathematical model is established according to the characteristics of LEO navigation signal, and then the influence of LEO navigation signal burst on Doppler and Pseudo-range errors is analyzed. Finally, the LEO constellation is established and the positioning performance boundary is simulated and analyzed. The research results of this paper can provide reference for new satellite navigation system.

2 Signal Modeling on LEO Signal Burst

2.1 Mathematical Model of LEO Signal Burst

The navigation signal generally includes three signal components: carrier, PRN code and navigation message. PRN code and navigation message are attached to the carrier through modulation, and satellites broadcast the modulated carrier signal. The continuous signal of traditional GNSS navigation satellite can be expressed as formula (1).

$$s(t) = \sqrt{2P}(x(t)D(t)\exp(j(2\pi ft + \theta))) \tag{1}$$

Where P is signal power, $x(t)$ is PRN code, $D(t)$ is navigation message, f is carrier frequency and θ is initial phase.

Different from traditional navigation satellite signals, LEO navigation signals are usually broadcasted by satellite paging channels. Paging signal burst have the feature of fixed time-frequency resources, one-way broadcasting, high landing power and comprehensive coverage, which are suitable for navigation information broadcasting. Therefore, the LEO navigation signal is discontinuous in time domain, which can be expressed as formula (2).

$$s(t) = \sqrt{2P}(x(t)D(t)\exp(j(2\pi ft + \theta)))(u(t - t_0) - u(t - t_1)) \tag{2}$$

Where, $u(\cdot)$ represents the step function, $T = t_0 - t_1$ represents the signal duration.

According to the signal model of LEO satellite, the signal burst parameters mainly include carrier frequency, signal power, signal duration, PRN code and navigation message. The carrier frequency is determined by the frequency of LEO communication satellite. The signal power, signal duration and chip duration are the main factors that affect the Doppler measurement error and Pseudo-range error of LEO satellite. Such errors will directly affect the user's positioning accuracy. Therefore, this paper will mainly analysis the influence of LEO signal burst parameters on Doppler error and Pseudo-range error.

2.2 Modeling of Doppler Error with LEO Signal Burst

When user terminal receives satellite signal, it will introduce frequency measurement error caused by time difference and signal power, and then affects positioning accuracy finally. Therefore, the design of LEO navigation signal needs to consider the influence of signal duration and SRN, and provide a reasonable and effective way for signal structure design.

The CRLB (Cramer-Rao Lower Bound) [10, 11] is a lower bound for the variance of unbiased estimation, which does not care about the specific estimation method. The CRLB only reflects the best result of using all useful information to estimate parameters.

Based on the mathematical expression of the LEO navigation signal in the previous section, the Fisher matrix can be obtained as formula (3).

$$J = \frac{1}{\sigma^2} \begin{bmatrix} A^2 T^2 (n_0^2 N + 2n_0 P + Q) & 0 & A^2 T (n_0 N + P) \\ 0 & N & 0 \\ A^2 T (n_0 N + P) & 0 & A^2 N \end{bmatrix} \tag{3}$$

Among them,

$$P = \sum_{n=0}^{N-1} n = \frac{N(N-1)}{2} \tag{4}$$

$$Q = \sum_{n=0}^{N-1} n^2 = \frac{N(N-1)(2N-1)}{6} \tag{5}$$

A is the amplitude of the signal, σ^2 is the variance of Gaussian white noise; $n_0 = t_0/T$, t_0 is the time of the first sampling, N is the number of samples collected, which is related to the sampling frequency f_s, signal time length T_{signal}, and the relationship is as formula (6).

$$N = f_s * T_{signal} \tag{6}$$

The CRLB of signal frequency estimation can be obtained as formula (7).

$$\text{var}(\hat{\omega}) = \begin{cases} \frac{\sigma^2}{A^2 T^2 (n_0^2 N + 2n_0 P + Q)}, & \text{Phase known} \\ \frac{12\sigma^2}{A^2 T^2 N(N^2 - 1)}, & \text{Phase unknown} \end{cases} \tag{7}$$

In this paper, we only consider the situation where phase is unknown. Further, formula (7) can be converted into frequency estimation as formula (8).

$$\text{var}(\hat{f}) = \frac{12}{(2\pi)^2 (SNR) T^2 N(N^2 - 1)} \tag{8}$$

SNR is the signal-to-noise ratio of the received signal. From the above formula, the larger the number of samples N is, the higher the SNR is, then the frequency estimation accuracy could be improved. In other words, longer signal duration result in more accurate frequency estimation, leading to less positioning error.

To verify the derivation, the sampling frequency is set to meet the Nyquist criterion. According to the data of Luojia-01, the range of C/N_0 of simulation analysis is set to be 25 dB·Hz to 55 dB·Hz, and the data length is set to be 5 ms to 30 ms. The estimated error of frequency is shown in Fig. 1.

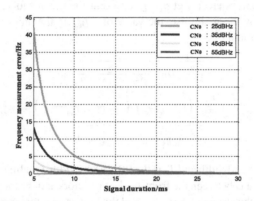

Fig. 1. Frequency error corresponding to duration of LEO signal

According to Fig. 1, with the increase of C/N_0, the signal duration required to achieve the same Doppler accuracy is gradually shortened; correspondingly, under the same received signal C/N_0, the Doppler accuracy improves with the increase of signal duration. Specifically, the relationship between the frequency estimation accuracy, the C/N_0 and the minimum signal duration required is shown in Table 1.

Table 1. Signal duration for different frequency estimation accuracy

C/N_0/dB·Hz	Frequency error/Hz					
	5	2	1	0.5	0.2	0.1
25	10.17 ms	13.8 ms	17.39 ms	21.91 ms	29.73 ms	30+ ms
35	6.52 ms	9.41 ms	11.85 ms	14.93 ms	20.26 ms	25.52 ms
45	√	6.41 ms	8.08 ms	10.17 ms	13.80 ms	19.39 ms
55	√	√	5.50 ms	6.93 ms	9.41 ms	11.85 ms

Simulation results show that when the required frequency estimation accuracy is set to be 1 Hz, the data length should be at least 5.50 ms under the condition of C/N0 as 55 dB·Hz, and more data is required for less signal power.

2.3 Modeling of Pseudo-Range Error with LEO Signal Burst

The signal power and chip duration of LEO signal burst will affect the SNR of receiver and the corresponding acquisition and tracking threshold, and then affect the positioning accuracy. Therefore, it is necessary to analyze the relationship between the signal power and chip duration of LEO navigation signal and the Pseudo-range measurement performance, and provide a reasonable and effective way for the signal parameters design.

The error sources of code loop mainly include code phase error caused by thermal noise and dynamic stress error. Let σ_{tDLL} represent the mean square error of the code phase error caused by thermal noise, the value of σ_{tDLL} in the unit of PRN chip can be estimated by the formula (9).

$$\sigma_{tDLL} = \begin{cases} \sqrt{\frac{B_L}{2 \cdot C/N_0} D \left(1 + \frac{2}{(2-D)T_{coh} \cdot C/N_0}\right)}, & D \geq \frac{\pi}{B_{fe}T_c} \\ \sqrt{\frac{B_L}{2 \cdot C/N_0} \left(\frac{1}{B_{fe}T_c} + \frac{B_{fe}T_c}{\pi-1}\left(D - \frac{1}{B_{fe}T_c}\right)^2 \left(1 + \frac{2}{(2-D)T_{coh} \cdot C/N_0}\right)\right)}, & \frac{1}{B_{fe}T_c} < D < \frac{\pi}{B_{fe}T_c} \\ \sqrt{\frac{B_L}{2 \cdot C/N_0} \frac{1}{B_{fe}T_c}\left(1 + \frac{1}{T_{coh} \cdot C/N_0}\right)}, & D < \frac{1}{B_{fe}T_c} \end{cases} \quad (9)$$

Where, B_{fe} is the RF bandwidth and T_c is the PRN code width. Qualitatively speaking, the reduce of the distance D between the front-back correlators and the loop noise bandwidth B_L, combining with the stronger the C/N_0 and the longer coherent integration time T_{coh}, results in smaller estimation error σ_{tDLL}.

Under the condition where B_L is 30 Hz, T_{coh} is 10 ms and $B_{fe}T_c$ is 17, the variation of thermal noise mean square error σ_{tDLL} with C/N_0 is simulated and analyzed under different correlator distance D, and the results are shown in Fig. 2.

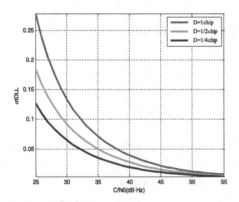

Fig. 2. Code loop thermal noise variance

Simulation results show that the mean square error of code phase measurement caused by thermal noise is about 0.005 chip.

Assuming that the chip duration is T_s, the code phase tracking accuracy is about $\sigma_{tDLL}T_s$, and the Pseudo-range error and signal bandwidth can be expressed as formula

(10) and formula (11).

$$\rho = \sigma_{tDLL} T_s \cdot c \tag{10}$$

$$B = \frac{2}{T_s} \tag{11}$$

Under the condition of $D = 1/2$ chip and C/N_0 ranging from 25 dB·Hz to 55 dB·Hz, the variation of Pseudo-range error with chip duration under different C/N_0 is simulated and analyzed, and the results are shown in Fig. 3.

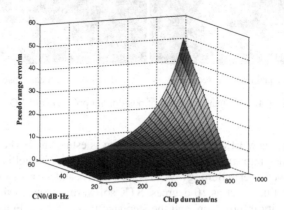

Fig. 3. Pseudo-error corresponding to chip duration and C/N_0

As can be seen from Fig. 3, with the increase of C/N_0, the chip duration required to achieve the same Pseudo-range accuracy is gradually lengthened; accordingly, under the condition of the same received signal C/N_0, the Pseudo-range error is improved with the extension of chip duration. It can be seen that there are two ways to achieve higher positioning accuracy, one is to improve the C/N_0, that is, to improve the on-board transmission power; the other is to improve the signal bandwidth and reduce the duration of a single chip. These two ways can achieve equivalent performances.

3 Positioning Error Analysis of LEO Signal Burst

Based on the analysis of LEO satellite signal modeling, this section establishes a new LEO satellite constellation to analyze the influence of LEO satellite signal parameters on positioning error.

3.1 Simulation Environment Construction

Firstly, the principle of LEO satellite positioning technology is briefly summarized. The positioning method of navigation system based on LEO satellite uses Doppler measurement positioning algorithm or Doppler/Pseudo-range joint positioning algorithm.

In space, based on the pseudo-range positioning equation, sphere with equal pseudo-range can be obtained. On the other hand, based on the Doppler positioning equation, cone with equal Doppler frequency can be obtained, as shown in Fig. 4. When there are at least four observations, the joint positioning equation can be used to solve the user position.

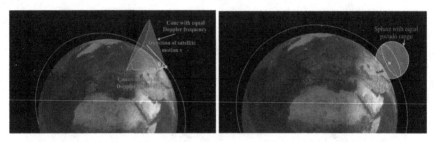

(a) Cone with equal Doppler frequency   (b) Sphere with equal pseudo-range

Fig. 4. Schematic diagram of positioning principle of LEO

In this paper, a new LEO satellite constellation is established. The orbit height is 780 km. It is divided into six orbital planes, each of which has 12 satellites. The position of the user's receiver is set in Beijing (39°56′N, 116°20′E), and the lowest elevation angle of the visible satellite is set as 10 degrees. STK software is used to simulate satellite position and velocity information, and the step size is set as 10 s. Figure 5 shows the simulation results of satellite visibility in a certain period. It can be seen that the number of visible satellites in this period ranges from four to seven, which can meet the multiple coverage requirements of large LEO navigation constellation.

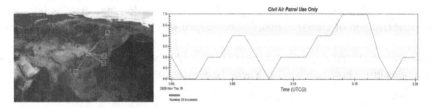

Fig. 5. The visibility of LEO satellite constellation

The orbit parameters of visible satellites in the period are derived from STK, and the influence of Doppler measurement error and Pseudo-range error on positioning accuracy under multi satellite condition is further analyzed.

3.2 Doppler Measurement Error Analysis

Doppler error is one of the most important parameters when the LEO satellite is positioning. Doppler error causes the change of the angle of cone with equal Doppler frequency, which causes the positioning result to deviate from the real position. The Doppler error has a great influence on the positioning results. This section will analyze the positioning error caused by the Doppler error by numerical simulation.

According to the relevant data analysis, the pseudo-range error is set to 10 m, the position error of the ephemeris is set to 1m, and the velocity error is set to 0.1 m/s. The change of the positioning error with Doppler error under the condition of multiple satellites positioning is analyzed respectively. The simulation results are shown in Fig. 6.

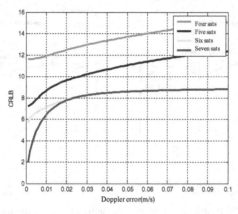

Fig. 6. Influence of Doppler error on positioning accuracy

It can be seen from Fig. 6 that with the increase of Doppler error, the positioning error becomes larger and then tends to be flat; with the increase of the number of satellites, the positioning accuracy is gradually improved. Specifically, the positioning error of 4 satellites is about 11.6–15.1 m, of 5 satellites is about 7.2–12.4 m, 6 satellites is about 5.6–8.9 m, and of 7 satellites is about 1.9–8.9 m.

Further, the simulation analysis is carried out on the change of positioning error with signal duration in the same scenario, and the simulation results are shown in Fig. 7. Simulation results show that with the increase of the C/N$_0$, the signal duration required to achieve the same positioning accuracy is gradually shortened; correspondingly, the positioning accuracy is improved with the increase of the signal duration under the same received signal C/N$_0$. In addition, the number of observable satellites also significantly affects the performance of positioning solution, that is, with the increase of the number of satellites, the positioning accuracy will be improved. It is important to note that the above simulation is the lower bound of positioning accuracy under ideal conditions, and some redundancy should be considered in the practical engineering application design.

3.3 Pseudo-Range Error Analysis

Pseudo-range error is also one of the most important parameters when LEO satellite is positioning. Pseudo-range error changes the radius of Sphere with equal pseudo-range, which leads to the deviation of positioning results. This section makes simulation analysis on the positioning error caused by pseudo-range error.

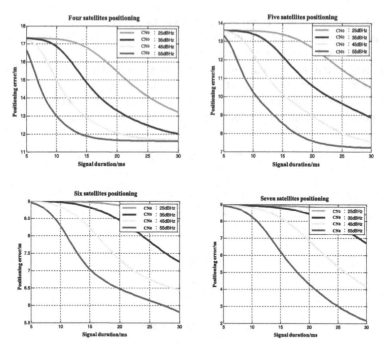

Fig. 7. Positioning error corresponding to signal duration

According to the relevant data analysis, the Doppler error, ephemeris position error and velocity error are set as 1.5 m/s, 1m and 0.1 m/s. The variation of positioning error versus pseudo-range error is analyzed respectively, and the simulation results are shown in Fig. 8.

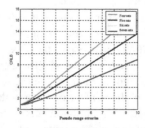

Fig. 8. Influence of pseudo-range error on positioning accuracy

As can be seen from Fig. 8, with the increase of pseudo-range error, the positioning error basically presents a trend of linear increasing. With the increase of the number of satellites engaged, the positioning accuracy gradually improves.

Furthermore, the positioning error versus chip duration is simulated and analyzed, and the simulation results are shown in Fig. 9. The simulation results show that with the increase of C/N0, the chip duration required to achieve the same positioning accuracy becomes longer. Accordingly, under the condition of the same received signal C/N0, the positioning error increases with the chip duration. In addition, with the increase of the number of visible satellite, the positioning performance can be significantly improved.

According to different functions of LEO satellite, there are different requirements for system service accuracy. When LEO is used as GNSS backup or anti-deception position verification, it usually needs only 50–100 m positioning accuracy to meet the positioning requirements. In this case, the number of visible satellites is 6–7, the C/N_0 is 25–55 dB·Hz, and the chip duration is less than 900 ns, that is, the bandwidth should be more than 2.22 MHz, which can meet the user's 50 m positioning requirements. When LEO satellites provide navigation and positioning services independently, the positioning accuracy is usually less than 10m. In this case, the number of visible satellites is 4 or more, the C/N_0 is 45–55 dB·Hz, and the bandwidth is more than 2.22 MHz, which can meet the 10m positioning accuracy to realize the independent navigation and positioning services of LEO satellites.

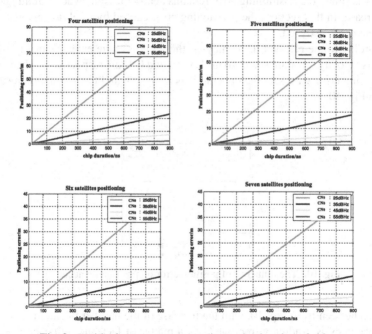

Fig. 9. Positioning error corresponding to the duration of chip

In conclusion, according to the analysis of Doppler error and pseudo-range error, the following conclusions can be drawn: Firstly, according to the formula of the angle of cone with equal Doppler frequency, Doppler measurement error is directly related with $\cos\theta$. Because of the nonlinear characteristics of cosine function, when Doppler measurement error is very low, small error increment can cause a large increase in positioning error. With the increase of measurement error, its influence on user positioning error gradually decreases, and finally tends to be flat; Secondly, with the increase of pseudo-range error, the radius of the sphere with equal pseudo-range increases linearly, so that the user error increases linearly with the pseudo-range error.

4   Error Analysis of Navigation Ephemeris

Usually, the user gets the position and speed information of the satellite from the navigation ephemeris. Due to the limitations of the satellite orbit determination algorithm and the navigation ephemeris, there exist deviation between the estimated position and the real position of the satellite, which may affect the positioning accuracy of the user. The influence of ephemeris error on positioning accuracy is analyzed below.

4.1   Satellite Position Error

Satellite position error will lead to changes of Cone with equal Doppler frequency and Sphere with equal pseudo-range, which results in the deviation of positioning results. Due to the fact that the influence of satellite position error on cone with equal Doppler frequency is small, the positioning error remains nearly the same when satellite position error increase. In this section, the positioning error caused by satellite ephemeris error is simulated and analyzed.

According to the relevant data analysis, the pseudo-range error, Doppler error and ephemeris velocity error are set as 10 m, 1.5 m/s and 0.1 m/s respectively. The variation of positioning error with satellite ephemeris is analyzed, and the simulation results are shown in Fig. 10.

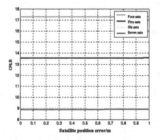

Fig. 10. The influence of position error on positioning accuracy

As can be seen from Fig. 10, with the increase of the number of satellites, the positioning accuracy is gradually improved. As a matter of fact, the influence of satellite position error on positioning is very small, which barely degrades the positioning accuracy. Specifically, the positioning error of four satellites is about 17.2 m, five satellites is about 13.5 m, six satellites is about 8.9 m, and seven satellites is about 8.8 m. When six satellites participate in the positioning calculation, the positioning accuracy of LEO satellites can be less than 10 m, which satisfies the precise positioning requirement.

4.2   Satellite Velocity Error

The satellite velocity error will cause the angle deviation of the cone with equal Doppler frequency, and then lead to the positioning error. In this section, the positioning error caused by satellite velocity error in ephemeris is simulated and analyzed.

According to the relevant data analysis, the pseudo-range error of the index item is set as 10 m, the Doppler error is set as 1.5 m/s, and the ephemeris position error is set as 1 m. The variation of positioning error with satellite velocity error is analyzed, and the simulation results are shown in Fig. 11.

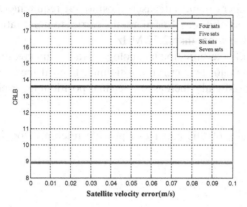

Fig. 11. The influence of velocity error on positioning accuracy

As can be seen from Fig. 11, similar to the influence of satellite position error on positioning accuracy, with the increase of the number of satellites, the positioning accuracy is gradually improved. As a matter of fact, the influence of satellite velocity error on positioning is very small, which barely degrades the positioning accuracy. Specifically, the positioning error of four satellites is about 17.29 m, five satellites is about 13.58 m, six satellites is about 8.99 m, and seven satellites is about 8.92 m. When six satellites participate in the positioning calculation, the positioning accuracy of LEO satellites can be less than 10 m, which satisfies the precise positioning requirement.

To sum up, according to the analysis of satellite position error and velocity error, as the current orbit determination technology is rather mature and already satisfies the positioning requirements, such errors are not the major limitation of user positioning accuracy, even if the satellite position and velocity error is increased, it has little impact on the user's final positioning results.

5   Conclusion

In this paper, we focuses on the navigation signal performance analysis. Firstly, the mathematical model of LEO signal burst is proposed. Then the estimation error of LEO navigation signal, including Doppler error and pseudo-range error are derived. Finally, the positioning service performance of large-scale LEO constellation is analyzed with numerical simulation. Main conclusions of this paper are drawn below.

1. The carrier to noise ratio and signal duration of LEO navigation signal can significantly affect Doppler error. With the increase of Doppler error, the positioning error increases. With the designed constellation in this paper, positioning accuracy better

than 10 m can be achieved with the number of visible satellites as 6 or more, the signal duration of 5-30 ms and carrier to noise ratio of 25–55 dB·Hz.
2. The carrier to noise ratio and chip duration of LEO navigation signal can significantly affect the pseudo-range error. With the increase of the pseudo-range error, the positioning error basically presents a trend of liner increasing. The designed constellation in this paper can meet the user's positioning requirements of 10m, with the number of visible satellites as 4 or more, the carrier to noise ratio as 45–55 dB·Hz, and the bandwidth is more than 2.22 MHz.
3. As the current orbit determination technology is rather mature, the ephemeris errors are no longer the major concern in positioning. Even if the satellite position and velocity errors are slightly increased, the final positioning results remains nearly unchanged.

The research results of this paper can provide reference for the design of LEO navigation signal.

References

1. Zhao, Y.: Brief probe on application of compass navigation satellite system in the fields of sea, land and air. In: Proceedings of 2017 2nd International Conference on Materials Science, Machinery and Energy Engineering. Dalian, China [s.n.], pp. 212–217 (2017)
2. Qin, H.L., Tan, A.A., Cong, L., et al.: Positioning technology based on ORBCOMM signal of opportunity. J. Beijing Univ. Aeronaut. Astronaut. **46**(11), 1999–2006 (2020)
3. Qin, H.L., Tan, Z.Z., Cong, L., et al.: Positioning technology based on IRIDIUM signals of opportunity. J. Beijing Univ. Aeronaut. Astronaut. **45**(9), 1691–1699 (2019)
4. He, F., Wu, L.: Spectral analysis and waveform optimization of signals for future GNSS. J. Harbin Inst. Technol. **44**(9), 101–106 (2012)
5. Meng, Y., et al.: A global navigation augmentation system based on LEO communication constellation. In: 2018 European Navigation Conference (ENC), pp. 65–71 (2018). https://doi.org/10.1109/EURONAV.2018.8433242
6. Ge, H., Li, B., Ge, M., et al.: Initial assessment of precise point positioning with LEO enhanced global navigation satellite systems (LeGNSS). Remote Sens. **10**(7), 984 (2018)
7. Benzerrouk, H., Nguyen, Q., Xiaoxing, F., Amrhar, A., Nebylov, A.V., Landry, R.: Alternative PNT based on iridium next LEO satellites doppler/INS integrated navigation system. In: 2019 26th Saint Petersburg International Conference on Integrated Navigation Systems (ICINS), pp. 1–10 (2019). https://doi.org/10.23919/ICINS.2019.8769440
8. Bofeng, L., Haibo, G., Maorong, G., et al.: LEO enhanced global navigation satellite system (LeGNSS) for real—time precise positioning services. Adv. Space Res. **61**, 2942–2954 (2018)
9. Khalife, J., Neinavaie, M., Kassas, Z.M.: Navigation With differential carrier phase measurements from megaconstellation LEO satellites. In: 2020 IEEE/ION Position, Location and Navigation Symposium (PLANS), pp. 1393–1404 (2020). https://doi.org/10.1109/PLANS46316.2020.9110199
10. Kay, S.M.: Fundamentals of Statistical Signal Processing: Estimation Theory. Prentice-Hall Inc., Upper Saddle River, pp. 193–197 (1993)
11. Rife, D., Boorstyn, R.: Single tone parameter estimation from discrete-time observations. IEEE Trans. Inf. Theory **20**, 591–598 **20**(5), 591–598 (1974)

An Analysis of Routing Simulation Technology of Unmanned Cluster Based on OPNET

Jiahao Dai[1,2(✉)], Yuhui Wang[1,2], Huijie Zhu[1,2], and Yongji Ren[3]

[1] Science and Technology on Communication Information Security Control Laboratory,
Harbin, China
[2] China Electronic Corporation NO. 36 Institute, Jiaxing, Zhejiang, China
[3] Naval Aviation University, Changzhi, China

Abstract. The military strategic guideline under the new situation points out that the base point of future war preparation is to win the informationized war mainly from the direction of unmanned cluster. Routing protocol is an important part of unmanned network communication system, and it is one of the most challenging tasks in unmanned network. This paper simulates five protocols, AODV, DSR, OLSR, TORA and GRP, analyzes the characteristics of each protocol under different circumstances, finds suitable protocols for unmanned trunking communication network under different environments, and provides suggestions for the establishment of a reasonable network.

Keywords: Routing protocol · Unmanned cluster · OPNET

1 Introduction

In modern wars, especially in recent local wars, unmanned aerial vehicles (UAVs) [1] have played a significant role with their accurate, efficient and convenient search capabilities and irregular operations. Because of UAVs in the field of military and scientific research are still on the stage of research in theory, the technology is not perfect, which means UAVs have not fully play its huge influence field and strength. However, only UAVs' performance in recent years is sufficient to demonstrate its great potential. Even some scholars think the future war is unmanned combat between cluster. Therefore, the major military countries in the world are stepping up the development and theoretical research of unmanned cluster network.

As an important development direction of military and civil communication networks in the future, unmanned communication is bound to play an important role in many fields and promote the development and change of many industries. However, this field is relatively new and rarely explored by researchers. Establish and maintain effective communication between the unmanned node is challenging, there are a lot of problems to be solved. Routing protocol of network layer is an important part of unmanned network communication system, and it is the basis of dynamic networking, multi-hop relay and other functions of unmanned nodes. The design of routing protocols is also one of the most challenging tasks in unmanned networks.

© ICST Institute for Computer Sciences, Social Informatics and Telecommunications Engineering 2021
Published by Springer Nature Switzerland AG 2021. All Rights Reserved
X. Wang et al. (Eds.): AICON 2021, LNICST 397, pp. 33–40, 2021.
https://doi.org/10.1007/978-3-030-90199-8_4

Ad Hoc On Demand Distance Vector (AODV) [2] is a reactive routing protocol for mobile Ad hoc networks. It adapts well to dynamic link conditions and has low processing and memory overhead with high network utilization. AODV can determine the unicast route to destination node in the self-organizing network. Each data packet has only the destination address, so the overhead is low. AODV only has the destination node's IP address, the source node and other relay nodes to store the next hop information for each data transfer. As routes are established on demand, routing traffic in the network is very small.

Dynamic Source Routing (DSR) [3] allows networks to self-organize and self-configure without the need for any existing network infrastructure, and is suitable for wireless self-organizing networks. The DSR works completely on demand and can scale automatically in response to changes in the path currently being used. Its route discovery and route maintenance mechanisms allow nodes to discover and maintain routes to any destination node.

Optimized Link State Routing (OLSR) [4] is one of the most commonly used Routing algorithms in Ad Hoc networks. After startup, routes to all destination nodes are determined, and the routing table is maintained and updated by the update process. Nodes broadcast their link states to neighboring nodes and other nodes through flooding to periodically exchange topology information with other nodes in the network. By collecting topology information about the network, OLSR enables nodes to use algorithms such as shortest paths locally to pre-compute paths from tables to be used for queries.

TORA [5] is a highly adaptive distributed algorithm. By introducing directed acyclic graph (DAG) and link reversal mechanism (LR), it can establish one or more routing paths between source and target nodes, which has the advantages of strong fault tolerance, high efficiency and strong scalability. The key idea of TORA is that when the topology structure of a certain region of the network is changed, the transmission of topology control information is well restricted to a small region and the routing control overhead is reduced.

GRP [6] is the most typical routing protocol based on geographic location. It is a passive routing protocol, that is, it does not need to maintain and update any routing path in advance. When any intermediate node receives the routing packet, it will immediately select the next hop node according to the relevant number packet forwarding algorithm, and this process will continue until the routing packet reaches the destination node. The GRP assumes that each node can obtain its current location via GPS.

Through the simulation of the above five protocols, this paper analyzes the characteristics of each protocol under different circumstances, finds out the suitable protocol for the unmanned trunked communication network under different environments, and provides suggestions for the establishment of a reasonable network.

2 Network Modeling

According to the characteristics of unmanned cluster and the three-layer modeling mechanism of OPNET, the simulation scenario of self-organizing network of unmanned cluster is defined respectively in the network model, the module functions of communication system of unmanned node are defined in the node model, and the routing protocol algorithm is implemented in the process model.

2.1 Network Model

As shown in the Fig. 1, in the free space with a length of 20 km and a width of 20 km, three simulation scenarios are realized successively, and the number of unmanned nodes is 10, 20 and 30 respectively. It is assumed that the movement of unmanned nodes is at the same height, and the X and Y coordinates of each node are generated randomly in the space range and move randomly at a certain speed. We simulate the unmanned communication network with five different routing protocols, and the parameters of network performance under different conditions were obtained.

The RXGroup Config module and the Mobility Config module are OPNET's own control modules, which provide rich built-in models and facilitate the simulation implementation. The RXGroup Config module is used to configure parameters such as the communication radius and path loss threshold of UAV nodes. The communication radius of UAV is set as 2 km without considering the path loss. The Mobility Config module is used to configure the node movement model in the simulation process. In order to test the performance lower limit of the routing protocol, the Random Waypoint model is adopted, that is, the node moves randomly, and the movement speed can be modified in different simulation scenarios. The actual UAV will not keep the random movement all the time during the execution of the task, and the working effect of the routing protocol will be better than the simulation result.

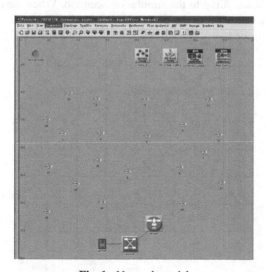

Fig. 1. Network model

2.2 Node Model

The unmanned nodes in the network are randomly distributed in a limited area and move randomly, so each unmanned node has the same node model as shown in Fig. 2. In order to obtain the network performance parameters in the simulation process in real time, the code in the WLAN_WKSTN node model is modified in this simulation, and the obtained data is written into the database. The process module in the node model has the following functions:

(1) RX module and TX module: located in the physical layer, wireless transceiver is used for signal receiving and sending. In the directionless receiving mode, data frames of other nodes are obtained and transmitted to MAC module to simulate the transmission process of grouping in the wireless channel.

(2) USAP module: a random access channel in the link layer protocol, distributed on multiple hops TDMA mobile multi-channel wireless network protocol, the protocol is used for node which has not been used in the free time slot allocation of one or more time slot. Time slot is used for communications between adjacent nodes, and through the coordinated control between the two hop node use time slot allocation, so as to ensure that the transmission between nodes do not conflict.

(3) TCP/IP module: located in the routing control layer, it is used to implement the routing protocol in this paper. The algorithm function realization of all routing protocols is written in this module.

(4) Application module: located in the application layer. It is used for used for data business generation and destruction. Data packets that need to be sent are generated according to Poisson distribution. The rate of generation and size of the packets can be adjusted according to the simulation scenario. When the data packet after a successful transmission to the destination node related statistic record grouping and will be destroyed.

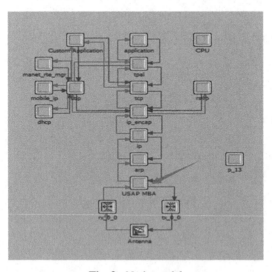

Fig. 2. Node model

2.3 Process Model

Each process module in the node model is implemented by a process model, and each process model is a finite state machine implemented by C code. In cluster, considered in the selection of MAC protocols need video, voice, data and other comprehensive service performance of the business. Network protocol of MAC layer simulation is a distributed coordination function of IEEE 802.11 MAC (DCF) model protocol, nodes in the model set USAP module process model of channel access protocol is shown in Fig. 3.

(1) Init state. This is the entry state of the entire USAP process model and is responsible for the initialization of some parameters and statistical variables. They are process ID, node ID, number of slots (num_lots), slot offset per node (my_offset), number of packets in and out of the queue, each statistic variable, protocol type, etc.

(2) BSS_INIT state. The purpose of these three states is to keep MAC processes moving in step with the emulation and prevent unexpected errors from occurring.

(3) Idle state. Only when a stream interrupt occurs is it transferred to another state depending on the interrupt type.

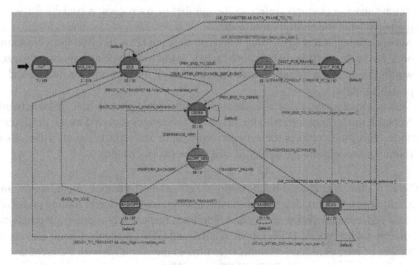

Fig. 3. Process model

(4) Transmit status. Receive handles packets sent from the ARP layer to the MAC layer. Inserts packets into the outgoing queue on a first-in, first-out basis.

(5) Backoff state. Process the data packets from the physical layer, and process them according to certain principles to decide whether to upload to the ARP layer.

(6) DEFER STATE. This state is the core implementation of the TDMA algorithm. Based on the current simulation time and slot length, you can get the number of slots that a frame has used (used_slots). From the number of slots already used for a frame (used_slots) and the total number of slots in the frame (num_slots), you can get the current slot offset. The packet can only be sent if the following two

conditions are met, otherwise an interrupt is scheduled for the node in the next slot. If a packet is successfully sent within its own time slot, it needs to be removed from the outgoing queue.

3 Simulation Result

On the basis of the above model and the simulation network, the network model is verified through the simulation experiment. In this simulation experiment, the number of different unmanned nodes is set to observe the change of network performance, and the simulation time is 10 min. We establish three-dimensional relationship diagram of the number of nodes, the simulation time and the network performance index, and analyze the simulation results. The performance evaluation, analysis and comparison among different routing protocols are complicated due to their different application scopes and performance evaluation criteria. The performance evaluation of routing in this paper mainly adopts the following indicators:

(1) Retransmission attempts: refers to the number of transmission packets for which the message is successfully transmitted.
(2) Network delay: refers to the time when message packet is received from the source node to the destination node. These include route lookup delays, message packets waiting in interface queues, retransmission delays, air transmission delays, and all possible delays.
(3) Network load: refers to the amount of data transmitted per unit time in the network.
(4) Network throughput: refers to the number of messages received by the destination node. This index reflects the network throughput and reflects the effectiveness of routing protocols and the ability to adapt to network changes.

Figure 4 shows the change relationship of network performance (including retransmission attempts, network delay, load and throughput) under different routing protocols, where the red, orange, yellow, green and blue lines respectively represent the network performance under AODV, DSR, OLSR, TORA and GRP protocols. Figure 4(a) shows the changes of retransmission attempts over time in the scenarios with different no-one nodes. It can be seen that under DSR, OLSR and GRP protocols, retransmission basically does not occur, while AODV and TORA increase retransmission requests as the complexity of the network increases. Figure 4(b) shows the changes of network delay with time in the scenarios with different no-one nodes. The network delay in the scenario using AODV is significantly higher than that of the other four protocols. Figure 4(c) shows the changes of network load with time under different no-node scenarios. It can be seen that the network load basically increases with the increase of the number of nodes in all protocol scenarios, but the network load carried by AODV scenario is far greater than that of other protocol scenarios. Figure 4(d) changes in network throughput are similar to those in network load. Based on the changes in the above four figures, it can be seen that AODV has higher performance than other routing protocols except for higher delay. Therefore, AODV can be said to be the most suitable protocol for

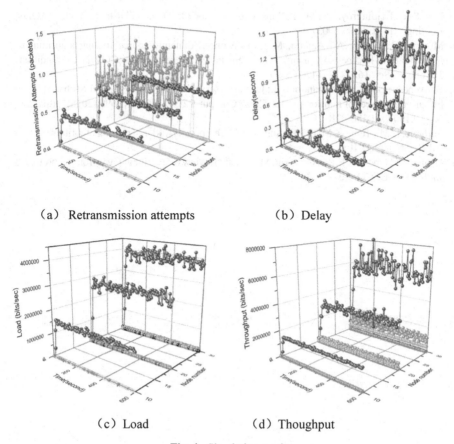

(a) Retransmission attempts   (b) Delay

(c) Load   (d) Thoughput

Fig. 4. Simulation result

unmanned trunked communication network. If the network needs low delay and high transmission rate, then choose TORA protocol.

4 Conclusion

In this paper, an OPNET-based unmanned trunking communication network model is established, the model can change the complexity of the network as needed. Then the results of network delay, load, throughput and retransmission attempts change under different protocols with different network complexity are obtained by simulation model. By comparing changes in network performance, we can get information about which protocols to use in different situations.

References

1. Zeng, Y., Zhang, R., Lim, T.J.: Wireless communications with unmanned aerial vehicles: opportunities and challenges. IEEE Commun. Mag. **54**, 36–42 (2016)

2. Das, S.R., Beldingroyer, E.M., Perkins, C.E.: Ad hoc On-Demand Distance Vector (AODV) Routing. RFC Editor (2003)
3. Moqimi, E., Najafi, A., Aajami, M.: An enhanced dynamic source routing algorithm for the mobile ad-hoc network using reinforcement learning under the COVID-19 conditions. J. Comput. Sci. **16**, 1477–1490 (2020)
4. Bhuvaneswari, R., Ramachandran, R.: Denial of service attack solution in OLSR based Manet by varying number of fictitious nodes. Clust. Comput. **22**(5), 12689–12699 (2018). https://doi.org/10.1007/s10586-018-1723-0
5. Surhone, L.M., Tennoe, M.T., Henssonow, SF.: Temporally-ordered routing algorithm. Mobile Ad Hoc Netw. (2010)
6. Usman, M., Oberafo, E.E., Abubakar, M.A, et al.: Review of interior gateway routing protocols. In: IEEE ICECCO (2019)

Research on Path Planning Optimization of Intelligent Robot in Warehouse Fire Fighting Scene

Qingshui Xue[✉], Zongyang Hou, Haifeng Ma, Xingzhong Ju, Haozhi Zhu,
and Yue Sun

School of Computer Science and Information Engineering, Shanghai Institute of Technology,
Shanghai 201418, China
xue-qsh@sit.edu.cn

Abstract. With the development of economy and society, the logistics industry is developing rapidly, and various types of warehouses are constantly emerging. At the same time, the fire safety problems of warehouses have become increasingly prominent. Intelligent fire-fighting robots can be used for warehouse fire-fighting monitoring and fire fighting 24 h a day. Multi-robots can perform the duty of patrolling and extinguishing fires. However, multi-robots often appear disorder and congestion during path planning. At the same time, when avoiding obstacles, there is a problem of insufficient smoothness of the path curve. This paper proposes an improved A-star algorithm to improve the ability of robots to avoid congestion in planning paths. Experimental data shows that this method can make the path distribution of multi-robots more uniform. At the same time, a curve obstacle avoidance strategy is proposed. When the robot encounters an obstacle, it performs the external ellipse or circle processing, and smoothes the obstacle avoidance according to the generated curve, which effectively solves the traditional A-star algorithm obstacle avoidance route with multiple turning points and unevenness.

Keywords: Robot navigation · Warehouse fire protection · Improved A-star algorithm · Curve obstacle avoidance

1 Introduction

With the development of artificial intelligence and distributed computing technology, the idea of intelligent distribution has emerged, and multi-agent system (MAS) is an important branch of its distributed intelligent control research. Agent is an autonomous agent, which can solve local problems and solve global problems cooperatively. As an application of MAS, distributed autonomous robot system is a complex multi intelligent system with high self planning and self-organization characteristics, which can work in unstructured environment. The multi robot system has a variety of high intelligent functional modules, such as task analysis, planning, decision-making, and so on. Each module can work well in coordination. The control methods of shared distributed multi

X. Wang et al. (Eds.): AICON 2021, LNICST 397, pp. 41–51, 2021.
https://doi.org/10.1007/978-3-030-90199-8_5

robot system are divided into centralized and distributed. There is a centralized coordination mechanism, so the efficiency is relatively high. However, because of the choice of centralized control to solve the conflict of all robots, it needs to add an administrator or choose the main control robot. This model has less practical application. However, there is no central controller in distributed control, such as a centralized robot or a server responsible for coordinating between machines [1].

It has a high risk in the fire fighting work. The fire robot can replace human to carry out high-risk fire fighting work. At the same time, it can carry out 24-h guard in the warehouse, and automatically navigate to the fire point to put out the fire when receiving the alarm. Multiple robots can position and navigate by central server or coordinated communication. In this paper, the fire fighting path planning of intelligent robot under distributed control and centralized control is optimized in the warehouse fire safety scenario.

2   Research on Path Planning of Improved A-Star Algorithm

2.1   Introduction of A-Star Algorithm

A-star algorithm is a heuristic search algorithm, which can be used for fast optimization. It belongs to a more flexible type of algorithm, while Dijkstra algorithm and BFS (breadth-first search) algorithm belong to its special variety. The formula of A-star algorithm is: $F(n) = g(n) + H(n)$, where $f(n)$ is the cost estimation from the initial state to the target state via state n, $G(n)$ is the actual cost from the initial state to state n in the state space, and $H(n)$ is the cost estimation of the best path from state n to the target state. For the path search problem, the state is the node in the graph, and the cost is the distance. The selection of $H(n)$ ensures to find the shortest path condition, and the key lies in the selection of the evaluation function $H(n)$. When $d(n)$ is used to express the distance between state n and target state, the selection of $H(n)$ can be divided into three cases:

(1)   If $h(n) < d(n)$ the actual distance to the target state, in this case, the number of search points is large, the search range is large, and the efficiency is low. But we can get the optimal solution.
(2)   If $h(n) = d(n)$, that is, the distance estimation $H(n)$ is equal to the shortest distance, then the search will strictly follow the shortest path, and the search efficiency is the highest.
(3)   If $h(n) > d(n)$, the number of search points is small, the search range is small and the efficiency is high, but the optimal solution cannot be guaranteed.

When $h(n) = 1$, $f(n) = g(n) + 1$, which is BFS algorithm, is a bad heuristic search algorithm. When $h(n) = 0$, $f(n) = g(n)$, that is Dijkstra algorithm, to find the single source shortest path algorithm.

$H(n)$ usually adopts European distance, Manhattan distance and Chebyshev distance. Euclidean distance, also known as Euclidean distance or Euclidean metric, is the shortest distance between two points based on space. It is a geometric term used in geometric

metric space to indicate the sum of absolute wheelbase of two points in standard coordinate system. Chebyshev distance is a measure in vector space. The definition of the distance between two points is the maximum of the absolute value of the difference between the coordinate values. When h(n) adopts Euclidean distance, the shortest path can be obtained. When Manhattan distance is used, the shortest path may not be obtained. In the application of the actual scene, the shortest route is often chosen, but the environmental factors are complex and diverse, so it is not the shortest route that is the optimal route, and the optimal route needs to be determined under the comprehensive analysis of various factors.

The process of A-star algorithm is to find the path by maintaining the openlist table and the Closelist table. Every time a node is visited, the node is put into the Closelist table, and then the node with the least estimated generation value is taken out from the openlist table for access. When the node is the target point, the path planning is completed, and the path trajectory is output reversely.

2.2 Research on A-Star Algorithm

The related researches on A-star algorithm are as follows: in reference [2], the criteria of deleting redundant points and adding new nodes are introduced to make the global path smoother and more consistent with the law of robot kinematics. Combined with the idea of rolling window method, the local path planning is carried out in each rolling window, and the local sub-target area is determined according to the previous node information, and then the local sub-target area is introduced Obstacle avoidance control strategy for real-time obstacle avoidance. In reference [3], an improved A-star algorithm combined with node load is proposed. The load of each node starts from the initial value, and dynamically updates the load of the node according to the corresponding dynamic load calculation formula. The load is introduced into the heuristic function of A-star algorithm to make the node load affect the AGV path selection and avoid high load nodes. In reference [4], the traditional A-star algorithm is improved by introducing the turning cost and the weighting coefficient of the heuristic function. The obstacle expansion coefficient is introduced in the process of grid map modeling, and the avoidance rule base is established. The result of a path planning is a global equilibrium solution. In reference [5], a hierarchical improved A-star algorithm guided path planning method in rainy days is proposed. Firstly, the grid map used in the traditional A-star algorithm is optimized to greatly reduce the number of processing nodes. Secondly, the risk factor related to the water depth of each section of the road is introduced as the actual cost to improve the original algorithm. Finally, different types of vehicles are classified and the priority of each vehicle is assigned. In reference [6], a two-stage search algorithm is used to guide the search towards the most promising direction by selecting the appropriate evaluation function, so as to obtain the optimal path. The improved algorithm in reference [7] extends the traditional 8-neighborhood search to 24 neighborhood, and uses the guidance vector to optimize the number of neighbors, eliminate redundant nodes, improve the search efficiency, and optimize the smooth path. In reference [8], jump point search (JPS) strategy is used to filter out the jump points, add them to openlist and Closelist instead of a large number of unnecessary neighbor nodes in A-star algorithm, and realize long-distance jump through jump points, so as to reduce memory consumption and evaluation of nodes until the final path is generated. In reference [9], a path planning algorithm with the constraint of necessary points is proposed. Combined with the distribution characteristics of obstacles, the algorithm can find the necessary points of the shortest path to constrain the search direction of a star, and then splice the shortest path segments to get the shortest path. A multi robot dynamic path planning algorithm based on reservation grid is proposed in reference [10]. Firstly, the collision between robots is prevented by using reservation grid and directed graph; secondly, the traffic congestion map is generated by using reservation grid to display the congestion status of current warehouse map in real time; finally, the dynamic path planning of multi robot is realized by improving A-star algorithm to solve the traffic congestion problem among robots and improve the system efficiency.

In this paper, a path planning method based on weighted improved A-star algorithm [11, 12] and curvilinear motion is proposed, and the path planning schemes of fire robot under centralized and distributed control situations are designed respectively. The obstacle avoidance strategy of elliptic curve and the turning mode of circular curve are adopted in the design, and the obstacle body is expanded to avoid safe collision. Through many experiments and comparisons [13, 14], the problems of route jam, multiple break points and unsmooth of traditional A-star algorithm are effectively solved.

3   Path Optimization of Improved A-Star Algorithm Combined with Curve Obstacle Avoidance

3.1   Weighted Improved A-Star Algorithm

When the fire happens, the fire-fighting robot needs to reach the warning point in the first time. This paper uses heuristic search A-star algorithm for planning, because this algorithm has high efficiency, and achieves the goal requirements of different scenarios by setting heuristic function [15].

The heuristic search algorithm of A-star is improved as follows: the algorithm formula $F(n) = g(n) + H(n)$, $G(n)$ is the actual cost from the starting point to the current point, $H(n)$ is the estimated cost from the current point to the target point, and $f(n)$ is the estimated cost from the starting point to the target point. The weight parameters w, $w = x/C$, $C = \max (density)$ are introduced into this formula; x is the series of road density, C is the series of maximum density. $g(n) = \sum_{0}^{i} w(i)d(i)$ $h(n) = \sum_{0}^{j} w(j)D(j)$

Parameter i is the number of road sections that have been passed. Parameter j is the number of road sections to be passed. w(i), w(j) are the weights of the corresponding road sections, D(i) is the path length of each road section, D(j) is the Chebyshev distance of the corresponding road section, that is, the distance between two points is defined as the maximum absolute value of the difference of coordinate values. Taking (x^1, Y^1)

and (X^2, Y^2) as examples, the Chebyshev distance is max $(|x^2-x^1|, y^2-y^1|)$. Compared with the traditional algorithm [16, 17], the improved weighted algorithm has the ability to avoid congestion. This paper uses the improved weighted A-star algorithm for path planning, and gives the specific scheme in Sect. 3.3 (Fig. 1).

3.2 Curve Obstacle Avoidance Ethod

As shown in Fig. 2 , when the robot encounters obstacles, the obstacles are regularized into rectangular shape, and then the weight parameters are added to expand the rectangle to increase the safe distance from the fire robot, When the fire robot encounters a rectangular obstacle in the direction of arrow, it can avoid the rectangular obstacle. This paper proposes a method as shown in Fig. 2 to generate the circumscribed ellipse P1 on the basis of the minimum rectangle. The method for generating the parameters of the elliptic curve is shown in Fig. 3: set up the rectangular coordinate system with the center of the rectangle as the origin o, and select the point F1 (C, 0) and the symmetrical position F2 (−C, 0) within the range of the abscissa axis, then $MF_1 + MF_2 = 2a$, a is the length of the major axis of the ellipse, and the standard equation of the elliptic curve is obtained: $x^2/a^2 + Y^2/b^2 = 1$. According to the function of the equation, the elliptic curve is planned. The expansion coefficient i is introduced into the ellipse P1 to generate a larger ellipse and increase the collision safety distance, so that the fire robot can smoothly bypass the obstacles. At the same time, as shown in Fig. 4, the method of generating external circular curve is proposed, and the same expansion coefficient is used to generate the curve obstacle avoidance path. Compared with the traditional path planning algorithm, the turning angle at the break point is too large. This paper uses the combination of elliptic curve path obstacle avoidance and circular curve turning and linear motion to plan the path and remove the break point. The specific scheme is given in Sect. 3.3.

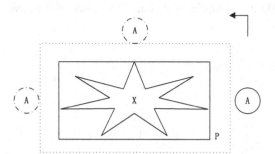

Fig. 1. Rectangular path obstacle avoidance

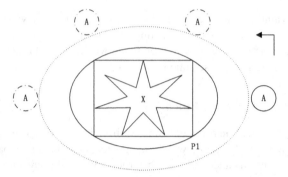

Fig. 2. Elliptic curve path obstacle avoidance

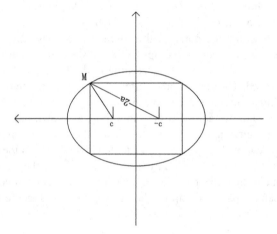

Fig. 3. Establishment of obstacle avoidance elliptic curve

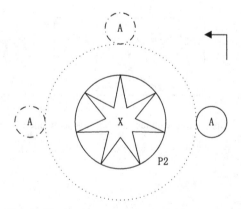

Fig. 4. Obstacle avoidance by circular curve path

3.3   Path Planning Scheme

According to the analysis and improvement of the traditional planning scheme in Sects. 3.1 and 3.2 [18], The schemes in centralized and distributed control situations are given respectively.

(1) In the centralized control situation, the weighted improved A-star algorithm is used to plan the path of the fire robot in turn. The improved A-star algorithm is used for path planning, and the starting point of the algorithm is from the center. Based on the position information of all the fire robots, the optimal route is planned in turn. When encountering obstacles, plan an elliptic curve path to avoid obstacles. When encountering no obstacles but turning, plan a circular curve path to avoid obstacles, as shown in Fig. 5, and move in a straight line at other times.

Suppose there is a set of fire robots o (A, B, C…) algorithm steps:
① The path planning of fire robot A is carried out, and the improved A-star algorithm is used to generate the path. At this time, the corresponding position of robot A at each time is recorded.
② The improved A-star algorithm is also used to generate the path of fire robot B. At this time, due to the existence of robot a path trajectory, according to the improved algorithm, due to the change of the density of each cell, the estimation function $H(n)$ and the actual cost function $g(n)$ will be affected by the former.
③ The path planning of fire robot C is carried out, and the improved A-star algorithm is used to plan the path under the influence of A and B paths.
④ Route planning is carried out for the remaining fire robots in turn, and the global route solution is finally generated.

(2) In the distributed control situation, the traditional A-star algorithm [19] is used for path pre planning of multiple fire robots, and the pass frequency of the planned road section is counted. According to the frequency value, the obstacle value of the current map feasible road section is assigned. Each fire robot uses the weighted improved A-star algorithm to plan its own path according to the assigned new map. The steering and obstacle avoidance methods are the same as those in scheme 1.

① In case of fire alarm, the center uses A-star algorithm for path planning of all fire robots according to the position of each robot, and generates corresponding N paths information.
② The N pieces of information are processed, and the map is weighted, that is, the map information at each time and location is transformed, and the density level is weighted.
③ Transfer the modified map to all robots, according to the embedded improved weighted A-star algorithm, the robot makes route planning to avoid potential dense road sections and generate their own paths (Fig. 5).

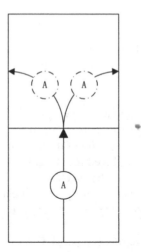

Fig. 5. Turning path of circular curve

4   Experimental Simulation

The grid environment model of warehouse map is established and simulated. Manually set the size of the map, take the current time of the system as the random seed, and use the random function to generate random numbers. In this way, the map obstacle points are generated randomly, and the number of obstacle points is set manually. Randomly generate the position of the fire robots, and manually set the number of fire robots, and set the fire point as the lower right corner of the map. In the experiment, the size of randomly generated grid is 10 * 10, the number of obstacles is 15, and the number of target fire robots is 15. Combined with the content of the third chapter, the path planning scheme, experimental design process and results of the fire robot are described as follows:

(1)   According to scheme 1, experiment 1 is described as follows:

   Program flow: in order to plan the path of the target in turn, record the space points and time of each target. According to the improved algorithm, theoretically the latter always avoids the former aggregation point.

   Experimental results: as shown in Fig. 6, the path trajectory of fire robot A using the traditional algorithm, as shown in Fig. 7, the route trajectory of fire robot a using the improved algorithm is compared. It is found that the route of fire robot A is not the shortest route, but a relatively short route. Fire robot A is more inclined to the low density short route, which indicates that the planning path using the improved algorithm has the effect of avoiding high-density road segments. Figure 8 shows the route map of linear motion planning using the improved algorithm. Compared with Fig. 7, the robot consumes more steering time and distance.

(2)   According to scheme 2, experiment 2 is described as follows:

Program flow: the traditional algorithm is used to simulate the route of the target points in turn, record the frequency of the passing points, and generate the spatial point

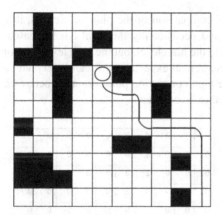 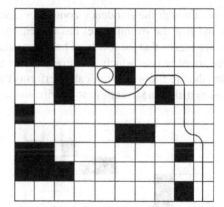

Fig. 6. Fire protection planning path of robot A before planning

Fig. 7. Fire protection planning route of robot A after planning

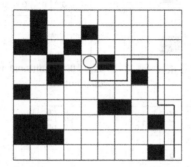

Fig. 8. Traditional linear motion planning route

coordinate frequency map after the planning. According to the spatial point coordinate frequency map, the map is modified, and the obstacle weights of the common walking points are set. Then, the improved algorithm is used to make a new round of path planning for the fire robots target set in random order. According to the spatial attributes, the path generated by each fire robot is unique and does not change with the planning sequence.

Experimental results: the map information randomly generated as Fig. 9. As shown in Fig. 10, which is the number of frequencies of robots passing through each node under the traditional A-star algorithm path planning. The H (n) function chooses the Manhattan distance. Figure 11 shows the frequency of the robot passing through each node under the improved A-star algorithm path planning. Figure 12 shows the results of congestion classification for the node frequencies planned by the traditional A-star algorithm and the improved A-star algorithm. It is obvious that the improved A-star algorithm has a good evacuation congestion ability compared with the traditional A-star algorithm.

After randomly distributing the positions of obstacles and robots for many times, the path planned by each target value is uniquely determined, and there is a detour phenomenon, which indicates that the introduction of obstacle weight on the map affects the shortest path selection of the fire robots, and tends to avoid congestion. At the same time, through the frequency congestion level comparison of the planning results, it is found that the overall level has decreased, and occasionally the level has increased, which means that the low level has increased to the high level, but the high level has not continued to rise, which is in line with the theoretical expectation. It can be explained that the fire robot automatically performs the high congestion point drainage behavior, which makes the overall flow distribution tend to be balanced.

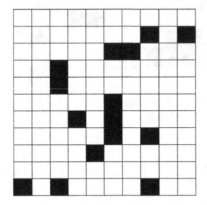

Fig. 9. Map information.

0	0	0	0	0	0	0	0	0	0
0	0	0	1	0	0	0	0	0	0
0	0	0	2	0	0	0	0	0	0
0	0	0	3	2	0	0	0	0	0
0	0	0	2	6	9	9	9	0	0
0	0	0	1	1	2	0	9	0	0
0	0	0	0	0	0	0	10	0	0
0	0	0	0	0	0	0	10	0	0
0	0	0	1	1	0	0	13	14	15
0	0	0	0	1	1	1	2	0	15

Fig. 10. Traditional algorithm - frequency distribution

0	0	0	0	1	2	2	2	2	0
0	0	0	0	1	1	0	0	2	0
0	0	0	1	1	0	0	1	3	1
0	0	0	2	2	3	2	2	3	1
0	0	0	1	1	4	3	3	3	1
0	0	1	2	3	2	0	3	3	1
0	0	2	0	1	0	0	4	3	4
0	0	2	1	2	1	0	4	0	4
0	0	0	1	2	0	1	9	10	15
0	0	0	1	3	3	3	3	0	15

Fig. 11. Improved algorithm frequency distribution

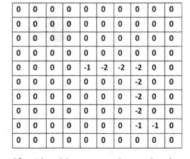

0	0	0	0	0	0	0	0	0	0
0	0	0	0	0	0	0	0	0	0
0	0	0	0	0	0	0	0	0	0
0	0	0	0	0	0	0	0	0	0
0	0	0	0	-1	-2	-2	-2	0	0
0	0	0	0	0	0	0	-2	0	0
0	0	0	0	0	0	0	-2	0	0
0	0	0	0	0	0	0	-2	0	0
0	0	0	0	0	0	0	-1	-1	0
0	0	0	0	0	0	0	0	0	0

Fig. 12. Algorithm comparison - density change chart

5 Conclusion

Through many random simulations of obstacle position and multi robot position, different maps are generated. The proposed scheme is used to compare the path planning of fire robots in centralized and distributed control situations. It is found that the weighted improved A-star algorithm makes the route distribution of multi fire robots more uniform. The route trajectory occupies most of the map, and has a good ability to avoid congestion. At the same time, the proposed curve obstacle avoidance and curve steering method can reduce the cost of robot steering and make the path more smooth. In the warehouse fire safety scenario, it can plan a better smooth route for multi intelligent robots, which has high application value.

References

1. Qing, Z., Xu, L., Li, P., Fengzeng, Z.: Path planning of mobile robot based on JPS and improved a * algorithm. Comput. Sci. Explor. 1–10 (2021)
2. Xiaojing, G., Zhuozheng, Y.: A* algorithm for static path planning based on neighborhood expansion. Comput. Eng. Appl. 1–9 (2021)
3. Zihan, L., Kuang, P., Mingyou, D., Jiang, Z., Wenfeng, W., Meilin, W.: Vehicle navigation method in rainy days based on improved hierarchical a * algorithm. Comput. Appl. **40**(S2), 210–214 (2020)
4. Baojian, W., Dasha, H., Yuming, J.: Application of improved a * algorithm in path planning. Comput. Eng. Appl.1–6 (2021)
5. Xiao, L., Zengwen, D., Kangqiang, Z.: Cooperative Path Planning of multiple fire fighting vehicles based on improved a ~ * algorithm. Comput. Simul. **37**(12), 276–282 (2020)
6. Dong, Z.W., Chao, J.: A ~ * global path planning algorithm for two-stage search. Comput. Appl. Softw. **37**(12), 249–253 (2020)
7. Hong, H., Zhian, Z., Wen, S.Z., Xing, C.G.: Robot path planning method based on multiple a * algorithm in dynamic environment. Comput. Eng. Appl. 1–9 (2021)
8. Lei, W., Lifan, S.: Research on path planning algorithm with necessary point constraint. Comput. Eng. Appl. **56**(21), 25–29 (2020)
9. Rui, D.C., Xin, G., Ning, L., Ning, S.X.: Multi robot dynamic path planning based on improved a ~ * algorithm. Hightech. Commun. **30**(01), 71–81 (2020)
10. Zhijun, L., Xiao, Z., Tiansheng, L.: Design and implementation of distributed multi robot communication system based on group cooperation. Robotics (04), 300–304 + 328 (2000)
11. Xu, Z., Liu, B., Zhe, S., Bai, H., Wang, Z., Neville, J.: Variational random function model for network modeling. IEEE Trans. Neural Netw. Learn. Syst. **30**(1) (2019)
12. Jia, Z.L., Wei, C., Ye, F.H.: AGV path planning combining A* and ant colony algorithm. J. Phys. Conf. Ser. **1948**(1) (2021)
13. Dhaniya, R.D., Umamaheswari, K.M.: Critical comparative study of robot path planning in grid-based environment. J. Phys. Conf. Ser. **1804**(1) (2021)
14. JinGu, K., DongWoo, L., YongSik, C., WooJin, J., JinWoo, J.: Improved RRT-connect algorithm based on triangular inequality for robot path planning. Sensors **21**(2) (2021)
15. Ni, X., Xinzhi, Z., Xiuqing, Y., Yong, X., Junyong, M.: Mobile robot path planning based on time taboo ant colony optimization in dynamic environment. Front. Neurorobot. **15**(5) (2021)
16. Shasha, T., Yuanxiang, L., Yilin, K., Jiening, X.: Multi-robot path planning in wireless sensor networks based on jump mechanism PSO and safety gap obstacle avoidance. Fut. Gen. Comput. Syst. **118** (2020)
17. Xiaoyong, X., Haitao, M., Yuanbin, Y., Pengyu, W.: Application improvement of A* algorithm in intelligent vehicle trajectory planning. Math. Biosci. Eng. MBE, **18**(1) (2020)
18. Ahmed, T., Teli, M., Wani, A.: A fuzzy based local minima avoidance path planning in autonomous robots. Int. J. Inf. Technol. (4) (2020)
19. Wang, H.-J, Yong, F., Zhao, Z.-Q., Yue, Y.-J.: An improved ant colony algorithm of robot path planning for obstacle avoidance. J. Robot. **2019**(5), 6097591 (2019)

Nonlinear Interference Cancellation Technique for Cellular Network with Time Slot Overlap

Boyi Tang[1], Xiangjie Xia[1], Zaitian Zhang[2], Wanmei Feng[3], Jie Tang[3,4], Shihai Shao[1], and Ying Liu[1(✉)]

[1] National Key Lab of Science and Technology on Communications, University of Electronic Science and Technology of China, Chengdu 611731, China
liuying850613@uestc.edu.cn
[2] Chuanrong Machinery Factory, Shenyang, China
[3] School of Electronic and Information Engineering, South China University of Technology, Guangzhou 510641, China
[4] National Mobile Communications Research Laboratory, Southeast University, Nanjing 210096, China

Abstract. The rapid development of the fifth generation (5G) wireless networks are facing challenges to meet the traffic demands of end users. Interference cancellation is considered as an important technique for implementing the full duplex and improving the frequency spectrum efficiency in 5G cellular networks. Because time slots are assigned differently to base stations in different networks, there exists time slot overlap problem that causes strong interference at the receiver base station. A digital-domain interference cancellation method is studied in this paper, which allows the receiver base station to extract the desired signal transmitted by its user equipment under influence of high-power signal from adjacent base station. The interference is rebuilt and suppressed after estimating the nonlinear components of power amplifier using the least-square method. The simulation results demonstrate that the proposed interference cancellation method is effective for interference signal modulated by different methods.

Keywords: Nonlinear interference cancellation · Base stations · Least-square estimation · Power amplifier · Full duplex

1 Introduction

With the development of economy and communication technology, the fifth generation (5G) of wireless communication networks would be widely used in the recent years and benefit people in many aspects of life [1]. As estimated, there are around thousand-fold higher mobile data volume per area and 10 times to 100 times more connected devices in 5G networks compared to 4G communication systems [1–5]. Therefore, the limited frequency spectrum resource is valuable.

Full duplex technique, which can transmit and receive data at the same time-frequency resource, is considered as an important application in the future from Wi-Fi

© ICST Institute for Computer Sciences, Social Informatics and Telecommunications Engineering 2021
Published by Springer Nature Switzerland AG 2021. All Rights Reserved
X. Wang et al. (Eds.): AICON 2021, LNICST 397, pp. 52–61, 2021.
https://doi.org/10.1007/978-3-030-90199-8_6

to ad-hoc networks [6, 7]. Theoretically, this technique can double the billions of dollar worth of frequency spectrum resources [2, 3, 6] and increase the throughput [8] compared to frequency division duplex (FDD) and time division duplex (TDD) in the fourth generation of wireless networks (4G), which has attracted significant attention in the research community and industry. However, the reason why full duplex technique did not be used in the previous generations is that there is strong interference when transmits and receives signals simultaneously [2, 3, 7, 9]. In order to solve this problem, many interference cancellation methods have been proposed to suppress the strong interference signal.

In general, interference can be suppressed in propagation domain, analog domain and digital domain [3, 7, 10]. Propagation-domain interference cancellation methods are divided into three main types, namely, passive approach, active approach and antenna interface approach. Passive methods include separation approach, phase control approach and surface treatments approach, while passive means contain transmit beamforming approach. In addition, electrical balanced duplexers and circulators are two interfaces that are widely used in antenna interface techniques. Interference suppression techniques in analog domain can be classified into time-domain approach, frequency-domain approach and digitally assisted approach, while channel modeling and receive beamforming are two common methods in digital domain [11]. However, propagation-domain interference cancellation methods may suppress the desired signal together with interference. Meanwhile, analog-domain techniques require additional analog circuit, which may limit the design of small-size devices. In comparison, digital-domain interference cancellation methods can simplify the complex processing process using digital signal processing techniques [7], which is adopted in this paper.

Since the interference signal generally has high power, it may overwhelm desired signal and beyond the dynamic range of analog-to-digital converter (ADC) at receiver side. In order to avoid saturating the ADC, the high-power interference signal should be subtracted from the received signals [8, 10]. It is difficult to subtract interference even when the intended transmit signal is known, because noise and nonlinear components are introduced to the received signal by communication channels. Such nonlinear interference is mainly caused by power amplifier (PA) [6, 11, 12]. As a result, a nonlinear model of interference is necessary in order to estimate the interference signal [9]. In this paper, we propose a digital domain approach to suppress the co-channel interference due to overlapping time slots of base stations. In the proposed method, we use a fiber link to transmit the original interference source, and then estimate the nonlinear distortion introduced by PA utilizing the least-square (LS) estimation method. Therefore, the interference is suppressed by subtracting the reconstructed interference signal from the received signal.

In the following parts, we firstly present the system model in Sect. 2, and then explain the proposed interference cancellation method in Sect. 3. The simulation results are presented in Sect.4 to show the efficiency of the proposed method. At last, the conclusion is discussed in Sect. 5.

2 System Model

There are a large number of base stations, user equipment in the 5G cellular networks. Here, we consider two base stations (BS1 and BS2) and two user equipment (UE1 and UE2) within two different networks as shown in Fig. 1, while all these BSs and UEs work in the same frequency. BS1 and BS2 are the serving base stations of UE1 and UE2 respectively, and these two BSs provide the best average propagation situation to their user equipment [13].

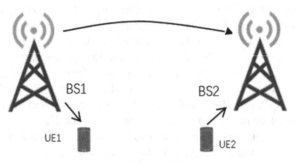

Fig. 1. System model

In order to minimize the interference and improve channel capacity, two BSs operate at the same frequency in different time slots [14]. However, as the number of base stations increases, the transmission time slots overlap in some specific scenarios which causes strong interference. For example, when BS1 is in downlink (DL) and BS2 is in uplink (UL), BS2 receives information from UE2 together with data transmitted from BS1. The interference from BS1 reduces the uplink capacity of the system [15]. When the same frequency is used in this case, there is inter-cell interference, which can be canceled by using the information transmitted through the backhaul network between base stations [16, 17]. The fiber link, which provides abundant capacity and high scalability [4], is an ideal choice for backhaul network and is used in the proposed method to transmit the original interference source.

Since signals transmitted by BSs are stronger than those transmitted by mobile users, the interference from BS1 to BS2 link is stronger than the interference from the user to BS2 link [14]. The high power interference signal leads to interaction problems in the ADC of BS2, such as desensitization, blocking as well as undesired intermodulation distortion products [18, 19] Even the intended interference signal is obtained through the fiber link, the high power interference still cannot be directly subtracted from the received signal since noise is added to the original interference source. The noise at the receiver side is mainly introduced by the nonlinear components of power amplifier (PA) at BS1, and such interference reduces the transmission efficiency and channel capacity of the communication system [12]. Therefore, we propose an interference cancellation method using the least-square method to estimate the nonlinear components of PA and reconstruct the interference signal.

3   The Proposed Interference Cancellation Method

Here, the transmitted signal from BS1 is $x(n)$ and it becomes $z(n)$ after a power amplifier (PA) which obeys the odd-order-only memory polynomial model

$$z(n) = \sum_{\substack{k=1 \\ k \text{ is odd}}}^{K} \sum_{q=0}^{Q} c_{kq} x(n-q) |x(n-q)|^{k-1},$$

(1)

where $K = 5$ and $Q = 2$, and c_{kq} is the nonlinear coefficient.

As for BS2, we consider the received signal from BS1 (interference signal) as $y(n)$ and the desired signal from UE2 as $u(n)$. Therefore, the signal received at BS2 can be written as $r(n) = y(n) + u(n)$. Because the interference signal $y(n)$ affects the process that BS2 correctly demodulates the wanted signal $u(n)$, in order to accurately obtain the desire signal $u(n)$ in digital domain, $y(n)$ needs to be identified and then subtracted from $r(n)$.

In this paper, the least-square (LS) method is used to estimate the nonlinear components generated by PA. Since the interference signal $y(n)$ is unknown to the BS2, we use an optical fiber link to obtain the original interference $x(n)$ to estimate $y(n)$ as required in the LS estimation.

As shown in Fig. 2, we use N samples to estimate $y(n)$, and then Eq. (1) can be written in vector form as

$$z = c\,X,$$

(2)

where $z = [z(0), z(1), \ldots, z(N-1)]^T$ is the collection of $z(n)$, $c = [c_{1Q}, \ldots, c_{KQ}]^T$ is the collection of nonlinear coefficients c_{kq}, $(\bullet)^T$ denotes the matrix transpose operation.

$$X = \begin{bmatrix} x_{10}(0) & \cdots & x_{K0}(0) & \cdots & x_{1Q}(0) & \cdots & x_{KQ}(0) \\ \vdots & \ddots & \vdots & \ddots & \vdots & \ddots & \vdots \\ x_{10}(N-1) & \cdots & x_{K0}(N-1) & \cdots & x_{1Q}(N-1) & \cdots & x_{KQ}(N-1) \end{bmatrix}$$

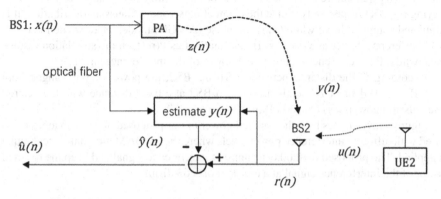

Fig. 2. The framework of the proposed interference cancellation method

is the matrix constructed by the collection of $x(n)$.

After transmission, the PA signal $z(n)$ is received at BS2 along with channel noise and becomes the interference signal $y(n)$, and thus the interference signal can be written as.

$$y = cX. \tag{3}$$

Since the interference signal $y(n)$ is normally independent of the desired signal $u(n)$ and $r(n) = y(n) + u(n)$, Eq. (3) can be expressed as.

$$r = aX, \tag{4}$$

where $r = [r(0), r(1), ..., r(N-1)]^T$ is the collection of received signal $r(n)$, and vector a is the estimation of vector c. Therefore, vector a can be estimated using the LS estimation, which is given by

$$\tilde{a} = (X^H X)^{(-1)} X^H r, \tag{5}$$

where $(\bullet)^H$ denotes the conjugate transpose of matrix.

By using Eq. (5), we can reconstruct the interference signal as $\hat{y} = \hat{a}X$, i.e.,

$$\hat{y}(n) = \sum_{\substack{k=1 \\ k \text{ is odd}}}^{K} \sum_{q=0}^{Q} \hat{a}_{kq} x(n-q) |x(n-q)|^{k-1}, \tag{6}$$

where $K = 5$, $Q = 2$. Then the desired signal is estimated as $\hat{u}(n) = r(n) - \hat{y}(n)$.

4   Simulations Results

The simulation results illustrate the effectiveness of the proposed interference cancellation method. The desired signal $u(n)$ is modulated using 16-quadrature amplitude modulation (16-QAM), while the modulation method of the intended interference signal $x(n)$ is 64-quadrature amplitude modulation (64 QAM) and Quadrature Phase Shift Keying (QPSK) respectively. Since the channel noise obeys Gaussian distribution, it is simulated using Additive white Gaussian noise (AWGN) model. Here we define residual interference power as $y(n) - \hat{y}(n)$, and marked as P(rest) in the simulation results. Meanwhile, P (Interference) refers to the power of the interference signal.

According to the distance between BS1 and BS2, the power of $y(n)$ ranges from -54 dBm to 0 dBm. UE2 sends message to BS2 at a fixed distance with the desired transmission power $u(n)$ of -30 dBm.

Figure 3 investigates how the residual power of our proposed method changes compared with different interference power levels where the 64-QAM modulation technique is applied. The proposed method can suppress interference signal and keep the residual power of the interference signal at a constant of -63 dBm.

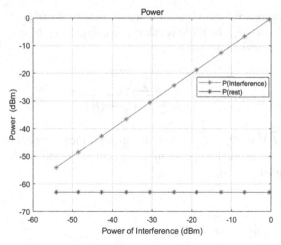

Fig. 3. Power of interference and residual power when the modulation method of interference is 64QAM.

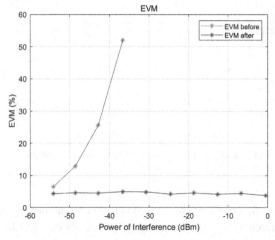

Fig. 4. EVM before and after interference cancellation for 64QAM as the power of interference signal increases.

Figure 4 studies the error vector magnitude (EVM) of our proposed method under different interference power levels. The line "EVM before" is the EVM between $u(n)$ and $r(n)$, which indicates how much the points in the constellation diagram of $r(n)$ differs from $u(n)$'s. "EVM before" increases exponentially with the increasing of the interference power levels without applying the proposed interference cancellation method. When EVM is more than 30%, the constellation diagram shows that the desired signal is completely covered by the interference signal. Therefore, the simulation results become meaningless, which is not drawn in the figures. The line "*EVM after*" shows the EVM between the original signal $u(n)$ sent by UE2 and the estimated signal $\hat{u}(n)$, which indicates that the proposed method can estimate the desired signal $u(n)$ successfully and achieve a low EVM of 4%. The EVM is calculated using the EVM measurement model in Matlab with the following formula

$$EVM = \sqrt{\frac{\frac{1}{N}\sum_{k=1}^{N} e_k}{\frac{1}{N}\sum_{k=1}^{N}(I_k^2 + Q_k^2)}} *100, \qquad (7)$$

where $e_k = (I_k - \tilde{I}_k)^2 + (Q_k - \tilde{Q}_k)^2$, I_k is the in-phase measurement of the kth symbol in the burst, Q_k is the quadrature phase measurement of the kth symbol in the burst, N is the length of signal.

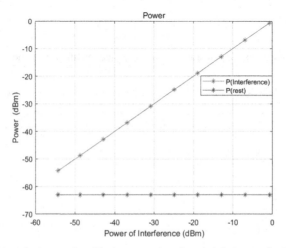

Fig. 5. Power of interference and residual power when the modulation method of interference is QPSK.

As shown in Fig. 5, when the interference signal is modulated by QPSK, the residual power of interference signal remains unchanged at about −63 dBm with different interference power levels.

Figure 6 presents the EVM before and after mitigating the interference when the interference signal is modulated using QPSK. Before canceling the interference signal, the EVM between $u(n)$ and $r(n)$ (the line "*EVM before*") increases exponentially as the power of interference increases, while the EVM between $u(n)$ and $\hat{u}(n)$ (the line "*EVM after*") is reduced to about 4% with the increasing interference power. This result shows that the QPSK-modulated interference signal can be suppressed to obtain the desired signal by the proposed method.

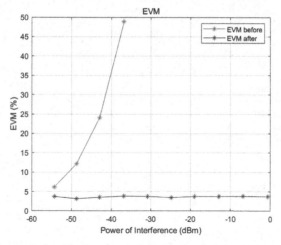

Fig. 6. EVM before and after interference cancellation for QPSK as the power of interference signal increases.

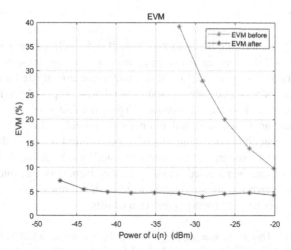

Fig. 7. EVM before and after interference cancellation for 64QAM as the power of desired signal increases.

In addition, when the location of two base stations is fixed and the power of interference signal $y(n)$ is −40 dBm, the power of desired signal $u(n)$ is ranged from −47 dBm to −20 dBm. In this case, for both 64QAM and QPSK as shown in Fig. 7 and Fig. 8 respectively, the EVM before interference suppression increases exponentially as the power of desired signal decreases, while the EVM remains stable at about 5% after canceling the interference signal. Therefore, it is demonstrated that the proposed algorithm can achieve significant performance gain in terms of mitigating the residual interference power and estimating the desired signal.

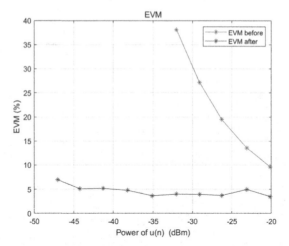

Fig. 8. EVM before and after interference cancellation for QPSK as the power of desired signal increases.

5 Conclusions

Time slots assigned to multiple BSs may be different in 5G cellular networks. However, when the number of BSs increases where time slots may overlap, the strong interference between end users needs to be tackled. In this paper, we investigated the interference problem where an interference cancellation method was proposed for mitigating the co-channel interference. This paper proposed a digital-domain interference cancellation method, which used an optical fiber link to obtain the intended interference source and estimated the nonlinear components introduced by power amplifier using the least-square method. The interference suppression was implemented by subtracting the reconstructed interference signal from the received signal. The effectiveness of this interference cancellation approach in terms of suppressing the residual interference power and estimating the desired signal was verified by the simulation results.

Acknowledgements. This work was supported by the National Key R&D Program of China under grant 2018YFB1801903, the National Natural Science Foundation of China under grants 62071094, U19B2014, 61771107, 61701075, 61601064, 61531009, and Sichuan Science and Technology Program 2020YFH0101. This work was also supported by the Open Research Fund of National Mobile Communications Research Laboratory, Southeast University, under Grant 2019D06.

References

1. Alnoman, A., Anpalagan, A.: Towards the fulfillment of 5G network requirements: technologies and challenges. Telecommun. Syst. **65**, 1 (2017)
2. Al-Saadeh, O., Sung, K.W.: A performance comparison of in-band full duplex and dynamic TDD for 5G indoor wireless networks. EURASIP J. Wirel. Commun. Netw. **2017**(1), 1–14 (2017). https://doi.org/10.1186/s13638-017-0833-3

3. Zheng, M.A., et al.: Key techniques for 5G wireless communications: network architecture, physical layer, and MAC layer perspectives. Sci. China (Inf. Sci.) **58**(4), 5–24 (2015)
4. Wei, L., Hu, R.Q., Qian, Y., Wu, G.: Key elements to enable millimeter wave communications for 5G wireless systems. IEEE Wirel. Commun. **21**(6), 136–143 (2014)
5. Li, Q.C., Niu, H., Papathanassiou, A.T., Wu, G.: 5G network capacity: key elements and technologies. IEEE Veh. Technol. Mag. **9**(1), 71–78 (2014)
6. Hong, S., et al.: Applications of self-interference cancellation in 5G and beyond. IEEE Commun. Mag. **52**(2), 114–121 (2014)
7. Liu, G., Yu, F.R., Ji, H., Leung, V.C.M., Li, X.: In-band full-duplex relaying: a survey, research issues and challenges. In: IEEE Commun. Surv. Tutor. **17**(2), 500–524, Q2nd (2015)
8. Liu, Y., Ma, W., Quan, X., Pan, W., Kang, K., Tang, Y.: An architecture for capturing the nonlinear distortion of analog self-interference cancellers in full-duplex radios. IEEE Microwave Wirel. Compon. Lett. **27**(9), 845–847 (2017)
9. Korpi, D., et al.: Nonlinear self-interference cancellation in MIMO full-duplex transceivers under crosstalk. EURASIP J. Wireless Commun. Netw. **2017** 1 (2017)
10. Ge, S., Meng, J., Xing, J., Liu, Y., Gou, C.: A digital-domain controlled nonlinear RF interference cancellation scheme for co-site wideband radios. IEEE Trans. Electromagn. Compat. **61**(5), 1647–1654 (2019)
11. Kolodziej, K.E., Perry, B.T., Herd, J.S.: In-band full-duplex technology: techniques and systems survey. IEEE Trans. Microw. Theory Tech. **67**(7), 3025–3041 (2019)
12. Suzuki, Y., Narahashi, S., Nojima, T.: Evaluation of non-linear compensation effect of base station power amplifier on adjacent channel interference between different mobile systems. In: 2010 IEEE International Conference on Communication Systems, Singapore, pp. 341–345 (2010)
13. Romero-Jerez, J.M., Ruiz-Garcia, M., Diaz-Estrella, A.: Interference statistics of cellular DS/CDMA systems with base station diversity under multipath fading. IEEE Trans. Wireless Commun. **2**(6), 1109–1113 (2003)
14. Uykan, Z., Jäntti, R.: Converged heterogeneous networks with transmit order and base-station-to-base-station interference cancellation. In: 2015 International Wireless Communications and Mobile Computing Conference (IWCMC), Dubrovnik, Croatia, pp. 469–473 (2015)
15. Weilin, J., Zhongzhao, Z., Yubin, X., Xuejun, S.: Interference mitigated receiver based on base station cooperation. In: 2009 International Forum on Information Technology and Applications, Chengdu, China, 2009, pp. 256-259 (2009)
16. Shin, B.K., Kim, H.S., Kim, S.S., Jang, J.W.: A simple transmission scheme to cancel co-channel interference within a cell in IEEE 802.16j relay networks. In: International Symposium on Wireless and Pervasive Computing, Hong Kong, China, pp. 1–5 (2011)
17. Teng, Z., Wu, J., Huang, X., Zhang, Z.: An iterative interference cancellation design and analysis for uplink cooperation among base stations. In: 2014 Sixth International Conference on Wireless Communications and Signal Processing (WCSP), Hefei, China, pp. 1–5 (2014)
18. Ahmed, S., Faulkner, M.: Interference issues at co-located base stations and an adaptive cancellation solution. In: 2010 Electromagnetic Compatibility Symposium - Melbourne, Melbourne, VIC, Australia, pp. 1–4 (2010)
19. Gomes, H.C., Carvalho, N.B.: Interference cancellation: new configuration technique for cancellation of strong interferences from adjacent frequency bands. In: 2008 Workshop on Integrated Nonlinear Microwave and Millimetre-Wave Circuits, Malaga, Spain, pp. 65–68 (2008)

Regression Capsule Network for Object Detection

Xiaofeng Zhang[1], Di Lin[1,2(✉)], Xiao Zhang[1,2], Hao Li[1,2], Chenyao Wu[1,2], Feng Liu[1,2], Shaotao Liu[1,2], Yuan Gao[1,2], and Jiang Cao[1,2]

[1] School of Information and Software Engineering, University of Electronic Science and Technology of China, Chengdu, China
lindi@uestc.edu.cn
[2] Military Academy of Sciences, Beijing, China

Abstract. In recent years, the emergence of capsule networks has brought new solutions to problems in various fields of computer vision. Capsule networks show the superiority of traditional convolution neural networks by using vectors and fusing the relationships between their different dimensions. Though prior work on object detection has shown their brilliant result, there is still a long way to improve in the detection results of multi-target and multi-classification tasks. Therefore, we consider that the combination of capsule networks and object detection can effectively improve the result of the prediction model. In this paper, 1. Our model utilizes the backbone structure of retinanet, using dynamic routing algorithm to ameliorate the structure of prediction subnet. 2. We test our model on MScoco 2017 datasets. mAP increases 0.8% and recall increases 0.4%.

Keywords: CapsNet · Squash · Object detection · FPN · CNN

1 Introduction

How to extract information from images that computers can understand is the central problem of computer vision tasks. In recent years, neural networks represented by CNN based model structure occupy the dominant position in the field of the computer vision task. Object detection, as an essential part of the computer vision task, needs to detect instances of visual objects of an identified category.

Object Detection needs to predict categories and mark the bounding boxes of objects in images of the given datasets. However, the 2D matrix is used to represent 3D images in reality. Besides different lighting and different shapes of the object. There are also elements like different perspectives that seriously bring about the result of object detection. How to accurately locate objects in complex environments is a challenge for object detection in the future.

Capsule network's original intention is to address some of the shortcomings of CNN [17]. Researchers widely believe that CNN makes good use of the characteristics of movement invariance, but it becomes a stumbling block effectiveness

© ICST Institute for Computer Sciences, Social Informatics and Telecommunications Engineering 2021
Published by Springer Nature Switzerland AG 2021. All Rights Reserved
X. Wang et al. (Eds.): AICON 2021, LNICST 397, pp. 62–73, 2021.
https://doi.org/10.1007/978-3-030-90199-8_7

of CNN. The Capsule network is based on the features detected by the CNN, and the strong relationship between the output channels can be expressed by capsule network. The relationship between the features of images is activated by squash function, which greatly improves the detection effect. The capsule network can be regarded as revolutionary network architecture. The output of a neuron has changed from a scalar to a vector, which gives the model ability to detect the relationship between different features. Each capsule neuron makes the information hidden in the original images richer. In addition, CNN and capsule network are not mutually exclusive. The bottom layer of capsule network is realized by CNN. After all, capsule network is good at integrating different features in the space of original images, and using abstract information to get more accurate results.

At this stage, object detection models [11,13,19,20,26] generally do not pay attention to the spatial relationship between image features. And researchers of capsule networks for object detection tasks are still very few. So in this paper, based on the structure of RetinaNet, we use capsule network to improve the subnet structure of regression part. We base on such a consideration: when the anchor is very close to the ground truth box, the update amplitude of the related parameters in the gradient descent is hard to reduce, so we use capsule network in regression subnet to use spatial relationship between different features to improve the above problems. The output dimension is extended by the last layer of the regression subnet. And we make an experimental improvement of dynamic routing algorithm to adapt to high dimension of the output of capsule layer. Finally, we use the conv1×1 convolution to reduce the activated matrix's dimension. Comparing to Retinanet, our model has a 0.8% improvement on mAP.

2   Related Work

From the perspective of the bottom logic, the biggest dilemma of deep neural networks is that gradient is difficult to converge. In order to make the model converge quickly, using pretrained model FPN [10] as backbone can reduce the risk of model unable to converge. Because the pretrained FPN as the backbone does extract features better than training model from scratch. We can use these features to complete the rest of object detection task, which will make the prediction process easier.

Considering the actual scene, the objects in the picture are usually at different depths of field, and the size and shape of the objects are also quite different. The feature map with a small size in the pyramid structure relates to small object, and the feature map with a large size relates a large object. So the pyramid structure has certain rationality. In fact, in [3,11], the small size feature map was extracted from Resnet [6], and the model's detection result on small object is also improved. It can be seen that the feature extraction result based on the pretrained backbone makes it very obvious.

[26] After pre-training, the model itself has the ability to predict. The next task is to make small adjustments to the rest of the model based on the specific input data so that it can adapt to the process of different tasks. In the past two years, most of the algorithms [9,11] based on one-stage are pyramid backbone based on FPN. Backbone networks above are usually from large pretrained models, such as VGG [18], ResNet [6], and ImageNet [2]. Researchers usually use one or more layers in the pretrained model to extract image features. According to the size of the feature map, different layers form a pyramid-like structure from large to small.

After FPN performs feature extraction, the subnet is usually used to process the extracted features. In [11,20], subnet is often divided into two parts, which are used for classification and regression problems. It is also feasible to use the subnet in [1,12–15], just the label processing is merely slightly different.

Now, all current mainstream detectors, such as R-CNN [4,16], YOLOv3 [15], RetinaNet [11] and SSD [12], are generally based on a set of predefined boxes to predict object category and bounding box's border offset in the anchor. In order to improve detection results, one of the preferred methods is to cluster the pictures, such as K-Means [23] and get a small number of different scale and ratio anchor boxes. Although this method reduces the amount of calculation in model training, there is still a strong connection between the model and the feature distribution of the images, and the robustness and credibility are difficult to prove of the model between different datasets. In another way, researchers often define anchors in the image for multiple specified anchor points (specific pixel points) [3,9], and each anchor point corresponds to multiple anchors of different sizes. Each anchor point corresponds to an object in label y. In the method above, a large number of predefined anchors are reflected by data labels, so there is still a long way to go of the accuracy improvement. Also, experiments [3,11] show that using ordinary loss function is difficult to make the model converge, and difficult to predict categories and border offset of bounding boxes.

Basically all recent research on capsule network like [21,22,24,25] rarely focus on capsule network for object detection tasks. Therefore, we think it is very promising to use the capsule network for object detection tasks.

3   Proposed Method

3.1   Outline

As shown in Fig. 1, our contains two parts, the top is the backbone of our model, and the bottom is the classification subnet and regression subnet of our model.

Considering that in the task of object detection, objects in the images need to be identified. Therefore, a straightforward idea is to take the pretrained model as backbone. In addition, with the rise and popularization of transfer learning, the concept of transfer learning and fine-tuning has become mature. Therefore, the pretrained network obtains parameters on pretrained dataset other than the training dataset, and continuing to participate in training can effectively extract some features of the target in the picture.

So, our backbone uses Resnet-50 as the pretrained model, and the pretrained model above is used as a part of the entire network to do feature extraction, which is used to extract image feature information and generate feature maps for the next step of classification and regression tasks. Generally, we think that backbone feature extraction ability is strong enough. We can load the model parameters that have been officially trained on large data sets (Pascal VOC, ImageNet [7]), and then connect them to our model for fine-tuning.

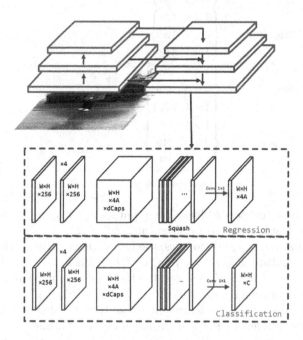

Fig. 1. The entire model structure. Top for backbone. Botton for classification subnet and regression subnet.

3.2 Backbone

As the structure mentioned above, we use Resnet-50 as the backbone. Table 1 shows the main structure of the backbone. As the picture shows us, backbone is divided into 6 layers according to the name of the layer to it belongs. For each stage, the output feature map size is twice smaller than the input feature map.

conv1 is the first block of Resnet-50. With zero padding and $step = 2$, it has 64 kernels of size 7×7. After conv1 is a Max Pooling layer, it does not change the number of channels of the feature maps.

Stage 1 is a composite block, which is composed of 3 residual modules composed of a multi-layer CNN structure. Each layer of the residual module is followed by the normalization function and Relu activation operation. And we use Relu to highlight object features. The range of the element is limited to [0,1).

Table 1. Our backbone structure

	Resnet-50
conv1	$7 \times 7, 64, padding = 0, step = 2, c = 64$
Max pooling	$3 \times 3, step = 2$
Stage1	$\left\{\begin{array}{l} 1 \times 1, \ 64 \\ 3 \times 3, \ 64 \\ 1 \times 1, \ 256 \end{array}\right\} \times 3$
Stage2	$\left\{\begin{array}{l} 1 \times 1, \ 128 \\ 3 \times 3, \ 128 \\ 1 \times 1, \ 512 \end{array}\right\} \times 4$
Stage3	$\left\{\begin{array}{l} 1 \times 1, \ 256 \\ 3 \times 3, \ 256 \\ 1 \times 1, \ 1024 \end{array}\right\} \times 6$
Stage4	$\left\{\begin{array}{l} 1 \times 1, \ 512 \\ 3 \times 3, \ 512 \\ 1 \times 1, \ 1024 \end{array}\right\} \times 3$

Stage 2 is also a composite block. The input feature map of size is $(w, h, 128)$, and the output feature map size will be $(w/2, h/2, 512)$.

Stage 3 contains 6 residual modules, the input feature map size is $(w, h, 256)$, and the output feature map size will be $(w/2, h/2, 1024)$.

Stage 4 contains 3 residual modules, the input feature map size is $(w, h, 512)$, and the output feature map size will be $(w/2, h/2, 2048)$.

As Fig. 1 shows, the three feature maps output by stages 2, 3 and 4 are merged to get three level FPN feature maps of P3, P4, and P5. To continue down-sampling, feature maps P6 and P7 are generated by the output of stage 4. The composition of the backbone is made up of P4, P5, P6 and P7.

3.3 Classification Subnet

As an alternative proposal to neural networks, our capsule network is equivalent to the Primary Capsule layer in [17] capsule network. Our capsule network's input is the output of backbone. In other words, the multi-channel feature map and the matrix are multiple capsules. The output of a normal CNN multi-channel feature map is grouped according to the dimension of the number of channels, and the multiple channels mentioned above are artificially divided into several capsules. Suppose the number of capsules is N, the number of output channels of CNN is C, and the number of channels inside each capsule is D, then the following relationship of N, C and D is blowing.

$$D = C/N$$

The classification subnet divides 320 channels into 80 groups according to the grouping convolution method, with 4 channels in each group. Here, 80 represents the final number of categories. Finally, the dimensionality of each capsule is reduced by *conv* 1×1. we do not use squash to activate in the classification subnet

There are two ways to implement the classification subnet with capsule network. The first way is to implement a stack of N parallel conventional convolution layers. The second implementation is to use convolution layer with the number of output channels of $N \times D$. And then artificially divide the output matrix with the number of channels C into N parts. If the implement is used by the first way, to a direct understanding, we need to define N convolution layers, and the number of output channels of each convolution layer is D. During training, N convolution layers are calculated serially, and the results are obtained in turn. It is conceivable that the training speed of this implementation method is pretty slow. We implement it in the second way. After the output matrix of the CNN layer is obtained, it needs to be subjected to a dimension conversion operation. As shown in Fig. 1, the number of channels inside each capsule is $D = 4$, and there are $N = 80$ capsules in total. The dimensional transformation process is shown in Fig. 1 Each of the 320 channels is divided into 80 parts in groups of four. Finally, the matrix is grouped and convolved by a convolution kernel with a convolution kernel size of 1×1. And the final result is obtained. In addition, the reason is that when calculating the loss function, each channel of the final output of the capsule network needs to correspond to each category. So, there are 80 categories of data in the MScoco 2017. 320 channels need to be split into 80 parts. The number of channels $D = 4$ in each convolution layer is to take into account the computing power of the experimental device D cannot be set too large. Otherwise, the storage limit of GPU devices will be exceeded during the calculation process. The calculation of the GPU device will be exceeded its computing ability.

3.4   Regression Subnet

The structure of the regression subnet is shown in Fig. 2. As shown in I in Fig. 2, the size of the input feature map received from backbone is (b, c, w, h), and b refers to batch size. In part II, the output of the backbone is divided into four capsules. Each capsule refers to an element of the prediction box. And we use the squash function to activate the four capsules respectively. In the activation, we get *routing* $= 1$ in our model. In Fig. 3, the ordinary CNN layer is replaced with a convolution layer with 4 grouped convolution. The output result is subjected to *conv*1×1 operation. The output channel number is 4, and the number of groups is also 4, which is corresponded to the prediction box of $P = (P_x, P_y, P_w, P_h)$ that indicate the center point of the object within the range of the anchor box. The offset of the distance anchor box in horizontal and vertical directions, as well as the offset of the upper and lower borders and the left and right borders. Each group has 4 independent channels. The output matrix size is $(b, 4, w, h)$.

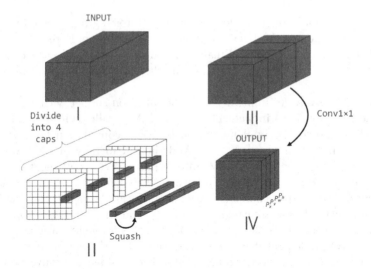

Fig. 2. Regression subnet structure diagram

3.5   Dynamic Routing Algorithm

Because the problem solved in [17] is the problem of image reconstruction. But we aimed at object detection task, which is different from the dynamic routing algorithm steps used in [17]. Our dynamic routing algorithm is shown in Algorithm 1. The input vector is $\hat{u}_{j|i}$, the number of iterations is r, and the output of the dynamic routing algorithm is *outputs*

Lines 1–2 initialize the intermediate linear offset matrix b, which is initialized to 0.

Line 3 executes lines 4–8 r times. We set $r = 1$, so the number of iteration is 1. The use of r = 1 is to take into account that object detection is a task with a high computational cost. Matrix multiplication and other complex matrix transformation operations will cause training time and the model's efficiency in processing pictures FPS performance In order to speed up the training speed, we set $r = 1$.

$$Squash(s_{ij}) = \frac{||s_{ij}||^2}{1 + ||s_{ij}||^2} \cdot \frac{s_{ij}}{||s_{ij}||}$$

In the loop of fourth line, we need to get each element s_{ij} in the vector matrix of size (W, H).

Line 5 uses b_{ij} to get c_{ij}, c_{ij} is a probability value. Because the output processed by $Softmax$ is a non-negative value, and the sum of each dimension of the vector c_{ij} is 1, which conforms to the concept of probability. c_{ij} can be understood as the existence probability between different channels in the capsule. Finally c_{ij} is learned during training.

Algorithm 1. Our dynamic routing algorithm

Input: input parameters $\hat{u}_{j|i}$, r
Output: *outputs*
1: **for** i in range(W) and j in range(H) **do**
2:      $b_{ij} = 0$
3: **for** iterations(r) **do**
4:      **for** i in range(W) and j in range(H) **do**
5:          $c_{ij} = Softmax(b_{ij})$
6:          $s_{ij} = c_{ij} \cdot \hat{u}_{j|i} + b_{ij}$
7:          $v_{ij} = Squash(s_{ij}))$
8:          $b_{ij} = b_{ij} + \hat{u}_{j|i} \cdot \hat{v}_{ij}$
9: **return** *outputs* $= (v)$

In line 6, we get s_{ij}, s_{ij} represents the total high-level features of the corresponding area of the anchor point and takes it as the input of Squash activation.

Line 7 uses Squash to get v_{ij}. While ensuring that s_{ij} remains unchanged, the length does not exceed 1.

Line 8 uses $\hat{u}_{j|i}$ and v_{ij} to get $\hat{u}_{j|i} \cdot v_{ij}$, and add b_{ij} to the sum of the result. The result is assigned to b_{ij}. And b_{ij} is updated during training.

Line 9 returns the *outputs*.

3.6 Loss and Activate Function

Loss is divided into two parts, the classification subnet $loss_{cls}$ and the regression subnet $loss_{reg}$. The method access to $loss_{cls}$ is as follows in [11], where $\gamma = 2$, $\alpha = 0.25$. And y' represents the predicted value. y represents the true value. The method access to $loss_{reg}$ is as follows, hyperparameters $s_a = 1/9$, $s_b = 1/18$. $diff_\omega$ represents the difference between the predicted frame and the real frame in the four dimensions $\omega \in x, y, w, h$.

$$loss_{cls} = \begin{cases} -\alpha \cdot 1 - y'^\gamma \cdot log(y'), & if \quad y = 1 \\ -\alpha \cdot y'^\gamma \cdot log(1 - y'), & otherwise \end{cases}$$

$$loss_{reg} = \begin{cases} mean(s_a \cdot diff_\omega{}^2), & if \quad diff_\omega < 1/9 \\ mean(diff_\omega - s_b), & otherwise \end{cases}$$

$$loss_{total} = loss_{cls} + loss_{reg}$$

4   Experiment

On MScoco 2017, the first step of our experiments is data preprocessing. In terms of data preprocessing, three different methods are used to enhance the images. Including the median filtering, mean filter, and Gaussian filter mentioned. The above three filtering methods are randomly selected to enhance image features, highlight edges and weaken image noise. 1/4 using the mean filter, 1/4 using the median filter, 1/4 using the gaussian filter. The remaining quarter will not be preprocessed.

After the above processing, the image is then scaled together with the tag y. Considering that our model is very sensitive to the output size of the heatmap, especially in MScoco 2017. The images of the large size usually above $1K \times 1K$, and most images are only a few hundred pixels multiply a few hundred pixels. Then the size of the final heatmap is quite different, which is not conducive to the training of the regression part of the model.

But the most important reason is that in the dynamic routing operation, the matrix multiplication shown in the Algorithm. 1 needs to be performed. If the image size is inconsistent, it will cause failure to determine the parameter ω in the dimensions of the length and width. The best case is to set the above hyperparameters to the dimensions of the heatmap formed by feature extraction of the largest image in the data set in both the length and width directions. However, when the above method is used to process smaller images, the heatmap needs to be filled. Then the filling part corresponding to ω is empty, which is very harmful to the model training. Especially when dealing with large images, because there are not so many large size images in the MScoco 2017, then the edge of ω (often processed The filled part of small images) will be very large, so the effect of processing large images will be not very well.

Correspondingly, after scale, some features in the image will be lost due to the scaling. However, based on the results of the above analysis, we adopt a compromise method to limit the size of the large image within the threshold range (500 × 500). In this way, the contradiction between the loss of image features and the training effect can be comprehensively considered.

Table 2. resnet50 as the result of the backbone network.

	AP	AP_{50}	AP_{75}	AP_s	AP_m	AP_l
Ours	30.6	47.6	32.2	13.9	33.9	43.2
Retinanet	29.8	47.6	31.4	13.7	32.9	42.6

As shown in Fig. 3 and Fig. 4, when the main network adopts Resnet50, the performance of the model is better than Retinanet, and mAP is 0.8% higher than Retinanet. In the detection of small objects, comparing to Retinanet the mAP is improved by 0.2%. In the detection of medium-sized objects, mAP is improved by 1.0%. And comparing to Retinanet the detection result of large objects is also improved by 0.6%. Due to the addition of the capsule network, It can be seen from the figure that the model is not effective than Retinanet at the first few epochs of the training period. As epochs go by, the training process enters the middle period. mAP of our model gradually exceeds Retinanet. Due to the efficacy of the capsule network, the model complexity has increased, and the training process is relatively slow. However, the capsule network can represent the spatial relationship between image feature information. After automatically stop triggered, the result of our model is better than Retinanet.

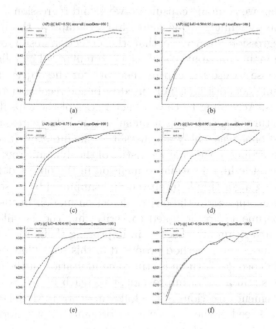

Fig. 3. Comparison chart of retinanet and ours in AP indicator

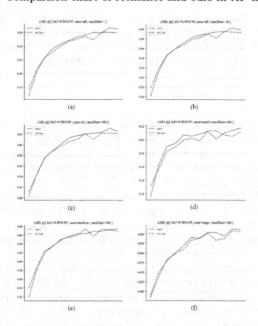

Fig. 4. Comparison chart of retinanet and ours in AR indicator

5 Conclusion

Based on the previous researches, for the two tasks of classification and regression in object detection, we combine capsule network and regression subnet together and improved the dynamic routing algorithm to adapt to the high dimension matrix in the regression subnet, so that the detection result overall reach a higher level. The main contributions of us are summarized as follows:

First, we propose to use the capsule network for the object detection task. The current capsule network is usually used in image reconstruction and image classification tasks. According to the characteristics of the capsule network, we improve the structure of the classification subnet and the regression subnet. We encapsulate the subnet reasonably and uses it as the input of the dynamic routing algorithm. According to the characteristics of the dynamic routing algorithm, and combined with the high heatmap dimension in the object detection model, the dynamic routing algorithm is improved and simplified by us so that the capsule network can be applied in the object detection model. In the experimental part, several experiments are designed to verify that the capsule network and dynamic routing algorithm are effective in improving the model result.

Although the model and method proposed in this paper have some improvement result in MS coco 2017, there is still some limitation in the experiment. In the future, there is still a lot of improvement to reach by us. So we summarize the future improvement directions of the following two: 1. Model complexity can be reduced. 2.The speed of the real-time performance of our model needs to be improved.

Acknowledgment. Partially Funded by Science and Technology Program of Sichuan Province (2021YFG0330), partially funded by Grant SCITLAB-0001 of Intelligent Terminal Key La-boratory of SiChuan Province, and partially Funded by Fundamental Research Funds for the Central Universities (ZYGX2019J076)

References

1. Bochkovskiy, A., Wang, C.Y., Liao, H.Y.M.: YOLOv4: optimal speed and accuracy of object detection. arXiv preprint arXiv:2004.10934 (2020)
2. Deng, J., Dong, W., Socher, R., Li, L.J., Li, K., Fei-Fei, L.: ImageNet: a large-scale hierarchical image database. In: 2009 IEEE Conference on Computer Vision and Pattern Recognition, pp. 248–255. IEEE (2009)
3. Duan, K., Bai, S., Xie, L., Qi, H., Huang, Q., Tian, Q.: Centernet: Keypoint triplets for object detection. In: Proceedings of the IEEE/CVF International Conference on Computer Vision, pp. 6569–6578 (2019)
4. Girshick, R.: Fast r-CNN. In: Proceedings of the IEEE International Conference on Computer Vision, pp. 1440–1448 (2015)
5. Girshick, R., Donahue, J., Darrell, T., Malik, J.: Rich feature hierarchies for accurate object detection and semantic segmentation. In: Proceedings of the IEEE Conference on Computer Vision and Pattern Recognition, pp. 580–587 (2014)
6. He, K., Zhang, X., Ren, S., Sun, J.: Deep residual learning for image recognition. In: Proceedings of the IEEE Conference on Computer Vision and Pattern Recognition, pp. 770–778 (2016)

7. Krizhevsky, A., Sutskever, I., Hinton, G.E.: Imagenet classification with deep convolutional neural networks. Adv. Neural Inf. Process. Syst. **25**, 1097–1105 (2012)
8. LaLonde, R., Bagci, U.: Capsules for object segmentation. arXiv preprint arXiv:1804.04241 (2018)
9. Law, H., Deng, J.: Cornernet: detecting objects as paired keypoints. In: Proceedings of the European Conference on Computer Vision (ECCV), pp. 734–750 (2018)
10. Lin, T.Y., Dollár, P., Girshick, R., He, K., Hariharan, B., Belongie, S.: Feature pyramid networks for object detection. In: Proceedings of the IEEE Conference on Computer Vision and Pattern Recognition, pp. 2117–2125 (2017)
11. Lin, T.Y., Goyal, P., Girshick, R., He, K., Dollár, P.: Focal loss for dense object detection. In: Proceedings of the IEEE International Conference on Computer Vision, pp. 2980–2988 (2017)
12. Liu, W., et al.: SSD: single shot multibox detector. In: Leibe, B., Matas, J., Sebe, N., Welling, M. (eds.) ECCV 2016. LNCS, vol. 9905, pp. 21–37. Springer, Cham (2016). https://doi.org/10.1007/978-3-319-46448-0_2
13. Redmon, J., Divvala, S., Girshick, R., Farhadi, A.: You only look once: unified, real-time object detection. In: Proceedings of the IEEE Conference on Computer Vision and Pattern Recognition, pp. 779–788 (2016)
14. Redmon, J., Farhadi, A.: Yolo9000: better, faster, stronger. In: Proceedings of the IEEE Conference on Computer Vision and Pattern Recognition, pp. 7263–7271 (2017)
15. Redmon, J., Farhadi, A.: Yolov3: an incremental improvement. arXiv preprint arXiv:1804.02767 (2018)
16. Ren, S., He, K., Girshick, R., Sun, J.: Faster r-CNN: towards real-time object detection with region proposal networks. arXiv preprint arXiv:1506.01497 (2015)
17. Sabour, S., Frosst, N., Hinton, G.E.: Dynamic routing between capsules. arXiv preprint arXiv:1710.09829 (2017)
18. Simonyan, K., Zisserman, A.: Very deep convolutional networks for large-scale image recognition. arXiv preprint arXiv:1409.1556 (2014)
19. Tan, M., Pang, R., Le, Q.V.: Efficientdet: scalable and efficient object detection. In: Proceedings of the IEEE/CVF Conference on Computer Vision and Pattern Recognition, pp. 10781–10790 (2020)
20. Tian, Z., Shen, C., Chen, H., He, T.: Fcos: fully convolutional one-stage object detection. In: Proceedings of the IEEE/CVF International Conference on Computer Vision, pp. 9627–9636 (2019)
21. Wang, Q., Xu, C., Zhou, Y., Ruan, T., Gao, D., He, P.: An attention-based bi-GRU-capsnet model for hypernymy detection between compound entities. In: 2018 IEEE International Conference on Bioinformatics and Biomedicine (BIBM), pp. 1031–1035. IEEE (2018)
22. Wang, X., Tan, K., Du, Q., Chen, Y., Du, P.: Caps-triplegan: Gan-assisted capsnet for hyperspectral image classification. IEEE Trans. Geosci. Remote Sens. **57**(9), 7232–7245 (2019)
23. Wong, J.A.H.A.: Algorithm as 136: a k-means clustering algorithm. J. R. Stat. Soc. **28**(1), 100–108 (1979)
24. Zhang, W., Tang, P., Zhao, L.: Remote sensing image scene classification using CNN-capsnet. Remote Sens. **11**(5), 494 (2019)
25. Zhu, C., He, Y., Savvides, M.: Feature selective anchor-free module for single-shot object detection. In: Proceedings of the IEEE/CVF Conference on Computer Vision and Pattern Recognition, pp. 840–849 (2019)
26. Zou, Z., Shi, Z., Guo, Y., Ye, J.: Object detection in 20 years: a survey. arXiv preprint arXiv:1905.05055 (2019)

Difficulty-And-Beauty Network Assessment Framework Based on Information Entropy Weight Principle

Jiachi Chen[1], Chenyiming Wen[1], Yu Zhang[1,2(✉)], Hong Peng[1], Guoxing Huang[1], Weidang Lu[1], and Yuan Gao[3,4]

[1] College of Information Engineering, Zhejiang University of Technology, Hangzhou 310023, China
yzhang@zjut.edu.cn
[2] National Mobile Communications Research Laboratory, Southeast University, Nanjing 210096, China
[3] Academy of Military Science of PLA, Beijing 100091, China
[4] Tsinghua University, Beijing 100084, China

Abstract. In this paper, we propose a difficulty-and-beauty network assessment framework based on information entropy weight principle. In the proposed framework, we divide the network performance indicators into two classes, namely "beauty" indicators and "difficulty" indicators. The weight of each indicator is generated from the experts' advices using the information entropy weight principle. On the other hand, the scoring of indicator is based on network measurement or expert rating. Then hierarchical non-linear weighted aggregation is performed on the indicators, through which we can obtain a final score as an assessment of the overall network performance. The proposed framework can inherently combine objective indicators and subjective indicators thus achieve an integrated network evaluation, and explicitly reflect the influence of each indicator during the evaluation process.

Keywords: Information entropy weight principle · Difficulty-and-beauty assessment · Non-linear aggregation

1 Introduction

In recent years, network system (especially complicated network system) has been widely investigated by researchers [1], e.g., OODA Loop model in the field of Command and Manipulation proposed by Boyd [2], Network Topology and Military Performance proposed by DSTO C[3]'s scholar Anthony Dekker [3] and so on. The above work has considered how to evaluate a certain network more accurately, which plays an important role in improving network efficiency. Therefore, this topic has become a vital subject in the field of network management.

X. Wang et al. (Eds.): AICON 2021, LNICST 397, pp. 74–84, 2021.
https://doi.org/10.1007/978-3-030-90199-8_8

Existing network evaluation methods can be divided into three classes, i.e., measurement, analysis, and simulation. Measurement method needs to acquire various types of parameters and related data through measurement tools. This method is easily affected by the circumstance and usage situation of the target network. Therefore, it is more suitable for existed and stable-running networks [4]. On the other hand, analysis method evaluates the network performance based on mathematic formulas. This obviously introduces two advantages: 1. faster analysis, 2. modelling with the help of explicit formulas. The relationship between the inherent parameters of the network as well as the relationship between the indicators and the acquired data can be expressed explicitly. Nevertheless, it requires math models like Queuing Theory and Probability Theory [5], which may cause over-complicated modelling. Finally, simulation method uses software programming to imitate total or partial behavior of the target network. The advantage lies in that with more specific programming parameter setting, one can obtain more accurate simulation result. Moreover, the influence of single indicator to the whole system can be also detected. Nevertheless, more specific simulation setting can lead to considerably high computational complexity. Since the result highly relies on the accuracy of programming model, it is difficult to guarantee the applicability in practice.

As one of the typical network evaluation methods, DoDAF was proposed by The United States Defense Department, which is a multi-view, multi-angle network description model [6]. However, with the increase of network structure complexity, it may not adapt to the rapidly changing application environment [7]. On the other hand, Analytic Hierarchy Process (AHP), first proposed by American scientist T.L. Saaty back to 1990, is a practical multi-criteria decision-making method combining qualitative with quantitative. It has been widely valued and applied in the field of performance evaluation [8]. For example, Jukka Korpela et al. demonstrated the important role of AHP method in the development of supply chain network system [9]. Ge Wanga et al. used AHP to redesign the supply chain network system [10].

In this paper, we propose the difficulty-and-beauty network evaluation framework that borrows idea from AHP. The evaluation process under this framework can be regarded as a process in which a group of experts make decisions based on their relevant experience under a restricted time requirement. Therefore, it is a human-oriented, systematic modeling and evaluation method that combines subjectivity with objectivity. We propose to introduce the information entropy weight principle into the difficulty and beauty assessment framework. The proposed framework takes into consideration both "Difficulty" (objective static indicators) and "Beauty"(subjective dynamic indicators), combined with the principle of information entropy theory. Specifically, the weight of each indicator is calculated using information entropy weight principle, which is used together with the data corresponding to the network performance to evaluate a whole network. The actual data can be collected through measurement method. Analysis method is applied during the calculation process of the proposed method, wherein the concept of interval numbers from fuzzy mathematics is involved. Furthermore, we apply the hieratical non-linear weighted aggregation in order to highlight the influence of single vital indicators on the overall evaluation of the network [11].

2 Difficulty-And-Beauty Network Assessment Framework

The establishment of difficulty-and-beauty network assessment framework is the precondition for the evaluation of the network. As shown in Fig. 1, the network assessment framework has four levels. First level consists of two indicators "Difficulty" and "Beauty". Under the "Difficulty" indicator, there are five second-level indicators, namely "Coverage", "Transmission", "Process", "Storage", "Defense". Under the "Beauty" indicator, there are three second-level indicators, namely "Situation Awareness", "Mission Planning", "Action Control". Under each second-level indicator, the corresponding third-level indicators are different. There are 56 third-level indicators in total.

Now we briefly introduce the third-level indicators under the "Coverage" indicator as an example:

Coverage Degree: A measure of the deployment of network nodes. It is defined as the ratio of the total area covered by all nodes to the total target area.

Coverage multiplicity: It indicates the degree of coverage redundancy in a certain area. If this area is within the coverage of K nodes, then its coverage multiplicity is K.

Weak coverage area: When the continuous coverage rate of a certain area is smaller than 96%, it can be considered that the area has weak coverage.

Cross-area coverage: When the signal of a cell can be detected outside the first neighboring cells around it, or the difference of the signal strength between that from this cell and the main serving cell is within 6 dB, the cell has a cross-area coverage issue.

Received signal strength: It reflects the distance between the mobile station and base station. So this value can be used to measure the size of the cell coverage.

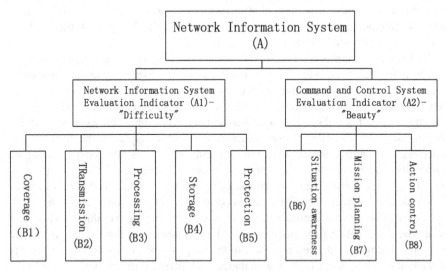

Fig. 1. Difficulty-and-beauty network assessment framework.

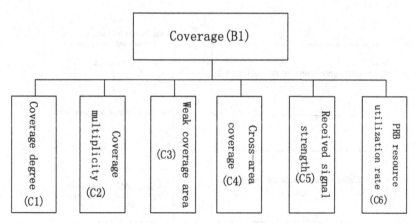

Fig. 2. Third-level indicators under "Coverage"

3 Network Evaluation Based on Information Entropy Weight Method

3.1 Overall Evaluation Procedure

The procedures for indicator weight calculation and final score calculation are in Fig. 3(a) and Fig. 3(b), respectively.

Figure 3(a) presents the 5 steps to calculate the indicator weights. Note that weight calculation for third-level, second-level and first-level indicators follows the same procedure.

Figure 3(b) presents the aggregation steps between each level to calculate the final score of the network performance.

More detail will be discussed in the following.

3.2 Calculation Rules of Interval Number

In the proposed network evaluation framework, fuzzy mathematic is involved, where the weight and score of each indicator are in the form of interval number. Therefore, we first introduce interval number calculation rules as follows:

A interval number is expressed as $\hat{x}_i = (x_i^l, x_i^r)$, where the superscript l indicates the lower bound of the interval number, and the superscript r indicates the upper bound of the interval number.

Definition 1: Interval number addition:

$$\hat{x}_i + \hat{x}_j = (x_i^l, x_i^r) + (x_j^l, x_j^r) = (x_i^l + x_j^l, x_i^r + x_j^r) \qquad (1)$$

Definition 2: Interval number subtraction:

$$\hat{x}_i - \hat{x}_j = (x_i^l, x_i^r) - (x_j^l, x_j^r) = (x_i^l - x_j^l, x_i^r - x_j^r) \qquad (2)$$

Definition 3: Multiplication of an interval number and a scalar:

$$n\hat{x}_i = (nx_i^l, nx_i^r) \qquad (3)$$

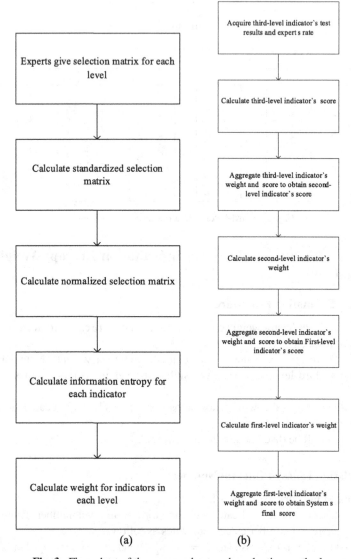

(a)   (b)

Fig. 3. Flow chart of the proposed network evaluation method

Definition 4: Interval numbers multiplication:

$$\hat{x}_i\hat{x}_j = \left(x_i^1, x_i^r\right)\left(x_j^1, x_j^r\right) =$$
$$\left(\min\left\{x_i^1 x_j^1, x_i^1 x_j^r, x_i^r x_j^1, x_i^r x_j^r\right\}, \max\left\{x_i^1 x_j^1, x_i^1 x_j^r, x_i^r x_j^1, x_i^r x_j^r\right\}\right) \tag{4}$$

Definition 5: Interval number division:

$$\frac{\hat{x}_i}{\hat{x}_j} = (x_i^1, x_i^r)(\frac{1}{x_j^r}, \frac{1}{x_j^1}) \tag{5}$$

Definition 6: Interval number exponentiation:

$$\hat{x}_i^{\hat{x}_j} = \left(x_i^1, x_i^r\right)^{\left(x_j^1, x_j^r\right)}$$
$$= \left(\min\left\{\left(x_i^1\right)^{x_j^1}, \left(x_i^1\right)^{x_j^r}, \left(x_i^r\right)^{x_j^1}, \left(x_i^r\right)^{x_j^r}\right\} \max\left\{\left(x_i^1\right)^{x_j^1}, \left(x_i^1\right)^{x_j^r}, \left(x_i^r\right)^{x_j^1}, \left(x_i^r\right)^{x_j^r}\right\}\right) \tag{6}$$

Definition 7: Interval number logarithm:

$$\log_a \hat{x}_i = \log_a(x_i^1, x_i^r) = (\log_a x_i^1, \log_a x_i^r) \tag{7}$$

3.3 Indicator Weight Calculation

In this section we explain in detail the steps and formulas involved in calculating weight of each indicator, as shown in Fig. 3(a).

In information theory, information entropy weight is used to measure the degree of disorder of a system. For an evaluation indicator, the smaller information entropy, the greater degree of variation of indicator value. Therefore, an indicator with smaller entropy can provide more useful information to assist the evaluation process, accordingly it should have larger weight. Here we use information entropy weight to reflect the performance of each indicator in the network [12].

The detailed steps of indicator weight calculation are as follows:

Step 1: Suppose the number of experts is N, and the number of indicators is M, then a $N \times M$ selection matrix can be generated, which is denoted as $\hat{\mathbf{A}} = \left(\hat{a}_{ij}\right)_{N \times M}$.

Step 2: Standardize the selection matrix. Set the maximum value in each column of the selection matrix to 1, and then divide all the elements in the matrix by the maximum value of the corresponding column. The resulted matrix is called standardized matrix, i.e., $\hat{\mathbf{R}} = \left(\hat{r}_{ij}\right)_{N \times M}$.

Step 3: Generate the normalized matrix $\hat{\mathbf{D}} = \left(\hat{d}_{ij}\right)_{N \times M}$ from the standardized matrix $\hat{\mathbf{R}} = \left(\hat{r}_{ij}\right)_{N \times M}$. Firstly, add each interval number of standardized matrix column-wisely. Then divide each element in standardized matrix by the sum of the corresponding column.

Let the normalized matrix be $\widehat{\mathbf{D}} = \left(\hat{d}_{ij}\right)_{N \times M}$. Then we have

$$\hat{d}_{ij} = \frac{\hat{r}_{ij}}{\sum\limits_{i=1}^{N} \hat{r}_{ij}}, \quad i \in N, j \in M \tag{8}$$

Step 4: According to the normalized matrix $\widehat{\mathbf{D}} = \left(\hat{d}_{ij}\right)_{N \times M}$, calculate the information entropy for each indicator as E_j:

$$\hat{E}_j = -\frac{1}{\ln N} \sum\limits_{i=1}^{N} \left(\hat{d}_{ij} \ln \hat{d}_{ij}\right), \quad j \in M \tag{9}$$

where $\hat{d}_{ij} = [0,0]$ is equivalent to the real number 0, and the corresponding information entropy is defined as $\hat{d}_{ij} \ln \hat{d}_{ij} = 0$.

Step 5: Use the following formula to calculate the information entropy weight $\hat{\delta}$ of each indicator at the same level:

$$\hat{\delta}_j = \frac{[1,1] - \hat{E}_j}{\sum\limits_{k=1}^{m} \left([1,1] - \hat{E}_k\right)}, \quad j \in M \tag{10}$$

the information entropy weight vector of current level is composed of the information entropy weight of each indicator. Aggregate weights and scores through weighted sum or weighted product to obtain the scores of upper-level indicators.

3.4 Score Calculation

This section explains the scheme for scoring the third-level indicators. We divide the indicators into two classes: qualitative indicator and quantitative indicator.

The score of qualitative indicators is obtained based on expert's rating on the actual performance of the network, which is an interval number. The detailed mapping scheme showed in following table.

Table 1. Mapping of qualitative assessment

Excellent	0.85–1
Good	0.75–0.85
Qualified	0.6–0.75
Unqualified	<0.6

The quantitative indicator scores are calculated as follows based on the network test results. Suppose that the quantitative evaluation criterions are given by: excellent (c, d), good (b, c), qualified (a, b), unqualified (0, a). Then a network test result (x^l, x^r) can be mapped to a score $(y(x^l), y(x^r))$ by

$$
y(x) = \begin{cases}
\dfrac{0.6}{a} \cdot x, 0 \leq x < a \\[2ex]
\dfrac{0.15}{b-a} \cdot (x-a) + 0.6, a \leq x < b \\[2ex]
\dfrac{0.1}{c-b} \cdot (x-b) + 0.75, b \leq x < c \\[2ex]
\dfrac{0.15}{d-c} \cdot (x-c) + 0.85, c \leq x \leq d
\end{cases} \tag{10}
$$

where in the score interval for excellent, good, qualified, unqualified are consistent with that of qualitative indicators as given in Table 1.

3.5 Nonlinear Aggregation Method

This section presents the method of aggregating lower-level indicators to upper-level and the involved detailed formulas.

Nonlinear aggregation usually includes two methods known as weighted sum and weighted product. Let g denotes the nonlinear aggregation method, $\hat{x}_i$ the score of upper-level indicator, $\hat{x}_{ij}, j = 1, 2, ..., m$ the scores of lower level indicators, $\hat{\delta}_{ij}, n = 1, 2, ..., m$ the weights of lower level indicators. Nonlinear aggregation can be presented as follow:

$$
\hat{x}_i = g\left(\hat{x}_{i1}, \hat{x}_{i2}, \cdots, \hat{x}_{im}; \hat{\delta}_{i1}, \hat{\delta}_{i2}, \cdots, \hat{\delta}_{im}\right) \tag{11}
$$

In the weighted sum method, every lower-level indicator is regarded as a component of upper-level indicator and the indicators under the same upper-level indicator are independent of each other and have equal importance. The aggregation is expressed as follows:

$$
\hat{x}_i = \sum_{j=1}^{m} \hat{x}_{ij}\hat{\delta}_{ij} \tag{12}
$$

where weight $\hat{\delta}_{ij}$ satisfies the normalization condition: $\sum_{j=1}^{m} \hat{\delta}_{ij} = [1, 1]$.

The weighted product method is also known as exponential function method, which is suitable for the situations where each lower-level indicator has different importance and indispensable to the upper-level indicator. The corresponding formula is given by:

$$
\hat{x}_i = \prod_{j=1}^{m} \left(\hat{x}_{ij}\right)^{\hat{\delta}_{ij}} \tag{13}
$$

weight $\hat{\delta}_{ij}$ satisfies normalization condition $\sum_{j=1}^{m} \hat{\delta}_{ij} = [1, 1]$.

4 Numerical Results

In this simulation, we consider a mobile communication networks that composed of multiple cells and a core network. The target network is tested and all the 56 third-level indicators are properly collected. We follow the procedures given in Sect. 3 to evaluate the network performance. In the following we plot the overall network score versus partial indicators to illustrate the influence of particular indicators on the network performance.

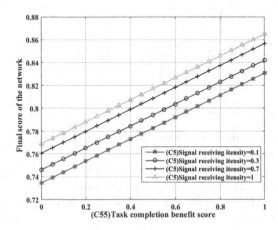

Fig. 4. Overall network score versus the score of (C55) "task completion benefit".

Figure 4 plots final score of the network versus the score of (C55) "task completion benefit". The "task completion benefit" indicator represents the weighted sum of the percentages of the completed tasks of different levels in the total number of task goals. With more important tasks completed, the "task completion benefit" indicator score becomes higher. "Task completion benefit" is a qualitative indicator using weighted sum aggregation method. Therefore, changes in the score of the indicator has a linear impact on the final evaluation of the target network. As for the influence of (C5) "signal receiving intensity" indicator, the higher the score of "signal receiving intensity", the higher the final score of the network.

Figure 5 plots final score of the network versus the score of (C2) "coverage multiplicity". The "coverage multiplicity" indicator indicates the degree of redundancy of coverage of a certain area. If this area is within the coverage of K nodes, then its coverage multiplicity is K. The "coverage multiplicity" indicator is a quantitative indicator using weighted product aggregation method. Therefore, changes in the score of the indicator has a nonlinear impact on the final evaluation of the system, under the same "signal receiving intensity", the growth will eventually converge.

The third-level indicators (C2) "coverage multiplicity" and (C10) "packet loss rate" belongs to the second-level indicators (B1) "Coverage" and (B2) "Transmission", respectively. The weights of the two indicators are (0.2227, 0.2421) and (0.1745, 0.6163),

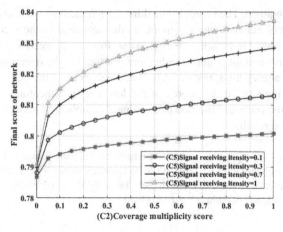

Fig. 5. Overall network score versus the score of (C2) "coverage multiplicity".

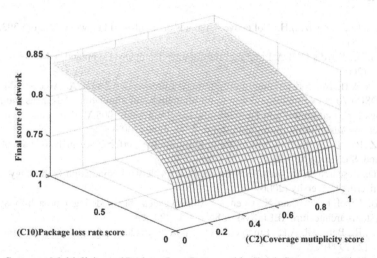

Fig. 6. Coverage Multiplicity and Package Loss Rate combination influence on system evaluation

respectively. As shown in Fig. 6, "packet loss rate" dominates the overall network evaluation compared with "coverage multiplicity". The reason is that "packet loss rate" has larger weight than "coverage multiplicity".

5 Conclusion

In this paper, we propose a difficulty-and-beauty assessment framework based on information entropy weight principle. In the framework, the weights are given in the form of interval numbers in the selection matrix of all levels of indicators based on the opinions of experts. After the standardization and normalization process, the information entropy of each indicator is calculated, with which the information entropy weight of each indicator is obtained. The scores of the third-level indicators are obtained according to expert opinions or network measurement, while the scores of the second-level indicators and the first-level indicators are aggregated from the lower-level indicators. For qualitative indicators and quantitative indicators, we use weighted sum aggregation and weighted product aggregation, respectively. The final score of the network is obtained by sequential aggregation of the scores of the lower-level indicators. The simulation results show that the proposed method can evaluate complicated networks and provide objective evaluation results.

Acknowledgement. This work was supported partially by Zhejiang Provincial Natural Science Foundation of China under Grant LY21F010008, by the open research fund of National Mobile Communications Research Laboratory, Southeast University (No. 2020D10), and the National Natural Science Foundation of China (No. 61871348).

References

1. Watts, D.J., Strogatz, S.H.: Collective dynamics of small-world networks. Nature **393**, 440–442 (1998)
2. Bazin, A.: Boyd's OODA Loop and the Infantry Company Commander. Mil. Rev. **18**(1), 17–19 (2005)
3. Dekker, A.H.: Network topology and military performance. In: Zerger, A., Argent, R.M. (eds.) MODSIM 2005 International Congress on Modelling and Simulation. Advances and Applications for Management and Decision Making; December 2005.Modeling and Simulation Society of Australia and New Zealand, pp. 2174–2180 (2007)
4. Liu, Z., Pan, J., Liu, S., Guodong, L.: Research on internet performance analysis and evaluation method. ShanDong Sci. **22**(4), 64–67 (2009)
5. Wu, D.: Research on Network Performance Base on Network Simulation Technology. Harbin Engineering University (2006)
6. Ge, B., Hipel, K.W., Yang, K., Chen, Y.: A novel executable modeling approach for system-of-systems architecture. IEEE Syst. J. **8**(1), 4–13 (2014)
7. Albert, R., Barabasi, A.L.: Emergence of scaling in random networks. Science **286**(5439), 509–512 (1999)
8. Satty, T.L.: How to make a decision: the analytic hierarchy process. Eur. J. Oper. Res. **48**(1), 9–26 (1990)
9. Korpela, J., Lehmusvaara, A.I., Tuominen, M.: An analytic approach to supply chain development. Int. J. Prod. Econ. **71**(1), 145–155 (2001)
10. Ge, W., Huangb, S.H., Dismukesa, J.P.: Product-driven supply chain selection using integrated multi-criteria decision-making methodology. Int. J. Prod. Econ. **91**(2), 1–15 (2004)
11. Zhu, W., Hou, G., Zhou, Y.: Performance evaluation in multi-sensors co-detection based on fuzzy comprehensive evaluation. J. Telemet. Tracking Command. **31**(4), 36–39 (2010)
12. Zhou, W., Li, X.: A comprehensive evaluation method based on information entropy. Sci. Technol. Eng. **23**(10), 1671–1815 (2010)

Network Information System Evaluation Based on Analytic Hierarchy Process

Qi Cheng[1], Yunxian Chen[1], Yu Zhang[1,2(✉)], Hong Peng[1], Yuxin Xu[1], Weidang Lu[1], and Yuan Gao[3,4]

[1] College of Information Engineering, Zhejiang University of Technology, Hangzhou 310023, China
yzhang@zjut.edu.cn
[2] National Mobile Communications Research Laboratory, Southeast University, Nanjing 210096, China
[3] Academy of Military Science of PLA, Beijing 100091, China
[4] Tsinghua University, Beijing 100084, China

Abstract. This paper investigates the evaluation method for network information system. We propose a "difficulty & beauty" evaluation method based on analytic hierarchy process (AHP) for communication networks. Due to the massive number of indicators in the communication network, it is non-trivial to assess the overall network performance. The proposed evaluation method in this paper can decompose the network evaluation problem into different constituent factors and establish a hierarchical structure according to the association and affiliation across these factors. Then according to the opinions of experts and the actual network behaviors, the weights and scores of the indicators can be obtained. By combining the indicator weights and scores, we can get the final score of the system. The proposed network evaluation method is feasible, and the evaluation process comprehensively considers qualitative and quantitative indicators.

Keywords: Communication network · Analytic hierarchy process · Difficulty-and-beauty evaluation system

1 Introduction

In recent years, researchers have tried novel modeling ideas for network evaluation. Based on the theory of network science, the method of modeling and investigating the network information system have emerged [1]. Literature [2] believed that the task model is very important in the construction of network information system, which can determine the capacity requirements of the system. Literature [3] proposed an executable network information system modeling method based on the Department of Defense Architecture Framework, which is committed to providing support for the analysis and verification of system requirements.

© ICST Institute for Computer Sciences, Social Informatics and Telecommunications Engineering 2021
Published by Springer Nature Switzerland AG 2021. All Rights Reserved
X. Wang et al. (Eds.): AICON 2021, LNICST 397, pp. 85–96, 2021.
https://doi.org/10.1007/978-3-030-90199-8_9

The evaluation of network information system is a complex system engineering, and the evaluation methods for different network systems are usually different. Currently commonly used methods are network data envelopment analysis (DEA) method, information entropy weight method, analytic hierarchy process (AHP), etc. The network DEA model does not need to assume the form of the production function in advance. The authors in [4] considered the cutting-edge production capacity of the network production process, and proposed an network model to calculate the efficiency of network systems; Literature [5] considered the structure of the network system and proposed three network DEA models: integrated model, distributed model and hybrid model. For the information entropy weight method, in 2006, the authors in [6] considered using uncertainty to measure combat effectiveness, decomposing the combat process into multiple nodes, using uncertainty self-information to measure the degree of completion of tasks by each node, and reforming information entropy function to obtain a suitable evaluation method for combat effectiveness. The AHP is a qualitative and quantitative multi-criteria decision-making method proposed by the famous American operations researcher T. L. Saaty [7]. Specifically, when using the AHP, the problem to be solved should be decomposed into related elements, and then further divided into goals, criteria, sub-criteria, etc. The authors in [8] demonstrated the important role of AHP in the development of supply chain network systems. The authors in [9] applied AHP to redesign the supply chain network system. Then the authors in [10] adopted the model of fuzzy analytic hierarchy process and made a good evaluation of the network system of Indian scientific research institutions; The authors in [11] combined the principal component analysis method and the AHP to evaluate the performance of the network system of 14 listed commercial banks, by which a certain basis for the bank's business decision-making was provided. At present, there are many research results on the evaluation methods of the network information system, but most of them are based on the traditional indicator system modeling methods. In addition, most existing evaluation methods only analyze the objective static indicators of the network information system, while ignoring the impact of subjective dynamic indicators.

In this paper, we introduced the "difficulty & beauty" evaluation system into the mobile network information evaluation problem and comprehensively consider the relationship between the indicators. We establish a mobile network "difficulty & beauty" evaluation system, wherein the objective static indicator (i.e., "difficulty") and the subjective dynamic indicator ("beauty") of the mobile network information system are comprehensively modeled and analyzed. Based on the above evaluation system, we propose a network evaluation method using AHP. In the evaluation process, qualitative and quantitative indicators can be inherently combined, and the calculation process requires less quantitative data, which depends more on the expert experience, thereby making up for the defect of the existing quantitative analysis methods. By this method, the opinions of experts and the actual network conditions are combined to obtain the indicator weights and scores for the target communication network. Finally, combining the indicator weight and score, the final evaluation score on the performance of the mobile communication network can be obtained.

2 "Difficulty & Beauty" Network Evaluation System

To evaluate the network system, we first need to establish a network evaluation system of "difficulty & beauty". The evaluation indicators of the network information system are divided into two categories: "difficulty" and "beauty". The network evaluation system has four levels. As shown in Fig. 1, the "network information system evaluation" indicator belongs to the first-level indicator namely "difficulty", under which "coverage", "transmission", "processing", "storage", and "protection" are the 5 s-level indicators; "the command and control system evaluation" indicator belongs to the first-level indicator of "beauty", under which "situation awareness", "mission planning", and "action control" are the 3 s-level indicators. A total of 56 third-level indicators are set up under the second-level indicators.

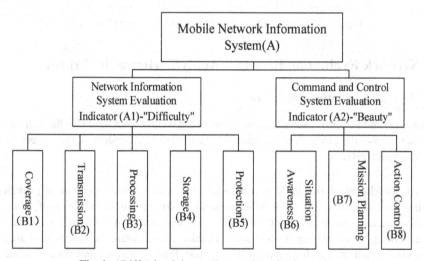

Fig. 1. "Difficulty & beauty" network evaluation system

As depicted in Fig. 2, there are 4 third-level indicators under the second-level indicator "mission planning". Due to the limited space, here we take B7 as an example to explain the meaning of corresponding third-level indicators.

"Resource requirements": After the algorithm performs mission planning, according to the planning results, this indicator reflects the bandwidth required to perform the missions.

"Dynamic adjustment ratio": It indicates the adjustment range of the original plan in the planning result.

"Emergency task completion rate": It indicates the completion of emergency tasks in the planning results.

"Node requirements": According to the network coverage planning, it indicates the number of nodes deployed to fulfill the three-dimensional space coverage planning.

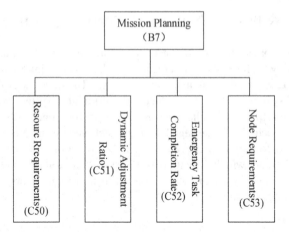

Fig. 2. Third-level indicators set under the "mission planning"

3   Network Evaluation Based on Analytic Hierarchy Process

3.1   Overall Evaluation Procedure

Figure 3(a) and Fig. 3(b) shown the procedure of the weight calculation for the indicators on each level in the evaluation system and the calculation procedure of the system final score, respectively.

1. The weight calculation of the hierarchical total sorting in Fig. 3(a) is mainly divided into 4 steps. Firstly, we establish the hierarchical structure of the indicators of network information system. Secondly, we give the judgment matrix of the all indicators according to the scoring from experts. Thirdly, we calculate the hierarchical single sorting results and perform the consistency test. Finally, we calculate the hierarchical total sorting results and perform the consistency test.
2. The procedure of obtaining the final score of the system is given in Fig. 3(b). Firstly, we obtain the test result or the expert scoring for each third-level indicator. Secondly, we calculate the score for each indicator, and then multiply them by their corresponding weights. With this, we get the final evaluation score of the network information system.

3.2   Indicator Weight Calculation

This section specifically introduces the detailed calculation scheme for calculate the single sorting weight and consistency test for the first-level, the second-level and the third-level indicators, and the total sorting weight and consistency test for all indicators using AHP.

The calculation procedure of weight calculation can be mainly divided into the following four steps:

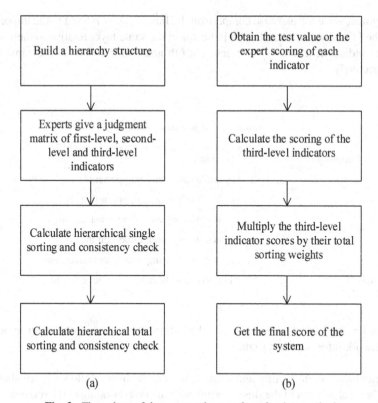

Fig. 3. Flow chart of the proposed network evaluation method

(1) Build a hierarchy structure

Firstly, a hierarchical structure model is established considering the relevant indicators and their affiliations in "difficulty & beauty" evaluation system. The entire hierarchical structure model is divided into four layers: target layer, criterion layer, sub-criteria layer and indicator layer. Only one evaluation object is allowed in the target layer, which is "mobile network information system" (A). The criterion layer is composed of two first-level indicators, namely "network information system evaluation" (A1) and "command and control system evaluation" (A2). Generally, "network information system evaluation" (A1) is evaluated from five perspectives: "coverage" (B1), "transmission" (B2), "processing" (B3), "storage" (B4) and "protection" (B5). Generally, "the command and control system evaluation" (A2) is evaluated according three lower-level indicators: "situation awareness" (B6), "mission planning" (B7) and "action control" (B8). The above eight second-level indicators constitute the sub-criteria layer. A total of 56 commonly used indicators are assigned below B1 to B8, which constitute the indicator layer (i.e., the third level) of the mobile network information system.

(2) Construct a judgment matrix: The importance of each indicator on the same layer relative to the corresponding upper-layer indicator is compared and scored by several experts. Here the pairwise comparison method is used. Table 1 shown the

judgment scale for pairwise comparison. In Table 1, α_{ij} is related to the importance of the i-th indicator over the j-th indicator in the same layer relative to their upper-layer indicator, α_i and α_j represent the i-th and j-th indicator in the same layer, respectively.

Table 1. The judgment scale

Intensity of importance	Definition
$\alpha_{ij} = 1$	α_i and α_j are equally important
$\alpha_{ij} = 3$	α_i is slightly more important than α_j
$\alpha_{ij} = 5$	α_i is obviously more important than α_j
$\alpha_{ij} = 7$	α_i is strongly more important than α_j
$\alpha_{ij} = 9$	α_i is extremely important compared to α_j
$\alpha_{ij} = 2, 4, 6, 8$	The mediums between the above 5 values

According to Table 1, one can obtain the judgment matrices for all layer indicators in the network information system.

(3) hierarchical single sorting and consistency check: In the following, we show the explicit calculation of the single sorting weight corresponding to the relative importance of indicators at the same layer to the upper-layer indicator and the consistency check scheme:

We use the judgment matrix derived before to calculate the single sorting weight by the square root method.

Step 1: we calculate the product of the elements on each row of the judgment matrix:

$$m_i = \prod_{j=1}^{n} \alpha_{ij}, i = 1, 2, \ldots, n, \tag{1}$$

where n denotes the dimension of the judgment matrix, α_{ij} denotes the element on the i-th row and j-th column of the judgment matrix. Then we calculate the nth root of m_i to get w_i':

$$w_i' = \sqrt[n]{m_i}, i = 1, 2, \ldots, n. \tag{2}$$

Then we normalized the column vector $W' = \left(w_1', w_2', \ldots, w_n'\right)^T$ as follows:

$$w_i = \frac{w_i'}{\sum_{i=1}^{n} w_i'}, i = 1, 2, \ldots, n, \tag{3}$$

Let $W = (w_1, w_2, \ldots, w_n)^T$, which is the single-sorting weight vector.

Step 2: we calculate the maximum eigenvalue of the judgment matrix:

$$\lambda_{\max} = \frac{1}{n} \sum_{i=1}^{n} \frac{\sum\limits_{j=1}^{n} \alpha_{ij} w_j}{w_i}, \tag{4}$$

where w_i and w_j are single sorting weight, respectively.

Step 3: we calculate the consistency indicator CI and random consistency ratio CR for the judgment matrix:

$$CI = \frac{\lambda_{\max} - n}{n - 1}. \tag{5}$$

Note that when $n = 2$, all the positive reciprocal comparison matrices are consistent, hence there is no need to perform a consistency check. When $n > 2$, we use the random consistency ratio CR to test the consistency of the n-dimensional judgment matrix. The calculation formula for CR is as follows:

$$CR = \frac{CI}{RI}, \tag{6}$$

where CI represents the consistency indicator, RI denotes the average random consistency indicator, which can be obtained according to Table 2. The values of 16-order average random consistency RI are shown in Table 2. When $n > 2$, $CR < 0.1$, the n-dimensional judgment matrix has acceptable consistency. If it does not meet the consistency requirement, the judgment matrix should be adjusted.

Table 2. 16-order average random consistency indicator value

Order	1	2	3	4	5	6	7	8
RI	0	0	0.58	0.9	1.12	1.24	1.32	1.41
Order	9	10	11	12	13	14	15	16
RI	1.45	1.49	1.52	1.54	1.56	1.58	1.59	1.5943

(4) hierarchical total sorting and consistency check:

We use the results of all the hierarchical single sorting for the indicators in the same layer to calculate their total sorting weights. This procedure is called hierarchical total sorting. The method is: Let B-layer be a second-level indicator and C-layer a third-level indicator, the total sorting weight of the indicators in C-layer is calculated by multiplying the weight of the single sorting of the indicators of C-layer by the weight of the total sorting of the indicators of the upper B-layer respectively. The above calculation is executed from the highest layer to the lowest layer, and finally the total sorting weight of the lowest layer relative to the uppermost layer can be obtained.

According to the judgment matrix of the indicators in the C-layer under the upper-layer indicator B_j, we obtain the consistency indicator of the C-layer single sorting, i.e., $CI(j), j = 1,\ldots,m$, and the corresponding average random consistency indicator is $RI(j), j = 1,\ldots,m$, where m is the number of B-layer indicators. Then the total sorting consistency test indicator of C-layer is as follows:

$$CR = \frac{\sum\limits_{j=1}^{m} CI(j) \cdot w_j}{\sum\limits_{j=1}^{m} RI(j) \cdot w_j}, \tag{7}$$

where w_j denotes the total sorting weight of B-layer. When $CR < 0.1$, the total sorting result of C-layer has acceptable consistency and the result is accepted. On the contrary, the structure of the judgment matrix needs to be adjusted to meet the consistency. The above consistency check follows the way of calculating from upper layer to lower layer.

3.3   Score Calculation of Indicator

In this section, we explain the scoring method of the third-level indicators. For qualitative indicators and quantitative indicators, the score is obtained in different ways as follows:

(1) The qualitative indicators are divided into four evaluation classes: "excellent", "good", "qualified" and "unqualified". As shown in Table 3, different scoring intervals are mapped for each evaluation class. According to the actual performance of the network, experts derive the interval number score of qualitative indicators.

Table 3. Mapping of qualitative evaluation

Qualitative evaluation class	Interval number score
Excellent	0.85–1
Good	0.75–0.85
Qualified	0.6–0.75
Unqualified	<0.6

(2) For quantitative indicators, we map the obtained test results of the network performance into a score. Let the test result of this indicator is the interval number (x^-, x^+), and the score $(y(x^-), y(x^+))$ is obtained by the calculation formula as follows:

$$y(x) = \begin{cases} \dfrac{0.6}{a} \cdot x, 0 \leq x < a \\ \dfrac{0.15}{b-a} \cdot (x-a) + 0.6, a \leq x < b \\ \dfrac{0.1}{c-b} \cdot (x-b) + 0.75, b \leq x < c \\ \dfrac{0.15}{d-c} \cdot (x-c) + 0.85, c \leq x \leq d \end{cases} . \tag{8}$$

where we assume that a certain quantitative indicator evaluation standard is divided into "excellent" (c, d), "good" (b, c), "qualified" (a, b), and "unqualified" (0, a), which are consistent with Table 3.

3.4 Calculation of System Final Score

According to the calculations from step (1) to step (4) in Sect. 3.2, the total sorting weight vector $\{w_1, w_2, \ldots, w_{56}\}$ of the third-level indicators C1– C56 can be obtained. By scoring 56 third-level indicators (refer to Sect. 3.3 for the scoring method) and then multiplying them by their total sorting weights, the final evaluation score of the network information system can be obtained. The formula is as follows:

$$C = \sum_{j=1}^{56} w_j \times C_j, \tag{9}$$

where w_j is the weight of the j-th third-level indicators and C_j is its score.

4 Numerical Results

This section presents numerical results of the proposed network evaluation method based on "difficulty & beauty" system and the analytic hierarchy process. In the simulation, we consider a compound mobile communication network including multiple cellular networks and a core network. A total of 56 indicators are assigned below second-level indicators. The simulation results and analysis are given in the following.

Figure 4 plots the overall network score versus the score of "task completion benefit" indicator. The "task completion benefit" (C55) indicates the weighted sum of the percentage of completed tasks of different classes to the total number of task goals. The task completion benefit increasing along with the number of important task objectives accomplished. The "received signal strength" (C5) indicates the distance between the mobile station and base station, therefore this value can measure the size of the cell coverage. As illustrated in Fig. 4, it can be observed that the variation of the overall

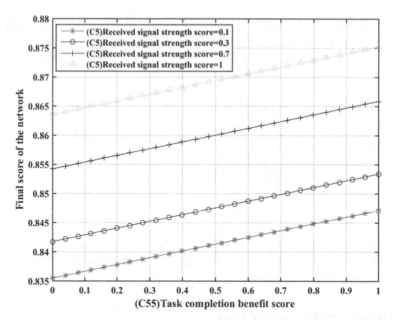

Fig. 4. Overall network score versus the "task completion benefit" indicator score

score along with C55 is considerably small, due to the fact that the weight of C55 is very small, indicating that the network evaluation result is very slightly affected by C55. Figure 4 also shows the network score under different scores of C5. It can be observed that the final score of the network increases along with the increase of the C5 score.

Figure 5 plots the overall network score versus the score of "coverage multiplicity" indicator. The "coverage multiplicity" (C2) indicates the degree of redundancy of coverage in a certain area. If this area is within the coverage of K nodes, then its coverage multiplicity is K. As shown in Fig. 5, it can be observed that the variation of the overall score along with C2 is small, due to the fact that the weight of C2 is small, indicating that the network evaluation result is slightly affected by C2. Figure 5 also shows the network score under different scores of C5. It can be observed that the final score of the network increases along with the increase of the C5 score.

Figure 6 plots the overall network score versus the score of "coverage multiplicity" (C2) and "packet loss rate" (C10) indicator. The "packet loss rate" (C10) indicates the ratio of the data packet loss to the total number of transmitted data packets under the steady load of the router. As demonstrated in Fig. 6, the network evaluation result changes quickly with C2, while it changes slowly with C10. The reason is that the weight of C2 is greater than the weight of C10, indicating that the C2 has a greater impact on the network evaluation result than the C10.

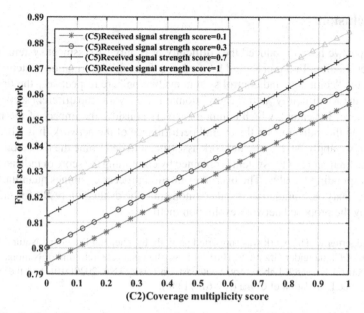

Fig. 5. Overall network score versus the "coverage multiplicity" indicator score

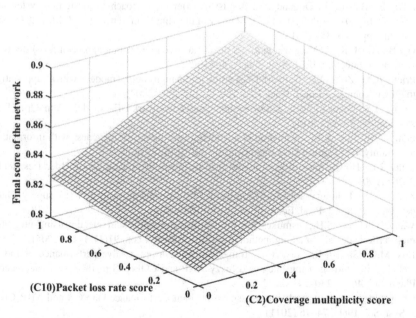

Fig. 6. Overall network score versus the "coverage multiplicity" and "packet loss rate" score

5 Conclusion

In this paper we have introduced the "difficulty & beauty" assessment system into the network evaluation. In the proposed method, the "network information system evaluation" and the "command and control system evaluation" are respectively the first-level indicators in the "difficulty" and "beauty" domain. Then we set up different second-level and third-level indicators, which comprehensively consider the impact of the interaction between the indicators on the overall performance of the network. It is worthwhile noting that we apply AHP to the network assessment to determine the indicator weight. Finally, the final score of the system is obtained by combining the score of indicators with their corresponding weights. The overall evaluation process combines quantitative and qualitative analysis. Simulation results demonstrate the evaluation result for the target network by the proposed network evaluation method.

Acknowledgement. This work was supported partially by Zhejiang Provincial Natural Science Foundation of China under Grant LY21F010008, by the open research fund of National Mobile Communications Research Laboratory, Southeast University (No. 2020D10), and the National Natural Science Foundation of China (No. 61871348).

References

1. Zeng, X.Z.: Network Science. Military Sscience, Beijing (2006)
2. Silva, E., Batista, T., Oquendo, F.: A mission-oriented approach for designing system-of-systems. In: 2015 10th System of Systems Engineering Conference, 17–20 May 2015, San Antonio, pp. 346–351 (2015)
3. Ge, B., Hipel, K.W., Yang, K., et al.: A novel executable modeling approach for system-of-systems architecture. IEEE Syst. J. **8**(1), 4–13 (2017)
4. Prieto, A.M., Zofío, J.L.: Network DEA efficiency in input-output models: with an application to OECD countries. Eur. J. Oper. Res. **178**(1), 292–304 (2007)
5. Chang, T.S., Tone, K., Wei, Q.: Ownership-specified network DEA models. Ann. Oper. Res. 214(March), 73–98 (2014)
6. Peng, Z.M., Luo, X.M.: A method of evaluating operational effectiveness with information uncertainty. Fire Control Command Control. **31**(8), 18–21 (2006)
7. Saaty, T.L.: How to make a decision: the analytic hierarchy process. Eur. J. Oper. Res. **48**(1), 9–26 (1990)
8. Korpela, J., Lehmusvaara, A., Tuominen, M.: An analytic approach to supply chain development. Int. J. Prod. Econ. 71(1/3), 145–155 (2001)
9. Wang, G., Huang, S.H., Dismukes, J.P.: Product-driven supply chain selection using integrated multi-criteria decision-making methodology. Int. J. Prod. Econ. **91**(1), 1–15 (2005)
10. Das, M.C., Sarkar, B., Ray, S.: A framework to measure relative performance of Indian technical institutions using integrated fuzzy AHP and COPRAS methodology. Socioecon. Plann. Sci. **46**(3), 230–241 (2012)
11. Chen, J.L., Li, X.J.: A study on assessment for bank performance via PCA and AHP. Chin. J. Syst. Sci. **19**(1), 74–76 (2011)

A Bio-inspired Geomagnetic Homing Navigation Method Based on Magnetotaxis Perception

Kun Liu[1](✉), Junfang Li[1], and Xinhui Wang[2]

[1] School of Electronic Engineering, Xi'an Aeronautical University, Xi'an 710077, China
[2] Shanxi Urban Economy School, Xi'an 710016, China

Abstract. As an important source of navigation information, the geomagnetic field is trusted by many animals. Different from the conventional geomagnetic matching navigation method, animal geomagnetic navigation can only use its own tactical perception of the magnetic field without a priori database, and reach the target point through the search of the target magnetic environment. It has high autonomy and concealment. Strong and other characteristics. Inspired by this behavior, this paper designs a geomagnetic bionic homing method based on magnetic taxis sensing. First, the tropism characteristics of the magnetic parameters are sensed through random walks; then, the multi-target search method is used to obtain the heading direction; as the movement progresses, the magnetic tropism characteristics are continuously updated to obtain new headings, and finally guide the individual to reach the target point. The simulation results verify the effectiveness of the method.

Keywords: Animal magnetotaxis · Bio-inspired navigation · Multi-objective search · Random walk model

1 Introduction

As one of the main survival skills of animals, navigation can ensure that they can safely, accurately and timely arrive at their destinations in different environments or in different environments [1].

There are many kinds of information sources that can be used for navigation scattered in nature. Due to the differences in their distribution characteristics, the applicable scenarios are also different. For example, the odor source is suitable for short-range navigation, and the polarized light is suitable for use in the daytime [2]. The geomagnetic field, which has unique distribution characteristics in near-Earth space, is a reliable navigation information source for animals to achieve long-distance migration, homing, and migratory tasks.

Mankind has used the geomagnetic field for a long time. Sinan was able to use the polarity characteristics of geomagnetic field to provide direction information [3, 4]. Then, the advent of compass was widely used in shipping. The modern geomagnetic navigation technology is mainly represented by matching navigation, which obtains carrier position information through correlation matching between measured data and a prior map. Its positioning accuracy and application range are related to the integrity of a prior database. Compared with the animal geomagnetic navigation behavior in nature, obviously, the existing geomagnetic navigation technology has a significant gap in flexibility, autonomy, reliability and other aspects.

Geomagnetic bionic navigation is bio-inspired by the behavior of animal geomagnetic navigation. It researched for a navigation method of homing which reached or returned to the established destination through independent search without a priori database reference.

In this paper, a geomagnetic bio-inspired navigation method is designed based on biological magnetotactic search. Firstly, the geomagnetic bio-inspired navigation problem is summed up as the geomagnetic field multi-parameter multi-objective convergence problem. Secondly, the individual random walk in the field is used to perceive and establish the trend characteristics of the magnetic field parameters. Then, multi-objective optimization method is used to obtain the navigation direction. In the process of navigation, combined with the change of individual displacement, the magnetotactic characteristics are constantly updated to obtain a new course and finally guide the individual to reach the target point. Through simulation analysis and comparison of different algorithms, the effectiveness and rationality of the proposed method are verified.

2   Navigation Model Design Based on Magnetotactic Search

2.1   Biological Implications of Magnetotactic Search

Taxis is a directional navigation movement that is driven towards or away from the excitation source. Common taxis include Phototaxis, Hydrotaxis, Chemotaxis, Rheotaxis (Amenota-xis), and Magnetotaxis. It plays an important role in the avoidance, foraging, nesting and migration of many animals.

Many scholars have paid much attention to the movement of tendency, and many effective models of tendency have been established for different stimuli. According to the behavioral characteristics of the worm approaching light source, literature [2] established the mechanism of rotation, which made the excitation uniform and the overall movement path approaching the stimulus source through regular alternating deviation from the stimulus source. Literature [3] proposed a temperature-tropic motion model based on behavioral decision, which controlled the direction of the temperature-tropic motion by adjusting the offset of the random walk. Alt W [4] proposed a drug-induced model based on biased random walk and correlated diffusion, in which cells approached the stimulus source according to the change of concentration gradient. Massimo [5] proposed an information orientation model for biological flavor orientation, in which the approach to odor source was regarded as the search of odor distribution information.

The geomagnetic field is an inherent resource of the earth, which covers a wide area and has long been a reliable source of navigation information in nature. According to the different biological cognition levels of the geomagnetic field, magnetic tropism has many manifestations. For example, magnetotactic bacteria have the ability to sense the magnetic field intensity, sense the magnetic field intensity through the magnetosome chain inside the cell, and move along the magnetic field intensity driven by flagella.

Migration bats have polar magnetic compasses to distinguish between north and south poles. Insects have the ability to know magnetic inclination and can move along both sides of the equator.

However, geomagnetic field has rich characteristic parameters, and biological use of geomagnetic field is far more than this. The results show that there are nano-magnetite particles at the end of trigeminal nerve in the skin tissue of homing pigeons' upper beak, which can provide more multidimensional perception of magnetic field parameters for homing pigeons. It has been proved that the geomagnetic field plays an important guiding role in the behavior process of homing pigeons, sea turtles migrating across the ocean, and salmon migrating over long distances.

2.2 Design for Navigation Model

At present, there are two academic hypotheses about the behavioral mechanism of bio-magnetic navigation. Lohmann K J [9] et al. believed that there is a priori geomagnetic map obtained by genetics in animals, which is used to continuously correct the direction of movement during their navigation and migration, so as to achieve the purpose of navigation. Wiltschko R [10] believed that the distribution of geomagnetic field was complex, and it was difficult for animals to obtain a priori geomagnetic map, and the establishment of their navigation direction depended on the acquisition of otactic movement [11].

Magnetotactic refers to the tendency of organisms to move towards or away from the stimulus source when stimulated by the geomagnetic environment. Taking magnetotactic bacteria as an example [12], the motion direction of each step has the random characteristics of typical Brownian motion, while from the perspective of the overall motion path, it can show the trend characteristics of approaching or away from the stimulus source. For more advanced animals, such as turtles and homing pigeons, magnetotactic behavior enables them to perform complex navigation behaviors such as orientation, homing, and migration. It is generally believed that when they leave the breeding ground or nest, they mark the complex magnetic environment there, and when they have physiological needs for migration and homing, they tend to reach the target position under the magnetic excitation [10].

From the bionic point of view, biomagnetic tendency behavior can be summed up as the problem of multiple parameters converging to their respective targets in the case of unknown parameter law.

$$
\begin{cases}
\min \ F(\mathbf{B}, k) = (f_1(B_1, k), f_2(B_2, k), \cdots, f_n(B_n, k)) \\
s.t. \quad g_i(S^k, \mathbf{B}^k, \mathbf{B}^T) \quad i \in n
\end{cases}
\tag{1}
$$

Where $k \in \mathbb{Z}^+$ meaning time variable, $\mathbf{B} =: (B_1, B_2, \cdots, B_n)^T \in \mathbb{R}^n$ meaning n dimensional geomagnetic field parameters, S represents the movement path of the carrier, g represents the constraint. Through the movement of the carrier, geomagnetic field parameters change, and subject to the constraints of function g, the objective function F will gradually decrease. When the objective function F takes the minimum value, it is considered that the target point has been reached and the navigation task is completed.

3 Biological Magnetotactic Navigation Model Based on Probabilistic Evolutionary Strategy

3.1 Biological Random Walk Behavior

Random walk model (RWM) [13] is a discrete time process. The variables at any time are independent and identically distributed random variables, which are often used in the analysis of biological locomotor behavior. If the biological movement strategy is taken as a random variable, the movement path at time n can be called a random walk process.

RWM is usually constructed by taking the variation of particle motion direction of two adjacent steps as a random variable. The weaker the correlation between variables, the stronger the randomness of motion. On the contrary, the stronger the correlation, the more obvious the directivity of the motion, also known as the biased random walk (BRWM).BRWM can be used to establish the directional movement trend effectively. However, due to the lack of storage and utilization of the historical information, its performance ability is still insufficient in the scene with relatively complex changes of navigation clues.

Therefore, the idea of population evolution is introduced, and RWM is constructed by the probability model of population, and the historical information is retained and utilized by the evolution and reproduction of population. Firstly, according to the carrier's motion model, the feasible motion schemes were extracted, and the limited schemes were taken as the population samples. Then, sample individuals were randomly selected as the carrier motion scheme to perform navigation movement. Finally, the environmental information obtained by the carrier movement is converted into the sample distribution probability and stored indirectly in the population through sample evaluation and population updating. If the population sample presents an equal probability distribution, the randomness of carrier movement is strong. If the sample distribution probability is not uniform, the carrier will show BRWM properties.

3.2 Magnetotactic Movements Based on Probabilistic Evolutionary Strategies

3.2.1 Probabilistic Evolution Strategy

Both evolutionary strategy and genetic probability model belong to the category of heuristic evolutionary algorithm.

Evolutionary strategy is an optimization method proposed by German I. Rechenberg [14] et al. referring to the idea of biological variation in biological evolution. The algorithm has the following two basic rules: (1) mutation, which randomly changes all the samples of the population at a certain probability to produce new individuals; (2) Survival of the fittest. For a certain sample to be executed, if it can reduce the objective function, the sample will be retained; on the contrary, the sample will be eliminated. Because the algorithm emphasizes the mutation operation of the sample individual, it has a strong exploration ability in the solution space, and is often used in the real value optimization problems in the complex engineering field.

Genetic probability model, also known as distribution estimation algorithm, was first proposed by scholars such as Muhlenbein [15]. The algorithm uses statistical learning method to establish the distribution probability model of excellent individuals in the solution space, according to the obtained model sampling to generate new solutions and update the probability model. The algorithm is to establish a mathematical model at the population level and describe the evolutionary trend of the population through the change of sample probability. In fact, it can be regarded as a mathematical modeling method at the macro level of biological evolution. Due to the lack of traditional genetic operations such as crossover and mutation, the algorithm focuses on sample sampling and execution, making it prone to exploitation search.

Considering the self-organizing characteristics of organisms in searching for unknown environments, the ability to explore equilibrium evolutionary strategies and the ability to develop genetic Probabilistic models, a trend movement model based on Probabilistic Evolution Strategy (PES) was proposed. Taking the motion parameters as the search strategy, the probabilistic model of various parameters was used to simulate the trend motion behavior in the population, and the temporal update of the motion parameters was realized through random sampling, mutation and other evolutionary operations, and then an individual trend motion system with self-organizing ability was constructed.

3.2.2 Design for Navigation Algorithm

1) Population sample
The carrier is regarded as a particle, and its two-dimensional plane kinematics model is as follows:

$$\begin{cases} \dot{x} = v \cos \theta \\ \dot{y} = v \sin \theta \\ \vec{u} = (v, \theta) \end{cases} \tag{2}$$

Where (x, y) meaning position of the carrier; $\vec{u}$ meaning feasible navigation scheme, which composed of velocity v and movement direction θ.

In a limited time, it is difficult for the carrier to search the complete space, so it is necessary to compress the navigation space appropriately. Assuming that the velocity v is constant, the navigation parameter u can be represented by M motion directions θ, where the I feasible heading is: $\theta_i = D_\theta \times i, i = 1, \cdots, M$, here $M = 2\pi / D_\theta$.

The compressed θ is taken as the motion parameter to construct the population sample, and the j-th sample individual is:

$$q_j = \theta_R = D_\theta \times R, \quad j = 1, \cdots, N \tag{3}$$

Where $R \in [1, \cdots, 2\pi / D_\theta]$ represents random numbers; N meaning the size of population, usually $N > (2\pi / D_\theta)$.

The$k$ time, the probability of q_i being selected is:

$$p(q_i, k-1) = \frac{\sum_{j=1}^{N} \delta_j(q_j = q_i)}{N} \tag{4}$$

Where, $\delta_j(q_j = q_i) = \begin{cases} 1, & q_j = q_i \\ 0, & \text{other} \end{cases}$.

At this point, the direction of magnetotactic movement is.

$$\Theta = \sum_i^N \mathbf{u}_i = \sum_i^N v(\cos(q_i) + j \cdot \sin(q_i)) \tag{5}$$

Where Θ meaning the direction of represents the magnetotactic search direction, $|\Theta|$ represents the search intensity of magnetotactic in this direction.

2) Fitness evaluation function

The difference of geomagnetic field parameters between the current environment and the target environment is the motivation of biological navigation and the difference is taken as the objective function.

The k times, the objective function constructed from the i-th geomagnetic parameter can be expressed as:

$$f_i(k) = (B_i^k - B_i^T)^2 \quad i \in n \tag{6}$$

With the movement of the carrier, the objective function changes accordingly. At the same time, the purpose of navigation is to reduce the objective function, so the fitness evaluation function of the sample can be constructed by the constraint function:

$$G(k, q^{k-1}) = \sum_{i=1}^n g_i(k)|q_j^{k-1} = \sum_{i=1}^n \frac{f_i(k)}{f_i(0)} \tag{7}$$

Here, 0 is the initial time. After the carrier executes sample q_j^{k-1}, the revenue of the carrier's tactile movement is the index to evaluate the performance of the sample.

3) Update the population

Different from other evolutionary algorithms, in the process of trend movement, the updating of population samples is constrained by the biological movement path, and only one sample can be evaluated in each generation, so large-scale parallel evaluation and updating cannot be performed.

Based on this, a time-series updating evolutionary rule is proposed. According to Eq. (7), "survival of the fittest" population reproduction is carried out. Perform individual mutation operation according to a certain proportion.

When $G(q_j, k) \leq G(q_j, k-1)$, it is considered that the carrier is approaching the target point, then it is determined that q_j is an excellent search scheme, and propagation operation is performed: the original sample is retained, and any sample q_r is selected and assigned as q_j; Conversely, when $G(q_j, k) > G(q_j, k-1)$, it is believed that q_j makes the carrier far away from the target point, and this individual is an inferior scheme. Elimination operation is performed: new samples are randomly generated to replace the original samples. And other individuals not involved do not change during the process.

$$\begin{cases} \left. \begin{array}{l} \hat{q}_j = q_j \\ \hat{q}_r = q_j \end{array} \right\} & G(k) \leq G(k-1) \\ \hat{q}_j = D_\theta \times R \ G(k) > G(k-1) \end{cases} \tag{8}$$

4) Mutation

Probability p_{mutation} is used to perform mutation operation on all samples. If a sample has mutation, a new sample will be randomly generated to replace the original sample.

4   Simulation and Experimental Analysis

In order to verify the effectiveness of the method in this paper, the following analysis is made from two aspects.

4.1   Analysis of the Relationship Between Population Diversity and Magnetotactic Behavior

The population diversity is measured by distribution entropy, which is defined as follows.

Definition 1. The distribution of entropy: The sample type is class L, and the sample individual can be expressed as $C_1, ..., C_L$. At a certain moment of population evolution, the proportion of sample individuals in the population is respectively $p_1, p_2, \cdots, p_L$, and satisfies $\sum_{i=1}^{L} p_i = 1$, then the distribution entropy is:

$$H(p_1, p_2, \cdots, p_L) = -\sum_{i=1}^{L} p_i \ln p_i \tag{9}$$

Background field of simulation experiment: the international geomagnetic field model IGRF2016 was used to simulate the actual geomagnetic field environment, and the simulation analysis was carried out in MATLAB.

Setting of experimental parameters: the x-direction component Bx, y-direction component By and total intensity Bf of the geomagnetic field were selected as magnetic field description. The algorithm parameters are: $D_\theta = 30°$, $N = 48$, $\sigma = 1$, $p_{mut} = 0.02$.

Test protocol: Assumed at k < 200, there is no magnetic excitation, and the carrier only performs the random walk motion RWM. When k > 200, the carrier is stimulated by a magnetic field. The carrier positions at 400 moments before and after collection are shown in the figure below:

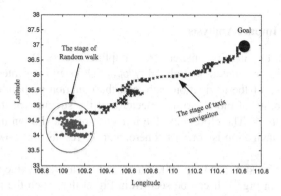

Fig. 1. Space trajectory of carrier (Color figure online)

In the figure, the red "O" represents the absence of magnetic excitation and the blue "X" represents the presence of magnetic excitation. It can be seen that when there is no magnetic excitation, the carrier makes a random walk, as shown in red "O". Under the magnetic excitation, the carrier will change from random movement to trend movement, as shown in blue "X".

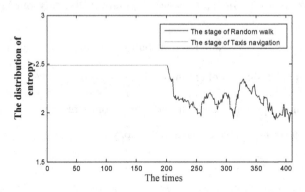

Fig. 2. Distribution entropy of population samples at different moments (Color figure online)

Figure 2 describes the population behavior entropy at the time of collection in Fig. 1. In the initial stage, the entropy value is the maximum, the samples in the population are distributed in equal proportion, and the carrier makes a random walk (RWM) movement behavior, which corresponds to the red "O" stage in Fig. 1. When excited by the magnetic field, the entropy value fluctuates, the population diversity decreases, and the movement trajectory presents a trend characteristic, which corresponds to the blue "X" stage in Fig. 1.

Combined with Fig. 1 and Fig. 2, it can be seen that the method proposed in this paper can be used to establish the magnetotactic motion behavior.

4.2 Parametric Impact Analysis

In PES algorithm, the main parameters are: sampling interval D_θ, population size N, number of breeding σ, mutation probability p_{mut}. The sampling interval D_θ affects the tortuous degree of the navigation path, and the mutation probability p_{mut} affects the exploration ability of the algorithm. Because of the structure of the algorithm, it often acts p_{mut} with N. Therefore, only the influence of N and σ on the performance of magnetotactic navigation is concerned here, and the results are shown in the figure below:

Each data bit was simulated for 1000 times, and the average value was taken. The results are shown in Fig. 3. It can be seen from Fig. 3 that when the population σ is small, the navigation time increases with the increase of the population size, and the movement time is mainly affected by the population size. However, with the σ increase of population size, the effect of population size on movement time will be weakened.

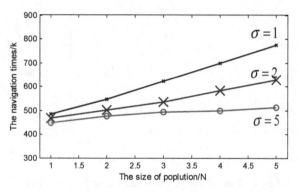

Fig. 3. Comparison of navigation time under different parameter settings

This result is consistent with the relevant conclusions in the paper, that is, the increase of population size will lead to the decrease of $p(q_i)$, and the decrease of $p(q_i)$ will increase the diversity of the population, making search more exploratory, and the movement time increases. The breeding number is proportional to $p(q_i)$, and the increase will reduce the population diversity, promote the search of the algorithm to develop, improve the navigation efficiency, and reduce the movement time. As $p(q_i)$ satisfies Eq. (13), the navigation time tends to be stable when the breeding σ and population size N increase to a certain extent, as shown in the figure.

4.3 Comparison and Analysis

Biased random motion (BRWM) is used to construct the magnetotactic navigation behavior, which makes the carrier move along the gradient direction of the multi-objective function. Its navigation mechanism is as follows:

$$\begin{cases} \theta_{k+1} = \theta_R & \dot{F} > 0 \\ \theta_{k+1} = \theta_k + \Delta\theta & \dot{F} <= 0 \end{cases} \tag{10}$$

Where $\theta_R \sim U[0, 2\pi]$, $\Delta\theta = \frac{\pi}{18} \cdot \varepsilon, \varepsilon \sim N(0, 1)$.

The ideal environment and the measuring noise environment were compared and analyzed respectively. In an ideal environment, three navigation tasks with different starting and stopping positions are respectively carried out, and the 100 navigation results of each task are counted, as shown in Fig. 4 below.

In order to simulate the actual environment more truly, noise interference is added to each geomagnetic field parameter, and the measured value is:

$$B' = B + \Delta B \cdot \varepsilon \tag{11}$$

Where B' is the measurement value, B is the ideal value, ΔB is noise intensity.

Task 1 was selected as the test object, repeated tests were conducted, and the test results were counted to obtain the success rate of navigation under different noise intensities, as shown in Fig. 5 below:

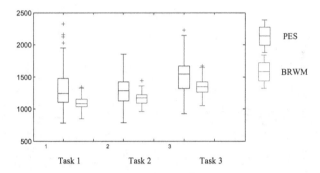

Fig. 4. Time of navigation in normal background field

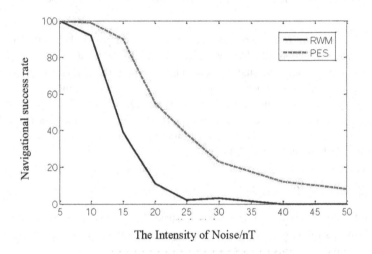

Fig. 5. Navigation success rate under different noises

A comprehensive comparison between Fig. 4 and 5 shows that, in an ideal environment, PES method proposed in this paper takes a long time to navigate, and the time length distribution is relatively scattered, and the effect is inferior to RWM method. However, contain measurement noise environment, with the increase of noise intensity of RWM method navigation success rate fell sharply, when the noise intensity is greater than 25 nT, almost impossible to realize the navigation task, while PES method able to work under the noise intensity of larger, even when the noise intensity is greater than 50 nT, can realize the navigation task at a certain probability.

In conclusion, the proposed method can effectively simulate the magnetotactic movement and bio-inspired navigation behavior.

5 Summary and Prospect

Based on probabilistic evolution strategy, this paper designs a magnetotactic motion model of organisms. A random walk model based on behavioral population was proposed, and the probability distribution of samples in the population was used to characterize the movement trend of organisms. Based on the evolutionary strategy of population renewal, the geomagnetic field information was obtained and used to simulate the magnetotactic movement behavior of organisms. Simulation results show that the method is effective.

Author Contributions. K. Li conceived and designed the experiments; J. Li performed and analyzed the data; X. W wrote the paper. All authors have read and agreed to the published version of the manuscript.

Funding. This work was supported in part by the Supported by National Science Foundation of China No. 61473233 and in part by the Scientific Research Foundation of Xi'an Aeronautical University under Grant No. 2020KY0208.

Conflicts of Interest. The authors declare no conflict of interest.

References

1. Anonymous: Animal behavior. Ecology **40**(7), 435 (2011)
2. Thimann, K.V., Curry, G.M.: Phototropism and phototaxis. Comparative Biochem. **1**, 243–309 (1960)
3. Klein, M., Afonso, B., Vonner, A.J., et al.: Sensory determinants of behavioral dynamics in Drosophila thermotaxis. Proc. Natl. Acad. Sci. **112**(2), 220–229 (2014)
4. Alt, W.: Biased random walk models for chemotaxis and related diffusion approximations. J. Math. Biol. **9**(2), 147–177 (1980)
5. Vergassola, M., Villermaux, E., Shraiman, B.I.: 'Infotaxis' as a strategy for searching without gradients. Nature **445**(7126), 406–409 (2007)
6. Lohmann, K.J., Luschi, P., Hays, G.C.: Goal navigation and island-finding in sea turtles. J. Exp. Mar. Biol. Ecol. **356**(1), 83–95 (2008)
7. Mora, C.V., Davison, M., Wild, J.M., et al.: Magnetoreception and its trigeminal mediation in the homing pigeon. Nature **432**(7016), 508–511 (2004)
8. Hays, G.C.: Animal navigation: salmon track magnetic variation. Curr. Biol. **23**(4), R144–R145 (2013)
9. Lohmann, K.J., Lohmann, C.M.F., Ehrhart, L.M., et al.: Animal behaviour: geomagnetic map used in sea-turtle navigation. Nature **428**(6986), 909–910 (2004)
10. Wiltschko, R., Wiltschko, W.: Magnetoreception. BioEssays **28**(2), 157–168 (2006)
11. Grünbaum, D.: Schooling as a strategy for taxis in a noisy environment. Evol. Ecol. **12**(5), 503–522 (1998)
12. Pan, Y.X., Zhu, R.X.: A review of biogeophysics: the establishment of a new discipline and recent progress (in Chinese). Chinese Sci. Bull. (Chinese Ver.) **56**, 1335–1344 (2011). https://doi.org/10.1036/972010-467
13. Pa Ng, B., Qi, J., Zhang, C., et al.: Analysis of random walk models in swarm robots for area exploration. In: 2019 IEEE International Conference on Robotics and Biomimetics (ROBIO). IEEE (2019)

14. Rechenberg I. Evolution strategy: nature's way of optimization. In: Bergmann, H.W. (ed.) Optimization: Methods and applications, possibilities and limitations. LNENG, vol. 37, pp. 106–126. Springer, Heidelberg (1989). https://doi.org/10.1007/978-3-642-83814-9_6
15. Claveria, O., Monte, E., Torra, S.: Evolutionary computation for macroeconomic forecasting. Comput. Econ. **53**, 833 (2019)

Homomorphic Encryption Based Privacy Preservation Scheme for DBSCAN Clustering

Wenbin Zhao[1]([✉]), Chenghao Zheng[1], Ye Zhang[2], and Zhilu Wu[2]

[1] Southeast China Institute of Electronic Technology, Nanjing, China
[2] Harbin Institute of Technology, Harbin, China

Abstract. In order to reduce the risk of privacy leakage during data outsourcing clustering operations, this paper proposed a privacy-preserving scheme for DBSCAN clustering learning based on homomorphic encryption, which implements homomorphic DBSCAN clustering operations on ciphertext datasets. Theoretical analysis and experimental results show that the proposed scheme can guarantee the privacy of data, has reliable data security, good clustering effect, and computational performance, and has high clustering accuracy and low time overhead.

Keywords: Privacy protection · Density clustering · Homomorphic encryption

1 Introduction

The rapid development of cloud services has provided users with more diverse ways to handle data. Due to the variety of users, the data sets they provide will also cover many types, and there is a risk of leakage of sensitive information contained in them when users outsource the information for processing. Therefore, how to protect the privacy contained in sensitive data is a current research hotspot.

When encrypting a data set, if a traditional encryption algorithm is used, the server cannot process the cryptomorphic data directly and requires the user to provide the server with a key or perform a decryption operation. Homomorphic encryption is a new cryptographic tool that supports arbitrary function operations on encrypted messages and the result obtained after decryption is the same as the result of performing the corresponding operation on the plaintext.

Homomorphic encryption satisfies both confidentiality and ciphertext manipulability making it more widely used in the field of privacy protection. The privacy protection model of outsourced computing based on homomorphic encryption is shown in Fig. 1. The user encrypts the data set to be outsourced and uploads it to the server-side (①), where the server performs data processing with higher computational complexity; then, the server returns the result to the user (②).

DBSCAN is a density-based unsupervised machine learning clustering algorithm that can find clusters of arbitrary shapes in the presence of noisy points. Compared

X. Wang et al. (Eds.): AICON 2021, LNICST 397, pp. 109–116, 2021.
https://doi.org/10.1007/978-3-030-90199-8_11

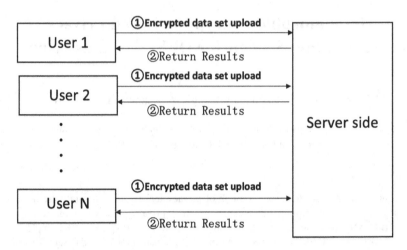

Fig. 1. Privacy-preserving model for outsourced computing based on homomorphic encryption.

with another common clustering algorithm K-means, it has a wider range of applications, such as for the implementation of advanced systems such as recommendation systems. DBSCAN can also be used for the design of a database structure in conjunction with accelerated range access (e.g. R*-tree). Therefore, the study of DBSCAN privacy protection issues is of great importance.

In this paper, we propose a privacy-preserving scheme for homomorphic encryption-based clustering learning, which implements homomorphic DBSCAN for clustering operations on ciphertext datasets.

2 Related Works

2.1 Homomorphic Encryption Algorithms

Definition 1. Homomorphic encryption. The homomorphic encryption algorithm consists of 4 main: KeyGen, Enc, Eval, and Dec.

① $(pk, sk) \leftarrow KeyGen(\lambda)$: Enter the security parameter λ and output the public key pk and the private key sk.

② $c \leftarrow Enc(pk, m)$: Enter the message plaintext $m \in M$ and the public key pk, and output the ciphertext c.

③ $m \leftarrow Dec(sk, c)$: Enter the ciphertext c and the private key sk and output the plaintext m of the message.

④ $c_{Eval} \leftarrow Eval(\mathcal{C}, \{c_1, \cdots, c_k\}, pk)$: Enter a Boolean circuit $\mathcal{C}$, a set of ciphertexts $\{c_1, \cdots, c_k\}$ and the public key pk, and output the resulting ciphertext c_{Eval}.

In this paper, we choose the BGV scheme proposed in the literature [1] and implement it with the help of the homomorphic encryption algorithm library HElib. The BGV programme consists of the following algorithms.

Setup $(1^\lambda, 1^\mu)$. The modulus q of μ bit is chosen randomly and $n = n(\lambda), N = N(\lambda)$, $\chi = \chi(\lambda), d = d(\lambda)$ is chosen. Such that $R = \mathbb{Z}[x]/f(x)$, where $f(x)$ is an n order partition polynomial. The above parameters should be chosen in such a way that the difficulty of the scheme can be based on the lattice difficulty problem GLWE (general learning with error) and can resist existing attacks.

KeyGen(λ). Choose $\mathbf{s} \leftarrow \chi^d$ such that the private key is $sk = (1, \mathbf{s}) \in R_q^{d+1}$. Randomly draw the matrix $\mathbf{A} \leftarrow R_q^{Nd}$, the vector $e \leftarrow \chi^N$, and compute $b \leftarrow As + te$, such that the public key is $\mathbf{B} = [\mathbf{b}, -\mathbf{A}]$. Clearly, $\mathbf{B}s = te$.

Enc (pk, m). Expand the plaintext $m \in R_t$ into p_{k+1}, pick $\mathbf{r} \leftarrow R_2^N$ at random, and output the ciphertext $\mathbf{c} = \mathbf{m} + \mathbf{B}^T\mathbf{r} \in R_q^{d+1}$.

Dec (sk, c). Output $m = \left[[\langle \mathbf{c}, \mathbf{s}\rangle]_q\right]_t$.

Eval (c_1, c_2). Ciphertext addition outputs $c_1 \oplus c_2$ and ciphertext multiplication outputs $c_1 \otimes c_2$.

In addition to the above algorithms, HElib also includes some processing procedures for implementing the FHE algorithm [2], such as key switching, modulus switching, and bootstrapping. The SWHE algorithm does not support infinite ciphertext operations, but its ciphertext and key size are smaller and it does not require bootstrapping to refresh the ciphertext, so it operates more efficiently. Since the scenario in this paper requires only a limited number of ciphertext operations, the SWHE algorithm is chosen to obtain high computational efficiency.

2.2 DBSCAN Algorithm

The DBSCAN algorithm is a common clustering algorithm used to construct clusters in a dataset and to discover noisy data [3, 4]. Compared to the equally common K-means clustering algorithm, the DBSCAN algorithm does not require a predefined number of clusters and is suitable for the construction of clusters of any shape, even unconnected cyclic clusters. Due to the minimum number of points restriction, the DBSCAN algorithm avoids the single-link effect compared to K-means and therefore has better clustering results for any shape of data distribution.

The DBSCAN algorithm itself has many variations, the original DBSCAN algorithm has a complexity of $O(n^2)$, and the $\rho -$ approximate DBSCAN algorithm has a complexity of $O(n)$, but it has some restrictions on the dimensionality of the data. the selection of the DBSCAN algorithm is related to the type of data. The two-dimensional DBSCAN algorithm was chosen to complete the experiments based on the data type of the data set of the scheme in this paper.

Some concepts of the DBSCAN algorithm are defined as follows: MinPts define the minimum number of data points required for a cluster, and the ε-neighbourhood represents the area covered by a circle with a point as its centre and ε as its radius. Centroids, i.e. the centres of clusters, contain more data points than MinPts in their ε-neighbourhood; edge points, i.e. nodes at the edges of clusters, contain fewer data points than MinPts in their ε-neighbourhood and are in the ε-neighbourhood of other centroids; and noise points, i.e. other data points in the dataset that are not centroids and edge points. An instantiated depiction of the node definition is shown in Fig. 2. In addition, Definition 2 and Definition 3 give the definitions of density reachable and density connected.

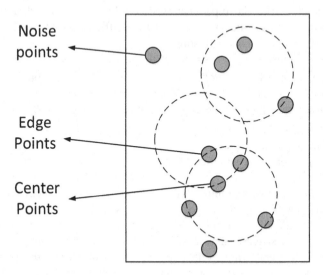

Fig. 2. Instantiated description of the node definition

Definition 2. The density can be reached. Let x_i, x_j be 2 data points. Let there exist a sequence of samples $p_1, p_2, \cdots, p_n$, where $p_1 = x_i$, $p_n = x_j$, if for $1 \leq k \leq n$, all have p_{k+1} in the ε-neighbourhood with p_k as the centriud, then x_j is said to be reachable by x_i density.

Definition 3. Density is connected. For a data point x_i, x_j, x_i is said to be density connected to x_j if there exists a point x_k such that x_i and x_j are density reachable after passing through x_k.

The flow of the DBSCAN algorithm is as follows.

Step 1 Enter a collection of data. Select an unlabeled observation x_I as the current node and label the first clustering cluster 1.

Step 2 Find all the nodes in the ε-neighbourhood centred on x_I, which are all neighbours of x_I. Perform the following operation.

① If the number of neighbouring nodes found is less than MinPts, then x_I is a noisy point and step 4 is performed.

② If the number of neighbouring nodes found is not less than MinPts, then x_I is a centroid and step 3 is executed.

Step 3 Separate all neighbouring nodes as centroids and repeat step 2 until there are no new neighbouring nodes to use as centroids.

Step 4 Select the next unlabelled point from dataset X as the current node, update the number of clusters and add 1.

Step 5 Repeat steps 2 to 4 until all points in the data set X have been marked.

3 DBSCAN Privacy Protection Solutions

In this paper, we construct a homomorphic clustering algorithm on encrypted datasets, which enables privacy-preserving of sensitive datasets during outsourcing computation.

Homomorphic DBSCAN algorithm

Input   Ciphertext set $X = \{[\![x_1]\!], [\![x_2]\!], \dots, [\![x_m]\!]\}$, ciphertext parameters $[\![\varepsilon]\!]$, MinPts

Output   Clustered clusters $C_1, C_2, \cdots, C_k$

1) Initialising a collection of centroids $\Omega = \varnothing$

2) for $j = 1, 2, \cdots, m$ do

3)   Obtain the $[\![\varepsilon]\!]$-neighbourhood of $[\![x_j]\!]$: $N_{[\varepsilon]}([\![x_j]\!]) = findneighbor([\![x_j]\!], [\![\varepsilon]\!]))$

4)   if $|N_{[\varepsilon]}([\![x_j]\!])| \geq MinPts$ then

5)   Put $[\![x_j]\!]$ into the set: $\Omega = \Omega \cup \{[\![x_j]\!]\}$

6)   end if

7) end for

8) Initialize the set of clusters $k = 0$

9) Initialise the set of unvisited data points $\Gamma = X$

10) while $\Omega \neq \varnothing$ do

11)   Record the unvisited data set $\Gamma_{old} = \Gamma$

12)   Pick a random centre point $o \in \Omega$, initialize the queue $Q = \langle o \rangle$ ($\langle \bullet \rangle$ for the queue, a first-in-first-out data structure)

13) $\Gamma = \Gamma \setminus \{o\}$

14)   while $Q \neq \langle o \rangle$

15)   Pick $[\![q]\!]$ from queue Q

16)   if $|N_{[\varepsilon]}([\![q]\!])| \geq MinPts$ then

17)   Let $\Delta = N_{[\varepsilon]}([\![q]\!]) \cap \Gamma$

18)   Put the sample from Δ into Q

19) $\Gamma = \Gamma \setminus \{\Delta\}$

20)   end if

21)   end while

22) $k = k + 1$, obtain the clusters $C_k = \Gamma_{old} \setminus \Gamma$

23) $\Omega = \Omega \setminus C_k$

24) end while

Common homomorphic encryption schemes only support additive (subtractive) and multiplicative operations, so complex operations need to be converted accordingly so that they can be expressed in additive and multiplicative terms.

4   Programme Realisation

In this paper, we verify the accuracy of the scheme by comparing the clustering results on plaintext data with the homomorphic clustering results on ciphertext data. The configuration used for the experiments was an Intel(R) Core(TM) i7–6700 CPU @ 3.40 GHz 3.41 GHz, 16 GB of RAM, and the Helib homomorphic encryption library for encryption and homomorphic clustering of datasets. In the experiments, the parameters ε and MinPts used in the execution of the DBSCAN algorithm are the same for both plaintext and ciphertext datasets, with ε denoted as *eps* and MinPts denoted as min _*Pts* in the experiments.

4.1   Data Set Explicit Clustering Results

The results of the clustering process are shown in Figs. 3 and 4. The parameters chosen for Data Set A were *eps* = 0.547 (5470 after coding) and min _*Pts* = 9; Data Set B was chosen with *eps* = 1.8 (180 after coding) and min _*Pts* = 11.

Data set A and data set B is encrypted by shifting and rounding, and then homomorphic clustering is performed on the encrypted data. The data in dataset A was shifted and rounded, and then the homomorphic clustering algorithm was performed on the ciphertext. The clustering results after decryption are shown in Fig. 5. The data set B is directly encoded by shift rounding, encrypted and homomorphic clustering is performed, and the clustering results obtained by decryption after the calculation are shown in Fig. 6.

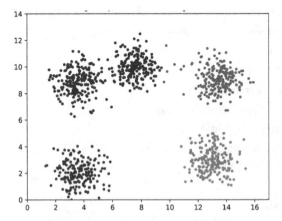

Fig. 3. Data set A plaintext clustering results

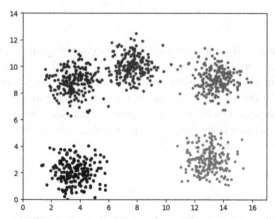

Fig. 4. Data set B plaintext clustering results

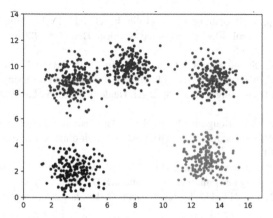

Fig. 5. Data set A ciphertext clustering results

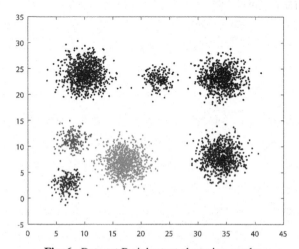

Fig. 6. Data set B ciphertext clustering results

5 Conclusion

In this paper, a scheme of homomorphic DBSCAN clustering algorithm on encrypted datasets is proposed for solving the privacy protection problem in the process of data outsourcing computation. The scheme selects the deformed Euclidean distance as the distance measure in the algorithm based on the type of operations supported by the homomorphic encryption algorithm and the experimental test results for different data set accuracies. The scheme in this paper has reliable data security, good clustering effect and computational performance.

References

1. Brakerski, Z., Gentry, C., Vaikuntanathan, V.: (Leveled) fully homomorphic encryption without bootstrapping. In: Innovations in Theoretical Computer Science, pp. 309–325. ACM Press, New York (2012)
2. Halevi, S., Shoup, V.: Bootstrapping for HElib. In: Oswald, E., Fischlin, M. (eds.) EURO-CRYPT 2015. LNCS, vol. 9056, pp. 641–670. Springer, Heidelberg (2015). https://doi.org/10.1007/978-3-662-46800-5_25
3. Kryszkiewicz, M., Skonieczny, Ł.: Faster clustering with DBSCAN. In: Kłopotek, M.A., Wierzchoń, S.T., Trojanowski, K. (eds.) Intelligent Information Processing and Web Mining. Advances in Soft Computing, vol. 31. Springer, Heidelberg (2005). https://doi.org/10.1007/3-540-32392-9_73
4. Chen, Y.W., Tang, S.Y., Bouguila, N., et al.: A fast clustering algorithm based on pruning unnecessary distance computations in DBSCAN for high-dimensional data. Pattern Recogn. **835**, 375–387 (2018)
5. Cheon, J.H., Kim, D., Kim, D., Lee, H.H., Lee, K.: Numerical method for comparison on homomorphically encrypted numbers. In: Galbraith, S.D., Moriai, S. (eds.) ASIACRYPT 2019. LNCS, vol. 11922, pp. 415–445. Springer, Cham (2019). https://doi.org/10.1007/978-3-030-34621-8_15
6. Tan, Z.W., Zhang, L.F.: Survey on privacy preserving techniques for machine learning. J. Softw. **31**(7), 2127–2156 (2020)

NS3-Based Simulation Study of UAV Routing Protocol in Plateau Environment

Fengbiao Zan[1], Jinze Huang[2(⌧)], Xin Liu[1], Tao Ye[1], and Wenting Li[1]

[1] School of Computer Science, Qinghai University for Nationalities,
Xining 810007, Qinghai, China
[2] School of Physics and Electronic Information Engineering, Qinghai University for
Nationalities, Xining 810007, Qinghai, China

Abstract. With the continuous social progress, ad hoc network protocol has attracted widespread attentions. Under this background, ad hoc network, especially UAV ad hoc network, has been extensively applied to various fields and entered a very mature stage. In this paper, by means of deploying the UAV ad hoc network in plateau environment, the simulation comparison between wireless ad hoc network protocol AODV and DSDV suitable for specific environment are conducted through NS3 simulation platform. Meanwhile, the three indicators including packet loss rate, end-to-end delay and average hop counts are selected simulation analysis, which shows that AODV protocol is more suitable for application scenarios.

Keywords: NS3 network simulator · Network simulation · Wireless ad hoc network

1 Introduction

Nowadays, the UAV ad hoc network is developing so rapidly that this technology has been widely used in various fields, but its application in plateau environment is still a brand-new attempt. The signal interference range, influenced by the climate and altitude, is relatively large during the sensor deployment, and effective communication between the sensors cannot be obtained. Therefore, it is a better method to deploy UAVs in the air. However, since the plateau sensor wireless communication technology is in its initial stage, it is of great significance to improve its network deployment.

In early phase of development, wireless network development was more concerned with the single-system fields that are more suitable for a large communication area but not practical in small communication areas [1]. Due to the high altitude and large temperature changes, traditional land wireless communication deployment cannot meet the requirements in plateau environment, but the wireless communication in the air is more appropriate. In view of this, the application of UAV for network communication and transmission has become the focus of study [2].

Since its first launch in the UK in early 20th century, UAV has been widely adopted in various fields as a key research object, and even became the focus of US military during

X. Wang et al. (Eds.): AICON 2021, LNICST 397, pp. 117–125, 2021.
https://doi.org/10.1007/978-3-030-90199-8_12

subsequent development [3]. On this basis, ad hoc network was proposed to be the key point in future research, so that UAV ad hoc network emerged. At present, in addition to the application in the military field, UAV ad hoc network also plays an important role in the communication. Compared to the mature UAV ad hoc network communication in foreign countries, this technology in China is relatively backward and imperfect [4]. Considering that the routing protocol is decisive in the ad hoc network, so the research on UAV routing protocol is of great significance for improving its network communication function.

The research focuses is the communication performance between UAV protocols. Generally, different application scenarios are simulated to test performance indicators, and key research is conducted on the routing protocol of UAV ad hoc network in plateau environment for performance analysis.

2   Overview of Study on UAV Ad Hoc Network Routing Protocol

The existing literatures mainly study UAV ad hoc network from the perspectives of MAC layer and the network layer, among which the selection of a reliable routing protocol for communication is the key point. In plateau environment, the effective communication between UAV transmission protocols affects the effective performance of the overall network. Therefore, during simulation, the mobile node is usually regarded as a UAV, and the IEEE802.11 protocol is adopted as MAC layer protocol because it maintains effective transmission distance of several hundred meters and is suitable for the directional transmission of communication protocols between UAVs. On the other hand, researches on routing protocols mostly focus on the on-demand routing protocols (AODV, DSR), active routing protocols (OLSR, DSDV) and geographic location-based routing protocols [5]. Thus, in this paper, the AODV protocol and the DSDV protocol are selected for simulation comparison so as to verify their performance. This kind of research not only helps screen out the communication protocol applicable to the UAV in the plateau environment, but also enhances the communication performance of UAV ad hoc network, so as to solve the problem of delayed sensor signal transmission and serious interference in the plateau environment.

3   Description of AODV Routing Protocol

In UAV ad hoc network, AODV protocol is a pure on-demand routing protocol which initiates work through a routing request [6]. In this way, when the request message is transmitted to the neighboring node, the node will first judge accordingly, and then send its response message if it is the target node; otherwise, it will continue to send messages to find the target node.

The target node, once being found, will make a routing response when receiving the message. Meanwhile, the target node will also send a response message to establish a path to respective target node, thereby building an effective route.

There is also a process of route maintenance in course of sending messages, which is mainly to detect the HELLO message frame sent between adjacent nodes, so as to judge the validity of the link between two nodes. If the link fails, then route repair is initiated.

4 Description of DSDV Routing Protocol

DSDV protocol is also a classic distance vector routing protocol [7]. Each node of DSDV has known routing table information, through which the DSDV protocol can dynamically update in real time to keep the information consistent.

DSDV protocol sends serial numbers through routing broadcasts, and gives priority to routes with larger serial numbers. In the case of the same sequence number, the hop count will be observed, and the route with the few hop count will be selected first.

DSDV protocol does not change the overall network topology when updating the route, but its route overhead consumption is extremely high because the algorithm takes a long time in each update.

5 NS3 Network Simulator

NS3 is mainly used for network simulation with various application levels such as in-vehicle networks, satellite communications, and underwater communications. Unlike NS2, NS3 is mainly compiled in C++. Of course, NS3 can also be compiled in python, which simplifies part of the language complexity compared to NS2. As the completely open source simulation software with many built-in modules, NS3 can call these modules for simulation when a simulation environment is simulated. In addition to mainly running under the Ubuntun system under the virtual machine, NS3 can also run under Windows, but many functions cannot be implemented due to version compatibility issues, so the Windows system is not considered.

6 Simulated Scenario Setting

In the scenario construction, the mobile node is regarded as a UAV. Considering that the study pays attention to small-scale network deployment in plateau environment, a 300 m * 300 m square area is used for simulation, with the simulation time of 300 s, the size of each data packet of 1024 bit, the sending rate of 2048 bps, and the MAC layer protocol of IEEE802.11b. In the two scenarios, the movement speed and pause duration of the UAV node are changed to observe the performance indicators of the two protocols. The scenario settings are shown as follows (Table 1 and 2):

Table 1. Scenario setting in different node movement speeds

Simulation parameters	Parameter values
System	Ubuntu 16.04
Software version	NS-3 (Version-3.26)
Movement range	300 * 300 m
Communication link	10
Node movement speed	10 m/s, 20 m/s, 30 m/s, 40 m/s
Node counts	50
Business source	CBR

Table 2. Scenario setting in different node pause durations

Simulation parameters	Parameter values
System	Ubuntu 16.04
Software version	NS-3 (Version-3.26)
Movement range	300 m * 300 m
Business source	CBR
Communication link	10
Node counts	50
Node pause durations	50 s, 100 s, 150 s, 200 s

7 Performance Indicator Setting

In this paper, the two protocols are verified and analyzed through three performance indicators, namely, packet loss rate, average end-to-end delay, and average hop counts.

The packet loss rate is calculated based on the ratio of the lost data packets to the sent data packets during the sending process. The lower the packet loss rate, the better the reliability of the routing. The formula is as follows:

$$q = \frac{lost\,packets}{lost\,packets + rxpackets} \tag{1}$$

The average end-to-end delay is calculated based on the ratio of (time to receive the data packet)−(the time to send the message)/the total number of data packets received. The size of the delay is closely related to the quality of the routing transmission. The greater the delay is, the more unstable the quality will be.

$$Delay = \frac{\sum_{i=1}^{packets}[endtime(i) - start\,time(i)]}{packetSum} \tag{2}$$

The average hop counts are calculated based on the ratio of the sum of the received data packet and the forwarded data packet to the received data packet. The average hop counts generally reflect the routing efficiency and network performance. The smaller the average hop counts, the higher the delivery rate of short-distance messages. Due to the harsh conditions in plateau environment, UAV ad hoc networks are generally concentrated, and the message transmission between each node is forwarded at most once. That means, under the same message delivery conditions, the smaller the average hop counts, the more suitable it is for dense UAV ad hoc networks.

$$\text{Hopcpunt} = \frac{times\,forwarded + rxpackets}{lost\,packets + rxpackets} \tag{3}$$

8 Analysis of Simulation Results

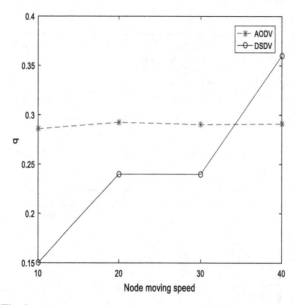

Fig. 1. Packet loss rate under the change of UAV moving speed

As can be learned from Fig. 1 and Fig. 2, in the change of the node movement speed and node pause duration, the packet loss rate of AODV has been relatively stable. In Fig. 1, the packet loss rate of AODV has been maintained at about 29%. The packet loss rate of AODV in Fig. 2 is also relatively stable despite slight fluctuation. In contrast, DSDV protocol is greatly affected, indicating that in the same scenario, the reliability of AODV is better than that of DSDV. The packet loss rate of DSDV will gradually increase as the node moves faster, which may because that frequent update of route in DSDV has gradually degraded its performance. In Fig. 2, as the node pause duration increases, the DSDV packet loss rate gradually decreases. The reason is that the number of data packets received by DSDV within a limited time increases thanks to the node survival time.

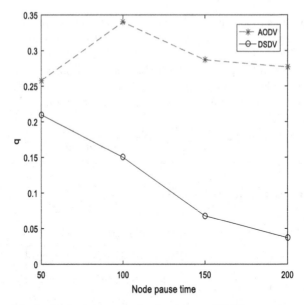

Fig. 2. Packet loss rate under the change of UAV pause time

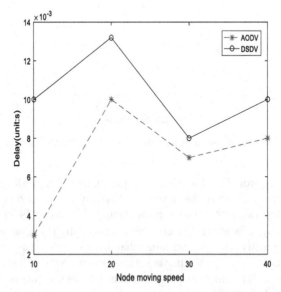

Fig. 3. Time delay under the change of UAV moving speed

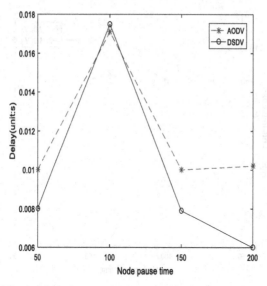

Fig. 4. Time delay under the change of UAV pause time

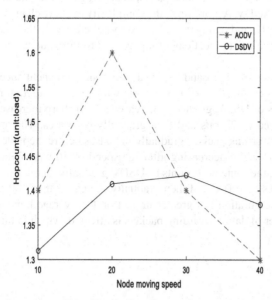

Fig. 5. Average number of hops when the moving speed of UAV changes

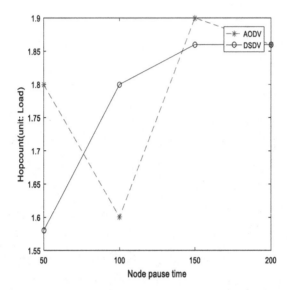

Fig. 6. Average number of hops under the change of UAV pause time

Figure 3 and Fig. 4 show that, the average end-to-end delay of AODV and DSDV varies with the node movement speed and pause duration. From the perspective of curve changes, the average end-to-end delay of DSDV has been lower than that of AODV. In Fig. 4, at the 100 s of node pause, the average end-to-end delay of DSDV is higher than that of AODV. According to the complexity of curve change, DSDV changes relatively dramatically, indicating that DSDV is more sensitive to the changes in network environment. To sum up, in most environments, the routing quality of DSDV is better than that of AODV.

From the analysis of Fig. 5 and Fig. 6, as the node movement speed increases, the average hop counts of AODV tend to be stable with small fluctuation range, while the average hop counts of DSDV gradually increases after a sharp increase, which reaches its peak at the speed of 20 m/s and then gradually decreases. This may because the number of data forwarding packets gradually increases before the node moves at speed of 20 m/s while gradually decreasing after the speed of 20 m/s. With the increase of the pause duration, the route hop counts of DSDV gradually increases, which gradually decreases from 50 s to 100 s, and then gradually increases after 100 s. This indicates that the node pause duration has greater impact on the average hop counts of AODV, because the number of data forwarding packets is affected, which in turn influences the average hop counts.

9 Conclusions

As can be concluded from above analysis, the reliability of AODV is better than DSDV to a certain extent, while DSDV is more sensitive to changes in network environment. With the change of scenarios, the average end-to-end delay of DSDV is lower than that of AODV, but there is no great difference between two protocols in terms of average hop counts. From the perspective of the overall curve analysis, the more complex the network environment, the greater the trend of DSDV curve change, indicating that DSDV is suitable for relatively simple and stable UAV networks rather than more complex UAV ad hoc networks. Besides, since AODV has stronger stability than DSDV, it can be applied to relatively complex UAV ad hoc networks to a certain extent.

By means of analyzing and studying the two protocols based on NS3, this paper clarifies the network environment suitable for AODV and DSDV. As can be observed from simulation, compared to DSDV, AODV is more adapted to the UAV ad hoc network environment in plateau environment.

Acknowledgement. This paper is supported by Qinghai Science and Technology Project (2018-ZJ-753), Qinghai Province, China. In addition, this paper is supported by the cooperation project of Qinghai University for Nationalities Tianjin University Independent Innovation Fund "Huangshui river monitoring and governance".

References

1. Zhu, M., Luo, Y.-J., Xing, M.-S.: Research on UAV ad hoc network system design. J. Appl. Sci. Eng. Innov. **7**(4) (2020)
2. Electronics - Electronics and Communications; Researchers at Peking University Report New Data on Electronics and Communications (Securing ICN-based UAV Ad Hoc Networks with Blockchain). J. Eng. (2019)
3. Fang, K., Ru, L., Yu, Y., Jia, X., Liu, S.: An energy balance and mobility prediction clustering algrithm for large-scale UAV ad hoc networks. Eng. Rev. Međunarodni časopis namijenjen publiciranju originalnih istraživanja s aspekta analize konstrukcija, materijala i novih tehnologija u području strojarstva, brodogradnje, temeljnih tehničkih znanosti, elektrotehnike, računarstva i građevinarstva (2019)
4. Kumar, S., Dutta, K.: Trust based intrusion detection technique to detect selfish nodes in mobile ad hoc networks. Wirel. Pers. Commun. **101**(4), 2029 (2018)
5. Chandan, R.R., Kushwaha, B.S., Mishra, P.K.: Performance evaluation of AODV, DSDV, OLSR routing protocols using NS-3 simulator. Int. J. Comput. Network Inf. Secur. (IJCNIS) **10**(7), 59 (2018)
6. Sharma, V., Kumar, R.: Teredo tunneling-based secure transmission between UAVs and ground ad hoc networks. Int. J. Commun. Syst. **30**(7), e3144 (2017)
7. Sharma, V., Kumar, R.: Cooperative frameworks and network models for flying ad hoc networks: a survey. Concurrency Comput. Pract. Exp. **29**(4) (2017)

Development Outlook of China's Navigational Data (NAVDAT) Maritime Digital Broadcasting System

Jinyu Zhao[✉], Fuzhai Wang, Zhongli Yi, and Shanshan Wang

Transport Planning and Research Institute, Ministry of Transport,
Beijing 100029, People's Republic of China

Abstract. This paper introduces the main functions and development trends of the domestic and foreign "Navigational Data" maritime digital broadcasting system (NAVDAT), and analyzes the basic conditions for promoting NAVDAT research and application in China. In addition, this paper makes a prediction for the development target of NAVDAT in China, and proposes the planning scheme and the coverage effect of NAVDAT stations.

Keywords: Digital broadcasting · Coastal radio station · NAVDAT · Prospect

1 Overview

1.1 Introduction to NAVDAT

In recent years, with the advancement of the Global Maritime Distress and Safety System (GMDSS) modernization process and e-Navigation construction, marine users have put forward higher demands for dissemination of maritime safety information, including content, speed, and timeliness. As a result, the "Navigational Data" Maritime Digital Broadcasting System (NAVDAT) came into being. Compared with the traditional NAVTEX system, the NAVDAT system has the advantages of digitalization, high bandwidth, high speed, and so on. International organizations such as the International Maritime Organization (IMO) have also vigorously promoted the application of NAVDAT [1], and NAVDAT becomes an important development of maritime safety information dissemination technology. Then in 2012, the International Telecommunication Union (ITU) promulgated the NAVDAT technical proposal – "Technical characteristics of a digital system called "Navigational Data" for implementing shore-to-ship maritime safety information broadcasting in the 500 kHz frequency band". (ITU-R 2010-0) [2]. From a technical point of view, the NAVDAT system is an intermediate frequency radio communication system for maritime safety communication services. It operates in the 500 kHz frequency band and uses digital transmission technology to provide a shore-to-ship broadcast link. The NAVDAT system can use a broadcast method similar to the NAVTEX system, with IMO-coordinated time slot allocation, and multiple radio stations broadcast in the same frequency band in time intervals; it can also use the Global Digital Radio mode, which can transmit by multiple radio stations at the same time, and utilize cross-cover radio signal range to achieve enhanced coverage of the targeted sea area.

© ICST Institute for Computer Sciences, Social Informatics and Telecommunications Engineering 2021
Published by Springer Nature Switzerland AG 2021. All Rights Reserved
X. Wang et al. (Eds.): AICON 2021, LNICST 397, pp. 126–135, 2021.
https://doi.org/10.1007/978-3-030-90199-8_13

1.2 Uses of NAVDAT

The NAVDAT system uses Orthogonal Frequency Division Multiplexing (OFDM) modulation to broadcast digital information on ships. It can achieve coverage from 100 to 400 nautical miles under different encoding modes. The effective data transmission rate is 12–18 kbps, which is about 300 times of NAVTEX system. The use of NAVDAT technology can effectively improve the efficiency of information transmission, and realize the timely and visual release of the meteorological information, hydrological information, as well as waterway information. Further, NAVDAT can be used to enrich and improve maritime safety information broadcast categories. And by publishing visual search and rescue information, it can display visually the location of surrounding ships in distress, and provide various information about the ship's cargo and personnel, which facilitates the rapid determination of ship positions, organization and rapid dispatch of search and rescue forces, and effectively improving the efficiency of maritime search and rescue emergency response. The use of digital information broadcasting technology can also realize the simultaneous broadcasting, directional broadcasting, and personalized broadcasting of maritime safety information, which is more in line with the actual needs of users. Therefore, NAVDAT has become one of the key systems supporting maritime broadband communication services in the modernization of GMDSS and e-Navigation, which is of great significance for improving the security communication coverage of the large coastal channels in China (Table 1).

Table 1. Comparison table of NAVDAT system and NAVTEX system

Communication characteristics	NAVDAT	NAVTEX
Transmit frequency	500 kHz	518/490/4209.5 kHz
Modulation	OFDM/NQAM	FIB
Modulation rate	25 kbps (Typical value)	100 bps
Effective data rate	12 k–18 kbps	50 bps
Coverage	A1, A2 Sea Area	A1, A2 Sea Area
Broadcast content	Navigational warning, meteorological and hydrological information, search and rescue information, port and pilotage services, ship traffic information, maritime safety and security, electronic chart data, etc	Navigational warning, meteorological and hydrological information, search and rescue information, pilotage services, etc
Broadcast format	Text message, file (text or image)	Text
Broadcasting method	General broadcast, selective broadcast, dedicated broadcast	General broadcast

1.3 NAVDAT System Composition

NAVDAT system is mainly composed of five parts: information management system, coast station network, intermediate frequency transmission equipment, transmission channel, and marine receiver.

Information Management System (SIM). Collecting and controlling various information; creating message files to be sent; creating a sending plan based on whether the message file needs to be sent repeatedly and its priority.

Coast Station Network. Ensuring the transmission of message files from the information source to the transmitter.

Intermediate Frequency Transmission-On Equipment. Receiving information from SIM; encoding and modulating information in OFDM mode to generate radio frequency signals; sending radio frequency signals to antennas to broadcast to ships.

Transmission Channel. The 500 kHz frequency band radio frequency signal transmission channel.

Marine Receiver. Demodulating the radio frequency OFDM signal; reconstructing the message file; organizing and making the message available on special equipment according to the type of the message file (Fig. 1).

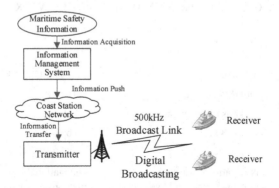

Fig. 1. Schematic diagram of NAVDAT system structure

2   International NAVDAT Development Trends

At the beginning of the 21st century, the United States, France, Japan and other countries began to study high-speed digital maritime safety information broadcasting systems. In 2009, France proposed the NAVDAT technical plan and conducted a relatively complete communication test. With the addition of the United States, Denmark, Japan and other countries, the basic research of NAVDAT technology has become more and more complete. Since the proposal of NAVDAT technology in 2009, NAVDAT has received great attention from many international organizations and countries. The research and preparation of relevant standards and recommendations are still ongoing. Below is a chronological summary of major research on this topic in the last decade.

In 2010, ITU released the report M.2201 "Digital Broadcasting of Shore-Ship Safety and Security Related Information in the 495–505 kHz Frequency Band for Maritime Mobile Services". The report is based on the preliminary research results of some European countries, and proposed a plan for digital broadcasting of maritime safety information using some equipment in the intermediate frequency band of the existing maritime mobile services.

In February 2012, the World Radio communication Conference (WRC-12) finally approved the revision of the current international "Radio Regulations", re-dividing the frequency band from 495 kHz to 505 kHz as dedicated to maritime mobile services.

In March 2012, ITU-R formally issued a new technical recommendation "Technical characteristics of a digital system called "Navigational Data" that implements shore-to-ship maritime safety information broadcasting in the 500 kHz frequency band" (ITU-R M.2010).

In July 2012, at the 58th meeting of the International Maritime Organization's Navigational Safety Subcommittee (NAV), Bulgaria, France, and Romania jointly come up with a proposal for the "Digital Broadcasting System for Maritime Safety Assurance Information in the Band 495–505 kHz" (NAV 58 /INF.17).

In 2013, COMSAR 17/4 "Report of the Eighth Meeting of the International Maritime Organization/International Telecommunication Union Maritime Radio communication Expert Group" (Section 44) listed the maritime security digital broadcasting system as one of the equipment, systems and technologies that may be applied in the modernization of GMDSS.

The 2015 IMO/ITU Joint Expert Working Group Report (NCSR 3/17) pointed out that NAVDAT can be introduced into the SOLAS Convention as a supplement or replacement for NAVTEX services.

The report (NCSR 3-29) of the 3rd meeting of the IMO Navigation, Communication, and Search and Rescue Subcommittee (NCSR) in 2016 argued that IMO and IEC should formulate recommendations on the necessary technical and operational services and performance standards for international NAVDAT.

In 2017, the 98th session of the IMO Maritime Safety Committee (MSC 98) approved the "GMDSS Modernization Plan Draft". As an important application of GMDSS modernization, the NAVDAT system will be gradually implemented along with the above-mentioned draft.

After 2018, the NAVDAT technical recommendation (ITU-R M.2010-0) is still being revised and improved, and the IMO plans to officially release the NAVDAT technical standard (ITU-R M.2010-1) in 2023.

3 Development Trends of China's NAVDAT

The Maritime Safety Administration of the People's Republic of China put the application of the NAVDAT system in the dissemination of China's maritime safety information in high priority. Since 2013, it has requested the Eastern Navigation Service Center of

China MSA to follow up relevant research. In 2015, the Eastern Navigation Service Center of China MSA established the NAVDAT test system to carry out test verification work [3], and formed the test report [4].Over the years, the research and application of China's NAVDAT system has advanced in many areas [5].

In the 19th ITU WP 5B meeting in May 2017, China submitted a proposal for the first draft of the revised M.2010-0. It proposes amendments to the positioning and requirements of selective broadcasting, monitoring functions of information and management systems, and OFDM parameter setting requirements.

In the 21st ITU WP 5B meeting in May 2018, China once again submitted a proposal on the preliminary manuscript for the revision of M.2010-0. The proposal focuses on revisions of and supplements to the operational characteristics, system structure, technical characteristics, and transmission structure of the NAVDAT system.

In the 22 ITU WP 5B meetings in November 2018, China continued to revise Recommendation M.2010-0, and proposed revisions to broadcast priority, synchronization header settings, and related parameter settings.

In December 2019, the NAVDAT test and verification platform of the Eastern Navigation Service Center of China MSA was mostly completed [6]. The construction includes a data source system, an information management and processing system, a broadcasting station, a shipboard terminal, and a land monitoring system. This is China's first NAVDAT test system. According to the parameter setting requirements stipulated in the ITU-R M.2010 standard, we carried out 3 real ship tests and long-term fixed point tests, through which we accumulated a wealth of test data, and verified the NAVDAT system in different encoding methods, broadcast conditions and other factors. The impact on the effect of system broadcasting provides empirical support for the further deepening of NAVDAT technology research. Among them, the communication coverage of the NAVDAT system under the conditions of 1 kW IF transmitter and 10 kHz bandwidth in Shanghai is shown in Table 2 [7]. At present, the project has been accepted by the Ministry of Transport, and the engineering effect and test results have also been fully recognized by the Ministry [8].

Table 2. NAVDAT system communication coverage

Antenna efficiency	Modulation (Bit Rate)	Coverage distance (Nautical Mile)
25%	4-QAM (0.5)	95.6–299.0
	16-QAM (0.5)	53.0–219.2
	64-QAM (0.5)	24.7–138.0
100%	4-QAM (0.5)	154.1–380.8
	16-QAM (0.5)	94.1–296.6
	64-QAM (0.5)	47.4–206.0

In addition, China's development plan for the transportation industry also puts forward requirements for the research and application of the NAVDAT system. In 2017, the "Thirteenth Five-Year Development Plan for China's Maritime and Navigation Security" [9] announced by the Maritime Safety Administration of the People's Republic of China clearly "expanded maritime broadband digital broadcast communications (NAVDAT)", and research on the layout of NAVDAT stations is currently underway.

In general, the construction and research of China's NAVDAT system has received strong support from the government and the industry, and has been at the world's leading level in terms of equipment development, testing/verification, and research on application layout. In recent years, the revision of the M.2010 Recommendation has also been led by China.

4 China's NAVDAT Development Outlook

4.1 China's NAVDAT Has Good Development Conditions

China is a major international shipping country, a Class A member of the International Maritime Organization (IMO), and a signatory to the 1974 International Convention for the Safety of Life at Sea (SOLAS) and the 1979 International Convention for Search and Rescue at Sea. Therefore, China aims to implement relevant international conventions and undertake international obligations. At the same time, China works actively to provide "Chinese solutions" in the field of international maritime security. Therefore, China should adapt to the latest development of international conventions and proposals, and respond to the call of IMO, ITU and other international organizations promptly. This includes continuing to develop based on the preliminary research of NAVDAT technology, further strengthening the leading role in the process of international standard formulation, and providing a valuable opportunity for China to go from "following" to ultimately "leading".

From the perspective of national development, the report of the 19th National Congress of the Communist Party of China puts forward the strategic development requirements of "accelerating the construction of a maritime power" and "building a transportation power". Guaranteeing maritime traffic safety is an important prerequisite for the smooth advancement of the national maritime strategy. However, the lack of coastal broadband communication means making it difficult to improve the quality of China's maritime safety communication services. Therefore, the transportation department places significant importance to the construction of maritime safety communication capabilities, and determines that the construction of the NAVDAT system is an important task in the future in multiple levels of planning. The transportation department also has dedicated policy support and financial guarantee for the construction and development of China's NAVDAT system.

From the perspective of user needs, maritime safety information broadcasting is the largest business in term of traffic volume of coast stations, providing important safety information services for ships sailing in medium-distance seas. At present, the traditional shipping industry is gradually developing toward the direction of intelligence. The requirements for the richness, timeliness and reliability of navigation-related information are constantly improving. However, the existing NAVTEX system is subject to many restrictions in terms of broadcasting mechanism, broadcasting rate, and broadcasting content. Moreover, it is difficult to meet the information acquisition needs of future intelligent shipping. The NAVDAT system, as an upgrade of the NAVTEX system, can realize the digital, graphical, and selective broadcast of navigation information, and can combine satellite positioning information and ship identification information to develop customized services. NAVDAT system has demonstrated economic efficiency while improving the effectiveness of information services, and therefore has a good user base (Table 3).

Table 3. 2017–2019 communication service data statistics of the three major coast stations

Unit: Times

Coast Station	Year	Distress Alarm	Maritime safety information dissemination			Regular Communication
			Navigation Warning	Weather Warning	Weather Forecast	Cordless Phone
Tianjin	2017	251	91116	10624	12078	39674
	2018	923	105156	11998	12782	29188
	2019	994	113592	14087	12775	20990
Shang-hai	2017	2850	111198	11386	12346	70109
	2018	3254	100362	10346	12354	25511
	2019	2228	119239	12263	11295	26293
Guang-zhou	2017	285	30324	8968	14028	45415
	2018	278	36972	12160	24160	37762
	2019	678	42468	11040	24192	32244

From the perspective of development infrastructure, China's GMDSS has 16 medium and high frequency coast stations in the coastal areas, of which seven coast stations in Dalian, Tianjin, Shanghai, Fuzhou, Guangzhou, Zhanjiang and Sanya have NAVTEX services. Over the years, China has gradually accumulated a wealth of infrastructure resources for coast stations, built a complete team of communications professionals, and formed a complete management mechanism for maritime safety information acquisition/coordination/broadcasting of multiple stations. Combined with a large number of studies and experiments carried out in the early stage, the construction and development of China's NAVDAT system has suitable hardware and software conditions (Fig. 2).

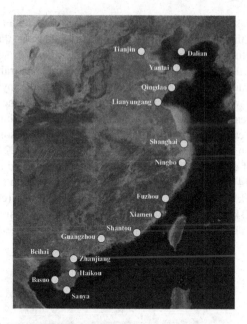

Fig. 2. Schematic diagram of overall layout of China's coast stations

4.2 Anticipated Goals of China's NAVDAT Development

As the NAVDAT technical proposal document is still being optimized, IMO plans to officially release technical standards in 2023. Therefore, a small number of NAVDAT system pilots should be appropriately deployed in the near future to strengthen the test and verification of the practicability, reliability and advanced nature of the NAVDAT system. Such pilots can also help form more complete and detailed test conclusions and high-quality technical proposals for the formulation of relevant technical standards in China. Further, the pilots can provide empirical support to promote the internationalization of domestic technical standards.

After the NAVDAT international technical standards are clarified, China's existing coast station resources can be relied on to actively promote the deployment and construction of NAVDAT stations and ultimately achieve continuous coverage of NAVDAT communications in China's coastal waters, and meet the relevant requirements of the latest international conventions and proposals. Finally, it can comprehensively improve internal management and external service capabilities, and provide mariners with digital, high-speed, customized maritime safety information broadcasting services.

4.3 NAVDAT Layout Planning Along the Coast of China

According to the NAVDAT test at home and abroad, the coverage of NAVDAT communication is about 200–250 nautical miles [10]. Combining with the current status of China's coast station construction and NAVDAT coverage capacity, this paper proposes an overall layout plan for China's coastal NAVDAT stations. Specifically, the deployment of three NAVDAT stations in Dalian, Tianjin and Qingdao in the northern sea area can achieve continuous coverage in the northern sea area of China and the key coverage of the Bohai Sea; the deployment of three NAVDAT stations in the eastern sea area, including Shanghai, Ningbo and Fuzhou, can achieve Continuous coverage and key coverage of the waters of the Yangtze River Estuary and the Taiwan Strait; and 5 NAVDAT stations, including Shantou, Guangzhou, Zhanjiang, Basuo and Sanya, are deployed in the southern sea area, which can achieve continuous coverage in the southern sea area of China and of the Pearl River Estuary, Qiongzhou Strait, and Beibu Gulf.

The coverage effect of NAVDAT station simulated by WRAP software is shown in Fig. 3. The calculation refer to ITU-R M.1467 [11] and ITU-R M.2201 reports on the calculation method of coverage and the ETSI ES 201 980 standard [12], ITU-R P.372 [13], ITU-R P.368 [14] reports related data. It is assumed that the NAVDAT system broadcast power is 5kW, the modulation method uses 16-QAM (code rate 0.5), the signal bandwidth is 10 kHz, the bit error rate (BER) is 10-5, the transmitting antenna and receiving The antenna height is 60 m and 10 m respectively, and the antenna efficiency is 50%.

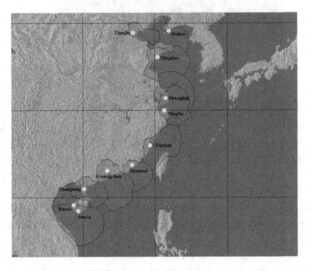

Fig. 3. NAVDAT layout plan along the coast of China

The above layout plan realizes the basic continuous coverage of NAVDAT communication in China's coastal waters, and can cover the main coastal channels of China, including the north-south route, coastal "six districts" and other key sea areas.

5   Conclusion

With the ongoing advancement of national maritime strategies and the transformation and development of shipping formats, the application of broadband digital communication technology in the field of maritime traffic safety protection has become more urgent. After years of research and implementation of NAVDAT system, the technical system has gradually matured, and IMO is currently advancing the research and formulation of international standards. As a category A member of the IMO, China should continue to deepen its applied research and maintain its international lead in the NAVDAT field. In the future, it is necessary to make full use of the good infrastructure, scientifically formulate the NAVDAT system construction and development plan, timely perform the contract, and provide better quality and safe communication services for the navigators.

References

1. ITU-R, Utilization of the 495–505 kHz band by the maritime mobile service for the digital broadcasting of safety and security related information from shore-to-ships, Report ITU-R M.2201 (2010)
2. ITU-R, Characteristics of a digital system, named Navigational Data for broadcasting maritime safety and security related information from shore-to-ships in the 500 kHz band, Recommendation ITU-R M.2010 (2012)
3. IMO NCSR, NAVDAT based maritime safety related information broadcasting tests conducted in China, NCSR 2/INF.4 (2015)
4. The Eastern Navigation Service Center of China MSA. Application Demonstration Test Report of NAVDAT for Maritime Safety Information Digital Broadcasting System (NAVDAT) (2015)
5. Youcheng, X., Difei, C.: China's participation in ITU NAVDAT research progress. China Commun. **11** (2019)
6. The Maritime Safety Administration of the People's Republic of China. Approval of the feasibility study report of the NAVDAT test verification platform project of the East China Sea Navigation Support Center (2018)
7. Youcheng, X., Difei, C.: NAVDAT coverage estimation. China Water Transp. **04** (2018)
8. The Maritime Safety Administration of the People's Republic of China. Completion acceptance certificate of NAVDAT test verification platform project (2020)
9. The Maritime Safety Administration of the People's Republic of China, Transport Planning and Research Institute Ministry of Transport. The 13th Five-Year Development Plan for China's Maritime and Navigation Guarantee (2015)
10. Kecheng, T.: High frequency NAVDAT system test and future application. Modern Inf. Technol. **09** (2020)
11. Recommendation ITU-R M.1467-1 Prediction of sea area A2 and NAVTEX ranges and protection of the A2 global maritime distress and safety system distress watch channel
12. ETSI ES 201 980 Digital Radio Mondiale (DRM): System Specification
13. Recommendation ITU-R P.372-13Radio noise
14. Recommendation ITU-R P.368-9 Ground-wave propagate ion curves for frequencies between 10 kHz and 30 MHz

Advances in AI and Their Applications in Information, Circuit, Microwave and Control

A Water Quality Data Correction Algorithm Based on Improved Wavelet Threshold Denoising Function

Hongcheng Zhao[1], Jun Ma[1,2]([✉]), Lingfei Zhang[1], Bohang Chen[1], and Haiming Lan[1]

[1] College of Physics and Electronic Information Engineering, Qinghai Normal University, Xining, China
[2] Academy of Plateau Science and Sustainability, Qinghai Normal University, Xining, China

Abstract. The water quality detection of natural water body is limited by working environment and measurement technology. The water quality data inevitably has random errors, which affects research of the natural water body. In order to obtain the water quality data that can accurately reflect the natural water body, this paper presents a water quality data correction algorithm based on improved wavelet threshold denoising function. Based on the theory of wavelet transform and the characteristics of robust estimation function, the algorithm realizes excellent correction of the water quality data with random errors. Through MATLAB simulation comparison and case analysis, the superiority of the improved wavelet threshold denoising function and the feasibility and accuracy of the algorithm are proved respectively. The corrected water quality data is more accurate and more consistent with the real data.

Keywords: Water quality · Natural water body · Random errors · Wavelet threshold denoising function · Robust estimation function · MATLAB

1 Introduction

The detection of natural water body [1], such as mountain springs, lakes, oceans and rivers [2, 3], has important guiding significance for the evaluation, prediction, planning and management of water resources [4, 5]. Accurate measurement data can directly reflect the real condition of natural water body [6], and it is also one of the prerequisites for water quality analysis [7, 8]. In the process of natural water body detection, some important water quality parameters, such as pH value, water turbidity, concentration of soluble solids and concentration of dissolved oxygen [9, 10]. Due to the limitation of bad detection environment and measurement technology, there is inevitably random error in the water quality detection data. If these error data are not processed, sometimes it will seriously affect the subsequent water quality analysis and research [11].

In data signal processing, the main methods are: Fourier transform and Wavelet transform [12]. Fourier transform is mainly used to analyze and process stable data signals,

X. Wang et al. (Eds.): AICON 2021, LNICST 397, pp. 139–150, 2021.
https://doi.org/10.1007/978-3-030-90199-8_14

while Wavelet transform is more suitable than Fourier transform in processing unstable data signals [13, 14]. Compared with the traditional data signal processing methods, wavelet transform has higher accuracy and performance. In view of the wavelet transform in different data signal denoising processing, scholars at China and abroad put forward many methods. For example, soft and hard threshold denoising function proposed by Donoho et al. [15]; Garrote threshold denoising function proposed by Gao et al. [16]; An asymptotic semi-soft threshold denoising function proposed by Anquan Wu et al. [17]. This paper proposes an improved wavelet threshold denoising function by combining with robust estimation function on the basis of in-depth study of wavelet transform theory. Through MATLAB simulation comparison, the superiority of the improved wavelet threshold denoising function be verified. In this paper, the improved wavelet threshold denoising function is used to process the water quality data of natural water body, and a water quality data correction algorithm is proposed. Through case analysis, the feasibility and accuracy of the water quality data correction algorithm be verified. The algorithm deals with random errors in water quality detection data, to provide convenience for subsequent water quality analysis and research.

2 Principle of Wavelet Threshold Denoising

2.1 Wavelet Transform

Wavelet transform is a method to analyze and study the time-frequency domain in the local form [18]. It combines the internal information in the time domain and frequency domain to summarize the characteristics of the signal, so it has a good localization property. Wavelet is a special waveform with finite length and zero mean value. Its precise definition is as follows: hypothesis $\psi(t) \in L^2(R)$, $\hat{\psi}(t)$ is $\psi(t)$ of Fourier transform, and satisfy Eq. 1, $\psi(t)$ is wavelet mother function [19].

$$C_\psi = \int_{-\infty}^{+\infty} \frac{\left|\hat{\psi}(t)\right|^2}{t} \, dt < \infty \tag{1}$$

By translating and stretching the wavelet mother function, the wavelet basis function can be obtained as follow,

$$\psi_{a,b}(t) = \frac{1}{\sqrt{a}} \psi\left(\frac{t-b}{a}\right) \qquad a, b \in R; a > 0 \tag{2}$$

Where a is the expansion factor and b is the translation factor.

By expanding the continuous function $f(t)$ under the wavelet basis function, the continuous wavelet transform of $f(t)$ as follow,

$$W_{a,b} = \int_R [f(t)\psi_{a,b}(t)]dt = \int_R \{f(t)[\frac{1}{\sqrt{a}}\psi\left(\frac{t-b}{a}\right)]\}dt \tag{3}$$

In the actual application process, In the practical application process, continuous function $f(t)$ is usually discretely sampled for the convenience of computer operation. The sampling results is N points of discrete signals, then the discrete wavelet transform function as follow,

$$W_{j,k} = \sum_{0}^{N-1} [f(n)\psi_{j,k}(n)] = \sum_{0}^{N-1} \{f(n)[\frac{1}{a_0^{j/2}} \psi \left(\frac{n-k}{a_0^j}\right)]\}$$ (4)

Where, $W_{j,k}$ is the wavelet coefficient of the discrete wavelet transform, j is the discretization scale parameter, and k is the discretization time delay parameter.

The corresponding inverse wavelet transform function as follow,

$$f(n) = \frac{1}{A} \sum_{j,k} W_{j,k} \psi_{j,k}(n)$$ (5)

Where, A is the bound of the wavelet frame constituted by $\psi_{j,k}(n)$.

2.2 Wavelet Threshold Function

The traditional threshold function is the soft and hard threshold function proposed by Donoho et al. The hard threshold function as follow,

$$\hat{W}_{j,k} = \begin{cases} 0, & |W_{j,k}| \leq \lambda \\ W_{j,k}, & |W_{j,k}| > \lambda \end{cases}$$ (6)

The soft threshold function as follow,

$$\hat{W}_{j,k} = \begin{cases} 0, & |W_{j,k}| \leq \lambda \\ sign(W_{j,k})(|W_{j,k}| - \lambda), & |W_{j,k}| > \lambda \end{cases}$$ (7)

Where, $\hat{W}_{j,k}$ is the wavelet coefficient processed by the threshold function, $W_{j,k}$ is the j-th wavelet coefficient on the k-th wavelet coefficient, and λ is the critical threshold.

The soft and hard threshold function image (see Fig. 1).

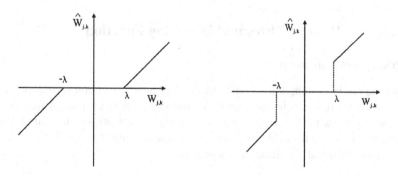

a. soft threshold function   b. hard threshold function

Fig. 1. The soft and hard threshold function image.

As can be seen from Fig. 1, the hard threshold function sets the wavelet coefficient with absolute value less than λ to zero directly. This function is discontinuous at image, which will make the denoised data signal oscillate continuously at image. On the basis of the hard threshold function, the soft threshold function shrinks the discontinuous threshold boundary to zero to avoid the generation of discontinuity points. However, the soft threshold function compared with the hard threshold function, there is a constant deviation λ.

In view of the shortcomings of soft and hard threshold function, experts and scholars put forward a variety of improvement methods.

Reference [16] proposed Garrote threshold function as follow,

$$\hat{W}_{j,k} = \begin{cases} 0, & |W_{j,k}| \leq \lambda \\ W_{j,k} - \frac{\lambda^2}{W_{j,k}}, & |W_{j,k}| > \lambda \end{cases} \tag{8}$$

Reference [17] proposed an asymptotic semi-soft threshold function as follow,

$$\hat{W}_{j,k} = \begin{cases} 0, & |W_{j,k}| \leq \lambda \\ sign(W_{j,k})(|W_{j,k}| - \frac{2\lambda^2}{|W_{j,k}| + \lambda e^{|W_{j,k}| - \lambda}}), & |W_{j,k}| > \lambda \end{cases} \tag{9}$$

The basic idea of the water quality data correction algorithm based on improved wavelet threshold denoising function. A set of water quality data with random errors is used as a signal, $f(n) = s(n) + c(n)$. $s(n)$ is the effective water quality data signal that needs to be obtained, and $c(n)$ is the random error data signal that needs to be eliminated or suppressed. The effective water quality data signal has continuity in time domain and the modulus of wavelet coefficient is relatively large after wavelet transform; random error data signal has discrete randomness in time domain, and the modulus of wavelet coefficient is relatively small after wavelet transform. By setting a threshold function to process the wavelet coefficient, zeroize the wavelet coefficient generated by the random error data signal, retain the wavelet coefficient generated by the effective water quality data signal. The processed wavelet coefficients are reconstructed to obtain the corrected water quality data.

3   Improved Wavelet Threshold Denoising Function

3.1   Principle of Improvement

The core idea of improving the wavelet threshold denoising function is to improve the wavelet threshold function in this paper. A class of unbiased estimation functions is constructed to deal with the wavelet coefficients by the robust estimation method. Under the premise of ensuring the continuity of the threshold function, the wavelet coefficients deviating from the ideal conditions are optimized.

Assume that from the distribution $f(\xi)$ to a set of data $(\xi_1, \xi_2, \xi_3, \ldots\ldots, \xi_n)$, T is used as an estimate of the variable θ, and $g(\xi)$ is an approximate model of the distribution of the variable ξ. The unbiased estimate of θ is $\hat{\theta} = T[f(\xi)]$, and the approximate estimate of θ is $\tilde{\theta} = T[g(\xi)]$, which can be get two distributions $\Gamma(\hat{\theta}, f)$ and $\Gamma(\tilde{\theta}, g)$. When Eq. 10 is satisfied, $T(\cdot)$ is robust [20].

$$\forall \varepsilon, \exists \delta : d(f, g) < \varepsilon \Rightarrow d\left[\Gamma(\hat{\theta}, f), \Gamma(\tilde{\theta}, g)\right] < \delta \tag{10}$$

Where, $d(\cdot)$ is a kind of distance measure in the function.

The influence function is an important function in robust estimation, which illustrates the importance of different measurement deviations ξ_0 in the estimation function. Its definition is as follow,

$$I(\xi_0) = \lim_{t \to 0} \frac{T\left[(1-t)f + t\delta(\xi - \xi_0)\right] - T[f]}{t} \tag{11}$$

Where, $\delta(\xi - \xi_0)$ is a Dirac function centered on ξ_0. If an estimate is robust, then the effect function of ξ_0 is bounded as it approaches infinity. The impact function is used in the robust estimation, then the impact of data point i is defined as follow,

$$I(\xi_i) = \frac{d\rho}{d\xi_i} \propto \begin{cases} \xi_i, & \text{if } \xi_i \text{ is small} \\ C, & \text{if } \xi_i \text{ is large} \end{cases} \tag{12}$$

Where, ρ is the objective function, and $\xi(i)$ is the deviation term.

The joint weight function is another important function of robust estimation. It is defined as follow,

$$\omega(\xi_i) = \frac{I(\xi_i)}{\xi_i} \tag{13}$$

In robust estimation, the larger the weight function corresponding to data point i, the smaller the degree of adjustment needed for the data point.

Through the analysis and comparison of the influence function and the joint weight function, various robust estimation functions that meet the requirements can be constructed. The objective function of robust estimation processes the wavelet coefficients which deviate from the ideal condition, so as to improve wavelet threshold function.

3.2 Improved Wavelet Threshold Function

From the influence function and the joint weight function in robust estimation, the characteristics of the objective function of robust estimation can be found, as follow,

$$\rho(\xi_i) \propto \begin{cases} 0.5\xi_i^2, & \text{if } \xi_i \text{ is small} \\ C\xi_i, & \text{if } \xi_i \text{ is large} \end{cases} \tag{14}$$

According to the characteristics of the objective function of robust estimation and the Correntropy function [21], an objective function of robust estimation is constructed, as follow,

$$\rho(\xi_i) = 1 - \frac{1}{C_0\sqrt{2\pi}} \exp\left[-2\left(\frac{\xi_i}{C_0}\right)^2\right] \tag{15}$$

Where, C_0 is a constant, which is set to $1/\sqrt{2\pi}$ in this paper. The range of $\rho(\xi_i)$ is on the interval 0 to 1. From 0 to infinity, $\rho(\xi_i)$ is monotonically increasing, and the increase is smaller and smaller. When the wavelet coefficient deviates from the threshold, the amplitude of adjustment becomes smaller. When the wavelet coefficient approaches the threshold from a direction greater than the threshold, it gradually approaches 0. The improved wavelet threshold function as follow,

$$\hat{W}_{j,k} = \begin{cases} W_{j,k}\left\{1 - \frac{1}{C_0\sqrt{2\pi}} \exp\left[-2\left(\frac{|W_{j,k}|-\lambda}{\lambda C_0}\right)^2\right]\right\}, & |W_{j,k}| \geq \lambda \\ 0, & |W_{j,k}| < \lambda \end{cases} \tag{16}$$

This improved wavelet threshold function image is compared with the hard and soft wavelet threshold functions (see Fig. 2).

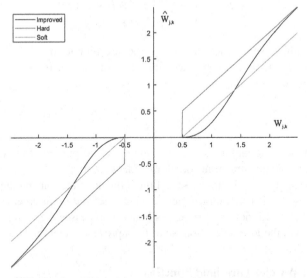

Fig. 2. Comparison between threshold wavelet functions.

$$\lim_{|W_{j,k}|\to 0} \hat{W}_{j,k} = \lim_{|W_{j,k}|\to 0} W_{j,k}\left\{1 - \frac{1}{C_0\sqrt{2\pi}}\exp\left[-2\left(\frac{|W_{j,k}|-\lambda}{\lambda C_0}\right)^2\right]\right\} = W_{j,k}\left[1 - \exp(0)\right] = 0$$

(17)

From the analysis Fig. 2 and Eq. 17, The improved threshold function can realize the smooth transition of wavelet coefficients well. This function not only has good continuity, but also has simple form for practical application.

4 Simulation and Analysis

4.1 The Simulation Comparison

In order to fully verify the superiority of the improved threshold denoising function proposed in terms of denoising, it is simulated and compared with several other threshold denoising functions.

In the simulation experiment, the SNR (signal-to-noise ratio) and RMSE (root-mean-square error) are selected as the evaluation criteria of the denoising effect. The SNR is expressed by the square of the real signal and the square of the difference between the denoised signal and the real signal. The SNR specific expression as follow,

$$SNR = 10\lg\frac{\sum_1^N f(n)^2}{\sum_1^N \left(f(n)-\hat{f}(n)\right)^2}$$

(18)

RMSE is represented by the square root of the variance between the real signal and the denoised signal. The RMSE specific expression as follow,

$$RMSE = \sqrt{\frac{\sum_1^N \left(f(n)-\hat{f}(n)\right)^2}{N}}$$

(19)

Where, $f(n)$ is real signal, $\hat{f}(n)$ is denoised signal, N is signal length.

The data signal of standard water quality data is similar to sine waveform, so sine wave is adopted as the real signal, and the sampling data is 2048 uniform sampling points. By adding Gaussian white noise into the real signal, the SNR of the test signals are 10 dB, 15 dB and 20 dB. The test signals are processed by the improved wavelet threshold denoising function and several other wavelet threshold denoising functions. Where the wavelet function is selected as db5 wavelet, the decomposition order is 4, the value of λ is 0.5. Compare the denoised signal with the real signal, results as follows,

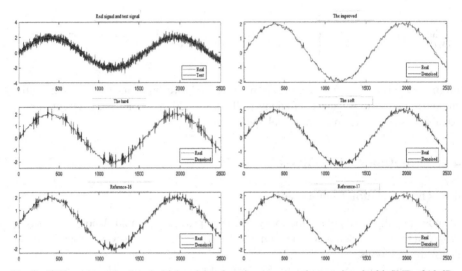

Fig. 3. Different wavelet threshold denoising functions process the test signal with SNR of 10 dB.

Table 1. Compare denoising effects of different wavelet threshold denoising functions on the test signal with SNR of 10 dB.

Test signal SNR = 10 dB	Wavelet threshold denoising function	Denoised signal SNR (dB)	RMSE
	The hard	18.3599	0.1669
	The soft	23.3679	0.0938
	Reference [16]	21.2748	0.1193
	Reference [17]	23.9252	0.0879
	The improved	24.9676	0.0780

Table 2. Compare denoising effects of different wavelet threshold denoising functions on the test signal with SNR of 15 dB.

Test signal SNR = 15 dB	Wavelet threshold denoising function	Denoised signal SNR (dB)	RMSE
	The hard	27.7657	0.0554
	The soft	29.0233	0.0491
	Reference [16]	29.0320	0.0501
	Reference [17]	29.1087	0.0467
	The improved	29.8161	0.0446

Table 3. Compare denoising effects of different wavelet threshold denoising functions on the test signal with SNR of 20 dB.

Test signal SNR = 20 dB	Wavelet threshold denoising function	Denoised signal SNR (dB)	RMSE
	The hard	34.0265	0.0260
	The soft	34.8150	0.0251
	Reference [16]	34.7265	0.0253
	Reference [17]	34.8165	0.0251
	The improved	34.8265	0.0250

As can be seen from the simulation in Fig. 3, due to the discontinuity at threshold point of the wavelet hard threshold denoising function, the reconstructed signal appears a spike mutation signal. The wavelet soft threshold denoising function has a constant difference value, which affects the approximation degree between reconstructed signal and real signal, and there is also a jump value in the local signal. The denoising results of several other wavelet threshold denoising functions are similar to those of wavelet soft and hard threshold denoising functions. The improved wavelet threshold denoising function proposed can overcome the above problems and achieve good denoising effect.

Analysis Table 1 , Table 2 and Table 3, With the increase of SNR of the test signal, the denoising effect of several wavelet threshold denoising functions is increased, and the evaluation tend to be consistent. The denoising effect of the improved wavelet threshold denoising function is still at a high level. In general, the improved wavelet threshold denoising function is better than several other wavelet threshold denoising functions.

4.2 Case Analysis

In order to verify the feasibility and accuracy of the water quality data correction algorithm base on the improved wavelet threshold denoising function, the above several data processing methods was used to correct the experimental samples water quality data.

Taking pH as the example, the experimental samples are obtained by adding random error to the standard sample of pH. Errors of the experimental samples are no more than 12.5% of the corresponding data in the standard sample. The experimental sample data is taken as the discrete signal, the improved wavelet threshold denoising function and several other denoising functions are used to correct the experimental sample respectively. Where the wavelet function is selected as db5 wavelet, the decomposition order is 4, the value of λ is 0.5. Take the processing of the three experimental samples as examples, results as follows,

Analysis Fig. 4 and Table 4, Table 5 and Table 6, the improved wavelet threshold denoising function is suitable for the correction of water quality data and is better than several other denoising functions. The water quality data correction algorithm not only inhibits the random errors in the data effectively, but also retains the dynamic characteristic of water quality data.

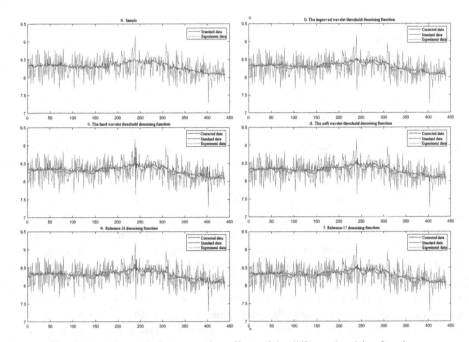

Fig. 4. Experiment-1: data correction effects of the different denoising functions.

Table 4. Experiment-1: comparison of data correction effects of the different denoising functions.

Experiment-1	Denoising function	Corrected data SNR (dB)	RMSE
	The hard	40.2447	0.0808
	The soft	41.7267	0.0681
	Reference [16]	41.0523	0.0736
	Reference [17]	41.9285	0.0678
	The improved	42.2762	0.0662

Table 5. Experiment-2: comparison of data correction effects of the different denoising functions.

Experiment-2	Denoising function	Corrected data SNR (dB)	RMSE
	The hard	39.1948	0.0857
	The soft	41.5267	0.0692
	Reference [16]	40.7523	0.0756
	Reference [17]	41.5195	0.0706
	The improved	41.8762	0.0675

Table 6. Experiment-3: comparison of data correction effects of the different denoising functions.

Experiment-3	Denoising function	Corrected data SNR (dB)	RMSE
	The hard	41.9575	0.0778
	The soft	42.0078	0.0672
	Reference [16]	41.5523	0.0717
	Reference [17]	42.1098	0.0669
	The improved	42.4559	0.0655

5 Conclusion

This paper focuses on problem of the random error of water quality data in natural water body. According to the characteristics of random errors in water quality data,, the paper presents a water quality data correction algorithm based on improved wavelet threshold denoising function. The algorithm combines wavelet transform and robust estimation function. Through MATLAB simulation comparison, the superiority of the improved threshold denoising function is verified. In experimental test, the water quality data is taken as the discrete signal, and the improved wavelet threshold denoising function is used to process the random error. Experimental results verify the feasibility and accuracy of the water quality data correction algorithm based on the improved wavelet threshold denoising function. To sum up, the water quality data corrected by this algorithm will be more accurate and more consistent with the real data.

Acknowledgments. The authors acknowledge the financial support of the Key Projects of the Natural Science Foundation of in Qinghai Province (Grant: 2021-ZJ-916).

References

1. Tian, Y., Li, C., Zhao, S., et al.: Assessment of water environmental quality in inner Mongolia section of yellow river based on fuzzy mathematics. Bull. Soil Water Conserv. **36**(05), 162–166 (2016)
2. Yang, F., Pan Yang, L., et al.: Water quality assessment of dongting lake based on principal component analysis. Yangtze River **50**(S2), 42–45 (2019)
3. Wang, J., Wang, C., Dong, Y., et al.: Investigation and analysis of water quality pollution characteristics and pollution sources in Guboshanhou River. Enviro. Monit. Warn. **13**, 39–43 (2021)
4. Sun, G., Shen, Y., Xu, Y., et al.: Time series analysis and forecast model for water quality of yellow river based on Box-Jenkins method. J. Agro-Environ. Sci. **30**(9), 1888–1895 (2011)
5. Yuan, H., Gong, L., Zhang, Q., et al.: Forecasting the water quality index in Zaohe River based on BP neural network model. J. Safety Environ. **2**, 106–110 (2013)
6. Chen, Q.: Determination of PH value, dissolved solids and total hardness of groundwater in Bayan Chagan Sammu of Hexigeteng Qi, Chifeng City. Chem. Enterpr. Manage. **30**, 199–200 (2018)

7. Liang, Y., Zhu, Y.: Environmental water quality analysis and monitoring technology and monitoring data processing analysis. Resour. Econ. Environ. Protect. (11), 93 (2016)

8. Li, JX., Xu, Y., Li, M., et al.: Water quality analysis of the Yangtze and the Rhine River: a comparative study based on monitoring data from 2007 to 2018. Bull. Environ. Contamin. Toxicol. **91**(2), 1–7 (2020)

9. Yu, B., Xiao, M., Wang, X., et al.: Study on the dynamic changes of spring water flow, conductivity and PH value Geol. Resour. **29**(04), 380–387 (2020)

10. Zhao, Z., Song, G., Zhao, L.: Characteristics of dissolved oxygen and PH variations in summer off the Qinhuangdao. Haiyang Xuebao **42**(10), 144–154 (2020)

11. Xiao, J., Dai, T., Liu, Z.: Analysis and evaluation of water quality of Yudong reservoir in Yunnan Province. Yangtze River **47**(S2), 14–18 (2016)

12. Shen, S.: Comparative analysis based on wavelet transform and Fourier transform and its application in signal denoising. J. Shanxi Normal Univ. (Nat. Sci. Edn.) **32**(03), 27–32 (2018)

13. Qin, C.X., Gu, X.H.: an image denoising method based on improved wavelet thresholding. IOP Conf. Ser. Mater. Sci. Eng. **452**(4), 42–59 (2018)

14. Zhao, G., Chen, A., Lu, G., et al.: Data fusion algorithm based on fuzzy sets and D-S theory of evidence. Tsinghua Sci. Technol. **25**(1), 12–19 (2018)

15. Donoho, D.L.: De-noising by soft-thresholding. IEEE Trans. Inf. Theory **41**(3), 613–627 (1995)

16. Gao, H.Y.: Wavelet shrinkage denoising using the non-negative garrote. J. Comput. Graph Stat. **7**(4), 469–488 (1998)

17. Wu, A., Shen, C., Xiao, J., et al.: Wavelet denoising based on an asymptotic semisoft thresholding function. Chinese J. Electron Devices **40**(2), 396–399 (2017)

18. Rathinasamy, M., Agarwal, A., Sivakumar, B., et al.: Wavelet analysis of precipitation extremes over India and teleconnections to climate indices. Stochastic Hydrol. Hydraul. **33**, 2053–2069 (2019)

19. Peng, R., Yao, Y.: Research on optical variable image fusion based on wavelet decomposition and reconstruction. Laser J. **42**(03), 145–148 (2021)

20. Jiang, C., Qiu, T., Chen, B., et al.: An improved dynamic data correction method based on robust estimation. Lect. Notes Electr. Eng. **24**(10), 1297–1301 (2007)

21. Xiong, Z., Zhu, X., Ren, S., et al.: A method for robust correction of thermal data based on interior point algorithm. Power Equip. **34**(05), 297–305 (2020)

Multi-sensor Information Fusion Algorithm Based on Power-Average Operator and D-S Evidence Theory

Bohang Chen[1], Jun Ma[1,2]($\boxtimes$), Zhou Yongjie[1], and Lingfei Zhang[1]

[1] The Computer College, Qinghai Normal University, Xining 810008, China
[2] Academy of Plateau Science and Sustainability, Qinghai Normal University, Xining 810008, China

Abstract. Data fusion algorithm based on power-average operator and D-S evidential theory is proposed to solve the problem of information loss or low accuracy in single sensor data acquisition, which is based on multi-sensor information. Firstly, the outliers of multi-sensor data are removed. Considering the problem of the increase of computation caused by the overuse of redundant information, a dynamic sliding window method is proposed to reduce the data usage. Then, the first data fusion is carried out by using the power average operator. Finally, a hierarchical decision-making method is proposed, according to the characteristics of wireless sensor networks, and the conflict of D-S evidence theory is processed by setting the evidence threshold. The simulation results show that this method can solve the problems of inaccurate information loss and D-S evidence theory conflict in single sensor information acquisition. compared with other algorithms, the recognition rate of H_1 is 0.81, the decision-making effect is good, and it has the advantages of relatively simple calculation.

Keywords: Information fusion · Power-average algorithm · D-S evidence theory · Sliding window · Hierarchical decision-making

1 Introduction

With the rapid development of artificial intelligence, robotics and big data industry, manual acquisition, analysis and decision of information are gradually becoming intelligent. As the main medium for external data access, the acquisition and processing of sensor information have become one of the hot-spots of research by many scholars [1]. Sensor data acquisition nodes are often deployed in the field as needed, which makes sensors vulnerable to external environment. When a single sensor collects data, the data is usually lost or inaccurate due to unknown reasons [2]. Nowadays, it has entered the information society, which puts forward higher requirements for the accuracy of sensor information collection, and a single sensor can no longer meet the application requirements.

Multi-sensor information fusion technology originated in the military field [3], used for battlefield environment monitoring, information acquisition and decision-making,

X. Wang et al. (Eds.): AICON 2021, LNICST 397, pp. 151–163, 2021.
https://doi.org/10.1007/978-3-030-90199-8_15

etc. After decades of development, its technology has been widely used in all aspects of production and life.The research on its algorithm is also gradually in-depth, from single sensor information calibration to information decision, various algorithms emerge in an endless stream.For example, Ref. [4] proposed a data fusion algorithm based on the fuzzy set and D-Sevidence theory for CPSs. This algorithm firstly uses the fuzzy set theory and attribute weight to determine the distribution of evidence, and combines the data fusion of attribute evidence with the reliability of sensor nodes in CPSs; In view of the high conflict of D-S evidence theory in Ref. [5], the similarity Jaccard coefficient matrix was segmented to calculate the weight of each sensor node to modify the evidence source, so as to reduce the decision risk of D-Sevidence theory. Reference [6] proposes to use the membership function to refine the missile's integrity state, which effectively overcomes the conflict problem in the fusion process. Reference [7] aiming at the problem of obstacle recognition for Unmanned Aerial Vehicles, the basic probability distribution of feature extraction is calculated by using camera and laser scanner, and finally a decision-making method is developed to identify obstacles. Test results show the validity of the proposed method and its application in cross-country environment perception. Reference [8] a belief divergence measure RB is proposed to measure the difference of basic probability distribution in D-S evidence theory, so as to solve the conflict problem in D-S evidence theory more effectively, this method can be effectively applied to practical problems. Reference [9] aiming at the conflict problem of D-S evidence theory, an improved strategy of evidence theory based on confidence degree is proposed. The algorithm extracts the weight from the initial prediction value of four neural networks, and reasonably constructs the BPAs function, the application effect of the system is verified by an example. Reference [10] a data fusion algorithm based on the fuzzy theory and the D-S evidence theory is proposed by combining the fuzzy theory and the attribute weight to determine the basic probability distribution and the reliability of sensor nodes, Experimental analysis shows that the proposed method has obvious advantages in the degree of the differentiation of the results. Reference [11] multi-sensor information decision-making is applied to power transformer fault detection, and a method combining the deep belief network classifier (DBNC) with D-S evidence theory is proposed, this method greatly improves the ability of fault detection. The above fusion algorithm has achieved certain effects, but it is all carried out under the condition that the data collected by each group of sensors are correct, and there is no analysis of the data collected by sensors. The calculation process of the modified D-S evidence theory is relatively complex.This article first analyzes the sensor data to eliminate the obvious error data, and then corrects the sensor data by setting a sliding window combined with the power average operator. After the basic probability assignment is completed in the D-S evidence fusion process, the conflict judgment and correction are carried out through the algorithm. Finally, the fusion result is obtained.

2 Multi-sensor Decision Information Fusion Model

The multi-sensor decision information fusion model is shown in Fig. 1. It can be seen from Fig. 1 that the fusion process of a wireless sensor network (WSN) network is divided into two steps. Firstly, the data queues collected by the same kind of sensors in the sub-network are preprocessed and the same kind of data fusion process is carried out, which is the same kind of data correction. Secondly, the different types of data are pre-processed to prepare for the next step of D-S evidence fusion. The pre-process is the basic probability assignment (BPA) process for sensor information. At the same time, the conflict judgment threshold is designed considering the conflict problem in D-S evidence theory. When there is no conflict of evidence, decision-making fusion can be carried out directly. On the contrary, it is necessary to process the conflicting data to get the fusion result.

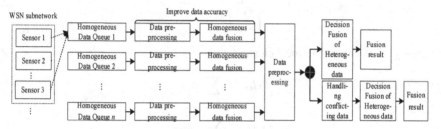

Fig. 1. Multi-sensor decision information fusion model

3 Power-Average Operator

The power-average operator is defined as follows [12].

$$
\begin{cases}
P_{(a_1,a_2,a_3,...,a_n)} = \dfrac{\sum\limits_{i=1}^{n}(1+T_{(a_i)})\,a_i}{\sum\limits_{i=1}^{n}(1+T_{(a_i)})\cdot 1} \\
T_{(a_i)} = \sum\limits_{\substack{j=1 \\ j\neq i}}^{n} \sup(a_i, a_j)
\end{cases}
\tag{1}
$$

$\sup(a_i, a_j)$ is a_i support for a_j, and $T_{(a_i)}$ is the sum of all a_j support for a_i of except a_i. Namely, a_j is synthetic support of a_i. And $\sup(a_i, a_j)$ satisfies the following condition:

(1) $\sup(a_i, a_j) \in [0, 1]$;
(2) $\sup(a_i, a_j) = \sup(a_j, a_i)$;
(3) When $|a_x - a_y| > |a_i - a_j|$, $\sup(a_i - a_j) \geq \sup(a_x, a_y)$;
(4) According to the power average operator equation, When $T_{(a_i)} = 0$, namely $\sup(a_i, a_j) = 0$, each a_j has no support for a_i, then the support function degenerates to: $P_{(a_1,a_2,...,a_n)} = \frac{a_1+a_2+...+a_n}{n}$.

(5) The distribution of the power-average operator is independent of the order of the acquisition data, that function is not monotonic. When the sensor data values are closer to each other, the support of the operator will be greater. Therefore, the error can be reduced by using the power-average operator to reduce the weight of the data.

4 D-S Evidence Theory

Definition. If the identification frame is $\theta = \{\theta_1, \theta_2, ..., \theta_n\}$ and the elements in θ are mutually exclusive, Then identify the power set formed by the frame θ and obey the function m of $2^\theta \to [0, 1]$. The function m is called the basic probability distribution, and m satisfies [13],

$$\begin{cases} m_{(\phi)} = 0 \\ \sum_{A \subseteq \theta} m_{(A)} = 1 \end{cases} \tag{2}$$

When $m_{(A)} > 0$, calls A the focal element, then,

$$Bel_{(A)} = \sum_{B \subseteq A} m_{(B)} \tag{3}$$

$$Pl_{(A)} = \sum_{B \cap A \neq \phi} m_{(B)} \tag{4}$$

Where the above equation can be calculated by $m_1 \oplus m_2 \oplus ... \oplus m_n(A) = \frac{1}{k} \sum_{A_1 \cap ... \cap A_n = A} m_1(A_1) \cdot m_2(A_2) \cdots m_n(A_n)$, where $\frac{1}{k}$ is the normalized coefficient:

$$k = \sum_{A_1 \cap ... \cap A_n \neq \varnothing} m_1(A_1) \cdot m_2(A_2) \cdots m_n(A_n) \tag{5}$$

5 Algorithm Improvement

5.1 Data Pre-processing

The reliability of Sensor data acquisition includes sensor fault and data acquisition error. This paper will be divided into two steps to ensure the correctness of sensor information acquisition. First, the first possibility is avoided by using the sensor parameters. Second, the second possibility is avoided by setting the support function.

(1) Multi-sensor information fusion technology can use multiple same sensors for data acquisition to ensure the accuracy of information Assuming that the raw data acquisition by the sensor is $A \in \{a | (a_1, a_2, a_3, ..., a_n), n \in (1, 2, ...)\}$, quickly sort A to get $B \in \{b | (b_1, b_2, b_3, ..., b_n), n \in (1, 2, ...)\}$. Get $b_{n'}$ by calculating $n' = \frac{n}{2}$, Assuming the accuracy of the sensor be $T \pm \Delta t$, then, when $b_i - b_{n'} \geq 2\Delta t$. it indicates that there is a problem in the data measured by the i-th sensor, and it is removed. When the data

acquired by each sensor node in the data acquisition area changes greatly, it can be processed by setting a threshold.

(2) **Definition 1** Assume that a certain sensor collects data as a queue. Set the dynamic virtual data window, the starting size of the window is c, the vector distance between the two sensors is d, then the support of historical data is defined as Eq. (6),

$$T_{(a_i)} = \sum_{\substack{j=1 \\ j \neq i}}^{n} \sup(a_i, a_j) \tag{6}$$

Where: $\sup(a_i, a_j) = \frac{1}{d_{ij}}$, $d_{ij} = d_j - d_i$, $(j \neq i, |j - i| < c)$ so, the result is,

$$\gamma = \frac{\sum_{i=1}^{n}(1 + T_{(a_i)})a_i}{\sum_{i=1}^{n}(1 + T_{(a_i)}) \cdot 1} \tag{7}$$

Note: When $a_j = a_i$, namely $d_{ij} = 0$, $\sup(a_i, a_j)$ loses its meaning. For this reason, specify that when $a_j = a_i$ has the most support is $u \cdot \max(\sup(a_i, a_j))$, where u is the same number of data.

Definition 2. On the basis of ensuring the accuracy of data, this paper adopts the method of setting virtual window to reduce the computation. Suppose that the virtual data window size of the sensor is c at moment t_0 that is, take c numbers from the median to both sides evenly. At this point, Through calculation a_i is an outlier. If an abnormal value occurs again on this basis, the window size will be expanded to c_1 at t_1. Similarly, if the abnormal value continues to increase, the window size will be expanded to c_2 at t_2 until the continuously collected correct data reaches a certain standard, and the sliding window will be reduced again to c. The reliability of the sensor is a stable value. The window change process is shown in Fig. 2.

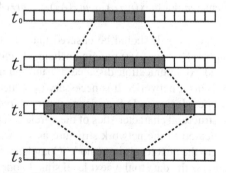

Fig. 2. Virtual data window change process

5.2 D-S Evidence Theory Fusion Process

BPA is not given in the D-S evidence theory. Therefore, most of them adopt the method of empirical assignment, but due to the limitation of experience, it has great limitations [14]. Since the data acquired by different types of sensors have certain similarities, this similarity is used to assign basic probabilities.

Definition 3. There are n decision schemes and e sensors in a sensor decision system. The value range of the i sensor corresponding to each scheme j is $a_i^j \pm \Delta t_i$ and its central value is a_i^j, so the scheme j can be represented by the vector $G^j = (a_1^j, a_2^j, ..., a_e^j)$ and the corresponding value of the sensor i is $G_i = (a_i^1, a_i^2, ..., a_i^n)^T$.

Definition 4. Assume that the maximum value measured by each sensor is $\max(a_i)$, the minimum value is $\min(a_i)$, and the actual measured value is b_i, then $\min(a_i) \le b_i \le \max(a_i)$.

Definition 5. Let N be the support of scheme j for each sensor measurement value, and $b_i - a_i^j$ is the distance from the measurement value b_i to the evaluation of j, then the basic probability is assigned as Eq. (8),

$$m_{(\theta)} = 1 - \frac{\left|b_i - a_i^j\right|}{\sum\limits_{j=1}^{n} \left|b_i - a_i^j\right|} \tag{8}$$

Where $\dfrac{1}{\sum\limits_{j=1}^{n}\left|b_i-a_i^j\right|}$ is the normalized coefficient.

Definition 6. If the evidence threshold is ∂, when there is $m_{(\theta)} \ge \partial$, it indicates that there is conflict in the current m, in order to avoid its influence on the fusion result, the D-S evidence conflict characteristic can be known, there is only one $m_{(\theta)} \ge \partial$, then assume $\max(m_Z(A_1), m_Z(A_2), ..., m_Z(A_i)) - \partial = k$, let $\frac{k}{i-1} = \Delta k$, Let vector $F = \max(m_Z(A_1), m_Z(A_2), ..., m_Z(A_{i-1}))$ be other elements except the maximum value. Update the data of evidence m, let $\max(m_Z(A_1), m_Z(A_2), ..., m_Z(A_i)) = \partial$ and the rest be $F + \Delta k$.

∂ basic principle of selection: It should be ensured that the size and order of the original $\max(m_Z(A_1), m_Z(A_2), ..., m_Z(A_i))$ remain unchanged, and not too small.

Data transmission and communication distance are the main reasons for energy consumption of wireless sensor networks. It is necessary to reduce the transmission of data and the possible data explosion in D-S evidence theory to reduce network energy consumption. Using the structural characteristics of the wireless sensor network, design the hierarchical fusion method of the network structure as shown in Fig. 3. The node $1, 2, ..., n$ sends the data to the next level sink 1 node. Complete the first-level fusion at the sink 1 node, then uploads the data to the next level sink 2 node, the fusion structure of sink 1 is used as the fusion data of sink 2 for Information Fusion, and so on until the final fusion result is obtained.

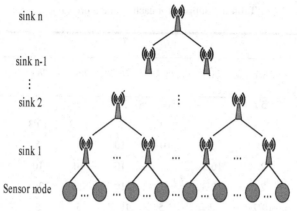

Fig. 3. Network structure diagram

Definition 7. Substitute the revised BPA into the D-S synthesis rule to get the final fusion result as Eq. (9),

$$m(A) = \begin{cases} \dfrac{\sum\limits_{A_1 \cap ... \cap A_n = A} m_1(A_1), m_2(A_2), ..., m_n(A_n)}{\sum\limits_{A_1 \cap ... \cap A_n \neq \varnothing} m_1(A_1), m_2(A_2), ..., m_n(A_n)}, A \neq \varnothing \\ 0, A = \varnothing \end{cases} \tag{9}$$

6 Case Studies

Example 1. Assume a temperature sensor is used to test the temperature change in an industrial production process. In order to improve the measurement accuracy, multiple temperature sensors can be used to measure data simultaneously.The measuring range of the temperature sensor is "-200 °C$-+150$ °C", and the precision is "$T \pm 0.5$ °C". Assuming there are 9 temperature sensors, the temperature measured at a certain moment is 78.5 °C, 78.6 °C, 78.6 °C, 78.8 °C, 78.1 °C, 0 °C, 78.4 °C, 78.3 °C, 80.3 °C.

The average method is used to calculate the result.

$$\overline{T_0} = {}^1\!/_9(78.5 + 78.6 + 78.6 + 78.8 + 78.1 + 0 + 78.4 + 78.3 + 80.3) \approx 69.96\,°C$$

Using the algorithm designed in this paper. First, sort the data from small to large to get (0 °C, 78.1 °C, 78.3 °C, 78.4 °C, 78.5 °C, 78.6 °C, 78.6 °C, 78.8 °C, 80.3 °C). the median is 78.5 °C, set the initial size of the virtual sliding window to 5, and compare the measured data with 78.5 °C, it can be seen that 0 °C and 80.3 °C are greater than "$2\Delta t$", therefore, remove the value. At this point, update the virtual sliding window size to 7. The support degree of the remaining temperature values are calculated as shown in Table 1.

The fusion result can be obtained by Equation $\gamma = \dfrac{\sum\limits_{i=1}^{n} (1+T_{(a_i)})a_i}{\sum\limits_{i=1}^{n} (1+T_{(a_i)})\cdot 1}$, that is, $\gamma_{temperature} =$

78.49 °C. Comparing $\gamma_{temperature}$ with $\overline{T_0}$, it can be shownthat $\overline{T}$ is obviously affected by temperature 0 °C. Therefore the error of the result is obvious.

Table 1. Support for each temperature value

$1/d_{ij}$ T $T(a_i)$	℃						
	78.1	78.3	78.4	78.5	78.6	78.6	78.8
	5	5	10/3	2.5	2	2	10/7
	10/3	10	10	5	10/3	10/3	2
	2.5	5	10	10	5	5	2.5
	2	10/3	5	10	10	10	10/3
	2	10/3	5	10	20	20	5
	10/7	2	2.5	10/3	5	5	5
$T_{(a_i)}$	683/42	86/3	215/6	245/6	76/3	76/3	809/42

Example 2. Assume a mechanical fault is divided into three levels: X_1, X_2, X_3 and the corresponding evidence is $m_1(A_i)$, $m_2(A_x)$, as shown in Table 2 [15].

Table 2. Example 2 evidence data

	$m_1(A_i)$	$m_2(A_x)$
X_1	0.99	0
X_2	0.01	0.01
X_3	0	0.99

The fusion results of the original D-S evidence theory are shown in Table 3.

Table 3. Fusion result of case 2 using D-S evidence theory

	$m_1(A_i)$	$m_2(A_x)$	m_{12}
X_1	0.99	0	0
X_2	0.01	0.01	1
X_3	0	0.99	0

The fusion result of Table 3 shows that the mechanical fault is X_2, According to experience, the result is obviously not in line with common sense.

Use the proposed algorithm in this paper to preprocess $m_1(A_i)$ and $m_2(A_x)$, set $\partial = 0.95$, then $\triangle k = \frac{0.99-0.95}{1-3} = 0.02$, at this time, the corresponding $m_1(A_i)$, $m_2(A_x)$, and m_{12} are shown in Table 4.

Table 4. The fusion result of method 2 in this paper

	$m_1(A_i)$	$m_2(A_x)$	m_{12}
X_1	0.95	0.02	0.49
X_2	0.03	0.03	0.02
X_3	0.02	0.95	0.49

From Table 4, we can see that the fusion result is better than that in Table 3.

Example 3. Assume a certain recognition frame θ is H_1, H_2, and H_3, and the corresponding evidence BPA is $m_1(A_1)$, $m_2(A_2)$, $m_3(A_3)$, $m_4(A_4)$, as shown in Table 5. The algorithm in this paper is set to $\partial = 0.7$. After preprocessing the original data, D-S evidence fusion is then carried out. Table 6 shows the comparison of the fusion results of different methods [16].

The analysis of the data in Table 5 shows that the evidence indicates that H_1 is the most likely result. In Table 6, the fusion result of the D-S evidence rule H_1 under the recognition framework is 0 and H_2 is the largest, which is obviously contrary to the facts. Analysis shows that the result is greatly affected by $m_2(A_2)$. Therefore, it has no reference value.

Table 5. Example 3 evidence data under recognition framework

	$m_1(A_1)$	$m_2(A_2)$	$m_3(A_3)$	$m_4(A_4)$
H_1	0.5	0	0.6	0.8
H_2	0.2	0.9	0.1	0.1
H_3	0.3	0.1	0.3	0.1

Table 6. Comparison of fusion results of different methods

Method	m_1, m_2	m_1, m_2, m_3	m_1, m_2, m_3, m_4
D-S evidence rule	$m(H_1) = 0$, $m(H_2) = 0.8571$, $m(H_3) = 0.1429$, $m(\theta) = 0$	$m(H_1) = 0$, $m(H_2) = 0.6667$, $m(H_3) = 0.3333$, $m(\theta) = 0$	$m(H_1) = 0$, $m(H_2) = 0.6667$, $m(H_3) = 0.3333$, $m(\theta) = 0$
Murphy	$m(H_1) = 0.1543$, $m(H_2) = 0.7469$, $m(H_3) = 0.0988$, $m(\theta) = 0$	$m(H_1) = 0.3912$, $m(H_2) = 0.5079$, $m(H_3) = 0.1008$, $m(\theta) = 0$	$m(H_1) = 0.7996$, $m(H_2) = 0.1752$, $m(H_3) = 0.0251$, $m(\theta) = 0$
Methods in literature [16]	$m(H_1) = 0.2627$, $m(H_2) = 0.4590$, $m(H_3) = 0.2088$, $m(\theta) = 0.0695$	$m(H_1) = 0.5938$, $m(H_2) = 0.1575$, $m(H_3) = 0.2487$, $m(\theta) = 0$	$m(H_1) = 0.8240$, $m(H_2) = 0.0682$, $m(H_3) = 0.1078$, $m(\theta) = 0$
In this paper methods	$m(H_1) = 0.2$, $m(H_2) = 0.56$, $m(H_3) = 0.24$, $m(\theta) = 0$	$m(H_1) = 0.4839$, $m(H_2) = 0.2258$, $m(H_3) = 0.2903$, $m(\theta) = 0$	$m(H_1) = 0.81395$, $m(H_2) = 0.08140$, $m(H_3) = 0.10465$, $m(\theta) = 0$

Figure 4 shows the relationship between the recognition rate of different fusion methods and the number of evidence.For this example, it can be seen from Fig. 4 that the fusion result using the D-S evidence theory, whether the number of evidence is 2, 3, or 4, the recognition rate of H_1 is 0. The reason for the analysis is that $m_2(A_2)$ corresponds to H_1 and is 0 at this time, which leads to greater conflicts only using D-S evidence theory fusion. The other three methods all have a better recognition effect on the result H_1. However, the method in this paper and the Ref. [16], compared with the Murphy method, the recognition rate is significantly higher when there are only 2 or 3 evidences. The difference between the method in this paper and the Ref. [16] is 0.06 when the number of evidence is 2, and only 0.01 when the number of evidence is 4. However, the calculation process of the method in this paper is relatively simple in the Ref. [16], and it has the characteristics of simple calculation, no need to sort the evidence, and probability assignment after calculating the weight of each evidence. Figure 5 shows the relationship between the number of evidences in the recognition framework θ and the recognition rate of the method in this paper. It can be seen from Fig. 5 that the recognition rate of the method in this paper is monotonous and the distinguishing effect is obvious.

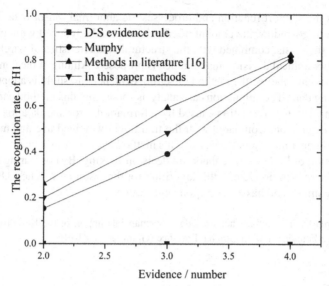

Fig. 4. Relationship between recognition rate and number of evidences for different fusion methods

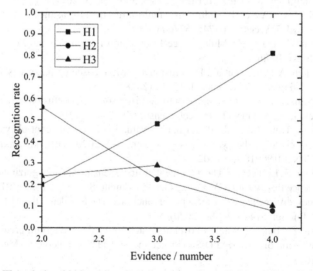

Fig. 5. The relationship between the recognition rate and the number of evidences

7   Conclusion

This study proposes a data fusion algorithm based on power-average operator and D-S evidence theory to improve the precision of sensor data acquisition and combine the characteristics of Wireless sensor network. The basic concepts of power-average operator and D-S evidence theory are introduced briefly in this paper. At the same time, the paper defines the support function and processes the abnormal sensor data. By setting a dynamic sliding window, the amount of calculation can be reduced without reducing accuracy. On this basis, combined with the structural characteristics of wireless sensor networks, a hierarchical decision-making idea is proposed. Aiming at the conflict problem of D-S evidence theory, the method of setting evidence threshold is adopted to deal with conflicting data. The simulation case analysis shows that this method can solve the problem of inaccurate information caused by information error and data loss in sensor information acquisition. Compared with the traditional weighted average method, the method in this paper has higher accuracy. This method paper has significantly improved the contradiction of D-S evidence theory in decision-making. By comparing with other algorithms, the recognition rate of this algorithm for the result H_1 reaches 0.81, and the calculation is simple and has certain application value.

Acknowledgments. The authors acknowledge the financial support of the Key Projects of the Natural Science Foundation of in Qinghai Province (Grant: 2021-ZJ-916).

References

1. Din, S., Ahmad, A., Paul, A., et al.: A cluster-based data fusion technique to analyze big data in wireless multi-sensor system. IEEE Access **5**, 5069–5083 (2017)
2. Liu, L., Ji, H., Zhang, W., et al.: Multi-sensor multi-target tracking using probability hypothesis density filter. IEEE Access **7**, 67745–67760 (2019)
3. Han, C., Zhu, H., Duan, Z.: Multi-source Information Fusion (Second Edition). Tsinghua University Press, Beijing
4. Zhao, G., Chen, A., Lu, G., et al.: Data fusion algorithm based on fuzzy sets and d-s theory of evidence. Tsinghua Sci. Technol. **1**, 12–19 (2018)
5. Zhang, Y., Sun, L., Zheng, G.: Approach to multi-sensor decision fusion based on improved Jousselme evidence distance. Instr. Tech. Sensor (7), 82–87 (2019)
6. Li, Y., Yue, R., Ding, C., et al.: Performance evaluation of missile control system based on improved D-S evidence theory. Electr. Opt. Contr., 1–6 (2020). http://kns.cnki.net/kcms/det ail/41.1227.TN.20190918.1536.002.html.
7. Zhao, Y., Ding, F., Li, J., et al.: The intelligent obstacle sensing and recognizing method based on D-S evidence theory for UGV. Future Gener. Comput. Syst. **97**, 21–29 (2019)
8. Xiao, F.: A new divergence measure for belief functions in D–Sevidence theory for multisensor data fusion. Inf. Sci. **514**, 462–483 (2020)
9. Si, L., Wang, Z., Tan, C., et al.: A novel approach for coal seam terrain prediction through information fusion of improved D-S evidence theory and neural network. Measurement **54**, 140–151 (2014)
10. Zhao, G., Chen, A., Lu, G., et al.: Data fusion algorithm based on fuzzy sets and D-S theory of evidence. Tsinghua Sci. Technol. **25**(1), 12–19(2020)
11. Li, G., Yu, C., Fan, H., et al.: Large power transformer fault diagnosis and prognostic based on DBNC and D-S evidence theory. Energy Power Eng. **9**, 232–239 (2017)
12. Wei, B., Shou, Y., Jiang, W.: A visibility graph information fusion method weighted average. J. XI'AN Jiaotong Univ. **52**(4), 145–149 (2018)
13. Yan, G., Meng, Z., Hao, L., et al.: Identifying vital nodes algorithm in social networks fusing higher-order information. J. Commun. **40**(9), 1–10 (2019)
14. Cao, J., Cao, W.: Fault diagnosis of large manufacturing equipment based on improve evidence fusion theory. J. Vibr. Meas. Diagn. **32**(4), 532–537 (2012)

15. Deng, Y., Shi, W.: A modified combination rule of evidence theory **37**(8), 1275–1278 (2003)
16. Hu, C., Si, X., Zhou, Z., et al.: An improved D-S algorithm under the new measure criteria of evidence conflict. Acta Electron. Sin. **37**(7), 1579–1583 (2009)

LED Nonlinear Compensation Method Based on Asymmetric Scaling Factor

Tao Wang[✉] and Chao Chen

School of Physics and Electronic Information Engineering, Qinghai Minzu University,
Xining 810007, China

Abstract. In visible light communication, the nonlinearity of the LED device will cause the nonlinear distortion of the signal. This paper proposes a nonlinear distortion mitigation method based on an asymmetric scaling factor, which is verified in the direct current biased optical OFDM (DCO-OFDM) system using 16-ary quadrature amplitude modulation (16QAM). Simulation results verify that the proposed scheme can obviously alleviate the nonlinear distortion, and the bit error performance is significantly improved. When the bit error rate (BER) is 10^{-5}, the signal-to-noise ratio gain can reach 3.6 dB.

Keywords: Visible light communications · LED nonlinearity · Nonlinear distortion mitigation · Optical orthogonal frequency division multiplexing

1 Introduction

Visible light communication (VLC) can use light-emitting diodes (LEDs) as signal transmitters to send signals. However, the nonlinearity of the LED device is one of the factors that limits the performance of the VLC system [1], the signals are affected by nonlinear effects during transmission [2]. In VLC systems, many physical devices will exhibit nonlinearity, such as LED nonlinearity, channel nonlinearity, receiving end device nonlinearity, amplifier nonlinearity. Among them, the most important nonlinear effect is the nonlinearity of the LED. Nonlinear distortion will cause system performance degradation, so mitigating LED nonlinear distortion is a problem that needs to be solved in the VLC system. The influence of LED nonlinear distortion can be mitigated in two ways. On the one hand, the input signal is selected or modified to make the signal insensitive to nonlinear distortion. For example, in [3], an optical orthogonal frequency division multiplexing (O-OFDM) scheme based on μ-law mapping (μ-OFDM) for the VLC system is proposed, which uses μ-law companding technology to alleviate LED nonlinear distortion. In [4], a scheme for the VLC-OFDM system that combines superimposed O-OFDM and μ-law mapping is proposed, under the constraints of the nonlinearity and limited dynamic range of the LED, the nonlinear influence of the LED is alleviated. Another method is distortion compensation. Several pre-distortion schemes have been suggested to counter the nonlinear characteristics of LED. The look-up table (LUT) method is the simplest solution, the nonlinear input-output of the LED is stored in the LUT, and it is

X. Wang et al. (Eds.): AICON 2021, LNICST 397, pp. 164–169, 2021.
https://doi.org/10.1007/978-3-030-90199-8_16

used to predistort the transmitted signal. In [5], a predistortion method using an adaptive normalized least mean square (NLMS) algorithm was proposed to estimate the LED distortion, instead of using a conventional memory look-up table (LUT) for nonlinear compensation. In [6], a nonlinear predistorter based on Chebyshev regression is proposed. There are also some distortion compensation methods that use a post-distorter at the receiver to compensate for LED nonlinearity. In [7], the linear post-equalization method (DD-LMS) and the nonlinear post-equalization algorithm (Volterra) are jointly used. However, with the increase of nonlinear complexity, the computational complexity of nonlinear post-equalization algorithms such as Volterra has increased dramatically, making the VLC system almost impossible to implement.

In recent years, with the rapid development of machine learning, methods based on machine learning have been successfully used in prediction, classification, feature extraction, behavior recognition, pattern recognition and other fields, and gradually used to solve the problems in the communication system. In the field of visible light communication, artificial neural networks (ANN), deep neural networks (DNN), support vector machines (SVM) and principal component analysis (PCA) can all be used for system nonlinear suppression and compensation, optical network performance monitoring, and modulation recognition and phase estimation, etc. Classical machine learning algorithms such as K-means have been tried by researchers to solve problems in visible light communication. In [8], the K-means algorithm is used to compensate the system nonlinearity and significantly reduce the system bit error rate. In [9], a clustering algorithms perception decision (CAPD) algorithm was proposed to reduce the nonlinear loss and complexity. With the continuous deepening of machine learning research, the application prospects of machine learning in the field of VLC will be very broad.

This paper proposes an LED nonlinear compensation method based on asymmetric scaling factor, which achieves the purpose of compensating LED nonlinearity. In the direct current biased optical OFDM (DCO-OFDM) system using 16-ary quadrature amplitude modulation (16QAM), the optimal asymmetric scaling factor is used for simulation verification. Simulation results show that this method significantly improves the bit error performance and the anti-nonlinear performance of the system.

2 Nonlinear Model of LED

The ideal LED is defined as a distortion-free diode, which transmits the signal from its input port (drive current) to its output port (emitted light power). In fact, LEDs exhibit nonlinearity, resulting in signal distortion during emission. In [10], a static nonmemory LED nonlinear model was proposed. The model studied the nonlinear characteristics of LED output light power and input current, and used polynomials to empirically model the static transfer function of the LED, which can be shown as

$$P_o(t) = b_0 + b_1(I_i(t) - I_D) + b_2(I_i(t) - I_D)^2 \tag{1}$$

Where P_o is the output power, t is the time, I_i is the drive current, I_D is the bias current, b_0, b_1 and b_2 are parameterized polynomial coefficients. In Eq. (1), $b_0 = \beta$, $b_1 = 1$,

$b_2 = -4\beta + 2$, and β is a parameter describing the degree of nonlinearity of the light source transfer function. The value of β varies according to the type of LED. Red LED is $\beta = 0.541$, and white LED is $\beta = 0.582$. When the normalized I_D is set to 0.5, the normalized nonlinear and linear static transfer function curves are shown in Fig. 1, and it can be seen that there is a nonlinear mapping between the output optical power of the LED and the input current.

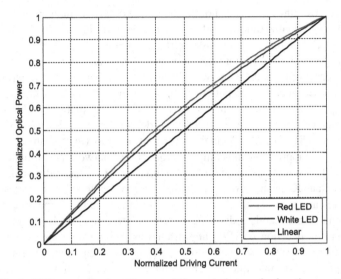

Fig. 1. LED normalized nonlinear and linear static transfer function curves.

3   Proposed Method

This paper proposes a method of LED nonlinear compensation based on asymmetric scaling factor. The LED nonlinear model proposed in [10] is adopted, the asymmetric scaling factor is used at the input port and output port of the LED nonlinear model. In this way, an approximately linear characteristic signal is output.

When considering LED nonlinearity and adopting symmetrical scaling factor, the input signal and output signal of the LED nonlinear model are shown in Fig. 2, it can be clearly seen that the LED output signal is significantly affected by the LED's nonlinearity, which is very different from the input signal curve.

When considering LED nonlinearity and adopting asymmetric scaling factor, the input signal and output signal of the LED nonlinear model are shown in Fig. 3, it can be clearly seen that the LED output signal can better approximate the linear characteristic.

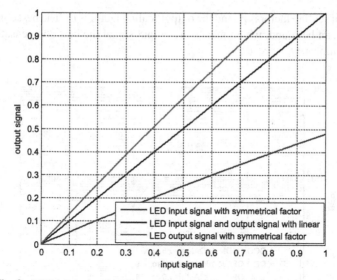

Fig. 2. LED input signal and output signal with symmetrical scaling factor.

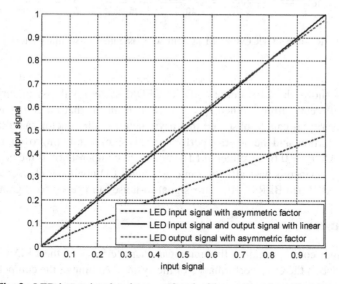

Fig. 3. LED input signal and output signal with asymmetric scaling factor.

4 Simulation Discussion

In this section, the proposed method is used in the DCO-OFDM system, and the error performance is analyzed through simulation. The simulation parameters are set as follows: the modulation format is 16QAM, the number of subcarriers is 512, and the DC offset is set to 7.5 dB, the LED nonlinear characteristic parameter $\beta = 0.582$.

The input scaling factor is r_i, and the output scaling factor is r_o. The best combination of r_i and r_o can be found, which makes the output signal the best compensation effect for LED nonlinearity.

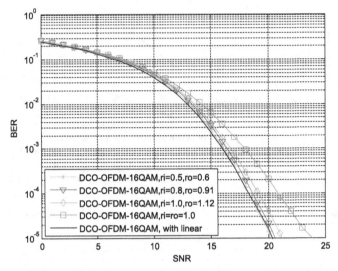

Fig. 4. The BER curve of DCO-OFDM system with asymmetric scaling factors of different settings.

Figure 4 shows the BER curve of DCO-OFDM system with asymmetric scaling factors of different settings. When $r_i = r_o = 1$, it means that no compensation for LED nonlinearity. It can be observed that asymmetric scaling factor can alleviate the nonlinear distortion, and the bit error performance is significantly improved. Especially when $r_i = 0.5$, $r_o = 0.6$, the effect of LED nonlinear compensation is the best, and the bit error performance is basically the same as when LED nonlinear characteristics are not considered. When BER $= 10^{-5}$, the signal-to-noise ratio gets 3.6 dB gain.

5   Conclusion

In visible light communication, the nonlinear characteristics of the LED will have a serious impact on the error performance of the system. Aiming at the compensation of LED nonlinear distortion, this paper proposes a nonlinear compensation method based on asymmetric scaling factor. The proposed method was simulated and verified in a DCO-OFDM system using 16QAM. The simulation results show that the proposed method effectively improves the bit error performance.

References

1. Elgala, H., Mesleh. R., Haas, H.: Predistortion in optical wireless transmission using OFDM. In: Proceedings 9th International Conference Hybrid Intelligent System (HIS), vol. 2, pp. 184–189 (2009)

2. Neokosmidis, I., Kamalakis, T., Walewski, J.W., et al.: Impact of nonlinear LED transfer function on discrete multitone modulation: analytical approach. J. Lightwave Technol. **27**(22), 4970–4978 (2009)
3. Yang, Y., Zeng, Z., Feng, S., Guo, C.: A simple OFDM scheme for VLC systems based on μ-law mapping. IEEE Photonics Technol. Lett. **28**(6), 641–644 (2015)
4. Wang, T., Ren, Y., Li, C., et al.: A PAPR reduction scheme combining superimposed O-OFDM and μ-law mapping for VLC-OFDM systems. Optics Commun. **460**, 125190 (2020)
5. Kim, J.K., Hyun, K., Park, S.K.: Adaptive predistorter using NLMS algorithm for nonlinear compensation in visible-light communication system. Electron. Lett. **50**(20), 1457–1459 (2014)
6. Mitra, R., Bhatia, V.: Chebyshev polynomial-based adaptive predistorter for nonlinear LED compensation in VLC. IEEE Photonics Technol. Lett. **28**(10), 1053–1056 (2016)
7. Wang, Y., Tao, L., Huang, X., et al.: 8-Gb/s RGBY LED-based WDM VLC system employing high-order CAP modulation and hybrid post equalizer. IEEE Photonics J. **7**(6), 1–7 (2015)
8. Ma, J., He, J., Shi, J., et al.: Nonlinear compensation based on k-means clustering algorithm for Nyquist PAM-4 VLC system. IEEE Photonics Technol. Lett. **31**(12), 935–938 (2019)
9. Lu, X.Y., Wang, K.H., Qiao, L., et al.: Nonlinear compensation of multi-CAP VLC system employing clustering algorithm based perception decision. IEEE Photonics J. **9**(5), 7906509 (2017)
10. Inan, B., Lee, S.C.J., Randel, S., et al.: Impact of LED nonlinearity on discrete multitone modulation. J. Opt. Commun. Networking **1**(5), 439–451 (2009)

Analysis of Human Body Comfort Based on Variable Precision Fuzzy Rough Set of Double Universe

Enfan Zhou[1], Jun Ma[2,1(✉)], Lingfei Zhang[1], and Bohang Chen[1]

[1] College of Physics and Electronic Information Engineering, Qinghai Normal University, Xining 810008, China

[2] Academy of Plateau Science and Sustainability, Qinghai Normal University, Xining 810008, People's Republic of China

Abstract. This paper proposes a human comfort analysis model based on variable precision fuzzy rough sets of dual universes. Firstly find out the relationship between temperature and humidity index (*THI*), wind efficiency index (*WEI*), clothing index (*ICL*) and human comfort. Divide the corresponding value range and assign the value according to the degree of the relationship between human body perception and *THI*, *WEI* and *ICL* values. Finally, according to the different values of α in the dual domain variable precision fuzzy rough set, the upper and lower approximations are obtained to obtain the human body comfort level. Because of the variable values of α and β in this method, the dual domain variable precision fuzzy rough set model has a wide range of applications and strong adaptability. It can analyze and process meteorological elements in different regions and at different times. It is helpful to analyze the time and space characteristics of human comfort.

Keywords: Rough set · Variable precision · Human comfort · Double universe

1 Introduction

People began to pay attention to the protection of the atmospheric environment in the 1960s. In 1972, the United Nations organized a global environmental conference, in which the conference formulated a plan for the protection of the global atmospheric environment to enhance people's awareness of the protection of the atmospheric environment. Since then, many scholars have carried out a series of studies on the evaluation and prediction of atmospheric environmental quality and the protection of the atmospheric environment. In recent years, a number of domestic and foreign researchers have put forward some basic theoretical models for the comprehensive evaluation of atmospheric environmental quality.

Wang Luping conducted a grid of Xi'an city and established an evaluation model of Xi'an air environmental pollution. It was concluded that the PM2.5 and PM10 particulate matter pollution was the most serious in 2013–2016. According to the temporal and

X. Wang et al. (Eds.): AICON 2021, LNICST 397, pp. 170–184, 2021.
https://doi.org/10.1007/978-3-030-90199-8_17

spatial distribution characteristics of pollutants, the air environment monitoring points are reasonably optimized, and the results show that the optimization model can well meet the actual needs of the air environment quality in Xi'an [1]. Wang Hongfang and others proposed an air pollution evaluation model based on BP neural network. Through the training of BP neural network, the accuracy of air pollution evaluation results is improved. The decision-making process of this model is not complicated and has a wide range of applications [2]. Cong Xiaonan et al. analyzed the different trends of China's climate and environment on people's tourist destinations based on the THI, WEI and ICL indexes, and concluded that there are fewer suitable travel periods in different regions at different times, and there are fewer cities suitable for travel in winter [3]. Yu Zhikang and others analyzed the THI, WEI, and ICL indexes of 212 high-latitude cities from 1980 to 2010, and found the places and months suitable for summer heat escape in space and time. The author has classified the best summer time period that is most suitable for the summer resort area in detail, and provided a favorable reference for related tourism departments [4].

2   Rough Set Theory Knowledge

2.1   Pawlak Rough Set

Let (U, R) be an approximate space, where U is a non-empty finite universe, and R is an equivalence relation on U. For any $X \subseteq U$, the lower and upper approximations of X are defined as [5]:

$$\underline{R}(X) = \{x \in U | [x]_R \subseteq X\} = \cup \{[x]_R | [x]_R \subseteq X\}; \tag{1}$$

$$\overline{R}(X) = \{x \in U | [x]_R \cap X \neq \varnothing\} = \cup \{[x]_R | [x]_R \cap X \neq \varnothing\} \tag{2}$$

Here $[x]_R$ represents the equivalence class of x. If $\underline{R}(X) = \overline{R}(X)$, then X is called an exact set; if $\underline{R}(X) \neq \overline{R}(X)$, then X is called a rough set. The upper and lower approximate representation of rough set is shown in Fig. 1. The entire box is the universe U, the black part is the lower approximation, and the black plus gray part is the upper approximation. The area within the red is the border area.

2.2   Rough Fuzzy Set

Let (U, R) be the equivalent approximate space of Pawlak rough set, F(U) is the fuzzy set, and $F(U) \subseteq U$, for $\forall A \subseteq F(U)$, the lower and upper approximations of A are respectively defined as [6]:

$$\underline{R}(A) = \min\{A(y) | y \in [x]_R\}; \tag{3}$$

$$\overline{R}(A) = \max\{A(y) | y \in [x]_R\} \tag{4}$$

Among them $[x]_R$ is the equivalence class of element x under the equivalence relation R. If $\underline{R}(A) = \overline{R}(A)$, then we call A an exact set. If the upper and lower approximations

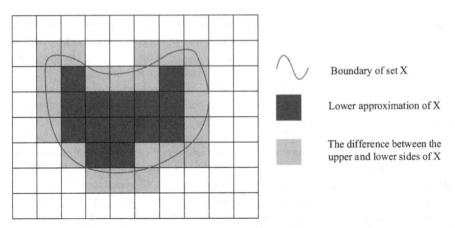

Fig. 1. Rough set upper and lower approximate representation

of set A are not equal, then we call the set $\left(\underline{R}(A), \overline{R}(A)\right)$ formed by the upper and lower approximations as a rough-fuzzy set. We call the lower approximation $\underline{R}(A)$ of A the positive domain of $POS_R(A)$, and $U-\overline{R}(A)$ is the negative domain of $NEG_R(A)$ of A under (U, R), Call $\overline{R}(A) - \underline{R}(A)$ be the $BND_R(A)$ boundary domain of A under (U, R).

2.3 Rough Set on the Double Universe

Take two finite non-empty sets U and V as two universes of compatible relation r, and for $\forall x \in U$, there must be $\exists y \in V$, so that x and y are related. The compatible relationship r from U to V can be expressed as: $U \to 2^V$, $R(x) = \{y \in V | x\ r\ y\}$, $x \in U$, R (x) is the x element in U and the x element has a collection of associated elements in V. According to this multi-valued mapping association, $\forall A \subseteq V$ can be represented by the elements in the equivalence class contained in U and the compatible elements in A. Then it is about the lower and upper approximation operator [7]:

$$\underline{R}_v(A) = \{x \in U | R(x) \subseteq A\}; \tag{5}$$

$$\underline{R}_v(A) = \{x \in U | R(x) \cap A \neq \varnothing\} \tag{6}$$

If $\underline{R}_v(A) = \overline{R}_v(A)$, then A is called an exact set in the dual universe; if $\underline{R}_v(A) \neq \overline{R}_v(A)$, then A is called a rough set on the dual universe.

2.4 Variable Precision Rough Set

In rough set theory, the upper approximation under the equivalence relation is the set of all elements in the set related to the object, and the lower approximation is the set of all elements related to the object 100%. This is due to the use of the upper approximation of the definition of existential quantifiers and the lower approximation of the definition of universal quantifiers. The definition of the upper approximation is too loose and can easily lead to a very large set, while the definition of the lower approximation is too strict and can easily lead to an empty set.

Ziarko proposed a variable precision rough set (VPRS) model to deal with these problems by introducing thresholds [8]. Generally, given $0 \leq 1 - \beta < \beta \leq 1$, if at least $100 * \beta\%$ of the elements related to y are in A, then element y is added to the lower approximation of set A. Similarly, if more than $100 * (1 - \beta)\%$ of the elements related to y are in A, then y belongs to the upper approximation of A. This is the generalization of the rough set model, using specific quantifiers with at least $100 * \beta\%$ and more than $100 * (1 - \beta)\%$ to replace universal quantifiers and existential quantifiers, respectively. In addition, this method is also used in the fuzzy rough set model. The common point is that they can rely on the use of specific threshold β and $(1 - \beta)$. Katzberg changed β and $(1 - \beta)$ to u and l on the basis of Ziarko, making the upper and lower approximations of variable precision rough sets more suitable for various situations.

The method in this paper inherits the flexibility of VPRS to deal with classification errors and expresses the fuzzy set of partial constraint satisfaction by relaxing the membership conditions of the lower approximation and tightening the membership conditions of the upper approximation.

Let (U, R) be an approximate space, where U is a non-empty finite universe, R is an equivalence relation on U, For any $A \subseteq U$, where $\{X_1, X_2, \cdots, X_m\}$, $[x]_R \in U/R$ is used to represent the equivalence class of object x under equivalence relation R. In addition, the rough membership function e(A) of A is [9]:

$$
e(A) = \begin{cases} \frac{[x]_R \cap A}{[x]_R} & [x]_R \neq \varnothing \\ 0 & [x]_R = \varnothing \end{cases} \tag{7}
$$

Since in real life, data may be affected by classification errors caused by humans or noise, the constraints in the upper and lower approximations are reduced, and the following parameterized definitions are obtained [10]:

$$
\underline{R}_u(A) = \cup \left\{ [x]_R | [x]_R \subseteq^u A, e(A) \geq u \right\} \tag{8}
$$

$$
\underline{R}_u(A) = \cup \left\{ [x]_R | [x]_R \subseteq^l A, e(A) > l \right\} \tag{9}
$$

The quantifiers used in rough set under equivalence relation are existential quantifier $\exists$ and universal quantifier $\forall$. The existence quantifier $\exists$ is when an element in the object is in the equivalence class, then all the elements in the equivalence class are combined and approximated. The universal quantifier $\forall$ is when all the elements in the object are in the equivalence class, then the equal All the elements in the price class are approximated as follows. The two threshold quantifiers in the variable precision rough set $> 100 * l\%$ and $\geq 100 * u\%$ respectively indicate that there are elements greater than $100 * l\%$ and greater than or equal to $100 * u\%$ in the object in the equivalence class, then equal all the elements in the valence class are combined with the upper and lower approximations respectively. Although the VPRS model relaxes the requirements for the lower approximation of the element and narrows the scope of the upper approximation, it still takes the value in an exact way. An element is either completely upper approximation or lower approximation, or does not belong to the upper approximation or lower approximation. When $l = 0$ and

$u = 1$, the variable-precision rough set degenerates into a general rough set. The values of l and u are very important. If the values of l and u are different, the results may be different [11].

Example 1. Let $U = \{x_1, x_2, \cdots, x_{30}\}$, the equivalence class under the equivalence relation: $X_1 = \{x_1, \cdots x_6\}$, $X_2 = \{x_7, \cdots x_{12}\}$, $X_3 = \{x_{13}, \cdots x_{18}\}$, $X_4 = \{x_{19}, \cdots x_{24}\}$, $X_5 = \{x_{25}, \cdots x_{30}\}$, object set $A = \{x_8, \cdots x_{20}\}$. For Pawlak rough set, $\underline{R}(A) = X_3$, $\overline{R}(A) = X_2 \cup X_3 \cup X_4$. Except for x_7, most of the elements in X_2 are in A, while X_2 is only in the upper approximation and not in the lower approximation. There is only one x_{19} in X_4 in A, but it is also in the upper approximation with X_2 and X_3. In variable precision rough set, we set $u = 0.8$, $l = 0.1$, then $\underline{R}(A) = X_2 \cup X_3$, $\overline{R}(A) = X_2 \cup X_3 \cup X_4$. But when $u = 0.9$ and $l = 0.1$, the result is the same as Pawlak rough set. Therefore, the values of l and u determine the accuracy of the result.

2.5   Variable Precision Fuzzy Rough Set on Double Universe

Suppose U and V are two non-empty finite domains, (U, V, R) is a double domain approximation space under fuzzy relations, $R \in F(U \times V)$, R is the fuzzy phase from U to V Content relationship. For $\forall A \subseteq V$, $\alpha \in (0, 1]$, the fuzzy compatibility relation R is:

$$R_\alpha(x) = \{y \in V | R(x, y) \geq \alpha, x \in U\} \tag{10}$$

The lower and upper approximations of A are:

$$\underline{R}_\alpha^\beta(A) = \{x \in U | (\frac{|R_\alpha(x) \cap A|}{|R_\alpha(x)|} \geq 1 - \beta) \cap (\frac{|R_\alpha(x) \cap A|}{|A|} \geq 1 - \beta)\} \tag{11}$$

$$\overline{R}_\alpha^\beta(A) = \{x \in U | (\frac{|R_\alpha(x) \cap A|}{|R_\alpha(x)|} > \beta) \cap (\frac{|R_\alpha(x) \cap A|}{|A|} > \beta)\} \tag{12}$$

We call the lower approximation $\underline{R}_\alpha^\beta(A)$ of A the positive field of $POS_R(A)$ of fuzzy set A in the fuzzy approximation space (U, V, R). $NEG_{R_\alpha}(A)$ negative domain and $BND_{R_\alpha}(A)$ boundary domain are expressed as follows:

$$BND_{R_\alpha}(A) = \overline{R}_\alpha^\beta(A) - \underline{R}_\alpha^\beta(A); \tag{13}$$

$$NEG_{R_\alpha}(A) = V - \overline{R}_\alpha^\beta(A) \tag{14}$$

The lower approximation of the improved rough set is shown in Fig. 2. The green part is the approximate increase below. The upper approximation of the improved rough set is shown in Fig. 3. The upper approximation reduces the orange part. Reduce the range of the upper approximation and increase the range of the lower approximation, making the range of the object A in the rough set more accurate.

The rough precision ρ_{R_α} and roughness μ_{R_α} of the variable precision fuzzy rough set on the dual universe of fuzzy set A are:

$$\rho_{R_\alpha}(A) = \frac{\left| \underline{R}_\alpha^\beta(A) \right|}{\left| \overline{R}_\alpha^\beta(A) \right|}; \tag{15}$$

$$\mu_{R_\alpha}(A) = 1 - \rho_{R_\alpha}(A) \tag{16}$$

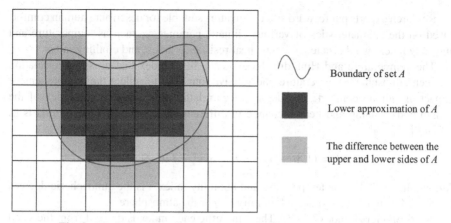

Fig. 2. The lower approximate representation of the improved rough set

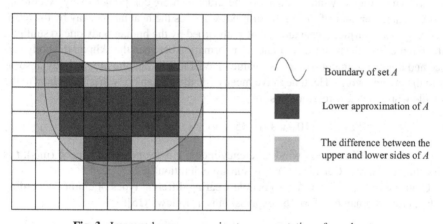

Fig. 3. Improved upper approximate representation of rough set

3 The Relationship Between Human Comfort and Meteorological Parameters

Because the human body's subjective sense of the external atmospheric environment is different from the results of meteorological data measured by the atmospheric environment sensor system. Since the human body does not have a specific index for the comfort of the current environment, the human body comfort index is used to describe the degree to which people can adapt to the environment. The human body comfort index is based on the temperature difference between the human body and the near-ground atmosphere, and is an index formulated to evaluate the human body's comfort level in different environments from the aspect of atmospheric meteorological parameters [12]. Human comfort not only affects people's daily life, but also plays an important role in the development of production, construction, sales and tourism.

Research experts put forward some indicators suitable for describing human comfort based on the characteristics of various climatic parameters, such as temperature and humidity index, wind efficiency index, heat resistance index, and clothing index.

The Temperature and Humidity Index (*THI*) is an index that uses the correlation between atmospheric temperature and relative humidity to reflect the comprehensive impact on human comfort. The degree of correlation is divided by the index of the human body's damp and heat exchange in different environments. The formula is as follows [13]:

$$THI = (1.8t + 32) - 0.55 \times (1 - f)(1.8t - 26) \tag{17}$$

Among them: THI is the temperature and humidity index, t is the atmospheric degrees Celsius (°C), and f is the relative humidity (%) of the atmosphere.

Wind Efficiency Index (*WEI*): The wind efficiency index is derived from the wind chill index. It is compared to the wind chill index obtained from experiments in Antarctica, the wind efficiency index considers the situation more comprehensively. According to some characteristics of the wind chill index, it adds the heat taken away by the evaporation of body surface sweat and the heat absorbed by the human body due to sunlight, which represents the heat transfer and transformation between the skin on the body surface and the environment. A positive value of WEI means that the human body absorbs from the outside world. Heat, negative means that the human body dissipates heat to the outside world. The expression is as follows [14]:

$$WEI = -(10\sqrt{v} + 10.45 - v) \times (33 - t) + 8.55 \times S \tag{18}$$

Among them, *WEI* is called wind efficiency index; v is average wind speed (m/s); t is atmospheric degrees Celsius (°C); S is sunshine duration (h/d).

Clothing Index (*ICL*): refers to people wearing different types of clothes according to the current human comfort, the expression is as follows [15]:

$$ICL = \frac{33 - t}{0.155H} - \frac{H + aR\cos\alpha}{(0.62 + 19\sqrt{v}H)} \tag{19}$$

In the formula: H refers to the human body's metabolic rate (W/m^2), where the human body's metabolic rate during small exercise is H = 87 W/m^2; t is degrees Celsius (°C); a refers to the amount of solar heat absorbed by the body's surface Degree, take 0.06; R refers to the heat absorbed per unit area of the land illuminated by the sun (W/m^2), generally R = 1367 W/m^2, α is the solar altitude angle, which will occur with the revolution of the earth Change, generally take the average value $a = 90°$.

The effect of a single climate factor on human comfort and thermal balance was introduced earlier. Actually, atmospheric temperature, humidity, wind, and sunshine time in daily life are not a single existence, but are interrelated and affect each other. The relative humidity in the atmosphere will affect the body's temperature regulation and the feeling of heat and cold. For example, when the temperature is 24–30 °C and the relative humidity in the atmosphere is 35%, the amount of heat exchange of the human body is significantly greater than the relative humidity of 75% Heat exchange rate [16], people feel hotter when the relative humidity of the atmosphere is 75%. This is because when the relative humidity is high, it will affect the evaporation rate of sweat on the surface of the human body, causing the heat to be unable to be discharged from the body in time, and people will feel sultry And the body temperature rises. When the temperature is too low, and the relative humidity is too high, it will increase the heat exchange contact area with atmospheric water molecules, thus speeding up the heat dissipation of the human body, making people feel damp and cold. When the ambient temperature is moderate, the relative humidity in the atmosphere has no obvious influence on the human body. When the atmospheric temperature is lower than the temperature of the human body, wind can accelerate the evaporation of sweat on the human body, making people feel that the temperature has dropped by 1–2 °C [17]. The faster the wind speed, the stronger the feeling.

Therefore, human comfort cannot be determined by a single atmospheric meteorological parameter. The relationship between the four main influencing parameters of temperature, relative humidity, wind speed and sunshine time must be considered comprehensively, and the temperature and humidity index (*THI*) obtained from these four main meteorological elements, Wind Efficiency Index (*WEI*), Clothing Index (*ICL*), these four parameters can be well connected to obtain the relationship between the comfort of the human body.

4 Experiment Analysis

Let $U = \{x_1, x_2, x_3\}$ be the set of three climate indexes, namely temperature and humidity index (*THI*), wind efficiency index (*WEI*), and clothing index (*ICL*), $P = \{A_1, A_2, A_3, A_4, A_5, A_6, A_7, A_8, A_9\}$ is the 9 kinds of human sensations, which are extremely cold and extremely uncomfortable, extremely hot and extremely uncomfortable, cold and uncomfortable, hot and uncomfortable, cold and relatively comfortable, warm and relatively comfortable, cool and comfortable, warm and comfortable, cool and very comfortable.

$B = \{b_1, b_2, b_3, b_4\}$ is the collection of temperature, humidity, average wind speed, and sunshine hours. The weather attribute set B and the climate index set U have a binary relationship. This paper obtains the average temperature (°C), average relative humidity (%), average wind speed (m/s) and sunshine hours (h/d) of Xining City from January to December 2020 from the Zhenqi website, as shown in Table 1 shown. The relationship between them is shown in Fig. 4.

From Fig. 4, it can be seen that the sunshine hours of Xining City will fluctuate the most from January to December 2020. This is because sunshine hours are not only related to the earth's revolution and latitude, but also related to the quality of the current atmospheric environment. The average temperature and average relative humidity fluctuate relatively greatly in May, June, July, August, and September, while the average wind speed level changes little, and it is in a long-term breeze state.

Bring the corresponding data in Table 1 into the formulas (17), (18), (19) to get the temperature and humidity index (*THI*), wind efficiency index (*WEI*) and clothing index (*ICL*). The average wind speed grade is converted into average wind speed according to the "Beauty Wind Rating Table" [18], and the sunshine hours

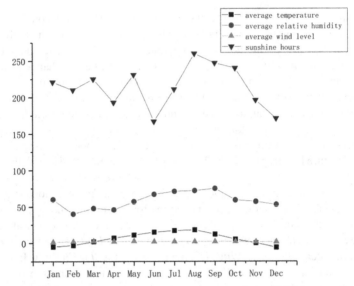

Fig. 4. Relationship between average temperature, average relative humidity, average wind level and sunshine hours

Table 1. Meteorological parameter data of Xining City from January to December 2020

Meteorological parameters	Jan	Feb	Mar	Apr	May	Jun	Jul	Aug	Sep	Oct	Nov	Dec
Average temperature (°C)	−5	−3	2	7	11	15	17	18	12	5	0	−6
Average relative humidity (%)	60	40	48	46	57	67	71	72	75	59	57	53
Average wind speed level	1.5	2	2.5	2	2.5	2	2	2	2	2	1.5	1.5
Sunshine hours (h/d)	221	210	225	193	231	167	211	260	247	240	196	171

need to be divided by the corresponding days of the month to get the daily average sunshine hours. Obtain the 12-month meteorological parameter index $V = \{y_1, y_2, y_3, y_4, y_5, y_6, y_7, y_8, y_9, y_{10}, y_{11}, y_{12}\}$, as shown in Table 2 Shown.

Human body sensation $P = \{A_1, A_2, A_3, A_4, A_5, A_6, A_7, A_8, A_9\}$, meteorological parameter index $U = \{x_1, x_2, x_3\}$, divide the corresponding range of values for *THI*, *WEI* and *ICL* according to human body feeling and assign values to them, as shown in Table 3.

Table 2. 12-month meteorological parameter index of Xining City.

Weather index	Jan	Feb	Mar	Apr	May	Jun	Jul	Aug	Sep	Oct	Nov	Dec
THI	30.7	37.0	42.0	48.6	53.3	58.8	61.9	63.4	54.2	44.8	38.2	30.7
WEI	−776	−796	−731	−563	−499	−380	−320	−282	−429	−597	−672	−812
ICL	2.9	2.7	2.3	1.9	1.6	1.3	1.2	1.1	1.6	2.1	2.5	2.9

Table 3. Value range and assignment of *THI*, *WEI* and *ICL*

Human sensation		*WEI*	*ICL*	Attribute assignment
Very cold, cold wind, down jacket	<40	<−1000	>2.5	0.1
Extremely hot, sweltering wind, thin singles	>80	>+60	<0.1	0.1
Cold, cold wind, cotton clothes	40–45	−700−−1000	1.8–2.5	0.3
Hot, hot air, single clothes	75–80	+ 160−+ 50	0.1–0.3	0.3
Colder, slightly cooler, thick coat	45–55	−500−−700	1.5–1.8	0.5
Too hot, slightly hot, short sleeves	70–75	+ 50−−100	0.3–0.5	0.5
Cool, cool breeze, spring and autumn clothing	55–60	−400−−500	1.3–1.5	0.9
Warm, warm air, light summer clothes	65–70	−100−−300	0.5–0.7	0.7
Cool, comfortable wind, long sleeves	60–65	−300−−400	0.7–1.3	1

Bring the previously calculated meteorological parameter index from January to December into Table 3 to calculate the relationship between the month and the meteorological parameter index $R(y_i, x_i)$, as shown in Table 4.

According to the classification under the relationship when $A = \{x_1, x_2\} \subseteq U, \alpha = 0.7$ under the fuzzy approximation space (U, V, R), the formula (10) is introduced:

$$R_{0.7}(y_5) = \{x_2\};$$

$$R_{0.7}(y_6) = \{x_1, x_2, x_3\};$$

$$R_{0.7}(y_7) = \{x_1, x_2, x_3\};$$

$$R_{0.7}(y_8) = \{x_1, x_2, x_3\};$$

$$R_{0.7}(y_9) = \{x_2, x_3\};$$

Table 4. Value range and assignment of *THI*, *WEI* and *ICL*

R(y_i, x_i)	THI	WEI	ICL
1	0.1	0.3	0.1
2	0.1	0.3	0.1
3	0.3	0.3	0.3
4	0.5	0.5	0.3
5	0.5	0.9	0.5
6	0.9	1	0.7
7	1	1	1
8	1	0.7	1
9	0.5	0.9	0.7
10	0.3	0.5	0.3
11	0.1	0.5	0.3
12	0.1	0.3	0.1

Take $\beta = 0.3$ and $\alpha = 0.7$ to calculate the lower approximation and upper approximation of A in the fuzzy approximation space (U, V, R), and the results of formulas (11) and (12) are as follows:

$$\underline{R}_{\alpha=0.7}^{\beta=0.3}(A) = \{y_6, y_7, y_8\};$$

$$\overline{R}_{\alpha=0.7}^{\beta=0.3}(A) = \{y_5, y_6, y_7, y_8, y_9\};$$

The boundary domain and negative domain of A in the (U, V, R) fuzzy approximation space are expressed as follows:

$$BND_{R_{0.7}}(A) = \overline{R}_{\alpha=0.7}^{\beta=0.3} - \underline{R}_{\alpha=0.7}^{\beta=0.3}(A) = \{y_5, y_9\};$$

$$NEG_{R_{0.7}}(A) = V - \overline{R}_{\alpha=0.7}^{\beta=0.3}(A) = \{y_1, y_2, y_3, y_4, y_{10}, y_{11}, y_{12}\};$$

The rough precision $\rho_{R_{0.4}}$ and roughness $\mu_{R_{0.4}}$ of the variable precision fuzzy rough set on the dual universe of fuzzy set A are:

$$\rho_{R_{0.7}}(A) = \frac{\left|\underline{R}_{\alpha=0.7}^{\beta=0.3}(A)\right|}{\left|\overline{R}_{\alpha=0.7}^{\beta=0.3}(A)\right|} = 0.6;$$

$$\mu_{R_{0.7}}(A) = 1 - \rho_{R_{0.7}}(A) = \frac{\left|\underline{R}_{\alpha=0.7}^{\beta=0.3}(A)\right|}{\left|\overline{R}_{\alpha=0.7}^{\beta=0.3}(A)\right|} = 0.4;$$

Analyzing the above data, we can conclude that with *THI* and *WEI* as the main indicators, the human body feels comfortable in June, July, and August, and the human body feels in May and September may be comfortable, while January, February, March, April, October, November, and December must be uncomfortable.

Classification under the relationship when $\alpha = 0.4$:

$$R_{0.4}(y_4) = \{x_1, x_2\};$$

$$R_{0.4}(y_5) = \{x_1, x_2, x_3\};$$

$$R_{0.4}(y_6) = \{x_1, x_2, x_3\};$$

$$R_{0.4}(y_7) = \{x_1, x_2, x_3\};$$

$$R_{0.4}(y_8) = \{x_1, x_2, x_3\};$$

$$R_{0.4}(y_9) = \{x_1, x_2, x_3\};$$

$$R_{0.4}(y_{10}) = \{x_2\};$$

$$R_{0.4}(y_{11}) = \{x_2\};$$

Take $\beta = 0.3$ and $\alpha = 0.4$ to calculate the lower approximation and upper approximation of A in (U, V, R) fuzzy approximation space, the results are as follows:

$$\underline{R}_{\alpha=0.4}^{\beta=0.3}(A) = \{y_4, y_5, y_6, y_7, y_8, y_9\};$$

$$\overline{R}_{\alpha=0.4}^{\beta=0.3}(A) = \{y_4, y_5, y_6, y_7, y_8, y_9, y_{10}, y_{11}\};$$

The boundary domain and negative domain of A in the (U, V, R) fuzzy approximation space are expressed as follows:

$$BND_{R_{0.4}}(A) = \{y_{10}, y_{11}\};$$

$$NEG_{R_{0.4}}(A) = \{y_1, y_2, y_3, y_{12}\};$$

The rough precision $\rho_{R_{0.4}}$ and roughness $\mu_{R_{0.4}}$ of the variable precision fuzzy rough set on the dual universe of fuzzy set A are:

$$\rho_{R_{0.4}}(A) = \frac{\left|\underline{R}_{\alpha=0.4}^{\beta=0.3}(A)\right|}{\left|\overline{R}_{\alpha=0.4}^{\beta=0.3}(A)\right|} = 0.625;$$

$$\mu_{R_{0.4}}(A) = 1 - \rho_{R_{0.4}}(A) = \frac{\left|\underline{R}_{\alpha=0.4}^{\beta=0.3}(A)\right|}{\left|\overline{R}_{\alpha=0.4}^{\beta=0.3}(A)\right|} = 0.375;$$

Analyzing the above data, compared to $\alpha = 0.7$, the months when the human body feels comfortable increased from June, July, and August to April, May, June, July, August, and September. $\underline{R}^{\beta=0.3}_{\alpha=0.7}(A) - \underline{R}^{\beta=0.3}_{\alpha=0.4}(A) = \{y_4, y_5, y_9\}$. Because the comfort level has been reduced, April, May, and September are added. The increased months are regarded as sub-comfortable months, which are called more comfortable, while those with lower comfort are less comfortable, and the last remaining months are uncomfortable. According to the formula (11), we get the comfort division diagram of each month, as shown in Fig. 5.

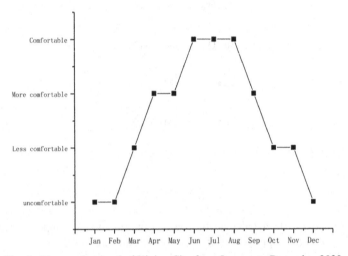

Fig. 5. The comfort level of Xining City from January to December 2020

Xining City is located in the northwest region with a higher altitude. June, July, and August are cool. Qinghai is known as the "Summer Capital", and the human body feels comfortable. However, December, January, and February are relatively cold, and the relative humidity of the air is low, and the air is relatively dry, and the human body feels uncomfortable. A humidifier can be placed at home as a spare. You need to add more clothes and pay attention to the cold when you go out.

5   Conclusion

By finding out the relationship between temperature and humidity index (*THI*), wind efficiency index (*WEI*), clothing index (*ICL*) and human comfort. According to the meteorological data of Xining City from January to December in 2020, such as average temperature, average relative humidity, average wind speed and sunshine hours, the 12-month *THI*, *WEI* and *ICL* indexes are obtained. Then divide the corresponding value range and assign the value according to the relationship degree of the human body to the *THI*, *WEI* and *ICL* values. Finally, we use the different values of α in the dual domain variable precision fuzzy rough set to obtain the upper and lower approximations to get the human comfort level from January to December, and analyze it. The results show that in the human body comfort level in Xining City in 2020, the months when the human body feels uncomfortable are January, February and December. The less comfortable months are October and November. The more comfortable months are April, May and September. The most comfortable months are June, July and August.

Acknowledgments. The authors acknowledge the financial support of the Key Projects of the Natural Science Foundation of in Qinghai Province (Grant: 2021-ZJ-916).

References

1. Liu, P.: Multiple attribute group decision making method 991 based on interval-valued intuitionistic fuzzy power Hero- nian aggregation operators. Comput. Ind. Eng. **108**, 199–212 (2017)
2. Zhan, J., Zhu, K.: A novel soft rough fuzzy set: Z-soft rough fuzzy ideals of hemirings and corresponding decision making. Soft Comput. **21**, 1923–1936 (2017)
3. Wang, C., Hu, Q., Wang, X., et al.: Feature selection based on neigh borhood discrimination index. IEEE Trans. Neural Netw. Learn. Syst. **29**(7), 2986–2999 (2018)
4. Sun, B., Qi, C., Ma, W., et al.: Variable precision diversified attribute multigranulation fuzzy rough set-based multi-attribute group decision making problems. Comput. Ind. Eng. **142**, 106–115 (2020)
5. Wu, J., Chang, J., Cao, Q., et al.: A trust propagation and collaborative filtering based method for incomplete information in social network group decision making with type-2 linguistic trust. Comput. Ind. Eng. **127**, 853–864 (2019)
6. Wang, C., He, Q., Shao, M., et al.: A unified information measure for general binary relations. Knowl.-Based Syst. **135**(1), 18–28 (2017)
7. Rehman, N., Ali, A., Inayat Ali Shah, S., et al.: Variable precision multi decision λ-soft dominance based rough sets and their applications in conflict problems. J. Intell. Fuzzy Syst., 1–16 (2019)
8. Wu, J., Chiclana, F., Liao, H.C.: Isomorphic multiplicative transitivity for intuitionistic and interval-valued fuzzy preference relations and its application in deriving their priority vectors. IEEE Trans. Fuzzy Syst. **26**, 193–202 (2018)
9. Ureña, R., Chiclana, F., Melancon, G., et al.: A social network based ap proach for consensus achievement in multiperson decision making. Inf. Fusion Vol. **47**, 72–87 (2019)
10. Rehman, N., Ali, A., Inayat Ali Shah, S.: Variable precision multi deci sion λ-soft dominance based rough sets and their applications in conflict problems. J. Intell. Fuzzy Syst. **132**, 1–16 (2019)
11. Xu, Z.S.: Multi-period multi-attribute group decision-making under linguistic as sessments. Int. J. General Syst. **38**(8), 823–850 (2009)
12. Wu, J., Chang, J., Cao, Q., et al.: A trust propagation and collabo rative filtering based method for incomplete information in social network group decision making with type-2 linguistic trust. Comput. Ind. Eng. **127**, 853–864 (2019)
13. Zhou, M., Liu, X., Yang, J., et al.: Evidential reasoning approach with multiple kinds of attributes and entropy-based weight assignment. Knowl.-Based Syst. **163**, 358–375 (2019)
14. Xu, Z., Zhao, N.: Information fusion for intuitionistic fuzzy decision making: an overview. Inf. Fusion, **28**, 10–23 (2016)
15. Sun, B., Ma, W., Qian, Y.: Multigranulation fuzzy rough set over two universes and its application to decision making. Knowl.-Based Syst. **123**, 61–74 (2017)

16. Yang, J., Zhang, Q., Xie, Qin.: Attribute reduction based on misclassification cost in variable precision rough set model. J. Intell. Fuzzy Syst., 1–14 (2018)
17. Yan, G., Li, X., Li, X.: Research on the correspondence between wind power level, wind speed and wind pressure. Doors Windows (08), 56–57 (2014)
18. Wu, J., Sun, Q., Fujita, H., et al.: An attitudinal consensus degree to control feedback mechanism in group decision making with different adjustment cost. Knowl.-Based Syst. **164**(15), 265–273 (2019)

Water Quality Assessment Model Based on Intuitionistic Fuzzy Multiple Attribute Decision-Making

Qianqian Wang[1], Jun Ma[1,2(✉)], and Lingfei Zhang[1]

[1] College of Physics and Electronic Information Engineering, Qinghai Normal University, Xining 810008, China
[2] Academy of Plateau Science and Sustainability, Qinghai Normal University, Xining 810008, China

Abstract. This paper uses intuitionistic fuzzy multi-attribute decision-making membership degrees and non-membership degrees for the interval values of water quality testing data. It can construct the water quality decision interval. Establish a dynamic evaluation model that can comprehensively reflect the interval values of each attribute of water quality. Achieve higher-precision assessment of water quality and comparison of pros and cons. Combined with the fuzzy comprehensive index method to verify the feasibility of the algorithm in the interval water quality evaluation research.

Keywords: Water quality attributes · Fuzzy comprehensive evaluation method · Intuitionistic interval multi-attribute decision-making matrix · Intuitionistic fuzzy multi-attribute decision-making

1 Introduction

With the rapid development of social economy, environmental problems have become more frequent and serious. Especially the problem of water pollution. It has triggered a series of tensions in the drinking water situation and outbreaks of water pollution-related diseases [1]. Therefore, it is necessary to regularly research and analyze the acquired water quality data [2] to complete the assessment and prediction of water quality. Today, facing the rapid development of water quality detection sensor research and development technology. Obtain a large amount of water quality data. Sorting out and refining these water quality data can be used as a potential, sharable, and long-term useable data resource [3]. Research on the use of multi-sensor information fusion algorithms. Process and analyze these data resources. And then get more reliable and more comprehensive water quality information. To achieve a more realistic assessment of water quality [4]. In the research of multi-sensor information fusion algorithm. Commonly used processing methods combining fuzzy sets and multi-attribute decision-making. Atanassov extends the intuitionistic fuzzy set based on the basic algorithm of fuzzy set. The concept of non-subscription and hesitation has been added. Makes the research of fuzzy multiple attribute

X. Wang et al. (Eds.): AICON 2021, LNICST 397, pp. 185–198, 2021.
https://doi.org/10.1007/978-3-030-90199-8_18

decision making more in-depth [5]. By reviewing the information fusion application of intuitive information decision-making involved in multiple development fields. It explained in detail the process of constructing attribute weights, aggregating intuitionistic fuzzy information, and ranking selection in the theory of intuitionistic fuzzy decision making. So as to select the best plan [6]. On the basis of intuitionistic fuzzy sets, two methods of entropy weight comparison and probability comparison are cited. It solves the problem that the commander can not directly express his opinions on the ground, but can fully take into account all the characteristic information of the target threat [7]. At the same time, design new intuitionistic fuzzy entropy to express. On the basis of intuitionistic fuzzy sets expressing uncertainty. Combine the similarity order preference closeness of the ideal solution to express the information content of the intuitionistic fuzzy set. Thus created the normalized sequence weight model [8]. In order to solve the problem of imperfect attribute weights, attribute values satisfy attribute decision-making. An optimization model of the ideal solution of the intuitionistic fuzzy set is established. Then the attribute weights in the ideal solution situation are obtained. And the total ranking of different schemes is realized. The example proves the superiority of the model creation [9]. The above research shows that the relationship between the pros and cons of water quality. Intuitionistic fuzzy multi-attribute decision algorithm can be used. Construct a water quality decision interval. Comprehensively consider the dynamic change information of each attribute interval of water quality. Make a comprehensive assessment of the quality of water. Effectively expand the research of interval water quality assessment algorithm.

2   Theoretical Basis

2.1   Definition

Definition 1: [10] Suppose a given non-empty set. Remember:

$$E = \{\langle x, u_E(x), v_E(x), x \in X \rangle\}$$

Then set E to be the intuitionistic fuzzy set on X. Among them, $u_E(x)$ and $v_E(x)$ are used to express the degree of membership and non-membership of X belonging to E. They meet the following conditions:

$$u_E(x) : X \in [0, 1], x \in X \rightarrow u_E(x) \in [0, 1]$$

$$v_E(x) : X \in [0, 1], x \in X \rightarrow v_E(x) \in [0, 1]$$

$$0 \leq u_E(x) + v_E(x) \leq 1, x \in X$$

In general, the intuitionistic fuzzy set can be simply recorded as:

$$E = \langle x, u_E(x), v_E(x) \rangle \text{ or } E = \langle u_E(x), v_E(x) \rangle / x$$

Known:

$$E = \{\langle x, u_E(x), 1 - u_E(x) \rangle | x \in X\}$$

Which is $\pi_E(x) = 1 - u_E(x) - v_E(x)$. It is called the intuitionistic index of the element x in the intuitionistic fuzzy set E, which is used to express the hesitancy degree of the element x to E. $x \in X 0 \leq \pi_E(x) \leq 1$.

$\pi_E(x) = 1 - u_E(x) - v_E(x)$ is called the intuitionistic index of element x in the intuitionistic fuzzy set E. This represents the hesitancy degree of element x to E. Namely: $x \in X 0 \leq \pi_E(x) \leq 1$.

If:

$$\pi_E(x) = 1 - u_E(x) - [1 - v_E(x)] = 0, x \in X$$

Then the intuitionistic fuzzy set degenerates into Zadeh's fuzzy set. Therefore, the special case of the direct fuzzy set is the fuzzy set.

Definition 2: Build a water quality sample set. The decision maker compares n water samples with each other. And construct the decision matrix $R = \{r_{ij}\}_{m \times n}$. Where $r_{ij} = [u_{ij}, 1 - v_{ij}]$, $i = 1, 2, ..., n$ u_{ij}. U represents the degree of preference for x_i when comparing the sample of decision makers x_i and x_j. And v_{ij} represents the degree to which decision makers prefer x_j.

Conditions met by $R = \{r_{ij}\}_{m \times n}$:

a) $\pi_{ij} = 1 - u_{ij} - v_{ij}$. The degree of hesitation of decision makers.
b) If $u_{ij} \in [0, 1], n_{ij} \in [0, 1], 0 \leq u_{ij} + v_{ij} \leq 1, i = 1, 2, ..., n; j = 1, 2, ..., n$.

Then R is called an intuitionistic interval fuzzy multi-attribute decision-making matrix.

2.2 Quantification and Standardized Treatment of Water Quality Attributes

Quantification and standardized treatment of water quality attributes: Quantification and standardization of water quality attributes: According to the characteristics of water quality attributes changing in a certain interval, use the given intuitionistic fuzzy interval judgment standard matrix $[r_{ij}]_{m \times n} = [u_{ij}, 1 - v_{ij}]$, The range of water quality attributes can be well constructed, combined with benefit and cost attribute types, and transformed into an intuitive interval judgment matrix representation to standardize water quality attributes. Set the water quality detection attribute value to $\left[X_{ij}^L, X_{ij}^U \right], i \in M, j \in N$ The attribute optimization formula [11] is:

Benefit attribute:

$$u_{ij} = \frac{X_{ij}^L}{\sqrt{\sum_1^m (X_{ij}^U)^2}}, v_{ij} = 1 - \frac{X_{ij}^U}{\sqrt{\sum_1^m (X_{ij}^L)^2}} \tag{1}$$

Cost attributes:

$$u_{ij} = \frac{1/X_{ij}^U}{\sqrt{\sum_1^m (1/X_{ij}^L)^2}}, v_{ij} = 1 - \frac{1/X_{ij}^L}{\sqrt{\sum_1^m (1/X_{ij}^U)^2}} \tag{2}$$

3   Intuitionistic Fuzzy Multi-attribute Water Quality Decision Steps with Unknown Weights

Step 1: Determine the water sample set $P = \{P_1, P_2, ...P_m\}$ and the water quality attribute set $Q = \{q_1, q_2, ..., q_n\}$ of the multi-attribute decision-making problem.

Step 2: Obtain water quality data through the water quality detection sensor. Different areas of the same river are aggregated to form water quality attribute measurement interval values, which can be represented by $\left[X_{ij}^L, X_{ij}^U\right]$. Refer to "Surface Water Environmental Quality Standard" (GB 3838–2002). Use interval mean to find fuzzy relation matrix.

Step 3: Use interval mean to form a fuzzy relationship matrix. Combine the excess weighting formula (3) to obtain the weight value.

$$w_i = \frac{X_i/X_{0i}}{\sum_{i=1}^m X_i/X_{0i}} \tag{3}$$

Step 4: Use the weighted average compound operation in the fuzzy comprehensive evaluation method. [12] As shown in formula (4). According to the principle of maximum degree of membership, the comprehensive grade of water quality is obtained. Screen water samples of the same grade.

$$B = A \circ R \tag{4}$$

Step: 5: Obtain the intuitionistic fuzzy feature information of the water sample $P_i \in P$ on the attribute $Q_j \in Q$ in the multi-attribute decision-making problem. Use formula (1) and formula (2) to regularize the attributes. Construct the multi-attribute decision matrix R' of intuition interval, namely:

$$r' = (u_{ij}, 1 - v_{ij})$$

Step 6: Convert the intuition interval multi-attribute decision-making matrix R' to the canonical intuitionistic multi-attribute decision-making matrix R. Namely:

$$r_{ij} = < u_{ij}, v_{ij} >$$

Step 7: Use formula (5) to determine the weight of each attribute. In the intuitionistic fuzzy multi-attribute decision-making method [13], the comprehensive attributes of water samples are worthy of comparison. The analysis is as follows: if the attribute value of all water samples under attribute $Q_j(j = 1, 2, 3, ..., n)$ is small, it indicates that the water quality attribute $Q_j(j = 1, 2, 3, ..., n)$ has a small effect on the pros and cons of the selected sample, and a small weight value is assigned; otherwise, a high weight value is assigned. Special case: If there is no difference in the attribute value of the water sample under the water quality attribute $Q_j(j = 1, 2, 3, ..., n)$, the attribute $Q_j(j = 1, 2, 3, ..., n)$ will not affect the ranking of the water sample, and its weight can be set to 0.

$$w_j = \frac{\sum_{i=1}^{m} \sum_{k=1}^{m} |u_{ij} - u_{kj}| + |v_{ij} - v_{kj}|}{\sqrt{\sum_{j=1}^{n} \sum_{i=1}^{m} \sum_{k=1}^{m} (|u_{ij} - u_{kj}| + |v_{ij} - v_{kj}|)}} \tag{5}$$

Step 8: Calculate the comprehensive attribute value c_i of P_i using formula (6).

$$c_i = < u_i, v_j >= IFWA_w(P_1, P_2, \ldots, P_n)$$

$$= < 1 - \prod_{j=1}^{n} (1 - u_j)^{w_j}, \prod_{j=1}^{n} (u_j)^{w_j} > \tag{6}$$

Step 9: Use formula (7) and formula (8) to calculate the score value $s(c_i)$ and the precise value $h(c_i)$ of the comprehensive attribute value c_i of scheme V_i. Generally, when the score value is the same, the exact value can be used to distinguish. Then determine the order of $c_i(i = 1, 2, ..., m)$. And use the permutation results to compare the pros and cons of the water sample P_i [14, 15] .

$$S(\xi) = u_E(x) - v_E(x) \tag{7}$$

$$H(\xi) = u_E(x) + v_E(x) \tag{8}$$

4 Data Processing

This article uses comprehensive data. Water sample data collected from different locations at the same time. In this way, it reflects the dynamic change characteristics of water quality detection data.

4.1 Data Collection

This article uses a comprehensive data sampling method. Twelve test water samples were obtained. The water quality data obtained by the five water quality detection sensors of dissolved oxygen, ammonia nitrogen, chemical oxygen demand, BOD5 and total nitrogen are selected as the water quality attributes of the research. As shown in Table 1.

4.2 Interval Aggregation of Water Quality Data

The measurement interval values are aggregated according to different areas of the same river to form water quality attribute measurement interval values. It can be represented by $\left[X_{ij}^L, X_{ij}^U\right]$. As shown in Table 2.

Table 1. Measured values of water quality attributes

Sample attributes	Sample 1		Sample 2	
	Detection point 1	Detection point 2	Detection point 1	Detection point 2
Dissolved oxygen	8.05	7.85	7.58	7.70
Ammonia	0.215	0.245	0.370	0.299
COD	17	16	24	21
BOD$_5$	2.25	2.39	2.4	2.3
Total nitrogen	1.8	1.96	4.30	4.53
Sample attributes	Sample 3		Sample 4	
	Detection point 1	Detection point 2	Detection point 1	Detection point 2
Dissolved oxygen	7.96	8.16	8.02	8.08
Ammonia	0.203	0.191	1.17	0.96
COD	16	19	13	11
BOD$_5$	2.2	2.1	1.435	1.605
Total nitrogen	2.71	2.99	0.412	0.432
Sample attributes	Sample 5		Sample 6	
	Detection point 1	Detection point 2	Detection point 1	Detection point 2
Dissolved oxygen	7.68	7.96	7.62	8.10
Ammonia	0.488	0.352	1.12	26.2
COD	19.9	16.5	18	20
BOD$_5$	1.49	2.35	2.1	2.4
Total nitrogen	0.814	1.15	6.14	39.9

Table 2. Measurement interval values of water quality attributes

Water sample	Dissolved oxygen	Ammonia	COD	BOD$_5$	Total nitrogen
Sample 1	<7.85, 8.05>	<0.215, 0.245>	<16, 17>	<2.25, 2.39>	<1.8, 1.96>
Sample 2	<7.58, 7.70>	<0.299, 0.370>	<21, 24>	<2.3, 2.4>	<4.30, 4.53>
Sample 3	<7.96, 8.16>	<0.191, 0.203>	<16, 19>	<2.1, 2.2>	<2.71, 2.99>
Sample 4	<8.02, 8.08>	<0.96, 1.17>	<11, 13>	<1.435, 1.605>	<0.412, 0.432>
Sample 5	<7.68, 7.96>	<0.352, 0.488>	<16.5, 19.9>	<1.49, 2.35>	<0.814, 1.15>
Sample 6	<7.62, 8.10>	<1.12, 26.12>	<18, 20>	<2.1, 2.4>	<6.14, 39.9>

4.3 Fuzzy Comprehensive Evaluation

Solve the interval mean by measuring the interval value. The results of the mean value of the water quality attribute measurement interval are shown in Table 3.

Table 3. Mean values of measurement intervals of water quality attributes

Water sample	Dissolved oxygen	Ammonia	COD	BOD$_5$	Total nitrogen
Sample 1	7.95	0.23	16.5	2.32	1.88
Sample 2	7.64	0.33	22.5	2.35	4.42
Sample 3	8.04	0.175	17.5	2.15	2.32
Sample 4	8.05	1.78	12	1.52	0.425
Sample 5	7.82	0.42	18.2	1.92	0.982
Sample 6	7.86	13.62	19	2.25	23.02

According to environmental factors, the pollution degree of each water quality attribute is classified. Refer to "Surface Water Environmental Quality Standard" (GB 3838–2002). As shown in Table 4 "Surface Water Environmental Quality Standards" basic project standard limits.

Table 4. Standard limits for basic items of "Surface Water Environmental Quality Standards"

	Dissolved oxygen	Ammonia	COD	BOD$_5$	Total nitrogen
I	7.5	0.15	15	2	0.2
II	6	0.5	15	3	0.5
III	5	1.0	20	4	1.0
IV	3	1.5	30	6	1.5
V	2	2.0	40	10	2.0

Carry out the construction of fuzzy relation matrix. The fuzzy relationship matrix formed by 6 water samples is shown in Table 5.

Refer to the over-standard weighting method of formula (3) for the interval mean value. Obtain the weight matrix. The results of the weight matrix are shown in Table 6.

Choose the weighted average compound operation model. Obtain the fuzzy comprehensive evaluation value of the water quality of 6 water samples. According to the principle of maximum degree of membership, the comprehensive grade of water quality is obtained. As shown in Table 7.

Table 5. Interval fuzzy comprehensive relationship matrix

Water sample	I	II	III	IV	V
Sample 1	1.00	0.00	0.00	0.00	0.00
	0.77	0.23	0.00	0.00	0.00
	0.00	0.70	0.30	0.00	0.00
	0.68	0.32	0.00	0.00	0.00
	0.00	0.00	0.00	0.24	0.76
Sample 2	1.00	0.00	0.00	0.00	0.00
	0.49	0.51	0.00	0.00	0.00
	0.00	0.00	0.75	0.25	0.00
	0.65	0.35	0.00	0.00	0.00
	0.00	0.00	0.00	0.00	0.00
Sample 3	1.00	0.00	0.00	0.00	0.00
	0.87	0.13	0.00	0.00	0.00
	0.00	0.50	0.50	0.00	0.00
	0.85	0.15	0.00	0.00	0.00
	0.00	0.00	0.00	0.00	1.00
Sample 4	1.00	0.00	0.00	0.00	0.00
	0.00	0.00	0.00	0.44	0.56
	1.00	0.00	0.00	0.00	0.00
	1.00	0.00	0.00	0.00	0.00
	0.25	0.75	0.00	0.00	0.00
Sample 5	1.00	0.00	0.00	0.00	0.00
	0.23	0.77	0.00	0.00	0.00
	0.00	0.36	0.64	0.00	0.00
	1.00	0.00	0.00	0.00	0.00
	0.00	0.04	0.96	0.00	0.00
Sample 6	1.00	0.00	0.00	0.00	0.00
	0.00	0.00	0.00	0.00	1.00
	0.00	0.20	0.80	0.00	0.00
	0.75	0.25	0.00	0.00	0.00
	0.00	0.00	0.00	0.00	1.00

Table 6. Weight matrix results

Water sample	Matrix
Sample 1	[0.311 0.045 0.162 0.114 0.368]
Sample 2	[0.191 0.041 0.141 0.074 0.553]
Sample 3	[0.292 0.032 0.159 0.097 0.421]
Sample 4	[0.336 0.371 0.125 0.079 0.089]
Sample 5	[0.359 0.096 0.209 0.110 0.225]
Sample 6	[0.040 0.343 0.024 0.014 0.059]

Table 7. Fuzzy comprehensive evaluation value of water quality

Water sample	Water quality classification					Max	Affiliation category
	I	II	III	IV	V		
Sample 1	0.423	0.160	0.049	0.088	0.280	0.423	I
Sample 2	0.259	0.047	0.106	0.035	0.553	0.553	V
Sample 3	0.402	0.098	0.080	0.000	0.421	0.421	V
Sample 4	0.415	0.067	0.000	0.163	0.208	0.415	I
Sample 5	0.491	0.149	0.350	0.000	0.000	0.491	I
Sample 6	0.051	0.008	0.019	0.000	0.922	0.922	V

4.4 Intuitionistic Fuzzy Multi-attribute Decision-Making Under the Same Water Quality

Select the water quality grade as V grade water. Compare the relationship between the pros and cons of the same level of water quality. According to the water quality attributes, continue the following analysis. According to the attribute type, the dissolved oxygen, ammonia nitrogen, chemical oxygen demand, BOD5, and total nitrogen in the water quality attributes are classified as quantitative attributes. Because the analysis of the data does not consider qualitative attributes for the time being. Among them, dissolved oxygen is a benefit-type attribute. Ammonia nitrogen, chemical oxygen demand, BOD5, and total nitrogen are cost-type attributes. Because there is generally a certain degree of contradiction among various indicators, the water quality attribute values are standardized. The normalization results are shown in Table 8.

Table 8. Multi-attribute quantitative results of V-level water quality intuition interval

Sample type	Dissolved oxygen	Ammonia	COD	BOD$_5$	Total nitrogen
Sample 2	<0.55, 0.58>	<0.43, 0.60>	<0.43, 0.57>	<0.52, 0.58>	<0.47,0.58>
Sample 3	<0.58, 0.61>	<0.78, 0.93>	<0.55, 0.75>	<0.57, 0.64>	<0.72,0.92>
Sample 6	<0.55, 0.61>	<0.01, 0.14>	<0.52, 0.66>	<0.52, 0.64>	<0.05,0.41>

In the same way, the multi-attribute quantification results of the intuitive interval of Grade I water quality are shown in Table 9.

Table 9. Multi-attribute quantification results of I-level water quality intuition interval

Sample type	Dissolved oxygen	Ammonia	BOD$_5$	BOD$_5$	Total nitrogen
Sample 1	<0.56, 0.59>	<0.74, 0.98>	<0.47, 0.57>	<0.39, 0.52>	<0.18, 0.22>
Sample 4	<0.58, 0.59>	<0.15, 0.22>	<0.61, 0.83>	<0.59, 0.81>	<0.83, 0.96>
Sample 5	<0.55, 0.59>	<0.37, 0.51>	<0.40, 0.56>	<0.40, 0.78>	<0.31, 0.49>

The multi-attribute quantification results of the intuitive interval constructed from Table 8. Construct standardized intuitionistic fuzzy multi-attribute results. As shown in Table 10.

Table 10. Intuitionistic fuzzy multi-attribute decision-making results for Grade V water quality

Sample type	Dissolved oxygen	Ammonia	COD	BOD$_5$	Total nitrogen
Sample 2	<0.55, 0.42>	<0.43, 0.40>	<0.43, 0.43>	<0.52, 0.42>	<0.47, 0.42>
Sample 3	<0.58, 0.39>	<0.78, 0.07>	<0.55, 0.25>	<0.57, 0.36>	<0.72, 0.08>
Sample 6	<0.55, 0.39>	<0.01, 0.86>	<0.52, 0.34>	<0.52, 0.36>	<0.05, 0.59>

In the same way, the normalized intuitionistic fuzzy multi-attribute result of Grade I water can be obtained. As shown in Table 11.

Calculate the weight of grade V water quality attributes by formula (5). The process is as follows:

$$j = 1: \quad \sum_{i=1}^{m} \sum_{k=1}^{m} (|u_{ij} - u_{kj}| + |v_{ij} - v_{kj}|)$$

$$k = 1: 0.00 + 0.06 + 0.03 = 0.09$$

Table 11. Intuitionistic fuzzy multi-attribute decision-making results of Grade I water quality

Sample type	Dissolved oxygen	Ammonia	COD	BOD$_5$	Total nitrogen
Sample 1	<0.56, 0.41>	<0.74, , 0.02>	<0.47, 0.43>	<0.39, 0.48>	<0.18, 0.78>
Sample 4	<0.58, 0.41>	<0.15, 0.78>	<0.61, 0.17>	<0.59, 0.19>	<0.83, 0.04>
Sample 5	<0.55, 0.41>	<0.37, 0.49>	<0.40, 0.44>	<0.40, 0.22>	<0.31, 0.51>

$$k = 2 : 0.06 + 0.00 + 0.03 = 0.09$$
$$k = 3 : 0.03 + 0.03 + 0.00 = 0.06$$

$$j = 1 : \sum_{i=1}^{m} \sum_{k=1}^{m} (|u_{ij} - u_{kj}| + |v_{ij} - v_{kj}|) = 0.09 + 0.09 + 0.06 = 0.24$$

In summary:

$$w_1 = \frac{0.24}{0.24 + 6.24 + 1.2 + 0.44 + 4.72} = 0.02$$

then: $w_1 = 0.02$, $w_2 = 0.49$, $w_3 = 0.09$, $w_4 = 0.03$, $w_5 = 0.37$.
The calculation process of formula (6) is as follows:

$$c_2 = \langle 1 - (1 - 0.55)^{0.02}(1 - 0.43)^{0.49}(1 - 0.43)^{0.09}(1 - 0.52)^{0.03}(1 - 0.47)^{0.37},$$
$$(0.42)^{0.02}(0.40)^{0.49}(0.43)^{0.09}(0.42)^{0.03}(0.42)^{0.37} \rangle$$
$$= \langle 0.45, 0.41 \rangle$$

In summary.

$$c_2 = \langle 0.45, 0.41 \rangle$$
$$c_3 = \langle 0.58, 0.22 \rangle$$
$$c_6 = \langle 0.36, 0.48 \rangle$$

In the same way, the comprehensive attribute values of Grade I water quality samples can be obtained.

$$c_1 = \langle 0.51, 0.14 \rangle$$
$$c_4 = \langle 0.62, 0.18 \rangle$$
$$c_5 = \langle 0.36, 0.44 \rangle$$

Use the score function formula (7) defined by the intuitionistic fuzzy number. Calculate the score value $s(c_i)$ of the water sample. Figure 1 shows the water sample score evaluation chart.

The water quality grade is obtained through the fuzzy comprehensive evaluation method. Using intuitionistic fuzzy multi-attribute decision-making, the relationship

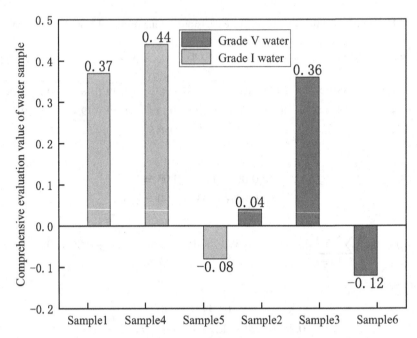

Fig. 1. Figure 1 evaluation diagram of water sample score value

between water quality under the same level is obtained. Shows the degree of discrimination of water samples more clearly. It can improve the accuracy of distinguishing water quality. At the same time, the comprehensive relationship between the pros and cons of the water quality in the interval is obtained.

5   Result Analysis

Combined with fuzzy comprehensive index method [16]. Calculate the comprehensive evaluation value of the selected water samples. And compared with the results of the algorithm in this paper. The comprehensive evaluation results of each water sample of the two algorithms are shown in Table 12.

Table 12. Comparison table of algorithm results

	Sample 1	Sample 2	Sample 3	Sample 4	Sample 5	Sample 6
Fuzzy comprehensive index method	2.64	3.58	2.94	2.24	1.84	4.73
The results of the algorithm	0.37	0.04	0.34	0.44	−0.08	−0.12

Figure 2 shows the comprehensive evaluation values of water samples under different algorithms. The 6 selected water samples can be clearly observed from the figure. Under the fuzzy comprehensive index algorithm and the algorithm of this paper. The order of the 6 water samples was basically the same. Among them, in order to facilitate the presentation of the pros and cons of water samples. This article reverses the fuzzy comprehensive index value. Due to the different algorithm principles and the same level of water quality, the pollution degree is closer. Therefore, the order of sample 1 and sample 5 is inconsistent under the two algorithms. In general, it is proved that the water quality assessment model of intuitionistic fuzzy multi-attribute decision-making is feasible.

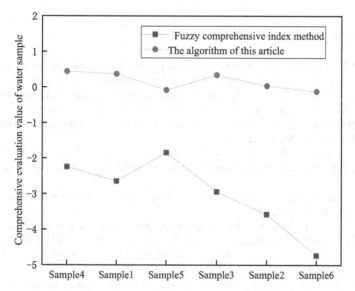

Fig. 2. Comprehensive evaluation values of water samples under different algorithms

6 Summary

This article starts from the dynamics of water quality testing data. The water quality attribute data fluctuates within a certain range because of multiple factors such as seasons and water conditions. The water quality data detection value is aggregated according to certain rules to form a water quality detection value interval. This can make full use of the water quality data interval change information. Through the water quality detection interval and the membership degree and non-membership degree of the intuitionistic fuzzy set, the intuitionistic interval multi-attribute decision matrix is constructed. According to the normalization and standardization of interval attributes, the intuition interval multi-attribute decision matrix is transformed. Then it turns into a standardized intuitionistic fuzzy multi-attribute decision-making matrix. Determine the attribute weight according to the relationship between the attributes of the water sample. Through calculation, the comprehensive attribute value of each water sample is obtained. Then use the score function to rank the water quality. Finally realize the water quality assessment. Construct a water quality assessment model based on intuitionistic fuzzy multi-attribute decision-making. It can describe the fuzzy characteristics of water quality in more detail. At the same time, the information that the water quality attribute value changes within a certain range is fully considered. Comprehensive comparisons can draw a more realistic relationship between pros and cons. So as to achieve a higher-precision assessment and judgment of water quality. Improved the reliability of the evaluation model.

Acknowledgments. The authors acknowledge the financial support of the Key Projects of the Natural Science Foundation of in Qinghai Province (Grant: 2021-ZJ-916).

References

1. Ren, Q.J.: High-precision automatic monitoring method and application of drinking water quality parameters. Xi'an University of Science and Technology, Xi'an (2019)
2. Tong, Y.X.: Multi-parameter water quality monitoring equipment and multi-layer monitoring station research. Dalian University of Technology, Dalian (2019)
3. Ji, B.: Resource utilization of testing data: water quality testing in the era of big data. Water Purif. Technol. **36**(09), 1–3 (2017)
4. Hall, L.D., Linas, J.: Handbok of Multisensor Data Fusion. CRC Press, Boca Raton (2001)
5. Atnassov, K.: Remarks on the intuitionistic fuzzy sets-III. Fuzzy Sets Syst. **75**(3), 401–402 (1995)
6. Xu, Z., Zhao, N.: Information fusion for intuitionistic fuzzy decision making: an overview. Inf. Fusion **28**, 10–23 (2016)
7. Xu, Y., Wang, Y., Miu, X.: Multi-attribute decision making method for air target threat evaluation based on intuitionistic fuzzy sets. J. Syst. Eng. Electron. **23**(6), 891–897 (2012)
8. Zhang, H., Xie, J., Lu, W., et al.: Novel ranking method for intuitionistic fuzzy values based on information fusion. Comput. Ind. Eng. **133**, 139–152 (2019)
9. Xu, Z.S.: Models for multiple attribute decision making with intuitionistic fuzzy information. Int. J. Uncertain. Fuzz. Knowl.-Based Syst. **15**(03), 285–297 (2007)
10. Atanassov, K.T.: Intuitionistic fuzzy sets. Fuzzy Sets Syst. **20**(1), 87–96 (1986)
11. Wang, Y., Liu, S., Zhang, W., et al.: Threat assessment method for intuitionistic fuzzy multi-attribute decision-making with uncertain attribute weights. Chinese J. Electron. **42**(12), 2509–2514 (2014)
12. Ma, Y.: Water quality evaluation and health risk analysis of Dagu River underground reservoir. Ocean University of China, Qingdao (2009)
13. Xu, Z.H.: Uncertain Multi-Attribute Decision-Making Method and Its Application. Tsinghua University Press, Beijing (2004)
14. Hong, D.H., Choi, C.H.: Multicriteria Fuzzy Decision-Making Problems based on Vague Set Theory, no. 3, pp. 158–165. Elsevier North-Holland, Inc. (2000)
15. Chen, S.M., Tan, J.M.: Handling multicriteria fuzzy decision-making problems based on vague set theory. Fuzzy Sets Syst. **67**(2), 163–172 (1994)
16. Xia, H.Q., Huo, X.X.: Water quality evaluation of the Jialing River in the Hanzhong section based on fuzzy comprehensive index method. Shaanxi Water Resour. **12**, 96–99 (2020)

Design of Virtual Amplitude Modulation System Based on LabVIEW

Haiming Lan[1], Jun Ma[1,2(✉)], Lingfei Zhang[1], Bohang Chen[1], and Zhao Hongcheng[1]

[1] College of Computer, Qinghai Normal University, Xining, China
[2] Academy of Plateau Science and Sustainability, Qinghai Normal University, Xining, China

Abstract. The traditional Oscilloscope has the problems of complex operation, long renewal period and inconvenient carrying. A virtual amplitude modulation system based on LabVIEW is designed. The system uses STC89C58 as MCU. The system combines RS232 serial port module, LCD display module, ADC module to form the lower computer of the system. LabVIEW software is used to write host computer of the system. Real-time reception, processing, display and adjustment of waveform signals can be realized. The test shows that the system runs well and can realize the preset function well. It has the characteristics of complete function, simple operation and strong expansibility.

Keywords: Virtual amplitude modulation · STC89C58 · LabVIEW · ADC module · RS232

1 Introduction

Oscilloscope is an electronic measuring instrument with a wide range of uses. An oscilloscope converts electrical signals into visible images and displays them. With the development of science and technology, technical requirements and accuracy have improved. The type of oscilloscope is constantly changing. The earliest analog oscilloscope is that the electron beam emitted by the cathode ray tube is biased according to the change of the signal. The corresponding waveform is displayed on the fluorescent substance [1]. Then the digital oscilloscope was invented. The signal transits the ADC (analog to digital converter) and the corresponding algorithm to display the corresponding waveform. The amplitude and frequency of the displayed waveform can be adjusted. But whether it is an analog oscilloscope or a digital oscilloscope, the required functions are limited. It is difficult to update in the short term. And traditional instruments are inconvenient to carry. So virtual instruments came into being. And it is an effective way to replace traditional instruments [2]. It can use the amplitude modulation function alone. In order to the amplitude of the signal is studied.

LabVIEW is a program that uses graphical language programming. The application is created by the icon. Each icon represents a corresponding function. It's straightforward to use. This is very different from text-based programming languages. LabVIEW uses data flow programming. The data flow determines the execution route. Therefore, the virtual

X. Wang et al. (Eds.): AICON 2021, LNICST 397, pp. 199–207, 2021.
https://doi.org/10.1007/978-3-030-90199-8_19

amplitude modulation system is written based on LabVIEW. It has many functions, strong expandability and high robustness [3].

This design uses a SCM (single-chip microcomputer) and LabVIEW to design a virtual amplitude modulation system. The SCM is a signal generator. The output waveform is transmitted to the application program written in LabVIEW using the serial port. Both the microcontroller and the host computer can adjust the amplitude of the waveform. And show it.

2   Overall System Structure

The virtual amplitude modulation system is composed of hardware design and software system. The hardware part is composed of the SCM of STC89C58, RS232 serial port module, ADC module, display of LCD12864 and buttons. The software part mainly includes application programs and hardware drivers of VISA. The design principle of the virtual amplitude modulation system is that the SCM of STC89C58 uses ADC module to output waveform signal. The signal is transmitted to the buffer of the RS232 serial port module. The RS232 serial port module is connected to the PC (Personal Computer). And the waveform signal is transmitted to the serial port buffer of the PC. So far, the steps of sending data from the SCM to the PC are completed. Finally, the waveform signal received by the PC is displayed in the virtual amplitude modulation system [4]. At the same time, the virtual amplitude modulation system can also send the waveform signal to the SCM of STC89C58 through the PC. The amplitude of the SCM output waveform is modulated. The overall block diagram of the system is shown in Fig. 1.

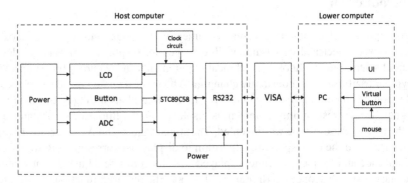

Fig. 1. Overall block diagram of the system

Full-duplex communication of serial port is the foundation when waveform amplitude is adjusted [5]. Both the PC and the SCM have a serial port buffer area. The waveform signals are stored respectively in the two serial port cache areas of the PC and the SCM. The data from both sides is transferred to each other using the serial port.

3   System Hardware Design

3.1   The Overall Design Principle of the System

The hardware system is the waveform signal generator. The SCM of STC89C58 is a super anti-interference, high-speed, low-power SCM launched by Hongjing Technology Co., Ltd. The instruction code is fully compatible with the traditional C51 microcontroller. Therefore, STC89C58 as the MCU of this design is selected. It is suitable for the design requirements and conforms to the ecological civilization concept of energy saving and emission reduction.

To control ADC module to output sine wave is used STC89C58. The waveform signal is connected to the PC utilizing the RS232 serial port, and the SCM communicates with PC. Four waveforms such as sine wave, square wave, triangle wave, and sawtooth wave can be changed by pressing the button. The amplitude of the waveform can be modulated separately. At the same time, it is equipped with a liquid crystal display of LCD12864 to display parameters such as the type and amplitude of the waveform [6]. Figure 2 is the overall circuit diagram of the system.

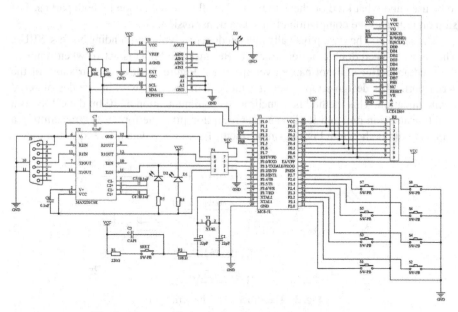

Fig. 2. The overall circuit diagram of the hardware system

3.2   ADC Module

The ADC module composed of PCF8591T is selected. PCF8591T is a single chip, single power supply, 8-bit CMOS data acquisition chip of low power consumption, with four interfaces of analog inputs, one interfaces of analog output and a serial I2C-bus. Three address pins A0, A1 and A2 of the ADC module based on PCF8591T can be used for hardware address programming. And eight devices are connected to the I2C bus were used, without additional hardware. The address bus, the control bus and the data bus are all transmitted serially through the two-wire bidirectional I2C bus.

The functions of the ADC module include analog input multiplexing, on-chip tracking and holding functions, 8-bit analog-to-digital conversion and 8-bit digital-to-analog conversion. In this design, the 8-bit digital-to-analog conversion function is selected. The waveform digital signal outputted is converted into an analog signal. The waveform is detected by the oscilloscope is smooth and beautiful.

3.3 Serial Port Module

The RS232 serial communication interface of the chip of MAX2323 is used to make the SCM communicate with the PC. Serial transmission is bit-oriented. A number of bits sent at once are called a frame. The structure of the frame is divided into start bit, data bit, parity bit, and stop bit according to the sequence of transmission [7]. Generally, the data transmitted by the serial port is of character type. The ASCII encoding is used. The data bit is the [5–8] binary number of the ASCII code value corresponding to the character, which are transmitted in order from low to high. Whether parity check bits to be used and what kind of check to be used shall be agreed upon by both parties. The stop bit indicates the completion of this data transmission.

The serial port has two physically independent receiving and sending buffers, SBUF. The receiver has a double buffer structure. Because the MCU is active when sending, the sending buffer will not cause overlap errors. Figure 3 shows the structure of the serial port. This design adopts working mode 1 of the four working modes of serial communication. This method is asynchronous communication of 10-bit data. TXD is a data transmission pin, and RXD is a data reception pin. The format for transmitting a frame of data is shown in Fig. 4. Among them, 1 start bit, 8 data bits, and 1 stop bit.

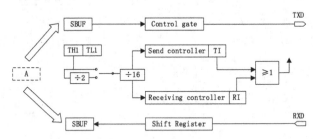

Fig. 3. The structure of the serial port

4   System Software Design

To design the software part of the virtual amplitude modulation system under the development environment of LabVIEW, it is necessary to configure the serial port first. Then the system has four functions, namely waveform display, waveform amplitude display, waveform adjustment and waveform amplitude adjustment. The system is designed according to the functional requirements [8]. Figure 5 is the flow chart of the virtual amplitude modulation system.

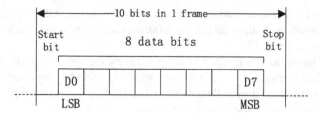

Fig. 4. The format of working mode 1 to transmit a frame of data

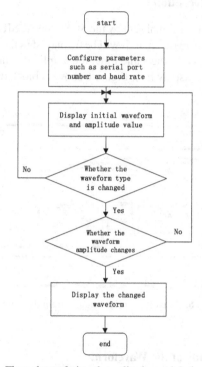

Fig. 5. Flow chart of virtual amplitude modulation system

4.1 Serial Communication

In the virtual amplitude modulation system, all the functions need to use the Visa driver of serial port to realize the communication between the SCM and the PC. Visa provides a consistent interface for applications and is a high-level API for calling the underlying driver [9]. Serial communication requires four parameters to be specified. The baud rate to be transmitted, the number of data bits of the encoded character, the number of optional parity bits, and the number of stop bits. Each transmitted character is encapsulated in a character frame, each frame consisting of a start bit, a data bit, an optional parity bit, and one or more stop bits [10]. When configuring the serial port, it is necessary to set the bit rate, data number and parity of the SCM and the PC to the same value. That is to say, the transmission rate and frame format of both sides can be the same before data transmission [11]. The serial port number corresponding to the SCM serial port module in the system is selected, the baud rate as 4800, the data bit as 8, the check bit as None, and the stop bit as 1 [12, 13].

Visa load function. The number of bytes loads by the specified serial port receive buffer [14]. The received data is ACSII code, which needs to be converted into decimal string. Then the received data will be displayed proportionally in the amplitude display frame of the virtual amplitude modulation system.

4.2   Waveform Signal Reception

When receiving the waveform signal sent by the SCM, the ACSII code is received. After the ACSII code is converted to decimal. It will be displayed in the waveform display box according to the signal type. At the same time, the amplitude value of the waveform is displayed in the amplitude display box. Figure 6 shows a block diagram of the received waveform.

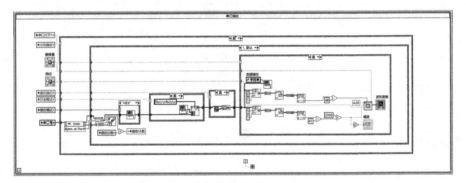

Fig. 6. Waveform receiving program diagram

4.3   Adjust the Amplitude of the Waveform

When amplitude modulation is required, a combination of the amplitude modulation knob and the amplitude modulation button is set to adjust the amplitude. The value of the amplitude modulation knob is displayed below the amplitude modulation knob [15]. After pressing the down amplitude button, the waveform amplitude of the SCM can be changed in real time. It should be noted that when sending data. The decimal array needs to be converted into ACSII code for the SCM identification to achieve real-time amplitude modulation. And the LCD screen is also real-time change amplitude. Figure 7 shows the program diagram for sending data.

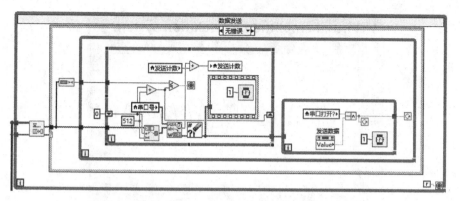

Fig. 7. Program diagram for sending data

5 System Test

In the virtual amplitude modulation system, the amplitude parameter displayed can be adjusted through the button in the middle of the lower part of the interface. The accurate amplitude value can be displayed through the display control below the corresponding position. The amplitude adjustment upper limit of the oscilloscope is 1000 mV and the lower limit is −1000 mV. The offset and phase parameters can be adjusted respectively in the same way. When the waveform signal generator changes the waveform and amplitude, the waveform amplitude of the virtual amplitude modulation system waveform display frame will also change in real time, real-time waveform display and amplitude value display. The waveforms are displayed at the same time are sine wave, square wave, triangle wave, and sawtooth wave. Figure 8 is the result of the system hardware. Figure 9 is the interface of the virtual amplitude modulation system with the amplitude of 255 mV.

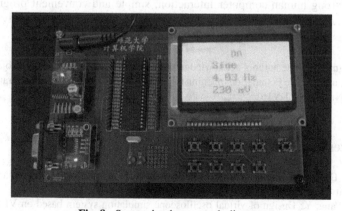

Fig. 8. System hardware result diagram

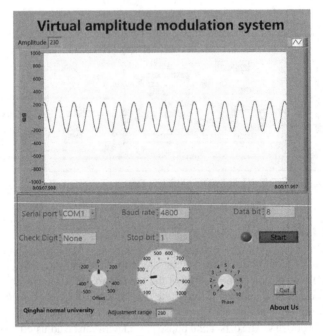

Fig. 9. Virtual amplitude modulation oscilloscope

6   Concludes

This paper designs a virtual amplitude modulation system based on LabVIEW. It can realize the function from signal generation to real-time signal reception, and then to real-time adjustment of signal amplitude. The software has a friendly interface, simple operation, strong human-computer interaction, simple and convenient programming, and good scalability, and no waveform distortion. This system can basically meet the requirements of virtual instruments.

Acknowledgments. The authors acknowledge the financial support of the Key Projects of the National Natural Science Foundation of China (Grant: 61761040), and the Key Laboratory of IoT of Qinghai (No. 2020-ZJ-Y16).

References

1. Guo, Z.: Design and implementation of virtual oscilloscope based on Windows platform. Jilin University, Jilin Province (2020)
2. Li, S., Wang, Y.: Design of virtual oscilloscope simulation system based on VB. Electron. World **18**, 126–127 (2020)
3. Wei, X., Li, J., Li, Y.: Signal modulation and demodulation simulation design based on LabVIEW. Digital Technol. Appl. **11**, 157–159 (2015)
4. Ma, J., Chen, X., Xinwen, D.: A digital amplitude modulation wave signal generator based on single-chip microcomputer. J. Qinghai Univ. (Nat. Sci. Ed.) **01**, 82–84 (2005)

5. Ma, Y., Wang, C., Ye, Z.: Design and implementation of serial communication system based on LabVIEW. Ind. Control Comput. **28**(12), 61–62 (2015)
6. Gao, Y.: Design and production of signal generator based on STC12C5A 60S2. J. Guilin Inst. Aerosp. Ind. **24**(02), 178–182 (2019)
7. Jan, M., Jiri, D.: Control of serial port (RS-232) communication in LabVIEW. In: International Conference Modern Technique and Technologies, pp. 36–40 (2008)
8. Wei, Y., Chen, L.: Research on serial communication based on LabVIEW-VISA mode. Electron. Design Eng. **23**(24), 129–131 (2015)
9. Zhixiong, W.: Virtualization of AM demodulator based on LabVIEW platform. J. Fujian Coll. Commer. **04**, 31–32 (2004)
10. Tang, J., An, W.: Serial communication program design of host computer based on LABVIEW. Electron. Design Eng. **26**(11), 86–90 (2018)
11. Lv, X., Gao, H., Ma, L., et al.: Research on serial communication based on LabVIEW. Foreign Electron. Measur. Technol. **28**(12), 27–30 (2009)
12. Song, M.: LabVIEW programming detailed explanation. Electronic Industry Press, Beijing, 605 (2017)
13. Zhou, H., Zhang, W., Zhang, C.: The realization of virtual instrument and serial communication based on LabVIEW. J. Shijiazhuang Vocat. Tech. Coll. **04**, 17–19 (2007)
14. Wang, H.M., Li, D.D., et al.: LabVIEW-based data acquisition system design. In: Proceedings of 2012 International Conference on Measurement, Information and Control, MIC 2012, pp. 689–692 (2012)
15. Ding, S.: Design of AM wave demodulator based on LabVIEW. Foreign Electron. Measur. Technol. **28**(03), 53–56 (2009)

Design and Implementation of Qinghai Intangible Cultural Heritage Handicraft Online Sales System Based on MVC

Decai Zhao[1] and Chunhua Pan[2(✉)]

[1] Physics and Electronic Information Engineering College of Qinghai Nationalities University, Xining 810007, Qinghai, China
[2] Computer College of Qinghai Nationalities University, Xining 810007, Qinghai, China

Abstract. Qinghai is a multi-ethnic gathering area. Various ethnic groups, especially ethnic minorities, have created unique and colorful arts and produced a large number of unique ethnic handicrafts, some of which are listed as national intangible cultural heritage. Due to its location on the Qinghai-Tibet Plateau, the promotion and dissemination of these outstanding ethnic intangible handicrafts are greatly restricted. Using SpringMVC technology and MySQL database management system to design and implement an online sales system for Qinghai intangible handicrafts can promote the market extension of ethnic handicrafts, and is also beneficial for the centralization of sales management in the country. The unified sales management of handicrafts can play a certain role in promoting the spread of Qinghai's multi-ethnic culture.

Keywords: Intangible cultural heritage · Online sales · Ethnic culture · MVC

1 Overview

Qinghai is a multi-ethnic area where more than 20 ethnic groups such as Han, Tibetan, Hui, Tu, Salar, Mongolia have lived and multiplied for generations. In their production and life cycles over time, the people of all ethnic groups in Qinghai have created their own history and culture, and formed unique and colorful customs and art forms. At the same time, a large number of unique ethnic handicrafts have also been produced, some of which are listed as national intangible cultural heritage, but because of their location on the Qinghai-Tibet Plateau, how to promote and spread Qinghai characteristic ethnic handicrafts is a question worth considering [1]. With the help of the Internet + background, integrating national arts and crafts masters and creators, the design and realization of an online sales system for Qinghai intangible cultural heritage can not only facilitate the promotion and dissemination of ethnic arts and crafts, but also bring a channel for economic growth in ethnic minority areas [2].

X. Wang et al. (Eds.): AICON 2021, LNICST 397, pp. 208–213, 2021.
https://doi.org/10.1007/978-3-030-90199-8_20

2 Analysis of System Function Requirements

2.1 Front-End Functional Requirements

1. Functional requirements of ordinary tourists.

The default identity of the majority of the network users is tourists. Tourist users can enter the system to get a preliminary understanding of the mall. Visitors can perform the following operations in the system: browse ethnic arts and crafts, view the history and culture of arts and crafts, search through keywords, search by category, browse ethnic arts and crafts they are interested in, and view website announcements.

2. Functional requirements of registered users.

When the user completes the registration operation and logs in to the mall, all functional modules of the mall can be used in the system. When registering, users need to fill in some information: name, gender, birthday, email, mobile phone number, etc. To prevent registered users from making mistakes, part of the information can be modified. In response to the shopping needs of registered users, the system provides shopping cart management, order management and other functions for registered users. Users can add their favorite crafts to the shopping cart, and then purchase after placing an order. Of course, users can also add, delete, modify, etc., the crafts in the shopping cart. Registered users can also search by keywords or find their favorite crafts by product classification, confirm whether the inventory is sufficient, and place orders. Of course, users can also add, delete, and modify all orders. Registered users will get certain points after purchasing handicrafts. After the consumption reaches a certain amount, the users will be upgraded to the members of the grades established by the system and enjoy certain rights and privileges. After the registered user places an order, the merchant user can obtain the details of the crafts order and process the delivery of the crafts. After the registered user receives the acceptance of the handicraft, click to confirm the receipt to complete the transaction, and the user can evaluate the purchased handicraft. In the later stage, if there is a problem with the crafts, the after-sale service can be submitted to the system.

2.2 Back-End Function Requirements

1. User administrator role

The user administrator is set in the background of the system to manage all users. After the user administrator is authenticated and logged into the background, he can obtain user management authority to perform corresponding operations. User administrators can obtain information about mall users, and can add, delete, and modify operations. User administrators can also change the status of users, disable and enable user accounts. User administrators can also obtain user's accumulated points information, upgrade and downgrade the user's membership, etc...

2. The role of commodity administrator

A commodity manager is set up on the backstage of the management system of crafts. After passing the verification and entering the background, the commodity manager can obtain the management authority of the crafts to perform corresponding operations. Commodity administrators can obtain related information about crafts, and can add, delete, and modify. Commodity administrators can also change the crafts' on and off the shelves status. Only the front desk of the crafts system can display their cultural and historical background, otherwise users will not be able to obtain relevant information.

3. The role of order administrator.
In the process of handicraft transaction, after the user places an order, the back office obtains the user's transaction information and delivers the goods. This operation is done by the order administrator. After the order administrator passes the verification and enters the background, he can obtain the order management authority to perform corresponding operations. The order administrator can check the order status and perform delivery processing. Under special circumstances, the user order can be cancelled. The order administrator can check the statistics of historical orders, etc.

4. The role of system maintainer.
In the process of system operation, preventing users from maliciously publishing messages brings some negative effects, and manual review is required. This is done by the system maintainer. System maintainers can view website announcements, user messages, and review them.

3   System Design

3.1   System Design Principles

The system design follows the principles of usability, integrity, operability, scalability, portability, and maintainability. The functional modules of the system are divided into two parts: the front-end functional subsystem structure diagram and the back-end management subsystem.

3.2   Front-End Function Module

The main functions of the front desk include: shopping for ethnic crafts (search by keywords); viewing popular and preferential ethnic crafts; auctioning and customizing your favorite crafts; adding your satisfied crafts to the shopping cart for viewing next time; viewing ethnic crafts detailed information such as history and culture; user registration and login; view user's order details; provide corresponding help for problems encountered in shopping; message board functions, etc. The structure is shown in Fig. 1.

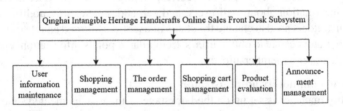

Fig. 1. The front-end function module diagram of the system

3.3   Main Background Functions

The system background management functions mainly include: setting the first-level classification of ethnic handicrafts, such as "Thangka, embroidery, black pottery", etc.; setting the lower-level classification of ethnic handicrafts, such as the "Black Tang, Cai Tang, Red Tang" classification under the Thangka; Maintain details of crafts; maintain details of news; user management; order management; user retention record management; message review, etc. The structure diagram is shown in Fig. 2.

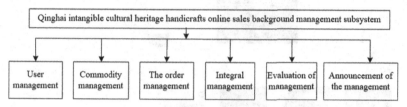

Fig. 2. System background function module diagram

4   System Database Design

Database design refers to the design of a suitable data storage mode in a specific application environment so that the system can efficiently access data in the database and meet the realization of the functional requirements contained in the system [4]. Therefore, the database design is the core part of the system design. A reasonably designed database design can greatly improve the operating efficiency of the system, and it is convenient for developers to perform post-maintenance of the system. After the functional requirements were clarified, the conceptual model was designed for the data requirements, using MySQL as the design and management tool for the back-end data, and the physical design was completed on the basis of the conceptual design.

5   System Implementation

The system uses SpringMVC as the web layer framework, MyBatis as the persistence layer framework, and uses the components in the container management project provided by Spring. Use MyBatis's PageHelper plug-in to implement paging, use Pagination on the page to implement digital page numbers, use SpringSecurity to manage project login, login checking, and permission verification, use Ajax to implement data interaction between the front-end and the server, use Boostrap as the front-end style framework, and layer as The pop-up component, zTree displays a tree structure on the page, and implements unified management of error messages in the project with the help of the exception mapping mechanism provided by SpringMVC. The system home page is shown in Fig. 3.

Fig. 3. System home page.

6 System Test

The system has undergone unit testing, integration testing, confirmation testing, and other quality factors such as system integrity, availability, reliability, and safety, which are all within acceptable ranges, and it is currently in operation.

7 Conclusion

This system takes "Internet + national culture" as the core guiding ideology, takes the online sales process of Qinghai national crafts as the design idea, and uses JAVA Spring MVC technology to develop the system. The system interface design is simple and generous, which is convenient for users to operate and meets the functional requirements. With the vigorous development of information technology and national culture [5], it is believed that the Qinghai ethnic arts and crafts online sales system will bring a broader sales market for Qinghai ethnic arts and crafts, and it will also play a certain role in the dissemination of Qinghai ethnic arts and crafts and culture.

Acknowledgements. Funded Project: Qinghai Provincial Department of Science and Technology Key Research and Development and Transformation Program, Qinghai Intangible Cultural Heritage Handicraft Digital Traceability System Development (No. 2020-GX-113).

References

1. Zhao, Y.: Research on the brand image design of ethnic handicrafts in northern Guangxi. Master, Guangxi Normal University (2017)

2. Zhuang, L.: Design and Implementation of Art Museum Art Management System. Master, Jilin University (2017)
3. Shuang, G., Yan, L., Guanyi, L.: Design and implementation of business intelligence system for enterprise sales and distribution. Softw. Eng. **23**(12), 36–38 (2020)
4. Xiaoyu, C.: The design and realization of the online shopping mall of traditional ethnic handicrafts with water phoenix horsetail embroidery. Internet Things Technol. **6**(3), 58–60 (2016)
5. Yanlong, Z.: Design and implementation of network sales system based on BS architecture. Jilin University, Master (2016)
6. Yanling, Q.: Research on the construction of digital resources of Thangka archives from the perspective of co-construction and sharing. Res. Nat. Cult. Heritage **4**(12), 1–5 (2019)
7. Cao, Y.: Research on platform design based on digital protection of intangible cultural heritage—taking shadow puppet art as an example. Master, East China University of Science and Technology (2016)
8. Yanru, L., Li, Z.: Innovative application of new media technology in the digital display of intangible cultural heritage. Packag. Eng. **37**(10), 26–30 (2016)
9. Ying, G.: The practice and thinking of new media technology in the protection of intangible cultural heritage. News Res. Guide **7**(2), 22–23 (2016)
10. Qiong, D.: Research on the protection of intangible cultural heritage by using new media technology—taking Shou County as an example. Commun. Copyright **1**, 116–117 (2016)
11. LNCS Homepage. http://www.springer.com/lncs. Accessed 21 Nov 2016

Research on the Identification of Hand-Painted Thangka and Printed Thangka Based on Computer Vision Processing Method

Chunhua Pan[1], Decai Zhao[2(✉)], Jinglong Ren[3], Shumin Cui[3], and Wenjing Li[3]

[1] Computer College of Qinghai Nationalities University, Xining 810007, Qinghai, China
[2] Physics and Electronic Information Engineering College of Qinghai Nationalities University, Xining 810007, Qinghai, China
[3] Qinghai Qianxun Information Technology Co. Ltd., Xining 810007, Qinghai, China

Abstract. Thangka is a unique painting art form in Tibetan culture. As Thangka was listed as the first batch of national intangible cultural heritage, it has received more and more attention. At the same time, many printed thangkas appeared on the market, and some merchants mixed printed thangkas with hand-painted thangkas and sold them at high prices. How to distinguish between hand-painted thangkas and machine-printed thangkas, and to guide the inheritance and protection of hand-painted thangkas is an important issue. Based on the analysis of the characteristics of thangkas, combined with related computer vision processing methods, this paper conducts method research and model construction, uses the LBP algorithm to analyze the texture of the canvas, identifies the canvas of the thangka based on the training results, and uses restricted Boltzmann's light transmittance analysis of thangkas, and the use of clustering method to analyze the gold line of thangkas and other methods combined, proposed a feasible method of identifying hand-painted thangkas and machine-printed thangkas. This method should play a significant role in the protection and inheritance of the country. This specification is set for scientific papers published in "Computer Applications and Software". The author is requested to read and implement one by one, if it does not meet the requirements, it will affect the publication of the article.

Keywords: Hand-painted thangka · Machine-printed thangka · LBP algorithm · Restricted Boltzmann algorithm · Clustering method

1 Overview

Qinghai is a multi-ethnic region. On the vast and mysterious plateau land of 720,000 km^2, more than 20 ethnic groups such as Han, Tibetan, Hui, Tu, Salar and Mongolia have lived and multiplied for generations. In the long-term production and life, the people of all ethnic groups in Qinghai have created their own history, their own culture, their own realizations and dreams, and have formed and maintained unique and colorful customs and art forms.

X. Wang et al. (Eds.): AICON 2021, LNICST 397, pp. 214–223, 2021.
https://doi.org/10.1007/978-3-030-90199-8_21

Thangka is a unique form of painting art in Tibetan culture. In 2006, thangka was approved by the State Council and the Ministry of Culture as the first batch of national intangible cultural heritage, which is increasingly attracting art lovers and collectors. At the same time, a lot of printed thangkas appeared on the market, and some merchants sold printed thangkas as hand-painted thangkas at high prices. How to distinguish hand-painted thangkas and machine-printed thangkas, so as to effectively protect and inherit this ancient and exquisite craftsmanship, and explore a development path suitable for oneself, let these exquisite national craftsmanship go to the world, and further promote national culture, is a problem that needs to be solved urgently.

2 The Cultural Value Difference Between Machine-Printed Thangka and Hand-Painted Thangka

The mystery of the thangka comes from the special rituals used when painting the thangka. The requirements for the painters are very high, including pre-bathing, chanting, and visualization. The completed thangka must go through the process of consecration and blessing. Therefore, every hand-painted thangka is condensed with blood, sweat and the protection of the gods. The finished thangka is regarded as a living Buddha, a Master, and a Three Treasure. Machine-printed thangka only needs electricity and machinery, and it loses all the artistic connotation and the meaning of vitality.

3 Identification of Machine-Printed Thangka and Hand-Painted Thangka

3.1 Use LBP to Analyze the Characteristics of the Canvas

The canvas of the hand-painted thangka uses a special cotton cloth, which is hand-polished, brushed on the cloth with a blend of cow glue and lime, and then repeatedly polished with Cha-Yang or white powder. The resulting canvas will show the color of the paint on it more evenly, and the polished canvas will not have to worry about being bitten by bugs.

The counterfeit machine-printed thangka generally chooses a ordinary canvas (a kind of special plastic cloth). Most of the counterfeit machine-printed thangka pigments are synthetic polymer pigments. These pigments are brighter in color and strong in adhesion. They can be painted on a variety of carriers and have great versatility in various painting techniques. However, the cotton cloth for machine printing has some shortcomings. It dries quickly and has water resistance, but after drying, the paint film is tough, feels stiff, has no stretchability, and will crack and drop slag. There will be a certain difference between the two canvases under the magnifying glass: the same equipment is used, and in order to avoid the color gap, the sampling is the same as the green background. The shooting effect, the machine-printed thangka is shown in Fig. 1, and the hand-painted thangka is shown in Fig. 2 as shown.

Through the renderings, it can be concluded that there are more obvious small dots on the machine-printed thangka. This paper uses the LBP algorithm to analyze the texture of the canvas. Proceed as follows:

Fig. 1. The machine-printed Thangka was taken at the maximum magnification of Huawei Honor 8

Fig. 2. Hand-painted thangka was taken at the maximum magnification of Huawei Honor 8

1. First, the detection window is divided into small 16 × 16 areas (cells).
2. For a pixel in each cell, compare the gray value of the adjacent 8 pixels with it. If the value of the surrounding pixel is greater than the value of the central pixel, the position of the pixel is marked as 1, otherwise it is 0. In this way, 8 points in the 3 * 3 neighborhood can be compared to produce an 8-bit binary number, that is, the LBP value of the center pixel of the window can be obtained. See the mathematic model in formula (1):

$$\text{LBP}(x_c, y_c) \sum_{p=0}^{p-1} 2^p s(i_p - i_c) \tag{1}$$

Wherein the (x_c, y_c) represents the central element of the 3 * 3 area, its pixel values is i_c. The value i_p represents the other pixels in the area. s(x) is a symbolic function, defined as in formula (2):

$$\text{s(x)} = 1(\text{if } x \geq 0, \text{ else s(x)} = 0) \tag{2}$$

Each image can be represented by an LBP feature vector, and the similarity of the image can be calculated using the similarity of the vector. There are many ways to calculate the similarity of vectors, such as cosine and distance. The following is this similarity calculation method based on histogram vector, Histogram intersection: as formula (3), Log-likelihood statistic as formula (4), Chi square statistic (x^2) as formula (5) as shown in the figure below.

$$\text{Histogram intersection: } D(S, M) = \sum_t \min(S_i, M_i) \tag{3}$$

$$\text{Log-likelihood statistic: } L(S, M) = \sum_t -S_i \log M_i \tag{4}$$

$$\text{Chi square statistic}(): x^2(S, M) = \sum_t \frac{(S_i, M_i)^2}{S_i + M_i} \tag{5}$$

The above method is only for one histogram, and in use, the image is divided into multiple regions to calculate the histogram separately. Therefore, in actual use, different regions can also be weighted. The model is as in formula (6):

$$x_w^2(S, M) = \sum_{i,j} w_j \frac{(S_{i,j}, M_{i,j})^2}{S_{i,j} + M_{i,j}} \tag{6}$$

3. Then calculate the histogram of each cell, that is, the frequency of occurrence of each number (assumed to be a decimal number LBP value); then normalize the histogram.
4. Finally, the obtained statistical histogram of each cell is connected into a feature vector, which is the LBP texture feature vector of the entire image. According to the above steps, the texture analysis of the machine-printed thangka and the canvas used in the hand-painted thangka is carried out. The results are shown in Fig. 3 for the texture analysis of the machine-printed thangka and Fig. 4 for the hand-painted thangka texture analysis. Use this analysis to record, perform predictive analysis

Fig. 3. Machine-printed thangka texture score results

Fig. 4. Hand-painted thangka texture analysis results

5. Training the SVM classifier, based on a very simple point of view, the distribution of different objects in the three-dimensional space of the pigment is different. The use of SVM can be constructed. First load the picture, Select representative points of different objects, Train the SVM classifier, Apply the trained classifier to the entire picture to create a classification surface, Use the SVM classifier to predict the image.

The forecast results are using this predictive model, the obtained image analysis shows that the machine-printed thangka images are neater and more regular than the hand-painted thangka images, and preliminary screening can be achieved by discriminating and analyzing the canvas.

3.2 Using Clustering Method to Analyze Thangka Gold Line

3.2.1 Analysis of Thangka Gold Line

The application of golden line in thangka paintings is considered to be thangka's most unique skill. Whether the main statue or the costumes of the characters in the surrounding story paintings, most of them are drawn with golden lines. Buildings, trees, and stones are often decorated with gold lines and dots. Tibetan painters are very good at using gold. They often use red gold for the base, and then use gold to depict patterns to increase the level of gold. Tibetan painters have strict requirements on the quality of gold. The gold powder used is pure gold and must be processed and polished in person. For cost reason the machine-printed thangka will not choose pure gold raw materials, but rather use chemical materials. Therefore, the gold line is one of the important bases for distinguishing between hand-printed thangka and machine-painted thangka.

In an environment with sufficient light, due to the specular reflection of the metal, it will be dazzling when viewed from the side. In a dark environment, after giving the thangka light source from the side, you can observe a very spectacular picture, which can be said to be magnificent. The hand-painted thangka effect after fill light is shown in Fig. 5, and the machine-printed thangka effect is shown in Fig. 6.

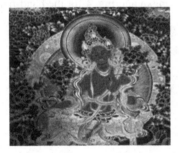   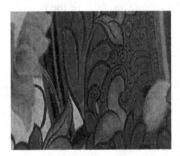

Fig. 5. Hand-painted Tangka   **Fig. 6.** Machine-painted Tangka

3.2.2 Application of Clustering Method

1. Obtain images of hand-painted thangkas and machine-printed thangkas.
2. Extract the feature values of the positive and negative samples and the color features of the thangka image.
3. Use the clustering method to cluster the variable number of feature values and color features into a fixed number of classes.
4. Normalize the fixed number of classes to obtain a histogram of 10 classes.
5. Train 10 classes in each picture as feature instances and positive and negative samples to obtain the features of the thangka picture.
6. Calculate the distance between each feature and 10 classes, and determine the class of each feature.
7. Normalize each eigenvalue, and make a histogram of the 10 classes.
8. Analyze the machine- printed thangka and hand-painted thangka gold line according to the above steps. The result is as shown in Fig. 7 for the machine-printed thangka gold line analysis, and the hand-drawn Thangka gold line analysis is shown in Fig. 8.

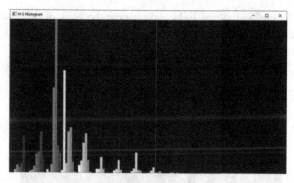

Fig. 7. Machine-painted Tangka gold line analysis results

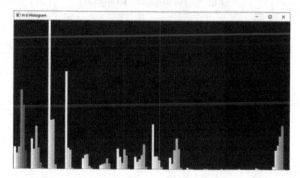

Fig. 8. Hand-painted Tangka gold line analysis results

Using this prediction model, the obtained image analysis shows that the hand-painted thangka image has a wider color gamut and a brighter yellow color gamut than the machine-printed thangka image. Through the identification and analysis of the gold line, it is judged whether the thangka is a hand-painted thangka or a machine-painted thangka.

3.3 Analysis of Thangka's Light Transmittance Using Restricted Boltzmann Machine

3.3.1 Analysis of Thangka Light Transmittance

The canvas of the hand-painted thangka uses a special cotton cloth, which is hand-milled, brushed on the cloth with a blend of cow glue and lime, and then repeatedly polished with Cha Yang or white powder. For simulation printing thangkas, canvases with common mechanisms are generally chosen. The difference between the two canvases is to point a Thangka at strong light and observe the back of the Thangka. If there are irregular marks on the back of the Thangka, this is generally the traces left by the hand-painted canvas during the polishing process. The hand-painted Thangka passes Manually painted colors cannot be absolutely uniform in the control of the amount of paint, while the machine-painted Thangka uses high-precision nozzles to control the uniformity of the paint quite strictly. Point a Thangka at strong light and observe the back of the Thangka, and you will find irregular marks (Figs. 9 and 10).

Fig. 9. Hand-painted Tangka

Fig. 10. Machine-painted Tangka

3.3.2 Restricted Boltzmann Machine

Restricted Boltzmann Machine (the RBM) is a class of stochastic neural network having two-layer structure, and no self-feedback symmetrical connection, all the interlayer connection, without connecting the inner layer. The model is shown in the following figure, v is the visible layer, which is used to represent the observation data, h is the hidden layer, which can be regarded as some feature detectors, and W is the connection weight between the two layers. Welling pointed out that the hidden and visible units in RBM can be arbitrary exponential family units, that is, given hidden units (visible units), the distribution of visible units (hidden units) can be any exponential family distribution, such as softmax units, Gaussian units, Poisson unit and so on.

Assuming that all visible units and hidden units are binary variables, that is, if an RBM has 'n' visible units and 'm' hidden units, use vectors 'v' and 'h' to represent the states of the visible and hidden units respectively, as shown in the figure, v_i represents the state of the i-th visible unit, and h_j represents the state of j hidden units. Then, for a given set of (v, h) states, the energy possessed by RBM as a system is defined as (7):

$$E(v, h|\theta) = -\sum_{i=1}^{n} a_i v_i - \sum_{j=1}^{m} b_j h_j - \sum_{i=1}^{n}\sum_{j=1}^{m} v_i w_{ij} h_j \qquad (7)$$

In the above formula, $\theta = \{w_{ij}, a_i, b_j\}$ are the parameters of RBM. They are all real numbers, which represent the neuron connection weight of the visible unit i and the hidden unit j, a_i represent the bias of the visible unit neuron (bias), and b_j represent the bias of the hidden unit j. When the parameter is determined based on the energy function, we obtain (V, H) the joint probability density distribution of formula (8):

$$P(v, h|\theta) = \frac{e^{-E(v,h|\theta)}}{Z(\theta)}, Z(\theta) = \sum_{v,h} e^{-E(v,h|\theta)} \tag{8}$$

For thangka's light transmittance, what we care about is the distribution of observation data v in $P(v|\theta)$ defined by RBM, that is, the distribution of the probability of the content can be correctly identified in the visible layer under the condition of trained weights. How to find this probability distribution? The marginal distribution can be obtained from Eq. (8), as follows (9):

$$P(v|\theta) = \frac{1}{Z(\theta)} \sum_h e^{-E(v,h|\theta)} \tag{9}$$

In order to determine the distribution, it is necessary to calculate the normalization factor $Z(\theta)$, which requires 2^{m+n} calculations (because the visible unit and the hidden unit are fully connected, and because there are n visible units and m hidden units), the amount of calculation is very large. Therefore, even if the parameters of the model W_{ij}, a_i, b_j, can be obtained through training, we still cannot calculate the distribution determined by these parameters. However, due to the special structure of RBM (i.e., inter-layer connection, intra-layer connection), it is known that when the state of the visible unit is given, the activation state of each hidden unit is conditionally independent. At this time, the activation probability of the j-th hidden unit is (10):

$$P(h_j = 1|v, \theta) = \sigma(b_j + \sum_i v_i w_{ij}) \tag{10}$$

Among them $\sigma(x) = \frac{1}{1+\exp(-x)}$ is the sigmod activation function.

Since the structure of RBM is symmetrical, when the state of the hidden unit is given, the activation state of each visible unit is also conditionally independent, that is, the activation probability of the i-th visible unit is Eq. (11):

$$P(v_i = 1|h, \theta) = \sigma\left(a_i + \sum_j w_{ij} h_i\right) \tag{11}$$

The probability that the state of a certain neuron j in the hidden layer equals to 1 is same as the probability of multiplying all the units and weights of all visible layers and then adding the bias value to obtain the sigmod function.

The difference between the image with sunlight and the image without sunlight is used to obtain the image sample after the difference; the feature extraction of the image after the difference is carried out, and the result is as shown in Fig. 11 for the machine-printed thangka processed image. The analysis of the hand-painted thangka processed image is shown in Fig. 12.

Fig. 11. Machine-painted Tangka gold line analysis results

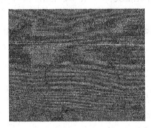

Fig. 12. Machine-painted Tangka gold line analysis results

Using this prediction model, the result is that the machine-printed thangka image is more uniform than the hand-painted thangka image.

4 Identification Steps

Analyze the characteristics of the canvas through the LBP algorithm, conduct a preliminary screening, determine the thangka type, and then analyze the thangka gold line through the clustering method, conduct a second screening, determine the thangka type, and finally pass the restricted Boltzmann Machine analyzes the light transmittance of the thangka, and conducts the third screening to determine the type of the thangka.

5 Conclusion

Through the research of hand-painted thangka and machine-printed thangka, it is found that there are differences in the light transmittance of the thangka canvas, the golden thread of the thangka, and the canvas under the light environment. For the research on the difference, the appropriate algorithm is selected. Carry out model construction, operation, and verification. In the end, it can be determined that the above method can be applied to the identification of hand-painted thangka and machine-printed thangka.

Acknowledgements. Funded Project: Qinghai Provincial Department of Science and Technology Key Research and Development and Transformation Program, Qinghai Intangible Cultural Heritage Handicraft Digital Traceability System Development (No. 2020-GX-113) project support.

References

1. Guan, L.: On the image dissemination of intangible cultural heritage in the new media era. Popular Lit. **462**(12), 177–178 (2019)
2. Kong, F.: Research on the construction of intangible cultural heritage database of public libraries. J. Libr. Inf. Sci. Univ. **37**(3), 83–86 (2019)
3. Feng, Y.: Thoughts on Qinghai intangible cultural heritage protection. J. Qinghai Normal Univ. (Philos. Soc. Sci. Ed.) **38**(1), 85–89 (2016)
4. Liu, P., Shi, R.: Protection and development of tibetan sports intangible cultural heritage in Qinghai Province. Fight Martial Arts Sci. **4**(2), 130–133 (2019)
5. Liu, P., Shi, R.: Protection and development of Tibetan sports intangible cultural heritage in Qinghai Province. Wushu Res. **4**(2), 136–139 (2019)
6. Zhe, Y.: Research on the protection of qinghai intangible cultural heritage inheritors. Pang Deng (Chin. Ed.) **37**(6), 127–131 (2018)
7. Xie, Y., Zhu, L.: Research on digital protection of intangible cultural heritage in the context of new media. Lantai World **552**(10), 87–89 (2018)
8. Tian, X., Ma, X.: Digital exploration in intangible cultural heritage inheritance. J. Cult. Stud. **99**(1), 158–160 (2019)
9. Hao, H.: Innovative research on digital development of intangible cultural heritage in the era of new media. Fujian Tea, vol. 219, no. 3, pp. 374–375 (2020)
10. Suárez, R., Alonso, A., Sendra, J.J.: Intangible cultural heritage: the sound of the Romanesque cathedral of Santiago de Compostela. J. Cult. Heritage **16**(2), 239–243 (2015)
11. Qiong, D.: Research on the protection of intangible cultural heritage by using new media technology—taking shou county as an example. Commun. Copyright **1**, 116–117 (2016)

Access State Detection for Serial Port Sensor Module in Micro Control System

Chengqiao Liu[⊠], Jun Ma, and Lingfei Zhang

School of Physics and Electronic Information Engineering of Qinghai, Normal University,
Xining 810008, China
Liuchq12@lzu.edu.cn

Abstract. An access state detection (ASD) method for the serial port sensor module in micro control system is proposed according to the work mechanism with which the micro control system gets data by serial port and the working feature of serial port sensor module. The micro control system detected the access state of serial port sensor module by examining the serial port receive flag of microcontroller, or by examining the serial port receive interruption of microcontroller. And based on these, the system determined the access state of sensor module, and then took effective measures to make sure the system ran well. Besides, the related safeguard mechanisms were also established to ensure the ASD was effective and reliable. The ASD method was applied to two micro control systems based on different serial port sensors, and good results were achieved. The practice indicates that, with the serial port sensor module ASD, the micro control system can detect the access state of serial port sensor module in micro control system accurately and taking effective measures in time for it, avoid suffering the adverse effects caused by the abnormal access state of serial port sensor module, and improve the comprehensive performance of micro control system.

Keywords: Access state detection (ASD) · Serial port sensor module · Serial port receive flag · Serial port receive interruption · Micro control system

1 Introduction

As we all know, the micro control system based on microcontroller and sensor module is simple in structure, and can be developed and maintained easily and less costly, so it is widely applied to industrial and agricultural production and daily life. For example, the road roughness measurement system [1] and the water temperature measurement system [2] in industry, the soil environmental monitoring system [3] and the irrigation system [4] in agriculture, the air monitoring system [5] and the smart home system [6] in daily life, etc. As one of the basic configurations of microcontroller, the serial port facilitates the communication between microcontroller and the other circuit modules, and the number of serial ports has been one of the main performance indexes of microcontroller. In order to be integrated with microcontroller more easily and be more convenient for operation, now many kinds of sensor modules have serial ports, which can be called

X. Wang et al. (Eds.): AICON 2021, LNICST 397, pp. 224–243, 2021.
https://doi.org/10.1007/978-3-030-90199-8_22

serial port sensor modules. For example, the SDS011, a PM2.5 sensor module which can be applied to the air monitoring system, the M-8729, a GPS receiver module which can be applied to the location system, and the US-100, a ultrasonic sensor module which can be applied to the distance measurement system, etc. The serial port sensor module data can be got with a proper operation on the serial port by system.

Running in good condition for the sensor module is one of the supporting conditions for micro control system to get sensor module data. However, in practice, the serial port sensor module may access the micro control system abnormally because of the environment factors [7–9], human factors or the serial port sensor module itself. For example, the sensor module disconnects from the microcontroller physically, the power for sensor module is abnormal, the sensor module is damaged, etc. These abnormities will cause some adverse effects to micro control system, and degrade the comprehensive performance of it. Detecting the abnormal access state of serial port sensor module accurately and taking effective measures instantaneously for it will improve the comprehensive performance of micro control system effectively.

2 Related Work

In recent years, a lot of work on sensor fault detection and diagnosis in many fields has been carried out by many researchers. For example, in the field of transportation, the principal component analysis (PCA), the contribution method based on reconstruction, and a modified fault Petri net (PN) model were applied to detect, isolate and diagnose the fault of multi-axle speed sensors for high-speed trains [10]. And an approach based on nonlinear disturbance observer (NDO) was proposed to detect and diagnose the aircraft inertial measurement unit (IMU) fault by using dynamic and kinematic relations of the aircraft [11]. In the field of unmanned aerial vehicle (UAV), for detecting UAV sensor faults, a new online detection strategy based on neural adaptive observer was developed [12], a fault detection and isolation (FDI) structure including faulty pitot tube, angle-of-attack sensor, sideslip sensor, accelerometer and gyro was designed and the fault detection filter (FDF) for proportional and multiple integral (PMI) was proposed [13], besides, interacting multiple model (IMM) approach which combined the IMM algorithm and the SA strategy was proposed [14]. The model-based FDI was applied to electric power system widely [15–17]. In the field of attitude control system (ACS), the fault tolerant extended Kalman Filter (FTEKF) [18] and a nonlinear observer which could detect any rate and attitude sensor fault [19] were proposed to detect the sensor faults for ACS. In the field of motor application, an algebraic equations-based analysis which derived the two admissible motor model solutions explicit expressions was presented to detect the steady-state speed sensor fault in induction motors with uncertain parameters [20], a differential algebraic estimation of fault dynamics and a scheme based on the combination of the Robust Integral Sign of the Error (RISE) observer with the algebraic approach were proposed for the current sensor FDI in induction motor drives [21]. In the field of battery management, a diagnosis system that relied on a dual unscented Kalman filter for residual generation was designed for both internal FDI and sensor FDI for Li-ion Batteries [22], and a hybrid system modeling and unscented particle filter based fault diagnosis method was proposed for voltage sensor and current sensor in

Li-ion battery pack system [23]. In the field of wireless sensor network, a Non-Negative Matrix Factorization (NMF) based machine learning method was applied to detect the sensor nodes fault in wireless sensor networks for agricultural [24], and a complete fault diagnosis methodology which included initialization phase, fault detection phase, fault classification phase, and fault tolerance phase was proposed for the sensor modules fault in wireless sensor network [25]. In other fields, an extended Kalman filter (EKF) based on concise algorithm, a strong tracking filter (STF) based on robust tracking ability, and the cubature Kalman filter (CKF) based on numerical precision were proposed to diagnose the electronically controlled air suspension (ECAS) sensor fault [26]. The partial adaptive kernel principal component analysis (AKPCA) was proposed for the sensor FDI of an industrial gas turbine [27]. A data-driven optimized statistical model was proposed for sensor fault detection and diagnosis (FDD) in water source heat pump air conditioning system [28]. The sensor fault detection based on the generalized likelihood ratio and correlation coefficient was applied to bridge structural health monitoring [29]. And the tolerance interval and modified measurement covariance were also introduced to the sensor fault detection [30], etc.

3   Problem Statement

All the work mentioned above provides technical supports for the sensor fault detection, isolation and diagnosis (FDID) in system, and plays a positive role in improving the performance of system. But these sensor FDID methods were based on a mountain of theoretical knowledge and algorithms. They may be effective on the sensor FDID of the powerful system with complex structure, but may not be effective on it of the simpler micro control system, even increase the burden of this system. Besides, none of them can be specially applied to the access state detection (ASD) for serial port sensor modules, which is not good for improving the performance of the micro control system based on microcontroller and serial port sensor module. Then a simple and useful method is urgent for the serial port sensor module ASD in micro control system.

We know that the microcontroller receives data by serial port in the inquiry way or in the interruption way. The Fig. 1a shows the work mechanism with which the micro control system gets serial port sensor module data in inquiry way, and the Fig. 1b shows the work mechanism with which the micro control system gets serial port sensor module data in interruption way.

According to Fig. 1a, when the microcontroller receives data by serial port in inquiry way, if the serial port receive flag of microcontroller is set to "1", it indicates that the microcontroller has received one frame of data, and the system can read data from the serial data buffer (SBUF), otherwise, the system can't read data from SBUF. In Fig. 1a, the "t" is the real time that the system needs to get complete data from serial port sensor module, and the "T" is the maximum time that the system sets for getting complete data from the serial port sensor module. The size of the data that the serial port sensor module transmits to microcontroller may be different due to the working environment, and the system always needs to read data from SBUF several times in order to get complete data from serial port sensor module, so the "t" may be also different. The system should get complete data from the serial port sensor module within "T" so that the other tasks can be performed in time. If the "T" is too short, the system possibly can't get complete data from serial port sensor module. And if the "T" is too long, the other tasks can't be performed in time, and the system work cycle will be extended. So, setting the "T" reasonably according to the performance characteristics of serial port sensor module will benefit the comprehensive performance of micro control system.

According to Fig. 1b, when the microcontroller receives data by serial port in interruption way, after the serial port receive interruption of the microcontroller is enabled, if the serial port receive interruption of microcontroller is generated, it indicates that the microcontroller has received one frame of data, and the system can read data from the SBUF, otherwise, the system can't read data from SBUF. As the Fig. 1b reveals, after the serial port receive interruption is enabled, the micro control system will not read data from the SBUF until the serial port receive interruption is generated. The micro control system will stop performing the current task immediately, and read data from the SBUF once the serial port receive interruption is generated. And the system will return to the breakpoint and continue the other tasks instantaneously after reading data from SBUF.

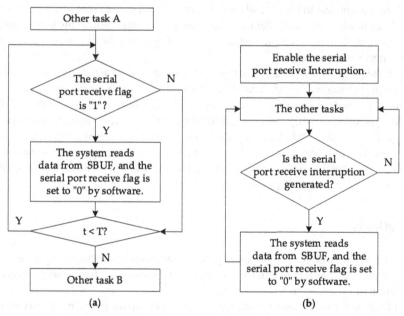

Fig. 1. Work mechanism for micro control system to get serial port sensor module data: (a) in inquiry way; (b) in interruption way.

No matter in which way the microcontroller receives data by serial port, the serial port receive flag of microcontroller must be set to "0" by software after the system read data from SBUF, otherwise the next frame of data will not be received regularly.

Comparing the work mechanism in Fig. 1a with the work mechanism in Fig. 1b, we can know that the micro control system should set an individual time for getting data from serial port sensor module when the system receives data by serial port in the inquiry way, and the system can get serial port sensor module data instantaneously without an individual time when the system receives data by serial port in the interruption way. The latter makes micro control system get serial port sensor module data in more timely manner, and run more efficiently.

When the serial port sensor module accesses system normally, the micro control system can get serial port sensor module data effectively with the existing work mechanism. But when the serial port sensor module accesses system abnormally, the comprehensive performance of micro control system will be influenced by these abnormities.

Once the serial port sensor module accesses the micro control system abnormally because of some reasons (the physical connection between microcontroller and serial port sensor module is disconnected, the serial port sensor module is powered off unexpectedly, the serial port sensor module is damaged, etc.), it does not transmit data to microcontroller, and the serial port receive flag of microcontroller is not set to "1", and the serial port receive interruption is also not generated. According to Fig. 1a, when micro control system receives data by serial port in inquiry way, system keeps inquiring the state of the serial port receive flag of microcontroller until the "T" is over, and then takes the other tasks. This work substantially makes the system keep running at the cost of "T". And according to Fig. 1b, when the micro control system receives data by serial port in interruption way, the system will keep taking the other tasks. This work substantially makes the system keep running at the cost of ignoring the abnormal access state of serial port sensor module.

With the analysis above, the existing work mechanism for micro control system to get serial port sensor module data can't detect the access state of serial port sensor module, and can't take effective measures instantaneously when serial port sensor module accesses system abnormally, which is a defect for the micro control system. In this paper, a simple and useful method based on the work mechanism with which the microcontroller gets data by serial port and the working feature of serial port sensor module is proposed to resolve this problem, and with this method, the comprehensive performance of micro control system is improved.

4   Methods

In this paper, the access state of serial port sensor module is detected by examining the serial port receive flag of microcontroller, or by examining the serial port receive interruption of microcontroller.

For the purposes of discussion, the serial port sensor modules can be categorized into two types according to the ways they work in: the automatic serial port sensor module and the instructions driven serial port sensor module. To the automatic serial port sensor module, it transmits the data to microcontroller instantaneously when it is powered on, and keeps going until it is powered off. For example, the M-8729 keeps transmitting the data that represents the location of micro control system to microcontroller until it is powered off [31]. And to the instructions driven serial port sensor module, when it is powered on, it does not transmit the data to microcontroller instantaneously until it gets the correct instructions from microcontroller, and transmits the data to microcontroller only once until it gets the correct instructions from the microcontroller again. For example, when the US-100 is powered on, if it gets "0X50" from the microcontroller, it transmits the data that represents the temperature to microcontroller instantaneously only once until it gets "0X50" from microcontroller again [32]. And if it gets "0X55" from microcontroller, it transmits the data that represents the distance to microcontroller instantaneously only once until it gets "0X55" from microcontroller again [32].

The ASD for these two types of serial port sensor modules will be elaborated as follows.

4.1 Detecting the Access State of Serial Port Sensor Module by Examining the Serial Port Receive Flag of Microcontroller

We know that, on the premise that the microcontroller works regularly, when he serial port sensor module accesses micro control system normally, the serial port receive flag of microcontroller is set to "1" automatically after the microcontroller receives one frame of data from serial port sensor module, otherwise the serial port receive flag of microcontroller is set to "0". And when the serial port sensor module accesses the micro control system abnormally, the serial port receive flag of microcontroller is always "0". According to this, the micro control system can decide whether the serial port sensor module accesses the system normally by examining the serial port receive flag of microcontroller. If the serial port receive flag of microcontroller can be set to "1" automatically, it is determined that the serial port sensor module accesses system normally, and if the serial port receive flag of microcontroller is always "0", it is determined that the serial port sensor module accesses system abnormally.

However, in a practical application, the hardware circuit of micro control system may suffer the adverse effects come from the surrounding environment, for example, the fluctuation of voltage and current, etc. These adverse effects may result in packet loss in the serial port sensor module data transmission, which can result in an error detection. A safeguard mechanism should be established for micro control system to make sure the detection is effective and reliable, and reduce the detection time. Because the ways that these two types of serial port sensor modules work in are different, the safeguard mechanisms for detecting their access state are also different.

To the automatic serial port sensor module, when it is powered on, it transmits data to microcontroller instantaneously, and in different application conditions, the data size may be different, and the system work cycles of different sensor modules may also be different, so the frequency for the serial port receive flag of microcontroller to be set to "1" automatically is uncertain. Given this, the micro control system detects the access state of the automatic serial port sensor module with the safeguard mechanism described as "Examining it within the required time, and stop examining it in time" (ERSE). The ERSE is explained by Eq. (1). In Eq. (1), the "S" expresses the access state of serial port sensor module, and the "t" expresses the real time that the system costs to examine the serial port receive flag of microcontroller until it is set to "1" automatically, and the "T" expresses the maximum time that the system costs to examine the serial port receive flag of microcontroller. The "T" is set by system according to the performance of automatic serial port sensor module. It indicates that the serial port sensor module accesses system normally when S = R, and the serial port sensor module accesses system abnormally when S = F.

$$S = \begin{cases} R & t < T \\ F & t = T \end{cases} \tag{1}$$

The Fig. 2 shows the work mechanism with which the micro control system detects the access state of automatic serial port sensor module by examining the serial port receive flag of microcontroller. According to Fig. 2, we can know that, with the ERSE, the micro control system records the "t", and compares it with the "T". If the serial port receive flag of microcontroller is set to "1" automatically and t < T, that is to say, the serial port receive flag of microcontroller can be set to "1" automatically within the maximum time that the system sets, it can be determined that the serial port sensor module accesses system normally. And if the serial port receive flag of microcontroller is "0" and t = T, that is to say, the serial port receive flag of microcontroller is always "0" within the maximum time that the system sets, it can be determined that the serial port sensor module accesses system abnormally. Once the access state of serial port sensor module is determined, the system will not examine the serial port receive flag of microcontroller again, but resets the related flags of system for taking the other tasks.

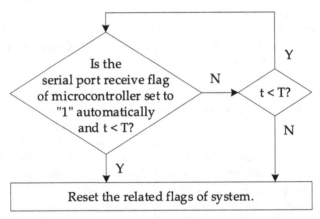

Fig. 2. Work mechanism for micro control system to detect the access state of automatic serial port sensor module by examining the serial port receive flag of microcontroller.

To the instructions driven serial port sensor module, when it is powered on, it does not transmit the data to microcontroller instantaneously until it gets the correct instructions from microcontroller, and then the serial port receive flag of microcontroller is set to "1" automatically. And the serial port sensor module transmits data to microcontroller only once until it gets the correct instructions from microcontroller again. Given this, the correct instructions can be available as the test signals for detecting the access state of serial pot sensor module. And the micro control system detects the access state of the serial pot sensor module with the safeguard mechanism described as "Examining it several times, and stop examining it in time" (ESSE). The ESSE is explained by Eq. (2). In Eq. (2), the "S" expresses the access state of the serial port sensor module, the "X" expresses the real number that the system sent test signal to serial port sensor module until the serial port receive flag of microcontroller is set to "1" automatically, and the "Y" expresses the maximum number that the system sent the test signal to serial port sensor module. The "Y" is set by system according to the performance of instructions driven serial port sensor module. It indicates that the serial port sensor module accesses system normally when S = R, and the serial port sensor module accesses system abnormally when S = F.

$$S = \begin{cases} R & X < Y \\ F & X = Y \end{cases} \tag{2}$$

The Fig. 3 shows the work mechanism with which the micro control system detects the access state of the instructions driven serial port sensor module by examining the serial port receive flag of microcontroller. According to Fig. 3, we can know that, with the ESSE, the micro control system records the "X", and compares it with the "Y". If the serial port receive flag of microcontroller can be set to "1" automatically and X < Y, that is to say, the serial port receive flag of microcontroller can be set to "1" automatically within the maximum number that the system sets, it can be determined that the serial port sensor module accesses system normally. And if the serial port receive flag of microcontroller is "0" and X = Y, that is to say, the serial port receive flag of microcontroller is always "0" within the maximum number that the system sets, it can be determined that the serial port sensor module accesses system abnormally. Once the access state of serial port sensor module is determined, the system does not send the test signal to serial port sensor module again, and also does not examine the serial port receive flag of microcontroller again, but resets the related flags of system for taking the other tasks.

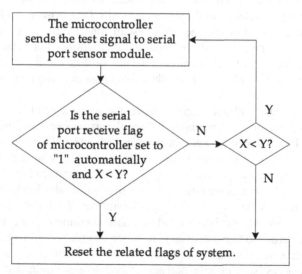

Fig. 3. Work mechanism for micro control system to detect the access state of instructions driven serial port sensor module by examining the serial port receive flag of microcontroller.

4.2 Detecting the Access State of Serial Port Sensor Module by Examining the Serial Port Receive Interruption of Microcontroller

We also know that, on the premise that the microcontroller works regularly, when serial port sensor module accesses micro control system normally and the serial port receive interruption of microcontroller is enabled, the serial port receive interruption of microcontroller is generated after the microcontroller receives one frame of data from serial port sensor module, otherwise the receive interruption of microcontroller is not generated. And when the serial port sensor module accesses the micro control system abnormally, the receive interruption of microcontroller is never generated. According to this, the micro control system can decide whether the serial port sensor module accesses the system normally by examining the serial port receive interruption of microcontroller. If the serial port receive interruption of the microcontroller is generated, it is determined that the serial port sensor module accesses system normally, otherwise it is determined that the serial port sensor module accesses system abnormally. It is similar to examining the serial port receive flag of microcontroller, the micro control system makes sure the detection is effective and reliable and reduce the detection time with a safeguard mechanism.

The ERSE is also available to detect the access state of automatic serial port sensor module by examining the serial port receive interrupt of microcontroller. The Fig. 4 shows the work mechanism with which the micro control system detects the access state of automatic serial port sensor module by examining the serial port receive interruption of microcontroller. According to Fig. 4, we can know that, after the serial port receive interruption of microcontroller is enabled, the micro control system records the "t", and compares it with the "T". If the serial port receive interruption of microcontroller is generated within the maximum time that the system sets, it can be determined that the serial port sensor module accesses the system normally. Otherwise, it can be determined that the serial port sensor module accesses system abnormally. Once the access state of serial port sensor module is determined, the system does not examine the serial port receive interruption of microcontroller again, but disables the serial port receive interruption of microcontroller and resets the related flags of system for taking the other tasks.

And the ESSE can be also available to detect the access state of instructions driven serial port sensor module by examining the serial port receive interruption of microcontroller. The Fig. 5 shows the work mechanism with which the micro control system detects the access state of instructions driven serial port sensor module by examining the serial port receive interruption of microcontroller. According to Fig. 5, we can know that, after the serial port receive interruption of microcontroller is enabled, the micro control system records the "X", and compares it with the "Y". If the serial port receive interruption of microcontroller is generated within the maximum number that the system sets, it can be determined that the serial port sensor module accesses system normally. Otherwise, it can be determined that the serial port sensor module accesses system abnormally. Once the access state of serial port sensor module is determined, the system does not send the test signal to serial port sensor module again, and also does not examine the serial port receive interruption of microcontroller again, but disables the serial port

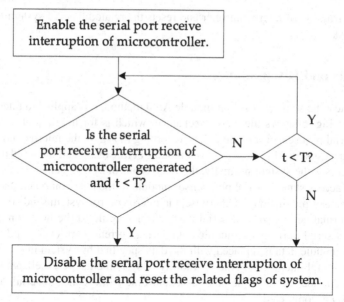

Fig. 4. Work mechanism for micro control system to detect the access state of automatic serial port sensor module by examining the serial port receive interruption of microcontroller.

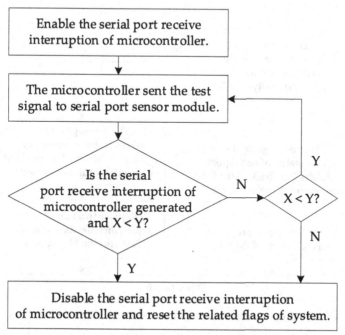

Fig. 5. Work mechanism for micro control system to detect the access state of instructions driven serial port sensor module by examining the serial port receive interruption of microcontroller.

receive interruption of microcontroller and resets the related flags of system for taking the other tasks.

5   Results and Discussion

In order to test the serial port sensor module ASD method, it is applied to micro control system. The Fig. 6 shows the work mechanism which is for micro control system to run with serial port sensor module ASD. According to Fig. 6, the micro control system detects the access state of serial port sensor module before using it. If the serial port sensor module accesses the system normally, the micro control system sends the message on the normal access state of serial port sensor module to the host computer, and then get serial port sensor module data. Otherwise, the micro control system sends the message on the abnormal access state of serial port sensor module to the host computer, and does not get serial port sensor module data during current work cycle, and this serial port sensor module data is replaced with the data specified by system in order to make sure the structural integrity and the operability of system data are excellent. The micro control system does not take the other tasks until the work relates to serial port sensor module ASD is completed.

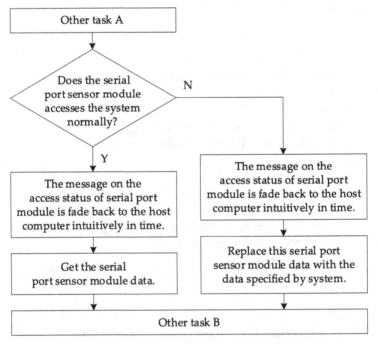

Fig. 6. Work mechanism for micro control system to run with serial port sensor module ASD.

In practice, the serial port sensor module ASD is applied to two micro control systems: "Location system based on MSP430F149 and M-8729" and "Distance measurement system based on MSP430F149 and US-100", and good results are achieved.

The MSP430F149 [33] is a 16-bit ultra-low power consumption microcontroller produced by the TI. There are some good features for the MSP430F149, For instance, low supply voltage range (1.8 V to 3.6 V), ultra-low power consumption (can be as low as 0.1 μA), from low-power modes to active mode in less than 6 μs, and two USARTs that make the data transmission more easier, etc. These good features make the MSP430F149 have an excellent performance, and be widely applied to micro control systems.

The M-8729 [31] is an automatic serial port sensor module, and it is a subminiature GPS engine module designed by low power consumption MTK GPS solution. The M-8729 can provide a highly sensitive (−165 dBm) and a quick first position time, which make the M-8729 have an excellent performance, and is widely applied to location system.

The US-100 [32] is an instructions driven serial port sensor module, and it is a distance measurement sensor module with an inner temperature sensor, which can correct the measuring results automatically, and the highest measurement range of the US-100 is 5000 mm. The US-100 can be triggered by the instructions from microcontroller, and there is a watchdog circuit in it. The US-100 works stably and reliably, and is widely applied to distance measurement system.

5.1 The Serial Port Sensor Module ASD Is Applied to "Location System Based on MSP430F149 and M-8729"

The Fig. 7 shows the schematic of location system based on MSP430F149 and M-8729. The system gets the M-8729 data by the USART1 of MSP430F149, and Communicated with the host computer by the USART0 of MSP430F149. Because the M-8729 is an automatic serial port sensor module, that is to say, the M-8729 only needs to transmit the data to the MSP430F149, it only needs to connect the TXD of M-8729 to the RXD1 of MSP430F149.

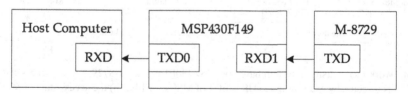

Fig. 7. The schematic of location system based on MSP430F149 and M-8729.

In this system, the access state of the M-8729 is detected by examining the USART1 receive flag (URXIFG1) of MSP430F149 and by examining the USART1 receive interruption of MSP430F149 respectively, and the message on the access state of M-8729 is fed back to the host computer in time. According to the performance characteristics of M-8729, the maximum time that the system costs to examine URXIFG1 was set to 10 s. The Fig. 8a and Fig. 8b show the work mechanism of this system. In Fig. 8a, the access state of the M-8729 is detected by examining the URXIFG1 of MSP430F149, which is shown in the dashed box of this figure. And in Fig. 8b, the access state of the M-8729 is detected by examining the USART1 receive interruption of MSP430F149, which is shown in the dashed box of this figure. In addition, the "t" expresses the real time that the system costs to examine the URXIFG1.

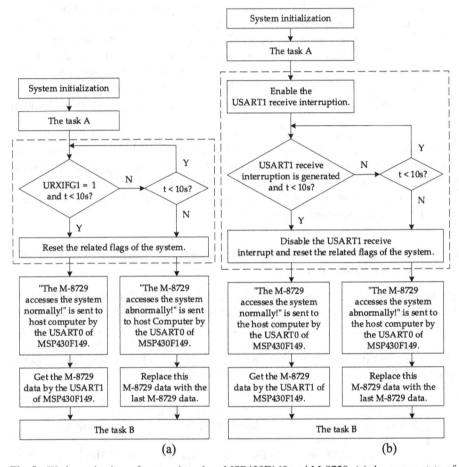

(a)   (b)

Fig. 8. Work mechanism of system based on MSP430F149 and M-8729: (a) the access state of M-8729 is detected by examining the URXIFG1 of MSP430F149; (b) the access state of M-8729 is detected by examining the USART1 receive interruption of MSP430F149.

We first test the several basic performance parameters of this system with the two detection mechanisms when all parts of this system work regularly. And then, on the premise that all parts of this system except the M-8729 work regularly, several abnormal access states of the M-8729 are simulated, and with the two detection mechanisms, the performance parameters of this system those have been tested when all parts of this system work regularly are tested again respectively by the control variates. The test results for the system with two detection mechanisms are the same (see the Table 1).

Table 1. The test results for the several basic performance parameters of the location system based on MSP430F149 and M-8729 with the two detection mechanisms.

Number	The access state of M-8729	Is the access state of M-8729 detected accurately?	Is the message on the access state of M-8729 fed back to the host computer intuitively in time?	Does the system get the M-8729 data effectively?	Is this M-8729 data replaced with the last M-8729 data?
1	M-8729 accesses system normally	YES	YES	YES	NO
2	Disconnect RXD1 from TXD	YES	YES	NO	YES
3	M-8729 is powered off	YES	YES	NO	YES
4	M-8729 is broken	YES	YES	NO	YES

From the Table 1, we can see that, with the serial port sensor module ASD, the micro control system can detect the access state of M-8729 correctly, and the message on the access state of M-8729 could be fed back to the host computer in time. When the M-8729 accessed the system normally (see the Number 1), the system can get the M-8729 data effectively, and implemented the location function. When the M-8729 accessed the system abnormally (see the Number 2, 3, 4), the system no longer gets the M-8729 data this work cycle, but replace this M-8729 data with the last M-8729 data. No matter the M-8729 accesses the system normally or abnormally, the structural integrity and the operability of the system data were excellent, and the system runs well.

5.2 The Serial Port Sensor Module ASD Is Applied to "Distance Measurement System Based on MSP430F149 and US-100"

The Fig. 9 shows the schematic of location system based on MSP430F149 and US-100. The system gets the US-100 data by the USART1 of MSP430F149, and communicate with the host computer by the USART0 of MSP430F149. Because the US-100 is an instructions driven serial port sensor module, that is to say, the US-100 not only needs to receive instructions from the MSP430F149, but also needs to transmit data to the MSP430F149, it needs to connect the RXD of US-100 to the TXD1 of MSP430F149, and connect the TXD of US-100 to the RXD1 of MSP430F149.

In this system, the access state of the US-100 is detected by examining the URXIFG1 of MSP430F149 and by examining the USART1 receive interruption of MSP430F149

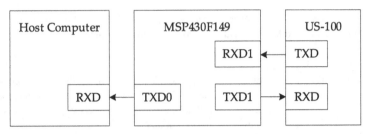

Fig. 9. The schematic of distance measurement system based on MSP430F149 and US-100.

respectively, and the message on the access state of the US-100 is fed back to the host computer in time. According to the performance characteristics of the US-100, the maximum number that the system sent the test signal to US-100 is set to 3. The Fig. 10a and Fig. 10b show the work mechanism of this system. In Fig. 10a, the access state of the US-100 is detected by examining the URXIFG1 of MSP430F149, which is shown in the dashed box of this figure. And in Fig. 10b, the access state of the US-100 is detected by examining the USART1 receive interruption of MSP430F149, which is shown in the dashed box of this figure. In addition, the "n" expresses the real time that the system costs to examine the URXIFG1.

We also first test the several basic performance parameters of this system with the two detection mechanisms when all parts of this system work regularly. And then, on the premise that all parts of this system except the US-100 work regularly, several abnormal access states of the US-100 are simulated, and with the two detection mechanisms, the performance parameters of this system those have been tested when all parts of this system work regularly are tested again respectively by the control variates. The test results for the system with two detection mechanisms are the same (see the Table 2).

From the Table 2, we can see that, with the serial port sensor module ASD, the micro control system can detect the access state of US-100 accurately, and the message on the access state of US-100 can be fed back to the host computer in time. When the US-100 accessed the system normally (see the Number 1), the system can get the US-100 data effectively, and implemented the distance measurement function. When the US-100 accessed the system abnormally (see the Number 2, 3, 4, 5), the system no longer gets the US-100 data this work cycle, but replace this US-100 data with "9999". No matter the US-100 accesses the system normally or abnormally, the structural integrity and operable of the system data were excellent, and the system runs well.

M-8729 and US-100 are the typical of serial port sensor modules in two different types, and their access state can be detected with the serial port sensor module ASD proposed in this paper. The test results show that the serial port sensor module ASD is applicable to the micro control systems based on microcontrollers and serial port modules. We also compare the basic performance parameters of micro control system with serial port sensor module ASD with that without serial port sensor module ASD, and the results are shown in Table 3.

From the Table 3, we can see that, with the serial port sensor module ASD (see the Number 1, 2), no matter the serial port sensor module accesses micro control system normally or abnormally, the access state of it can be detected correctly, the message on

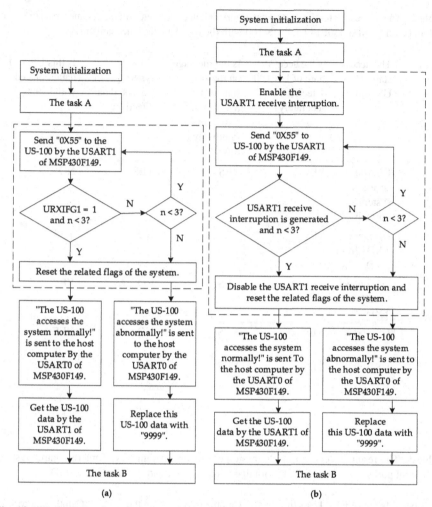

Fig. 10. Work mechanism of system based on MSP430F149 and US-100: (a) the access state of US-100 is detected by examining the URXIFG1 of MSP430F149; (b) the access state of US-100 is detected by examining the USART1 receive interruption of MSP430F149.

the access state of serial port module can be fed back to the host computer intuitively in time, and the system can take effective measures for data processing instantaneously. But the micro control system can only take effective measures for data processing instantaneously when the serial port sensor module accesses micro control system normally without the serial port sensor module ASD (see the Number 3, 4).

The serial port sensor module ASD method is tested successfully by being applied to two common micro control systems. According to the test results (see the Tables 1, 2, 3), with the serial port sensor module ASD safeguarded by the ERSE and ESSE, the micro control system can detect the access state of serial port sensor module correctly and

Table 2. The test results for the several basic performance parameters of the distance measurement system based on MSP430F149 and US-100 with the two detection mechanisms.

Number	The access state of US-100	Is the access state of US-100 detected accurately?	Is the message on the access state of US-100 fed back to the host computer intuitively in time?	Does the system get the US-100 data effectively?	Is this US-100 data replaced with "9999"?
1	US-100 accesses system normally	YES	YES	YES	NO
2	Disconnect TXD1 from RXD	YES	YES	NO	YES
3	Disconnect RXD1 from TXD	YES	YES	NO	YES
4	US-100 is powered off	YES	YES	NO	YES
5	US-100 is broken	YES	YES	NO	YES

Table 3. The results of comparing the basic performance parameters of micro control system with serial port sensor module ASD with that without serial port sensor module ASD.

Number	Is the serial port sensor module ASD applied to the micro control system?	Does the serial port sensor module access the micro control system normally?	Can the micro control system detect the access state of serial port sensor module correctly?	Can the message on the access state of serial port module be fed back to the host computer intuitively in time?	Can the micro control system take effective measures for data processing instantaneously?
1	YES	YES	YES	YES	YES
2	YES	NO	YES	YES	YES
3	NO	YES	NO	NO	YES
4	NO	NO	NO	NO	NO

take effective measures instantaneously, and the comprehensive performance of micro control system is improved.

6   Conclusions

With the serial port sensor module ASD, the micro control system can detect the access state of serial port sensor module accurately, and take effective measures. The micro control system can detect the access state of the serial port sensor module by examining the serial port receive flag of microcontroller, or by examining the serial port receive interruption of microcontroller, and can feed back the message on the access state of serial port sensor module to the host computer intuitively in time. When the serial port sensor module accesses the system normally, the system can get the sensor module data effectively, and implements the intended function. And when the serial port sensor module accesses the system abnormally, the system no longer gets the sensor module data in current work cycle, and replace this sensor module data with the data which is specified by system. The serial port sensor module ASD is simple and useful, and with it, the micro control system avoids the adverse effects come from the abnormal access state of serial port sensor module, runs more steadily and reliably, and the comprehensive performance of micro control system is improved effectively.

Fundings. The author(s) disclosed receipt of the following financial support for the research, authorship and/or publication of this: This research was funded by the Natural Science Foundation of Qinghai Normal University with grant number 2018zr009 and the National Natural Science Foundation of China with grant number 61761040.

References

1. Arbabpour Bidgoli, M., Golroo, A., Sheikhzadeh Nadjar, H., et al.: Road roughness measurement using a cost-effective sensor-based monitoring system. Autom. Constr. **104**, 140–152 (2019)
2. Holler, D., Vaghetto, R., Hassan, Y.: Water temperature measurements with a Rayleigh backscatter distributed sensor. Opt. Fiber Technol. **55**, 102160 (2020)
3. Deng, F., Zuo, P., Wen, K., et al.: Novel soil environment monitoring system based on RFID sensor and LoRa. Comput. Electron. Agric. **169**, 105169 (2020)
4. Barkunan, S.R., Bhanumathi, V., Balakrishnan, V.: Automatic irrigation system with rain fall detection in agricultural field. Measurement **156**, 107552 (2020)
5. Krzysztof, B., Artur, R., Andrzej, M.: The use of low-cost sensors for air quality analysis in road intersections. Transp. Res. Part D: Trans. Environ **77**, 198–211 (2019)
6. Surantha, N., Wicaksono, W.R.: Design of smart home security system using object recognition and PIR sensor. Procedia Comput. Sci. **135**, 465–472 (2018)
7. Salahinejad, E., Eslami-Farsani, R., Tayebi, L.: Corrosion failure analysis of printed circuit boards exposed to H 2 S-containing humid environments. Eng. Fail. Anal. **79**, 538–546 (2017)
8. Xiao, K., Gao, X., Yan, L., et al.: Atmospheric corrosion factors of printed circuit boards in a dry-heat desert environment: salty dust and diurnal temperature difference. Chem. Eng. J. **336**, 92–101 (2018)
9. Jirui, W., et al.: Influence of atmospheric particulates on initial corrosion behavior of printed circuit board in pollution environments. Appl. Surface Sci. **467–468**, 889–901 (2019)

10. Niu, G., Xiong, L., Qin, X., et al.: Fault detection isolation and diagnosis of multi-axle speed sensors for high-speed trains. Mech. Syst. Signal Process. **131**, 183–198 (2019)
11. Qizhi, H., Zhang, W., Lu, P., et al.: Performance comparison of representative model-based fault reconstruction algorithms for aircraft sensor fault detection and diagnosis. Aerosp. Sci. Technol. **98**, 105649 (2020)
12. Abbaspour, A., Aboutalebi, P., Yen, K.K., et al.: Neural adaptive observer-based sensor and actuator fault detection in nonlinear systems: application in UAV. ISA Trans. **67**, 317–329 (2017)
13. Guo, D., Wang, Y., Maiying, Z.Y., et al.: Fault detection and isolation for unmanned aerial vehicle sensors by using extended PMI filter. IFAC PapersOnLine **51**(24), 818–823 (2018)
14. Zhong, Y., Zhang, Y., Zhang, W., et al.: Actuator and sensor fault detection and diagnosis for unmanned quadrotor helicopters. IFAC PapersOnLine **51**(24), 998–1003 (2018)
15. Saha, S., Roy, T.K., Mahmud, M.A., et al.: Sensor fault and cyber attack resilient operation of DC microgrids. Int. J. Electr. Power Energy Syst. **99**, 540–554 (2018)
16. Haes Alhelou, H., Hamedani Golshan, M.E., Askari-Marnani, J.: Robust sensor fault detection and isolation scheme for interconnected smart power systems in presence of RER and EVs using unknown input observer. Int. J. Electr. Power Energy Syst. **99**, 682–694 (2018)
17. Li, J., Pan, K., Su, Q.: Sensor fault detection and estimation for switched power electronics systems based on sliding mode observer. Appl. Math. Comput. **353**, 282–294 (2019)
18. Adnane, A., Foitih, Z.A., Mohammed, M.A.S., et al.: Real-time sensor fault detection and isolation for LEO satellite attitude estimation through magnetometer data. Adv. Space Res. **61**(4), 1143–1157 (2018)
19. Nasrolahi, S.S., Abdollahi, F.: Sensor fault detection and recovery in satellite attitude control. Acta Astronaut. **145**, 275–283 (2018)
20. Verrelli, C.M., Lorenzani, E., Fornari, R., et al.: Steady-state speed sensor fault detection in induction motors with uncertain parameters: a matter of algebraic equations. Control Eng. Pract. **80**, 125–137 (2018)
21. Rkhissi, Y., Ghommam, J., Boukhnifer, M., et al.: Two current sensor fault detection and isolation schemes for induction motor drives using algebraic estimation approach. Math. Comput. Simul. (2018)
22. Couto, L.D., Kinnaert, M.: Internal and sensor fault detection and isolation for Li-ion batteries. IFAC PapersOnLine **51**(24), 1431–1438 (2018)
23. Zhen, C., Chen, Z., Huang, D.: Fault diagnosis of voltage sensor and current sensor for lithium-ion battery pack using hybrid system modeling and unscented particle filter. Energy **191**, 116504 (2020)
24. Jimmy, L.C., Juan, J.C.Z., Efraín, M.L.: Sensor nodes fault detection for agricultural wireless sensor networks based on NMF. Comput. Electron. Agric. **161**, 214–224 (2019)
25. Swain, R.R., Dash, T., Khilar, P.M.: A complete diagnosis of faulty sensor modules in a wireless sensor network. Ad Hoc Netw. **93**, 101924 (2019)
26. Xu, X., Wang, W., Zou, N., et al.: A comparative study of sensor fault diagnosis methods based on observer for ECAS system. Mech. Syst. Signal Process. **87**(Part B), 169–183 (2017)
27. Navi, M., Meskin, N., Davoodi, M.: Sensor fault detection and isolation of an industrial gas turbine using partial adaptive KPCA. J. Process Control **64**(21), 37–48 (2018)
28. Zhang, H., Chen, H., Guo, Y., et al.: Sensor fault detection and diagnosis for a water source heat pump air-conditioning system based on PCA and preprocessed by combined clustering. Appl. Therm. Eng. **160**, 114098 (2019)
29. Li, L., Liu, G., Zhang, L., et al.: Sensor fault detection with generalized likelihood ratio and correlation coefficient for bridge SHM. J. Sound Vib. **442**, 445–458 (2019)
30. Xu, C., Zhao, S., Liu, F.: Sensor fault detection and diagnosis in the presence of outliers. Neurocomputing **349**, 156–163 (2019)

31. M-8729 DataSheet. https://download.csdn.net/download/wangchunfeng/5080052. Accessed 12 Mar 2020
32. Instructions on US-100. https://www.docin.com/p-356658570.html?_t_t_t=0.281875516658 72035. Accessed 12 Mar 2020
33. MSP430F149 Datasheet (PDF) - Texas Instruments. https://pdf1.alldatasheet.com/datasheet-pdf/view/82012/TI/MSP430F149.html. Accessed 12 Mar 2020

Image Fine-Grained for Non-uniform Scenes Deblurring

Qing Qi[✉]

Qinghai MinZu University, Xining, China
qiqing@tju.edu.cn

Abstract. Recently, image deblurring has been made advanced progress by various priors and networks. However, it still has room for promoting the image quality of deblurred images, such as details and visual effects of latent images. Therefore, we present an image deblurring method for non-uniform scene deblurring based on image fine-grained strategy. Specifically, we develop building blocks of multi-path fusion blocks (MPFB) and enhancement scale attention modules (ESAM) to recover the fine-grained features of the deblurred image as much as possible. Moreover, we propose multiple loss functions to optimize network training and promote convergence. To demonstrate the effectiveness of the proposed method, subjective and objective comparison experiments are conducted on different datasets. Our method surpasses state-of-the-art (SOTA) methods on synthetic datasets and real images.

Keywords: Non-uniform scenes · Image deblurring · Fine-grained deblurring

1 Introduction

High-quality images not only present pleasant visual effects for people but also have significant value in practical application. However, in the process of imaging, due to camera shake, object motion, and other complex factors, images are inevitably blurred and degraded.

Since the image deblurring task is highly ill-posed, it is challenging to estimate kernels and compute latent images. Generally, traditional methods exploit various related priors [1–3, 12–14, 30] to estimate kernels and then adopt off-the-shelf deconvolution methods to obtain deblurred images. However, those priors may not always suitable for solving the realistic and challenging dynamic scene deblurring problem. By contrast, to mitigate the potential effects of the "kernel estimation-deconvolution" operation, the learning-based methods are adopted for investigating the blurry degraded process in a data-driven manner. Early learning-based methods [20, 27] respectively employ a single Convolutional Neural Network (CNN) to predict blur kernels in pixel-level and non-blind deconvolution algorithms to obtain deblurred images. Methods [15, 16] utilize multiple CNNs to estimate latent images directly. Although learning-based methods and traditional methods have their advantages, accumulated errors are amplified by

© ICST Institute for Computer Sciences, Social Informatics and Telecommunications Engineering 2021
Published by Springer Nature Switzerland AG 2021. All Rights Reserved
X. Wang et al. (Eds.): AICON 2021, LNICST 397, pp. 244–256, 2021.
https://doi.org/10.1007/978-3-030-90199-8_23

separately estimated kernels and latent images in a blended learning manner. Lately, inspired by end-to-end training manner, methods [8, 9, 11, 21, 33] build networks to recover deblurred images from the degraded observations. However, the multi-scale framework has several limitations. First, the multi-scale network structure tends to be over-fitting at a specific scale. Second, multi-scale networks focus on the dependencies between the scales rather than the corresponding relationship between the original input and the clean counterpart.

Very recently, inspired by Generative Adversarial Network (GAN) [34], image deblurring task [17, 18, 25] can be reconsidered as an image translation problem that transforming blurry images into sharp ones. Existing image deblurring methods obtain image features with various priors. However, fine-grained details of deblurred images have not been considered. In order to solve this limitation, the dependence of scale context information as well as large receptive fields of images is taken into account. Therefore, we investigate a network based on the fine-grained strategy to facilitate the visual quality of deblurred images.

The main contributions of this paper are presented as follows:

Firstly, we propose a GAN for image deblurring with MPFB and enhancement scale attention modules. The proposed network has the ability to provide favorable features that can be employed to generate deblurred images with fine-grained details.

Secondly, we introduce the multi-path fusion block to learn fine-grained features. It provides additional flexibility in dealing with details of blurry images.

Third, we develop an enhancement scale attention module to emphasize scale attention information to enhance the representational ability of the proposed network.

Finally, experimental results show that the proposed method can produce high-quality deblurred images compared with state-of-the-art (SOTA) methods.

The rest chapters of this paper are organized as follows. The related work is described in Sect. 2. The proposed method is introduced in Sect. 3. Section 4 presents datasets, experimental settings, as well as image deblurring performance. Finally, this paper is concluded in Sect. 5.

2 Related Work

In recent years, a great deal of image deblurring methods have been proposed. We mainly introduce image deblurring methods from aspects of traditional segmentation-based methods and learning-based methods.

Traditional Segmentation-Based Methods. Dynamic blurry scenes are spatially varied in pixel-level, and solutions for the uniform blurry task may not fit for the complicated dynamic scene task. According to blurry regions in a dynamic scene, Kim et al. [5] adopt an image segmentation method to separate blurry regions and then deal with each of them respectively. However, motion segmentation segments cannot accurately separate blurry regions. Since the limitation of the method [5], Kim and Lee [6] propose an alternative segmentation-free approach by exploiting the deblurring strategy locally linearly to solve this challenging task. This scheme avoids drawbacks bring by inaccurate segmentation. However, the dynamic blurry scene is spatially varied in pixel-level in extreme cases.

Especially, when object motion and camera shake simultaneously occur in the imaging process. As a compromise, Pan et al. [7] propose a method based on the segmentation confidence map for enhancing the segmentation accuracy of different regions of the degraded images.

Learning-Based Methods. In recent years, deep learning has been applied in computer vision fields, such as [38–43], since it was proposed. Because of the strong feature extraction ability of CNN, it has been fully employed in the image deblurring task. Early learning-based image deblurring algorithms can be categorized as the following situations: (1) Multiple CNNs are constructed [15, 16] to achieve kernel estimation and non-blind deconvolution, so as to obtain deblurring images; (2) CNNs can be used to estimate the information of kernels, and then deconvolution algorithms can be adopted to get latent images. However, kernels are estimated by CNNs are limited to local linear blurs, which cannot reveal the essence of image blur well.

To overcome the limitations of the above algorithms, researchers further propose an end-to-end learning manner to directly construct the essential relationship between blurry and clean images. Nah et al. [8] follow the "coarse-to-fine" image deblurring strategy and propose a multi-scale deblurring method. Although the multi-scale network reduces the difficulty of image deblurring by a divide-and-conquer manner, weight parameters of multiple scales are independent, and each scale of the network only deals with the image of the current resolution. Based on the literature [8], Tao et al. [21] propose a multi-scale CNN with shared parameters. On the one hand, this network takes advantage of the dependence of weight parameters among multi-scales; On the other hand, it can reduce network parameters and stabilize network optimization. In order to acquire high-dimensional feature representations, Gao et al. [10] proposed an image deblurring method based on selective parameter sharing and nested connections, which can effectively extract high-order nonlinear features. Furthermore, Zhang et al. [19] propose an image deblurring method based on Recurrent Neural Network (RNN) to learn the high-dimensional features used in image reconstruction and deblurring by indirectly expanding receptive fields. However, image deblurring algorithms based on CNN do not consider the semantic information between blurry images and clean images.

GAN [34] is a machine learning architecture proposed by Ian Goodfellow in 2014. GAN has been applied in the computer vision community. Inspired by CycleGAN [36], image deblurring can be considered as an image translation task by translating blurry degraded input to the blurry-free one. Since the highly unstable property of GAN, it is difficult to simultaneously train two pairs of GAN models. Furthermore, directly transfer this recycling framework to image deblurring task unsurprisingly generates poor results. Nimisha [25] propose a GAN for tackling class-specific image deblurring task with unsupervised fashion. Due to a lack of ground truths, they utilize blurry images themselves to guide the network to acquire image color information. Kupyn et al. [17] develop a conditional GAN named DeblurGAN. They propose a content loss to capture the semantic correspondence difference between blurry images and corresponding ground truths. Lately, to satisfy the different requirements of real-time processing and deblurring performance, Kupyn et al. [18] propose three models with feature pyramid network architecture. By contrast, we propose a multi-path attention network to acquire non-local information rather than local feature achieved by receptive fields. The proposed network jointly estimates the image content, salient structures, and fine details for solving non-uniform image deblurring.

3 Proposed Method

3.1 Network Architecture

In Fig. 1, we specially tailor an architecture for the challenging non-uniform scenes deblurring.

Generator. In the proposed network, the generator is adopted to map degraded blurry images to clean counterparts. In the part of image encoding, the blurry degraded inputs are spatially compressed and encoded. Correspondingly, in the part of image decoding, the decoded feature representations of blurry images are available for recovering deblurred images. Afterward, 5 MPFB arrange in the residual form are appended. Furthermore, we integrate ESAM into skip connections to bridge the semantic gap between encoded features and corresponding decoded features. Improved skip connections make the network easier to optimize. Finally, decoded features are activated by a Tanh function to obtain the deblurred image. Specific structures and parameters of the proposed model are shown in Fig. 1. Next, we particularly introduce two backbones of MPFB and ESAM.

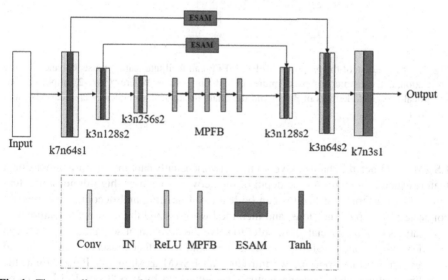

Fig. 1. The overall structure of the generator in the proposed GAN-based network. Where "Conv" implies a convolutional layer, indicates element-wise sum operation, "IN" denotes instance normalization, "ReLU" implies ReLU activation function, "Tanh" implies Tanh activation function, "k" is the kernel size, "n" indicates the number of feature maps, and "s" is the stride.

MPFB. For the image deblurring problem, it requires large receptive fields to capture more features for deblurred images recovery. Therefore, stacking more convolution layers is a straightforward approach. However, this idea is not feasible, since the overly deep network discourages gradient backpropagation and network convergence. To recover fine-grained features of deblurred images as much as possible, we develop MPFB, as shown in Fig. 2. Specifically, the first convolution layer on the left of MPFB progressively reduces the feature dimensions to 64 × 64, afterwards these enhanced features are passed to four branches to extract fine-grained features by using convolutions with different dilation factors. More importantly, the acquired fine-grained features are further integrated and enhanced between every two different branches by the element-wise summation operation and another convolutional layer. Finally, all fine-grained feature representations are processed and fused. In addition, the kernel size of all convolution layers is 3 × 3, and each convolutional layer is followed by IN and ReLU activation function [29].

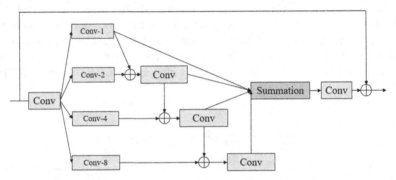

Fig. 2. The pipeline of the proposed MPFB. MPFB can facilitate feature reuse, enhance feature correlation, and construct complex features in high dimensions. Where "Conv-2" implies a convolutional layer with kernels of 3 × 3 and the dilation rate of 2, ⊕ indicates element-wise sum operation.

ESAM. In U-net, the shallow layer of the network usually captures the low-dimensional features such as texture. As the depth of the network increases, high-dimensional features of characteristic structures can be learned. Encoding and decoding features are connected by skip connections, and then the low-order and the high-order feature representations can be associated. In order to solve the problem of semantic gaps between encoded and decoded feature representations, and to further preserve significant and suppress irrelevant responses, we introduce an ESAM as shown in Fig. 3. First, the encoding features and decoding features are enhanced by two "Conv-ReLU" layers; Second, the enhanced feature are fused by element-wise summation; Afterward, features pass through three "Conv-ReLU" layers; Finally, the enhanced fusion features are obtained by a "Conv-IN-Sigmoid" layer.

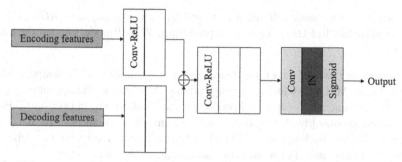

Fig. 3. The structure of the proposed ESAM. ESAM is designed for incorporating it into the generator for highlight clean features that are passed through skip connections. Where "Conv-ReLU" indicates a convolutional layer followed by ReLU function, "Sigmoid" represents Sigmoid activation function.

Discriminator. Unlike high-level computer vision processing, the sharpness judgment of an image depends on local features of the image. Thus, we adopt PatchGAN [35] for the discriminator D, rather than a general full-image discriminator. Details descriptions of PatchGAN [35] will not be repeated.

3.2 Loss Functions

We employ four loss functions of reconstruction loss, content loss, edge loss, and adversarial loss to constrain the entire GAN framework. In this paper, and weight coefficients of each constraint item are constrained as: $\alpha = 1, \beta = 10, \lambda = 12, \gamma = 1$. Each loss function is illustrated in detail as follows.

$$L(G, D) = \alpha L_{reconstruction} + \beta L_{content} + \lambda L_{edge} + \gamma L_{adv}(G, D) \tag{1}$$

Content Loss. The purpose of introducing $L_{content}$ [22] is to make the generated image and clean image consistent in terms of high-level semantic and perceptual differences, which can facilitate network optimization and improve the visual effect of the generated images. The pre-trained VGG19 model [28] has been proved to have good structure preservation ability. In this paper, we exploit the pre-trained VGG19 model to extract the perceptual features of the generated image and the clear image respectively, and the difference between them is calculated by solving the L_2 norm. The mathematical expression of $L_{content}$ is shown as follows:

$$L_{content} = \frac{1}{CWH} \sum_{x=1}^{W} \sum_{y=1}^{H} \left\| \phi(s_k)_{x,y} - \phi(G(b_k))_{x,y} \right\|_2 \tag{2}$$

where s_k and $G(b_k)$ indicate the clean image and the generated image; C, W, and H denote numbers, heights, and widths of feature representations respectively; ϕ is the feature map obtained by the activated convolutional within the pre-trained VGG19 network.

We regularize the semantic difference of s_k and $G(b_k)$ via $\|\phi(s_k)_{x,y} - \phi(G(b_k))_{x,y}\|_2$. Here, we chose the "ReLU3–2" layer in the pre-trained VGG19 model to extract semantic features.

Reconstruction Loss. Most of the learning-based methods mainly adopted Mean Squared Error (MSE) loss for optimizing training. MSE drives the appearance similarity between generated images and corresponding ground-truths at pixel-level. However, results optimized by MSE produce an over-smooth phenomenon. In this paper, we employ Mean Absolute Error (MAE) loss for facilitating the sparsity of deblurred images. The mathematical expression of $L_{reconstruction}$ is shown as follows:

$$L_{reconstruction} = \frac{1}{WH} \sum_{x=1}^{W} \sum_{y=1}^{H} \|L_1(s_k)_{x,y} - L_1(G(b_k))_{x,y}\| \tag{3}$$

Edge Loss. The purpose of L_{edge} is to drive the generated image to have significant structural features. The consistency of edges information between the generated image and the clean image in horizontal and vertical directions is achieved through solving L_1 norm. The mathematical expression is as follows:

$$L_{edge} = \frac{1}{WH} \sum_{x=1}^{W} \sum_{y=1}^{H} \left[\|\nabla_h(s_k)_{x,y} - \nabla_h(G(b_k))_{x,y}\|_1 + \|\nabla_v(s_k)_{x,y} - \nabla_v(G(b_k))_{x,y}\|_1 \right] \tag{4}$$

where ∇_h and ∇_v imply gradient operations in horizontal and vertical directions, respectively.

Adversarial Loss. The purpose of $L_{adv}(G, D)$ is to maximize the probability of assigning correct labels to the generated image and the clean image so that the generator can correctly convert the blurry image into the blurry-free one. WGAN-GP [32] is demonstrated to be more stable with the generator. We also exploit it as the critic function to stabilize optimization training. The mathematical expression of adversarial loss function is as follows:

$$L_{GAN} = E[D(G(b_k))] - E[D(s_k)] + \eta E_{\hat{x} \sim p_{\hat{x}}}[(\|\nabla \hat{x} D(\hat{x})\|_2 - 1)^2] \tag{5}$$

where $E[D(G(b_k))]$ implicates the expectation that the generated image is false, $E[D(s_k)]$ expresses the expectation that the clean image is true, $\eta E_{\hat{x} \sim p_{\hat{x}}}[(\|\nabla \hat{x} D(\hat{x})\|_2 - 1)^2]$ denotes a sample uniformly sampled on the line between s_k and $G(b_k)$.

4 Experiments

In this section, datasets and implementation details are elaborately introduced in Sect. 4.1 and Sect. 4.2. Then, we qualitatively and quantitatively compare the results of the proposed method with SOTA methods on synthetic and real datasets in Sect. 4.3.

4.1 Datasets

In this paper, we utilize standard datasets of GOPRO [8], Köhler [23], and Lai [24] to train and test the proposed model.

GOPRO. The GOPRO dataset consists of 3214 pairs of blurry images and clean images with a resolution of 1280 × 720. Among them, 2103 pairs of images are used as the training dataset, and the remaining images are used as the test dataset.

Köhler. The dataset of Köhler set up an experimental environment for recording the motion trajectory of the six-dimensional camera and record a series of clear photos by sampling the motion trajectory of the six-dimensional camera. The Köhler dataset consists of 4 clean images and each clean image corresponds to 12 blurry degraded images. In total, the dataset consists of 48 blurry images.

Lai. In 2016, Lai et al. develop a dataset [24] for validating the performance of image deblurring methods, which include two synthetic datasets and one real dataset. Images in the real dataset include natural images, class-specific images, and so on.

4.2 Experimental Setting

Training Details. The hardware configuration of experiments is as follows: the operating system is Unbuntu 14.04, the deep learning framework is PyTorch, and the hardware configuration is NVIDIA 1080Ti, Intel(R) Core(TM) i7 CPU (16G RAM). Adam optimizer [31] is adopted to perform network optimization training, where $\beta1$ and $\beta2$ are set as values of 0.5 and 0.999, respectively. The learning rate of the generator and the discriminator are both 0.0001, and the batch size is 4. During the training process, the generator is updated once, and the discriminator is updated 5 times.

Quality Measures. We employ quantitative evaluation metrics in terms of Peak Signal to Noise Ratio (PSNR), and Structural Similarity Index (SSIM) [37] to demonstrate the robustness and effectiveness of our method.

4.3 Comparisons with SOTA Methods

We select several representative learning-based methods for comparison. Gong [20] and Sun [27] replace the operator of kernels estimation in the traditional deblurring framework with a data-driven manner. [4] and [8] are CNNs-based methods. Furthermore, GANs-based methods of [17] and [18] are also taken into account. We reproduce these image deblurring methods with default settings and parameters provided by the authors.

Results on Synthesis Dataset. Quantitative values of the proposed network and SOTA methods on synthesis datasets of GOPRO are displayed in Table 1. In Table 1, our method achieves the best performance on PSNR and SSIM, which surpasses the second place 0.41 dB and 0.01 respectively. As shown in Fig. 4, the deblurred result obtained by the proposed model is competent for removing the blur on the degraded inputs and restoring the clean appearance. We can observe that SOTA deblurring methods have disadvantages. Due to the inaccurate kernels estimation operations, the results of Sun [27] and Gong [20] lead to indiscriminate blurry results. Though Nah [8] build a multi-scale CNN network over 120 convolution layers, they are incompetent at solving blurry scenes caused by extreme camera shake. DeblurGAN [17] construct a Resblocks-based CNN, but it is incapable of handling extremely camera shake blur. As an advanced version of it, DeblurGAN-v2 [18] has some deblurring performance, however the deblurred image still has blurry effects.

Table 1. Performance comparison with SOTA methods evaluated by quantitative assessment of PSNR (dB) and SSIM. We calculate average values on synthetic datasets of GOPRO and Köhler.

	GOPRO		Köhler	
	PSNR	SSIM	PSNR	SSIM
Sun [27]	18.7062	0.5391	18.5892	0.5371
Gong [20]	27.2778	0.8187	21.3371	0.6590
Nah [8]	28.3225	0.8588	20.8507	0.6340
Mustaniemi [4]	25.9563	0.8285	20.4833	0.6442
Kupyn [17]	25.2363	0.7773	19.0843	0.5838
Kupyn [18]	27.8086	0.8664	21.2987	0.6544
Ours	28.7373	0.8714	21.3632	0.6575

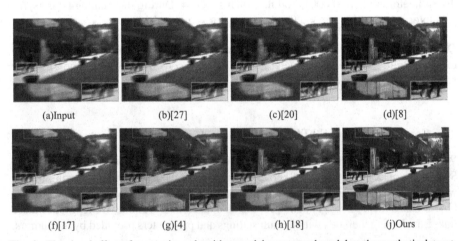

(a)Input   (b)[27]   (c)[20]   (d)[8]

(f)[17]   (g)[4]   (h)[18]   (j)Ours

Fig. 4. The visual effect of comparison algorithms and the proposed model on the synthetic dataset of GOPRO [8]. This method has satisfactory visual effects and good details.

Results on Real-World Dataset. Although our model has been evaluated on synthetic blurry datasets and achieved decent results, real blurry images are usually caused by more complex reasons. To further verify the effectiveness and generalization of the developed model, the dataset of Lai [24] is used as test dataset for this part. Figure 5 and Fig. 6 show two groups of results of comparison algorithms and our model on [24] respectively.

Method [27] conducts a non-blind deconvolution algorithm to obtain latent images, consequently, the accurate estimated kernels result in the latent images with blurry visual effects. It is demonstrated that separately estimate the kernels and latent images breaks the overall consideration of image deblurring strategy. Consistent with the performance on synthetic datasets, methods of [17] and [18] have weak generalization on real-world images. In comparison, benefiting from MPFB and ESAM, the proposed network has excellent performance and visual pleasant effect even in the challenging low-light condition.

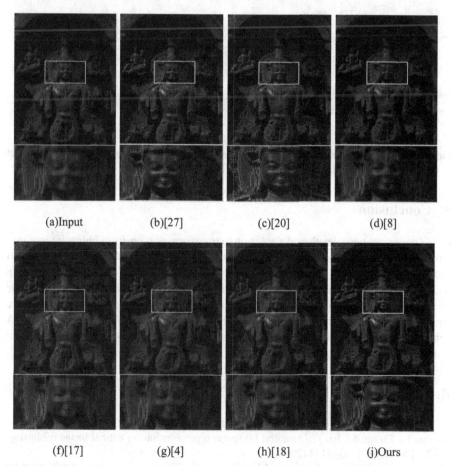

Fig. 5. The visual effect of comparison algorithms and the proposed model on the synthetic dataset of Lai [24]. This method has satisfactory visual effects and good details.

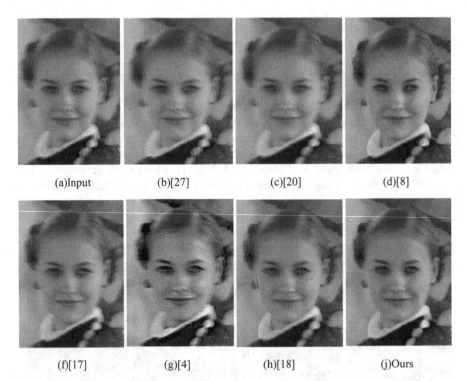

| (a)Input | (b)[27] | (c)[20] | (d)[8] |

| (f)[17] | (g)[4] | (h)[18] | (j)Ours |

Fig. 6. The visual effect of comparison algorithms and the proposed model on the synthetic dataset of Lai [24]. This method has satisfactory visual effects and good details.

5   Conclusion

In this paper, we have developed a solution to transform non-uniform blurry images into blurry-free counterparts. We introduce a network that includes building blocks of MPFB and ESAM to learn fine-grained feature representations as well as effective loss function which consists of reconstruction loss, content loss, and edge loss. To demonstrate the robustness of the proposed network, subjective and objective comparison experiments are conduct on different synthetic image datasets and real images. Comparing with SOTA deblurring methods, our model achieves satisfactory quantitative values and pleasant visual effects.

References

1. Cho, S., Lee, S.: Fast motion deblurring. ACM Trans. Graph. **145** (2009)
2. Xu, L., Zheng, S., Jia, J.: Unnatural L0 sparse representation for natural image deblurring. In: CVPR, pp. 1107–1114 (2013)
3. Pan, J., Sun, D., Pfister, H., Yang, M.H.: Blind image deblurring using dark channel prior. In: CVPR, pp. 1628–1636 (2016)
4. Mustaniemi, J., Kannala, J., Sarkka, S., et al.: Gyroscope-aided motion deblurring with deep networks. arXiv: Computer Vision and Pattern Recognition (2018).

5. Hyun Kim, T., Ahn, B., Mu Lee, K.: Dynamic scene deblurring. In: CVPR, pp. 3160–3167 (2013)
6. Hyun Kim, T., Mu Lee, K.: Segmentation-free dynamic scene deblurring. In: CVPR, pp. 2766–2773 (2014)
7. Pan, J., Hu, Z., Su, Z., Lee, H.Y., Yang, M.H.: Soft-segmentation guided object motion deblurring. In: CVPR, pp. 459–468 (2016)
8. Nah, S., Kim, T.H., Lee, K.M.: Deep multi-scale convolutional neural network for dynamic scene deblurring. In: CVPR, pp. 257–265 (2017)
9. Hradiš, M., Kotera, J., Zemcí, P., Sroubek, F.: Convolutional neural networks for direct text deblurring. In: BMVC (2015)
10. Gao, H., Tao, X., Shen, X., et al.: Dynamic scene deblurring with parameter selective sharing and nested skip connections. In: CVPR, pp. 3848–3856. IEEE Computer Society, Long Beach (2019)
11. Jin, M., Hirsch, M., Favaro, P.: Learning face deblurring fast and wide. In: CVPR Workshops, pp. 745–753 (2018)
12. Zhang, H., Yang, J., Zhang, Y., Huang, T.S.: Sparse representation based blind image deblurring. In: ICME, pp. 1–6 (2011)
13. Sun, L., Cho, S., Wang, J., Hays, J.: Edge-based blur kernel estimation using patch priors. In: ICCP, pp. 1–8 (2013)
14. Ren, W., Cao, X., Pan, J., Guo, X., Zuo, W., Yang, M.H.: Image deblurring via enhanced low-rank prior. TIP **25**, 3426–3437 (2016)
15. Chakrabarti, A.: A neural approach to blind motion deblurring. In: Leibe, B., Matas, J., Sebe, N., Welling, M. (eds.) ECCV 2016. LNCS, vol. 9907, pp. 221–235. Springer, Cham (2016). https://doi.org/10.1007/978-3-319-46487-9_14
16. Schuler, C.J., Hirsch, M., Harmeling, S., Schölkopf, B.: Learning to deblur. TPAMI **38**, 1439–1451 (2016)
17. Kupyn, O., Budzan, V., Mykhailych, M., Mishkin, D., Matas, J.: DeblurGAN: blind motion deblurring using conditional adversarial networks. In: CVPR, pp. 8183–8192 (2018)
18. Kupyn, O., Martyniuk, T., Wu, J., Wang, Z.Y.: DeblurGAN-v2: deblurring (ordersof-magnitude) faster and better. In: ICCV, pp. 8878–8887 (2019)
19. Zhang, J., Pan, J., Ren, J., et al.: Dynamic scene deblurring using spatially variant recurrent neural networks. In: CVPR, pp. 2521–2529. IEEE Computer Society, Salt Lake City (2018)
20. Gong, D., Yang, J., Liu, L., Zhang, Y., et al.: From motion blur to motion flow: a deep learning solution for removing heterogeneous motion blur. In: CVPR, pp. 3806–3815 (2017)
21. Tao, X., Gao, H., Shen, X., Wang, J., Jia, J.: Scale-recurrent network for deep image deblurring. In: CVPR, pp. 8174C-8182 (2018)
22. Johnson, J., Alahi, A., Fei-Fei, L.: Perceptual losses for real-time style transfer and super-resolution. In: Leibe, B., Matas, J., Sebe, N., Welling, M. (eds.) ECCV 2016. LNCS, vol. 9906, pp. 694–711. Springer, Cham (2016). https://doi.org/10.1007/978-3-319-46475-6_43
23. Köhler, R., Hirsch, M., Mohler, B., Schölkopf, B., Harmeling, S.: Recording and playback of camera shake: benchmarking blind deconvolution with a real-world database. In: Fitzgibbon, A., Lazebnik, S., Perona, P., Sato, Y., Schmid, C. (eds.) ECCV 2012. LNCS, vol. 7578, pp. 27–40. Springer, Heidelberg (2012). https://doi.org/10.1007/978-3-642-33786-4_3
24. Lai, W.S., Huang, J.B., Hu, Z., Ahuja, N., Yang, M.H.: A comparative study for single image blind deblurring. In CVPR, pp. 1701–1709 (2016)
25. Madam, N.T., Kumar, S., Rajagopalan, A.N.: Unsupervised class-specific deblurring. In: Ferrari, V., Hebert, M., Sminchisescu, C., Weiss, Y. (eds.) ECCV 2018. LNCS, vol. 11214, pp. 358–374. Springer, Cham (2018). https://doi.org/10.1007/978-3-030-01249-6_22
26. Lee, Y., Hwang, J., Lee, S., et al.: An energy and GPU-computation efficient backbone network for real-time object detection. In CVPR (2019)

27. Sun, J., Cao, W., Xu, Z., Ponce, J.: Learning a convolutional neural network for non-uniform motion blur removal. In: CVPR, pp. 769–777 (2015)
28. Simonyan, K., Zisserman, A.: A very deep convolutional networks for large-scale image recognition. ArXiv, arXiv:1409.1556 (2014)
29. Maas, A.L., Hannun, A.Y., Ng, A.Y.: Rectifier nonlinearities improve neural network acoustic models. In: ICML, p. 3 (2013)
30. Xu, L., Jia, J.: Two-phase kernel estimation for robust motion deblurring. In: Daniilidis, K., Maragos, P., Paragios, N. (eds.) ECCV 2010. LNCS, vol. 6311, pp. 157–170. Springer, Heidelberg (2010). https://doi.org/10.1007/978-3-642-15549-9_12
31. Kingma, D.P., Ba, J.: Adam: a method for stochastic optimization. ArXiv, arXiv:1412.6980 (2014)
32. Gulrajani, I., Ahmed, F., Arjovsky, M., et al.: Improved training of Wasserstein GANs. ArXiv, arXiv:1704.00028 (2017)
33. Mao, X., Shen, C., Yang, Y.B.: Image restoration using very deep convolutional encoder-decoder networks with symmetric skip connections. In: NIPS, pp. 2802–2810 (2016)
34. Goodfellow, I., et al.: Generative adversarial nets. In: NIPS, pp. 2672–2680 (2014)
35. Isola, P., Zhu, J.Y., Zhou, T., Efros, A.A.: Image-to-image translation with conditional adversarial networks. In: CVPR, pp. 1125–1134 (2017)
36. Zhu, J.Y., Park, T., Isola, P., Efros, A.A.: Unpaired image-to-image translation using cycle-consistent adversarial networks. In: ICCV, pp. 2223–2232 (2017)
37. Wang, Z., Bovik, A.C., Sheikh, H.R., Simoncelli, E.P.: Image quality assessment: from error visibility to structural similarity. TIP **13**, 600–612 (2004)
38. Li, C., Cong, R., Hou, J., Zhang, S., Qian, Y., Kwong, S.: Nested network with twostream pyramid for salient object detection in optical remote sensing images. arXiv preprint arXiv: 1906.08462 (2019)
39. Li, C., et al.: An underwater image enhancement benchmark dataset and beyond. arXiv preprint arXiv:1901.05495 (2019)
40. Li, C., Guo, J., Guo, C.: Emerging from water: underwater image color correction based on weakly supervised color transfer. SPL **25**, 323–327 (2018)
41. Li, C., Guo, C., Guo, J.C., Han, P., Fu, H.Z., Cong, R.: PDR-net: perception-inspired single image dehazing network with refinement. IEEE Trans. Multimedia **22**, 704–716 (2020)
42. Li, C., Anwar, S., Porikli, F.: Underwater scene prior inspired deep underwater image and video enhancement. Pattern Recogn. **98**, 107038 (2020)
43. Li, C., Guo, C., Guo, J., Han, P., Fu, H., Cong, R.: Underwater image enhancement by dehazing with minimum information loss and histogram distribution prior. IEEE Trans. Image Process. **25**(12), 5664–5677 (2016)

Image-Edge Detection System Based on Supervised Machine Learning Algorithm

Kaiyong Li, Haixia Wang[✉], Linwei Ouyang, and Bo Zhao

School of Physics and Electronic Information Engineering, Qinghai Minzu University, Xining 810007, China

Abstract. In view of the low detection quality of traditional image detection system, which is prone to fuzzy edge details, An image-edge detection system based on supervised machine learning algorithm is proposed. The overall framework of image edge detection system was constructed through supervised machine learning calculation. Based on the framework of the system, images that cannot be classified linearly or approximately in the normal sample space are classified by the support vector machine (SVM) model, According to the fitting results, every pixel in the image, As a training sample, So that the two-dimensional image can be represented by the corresponding Lagrangian function, It can also represent linear combinations of nucleated functions, Finally, the image edge can be detected by zero cross detection. The experimental results show that the proposed system can detect the image edges well and the target details are clear.

Keywords: Supervised machine learning algorithm · Detection system · Support vector machine · Image overlapping

1 Introduction

Existing image processing methods are becoming more and more convenient. The use of computers to analyze and process images can easily achieve the required results. Therefore, image processing technologies are applied to various industries [1], such as: electronic documents, ID cards Recognition, face recognition, housing management, etc. However, because the source of many images is uncertain, it is easy to make some errors when processing these images, causing unnecessary losses [2], and then edge detection is required. To highlight the target individual.

Currently commonly used image detection systems mainly include UV-visible image superposition accuracy test system based on UV imager and DSP-based two-frame difference and improved semi-causal weak target detection research. The former measures the cross-image center of the UV image and the visible light image. The offset generated by the point coordinates realizes the test of the accuracy of the image superposition, and the system can provide a reliable detection basis [3]. The latter uses the semi-causal support domain model to predict the background of the original image, and uses the two-frame difference to process the original image to obtain a binary image. On this

X. Wang et al. (Eds.): AICON 2021, LNICST 397, pp. 257–267, 2021.
https://doi.org/10.1007/978-3-030-90199-8_24

basis, the real weak target is obtained based on the principle of morphology. Analysis of experimental results shows that this method can quickly and effectively detect small and weak targets [4]. However, when the above-mentioned system detects blurred images, uneven illumination, or even damaged images, situations such as edge detail loss will occur, and the detection quality is not high.

To this end, this paper proposes a supervised machine learning algorithm image edge detection system. First, the image detection system is constructed using hardware such as image collection, low-level processing, high-level processing, and subsequent processing of detection results, and then the support vector machine is used to process the image data in the feature space. Linear classification, and for the parts that cannot be divided, through nonlinear mapping, from low-dimensional space to high-dimensional space, after kernel function conversion, it can be solved in high-dimensional space. Finally, the support vector machine regression domain is used to enable the kernel function to replace the inner product operation, that is, nonlinear fitting can be completed, and the zero-cross detection method can be used to complete the image detection. The experimental verification shows that the above process can effectively enhance the detection quality. The details are kept intact.

2   An Image-Edge Detection System Based on Supervised Machine Learning Algorithm

2.1   Principle Analysis of Supervised Machine Learning Algorithm

Machine learning algorithms are mainly divided into two learning methods, supervised and unsupervised [4]. The supervised learning algorithm builds a model based on the known training set (learning set) information, and classifies and estimates new information based on the model. Supervised machine learning algorithms include decision trees, artificial neural networks and support vector machines. This research uses the support vector machine method [5]. The support vector machine is based on the VC dimension principle and the principle of minimum structural risk [6]. Because the support vector machine has the advantages of effectively handling small sample problems, high dimensionality, and generalization capabilities, it is widely used in the classification process. For two types of classification problems, first construct a support vector machine function model, namely

$$\Phi(\omega, \xi) = min\frac{1}{2}\|\omega\|^2 + C\sum_{i=1}^{n} \xi_i \tag{1}$$

Need to satisfy the relationship $y_i[(\omega \cdot a_i) + B] \geq 1 - \xi_i, i = 1, 2, 3, ..., n, 0 \leq a_i \leq C$.

Perform quadratic programming calculation according to the function of the mechanics system and its motion conditions, and transform the dual problem.

Available $min\frac{1}{2}\sum_{i=1,j=1}^{n} a_i a_j y_i y_j (x_1 \cdot x_j) - \sum_{i=1}^{n} a_i$ Also need to meet $\sum_{i=1}^{n} y_i x_i = 0, a_i \geq 0, i = 1, 2, 3, ...n$ The following figure describes the basic principles of support vector machine classification (Fig. 1).

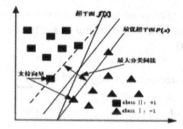

Fig. 1. Basic principles of support vector machine classification

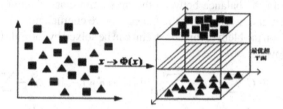

Fig. 2. The projection function of kernel function

For the problem of linear inseparability, related researchers generally use kernel functions Φ to project samples into high-dimensional space. At this time, the samples become linearly separable. The detailed process is shown in the following Fig. 2.

According to the principle of dual problem transformation, $(x_1 \cdot x)$ can be replaced with $(\Phi(x_i) \cdot \Phi(x))$. Generally, $K(x_1 \cdot x) = (\Phi(x_i) \cdot \Phi(x))$, $K(x_1 \cdot x)$ is regarded as a kernel function. The kernel function in this paper uses the radial basis function to obtain the following formula [7]:

$$K(x_1 \cdot x) = exp\{\frac{|x_i - x|^2}{\sigma^2}\} \tag{2}$$

Finally, the optimal hyperplane is:

$$F(x) = sgn\{\sum_{i=1}^{n} a_i^* y_i K(x_1 \cdot x) + b^*\} \tag{3}$$

2.2 Implementation of Image Edge Detection

2.2.1 Support Vector Machine Principle

The method of support vector machine is used to map the images in the normal sample space that cannot be linearly classified or approximated classified to the high-dimensional space. This method is developed based on the statistical learning theory. The formula for a given training number set is $\{x_i, y_i\}$, in the above formula $i = 1, 2, \cdots, l, x_i \in R^d, y_i \in \{+1, -1\}$.

Set the training set to be linearly divided by hyperplane wx + b = 0 then according to the statistical theory knowledge, the largest hyperplane of the classification interval is the best hyperplane, and the promotion performance is good. At the same time, in order to make the data linearly classified in the feature space, the decision function must meet the following constraints [8]:

$$Minimize\ \phi(x_i, y_i) = \frac{1}{2}\|w\|^2 + C\sum_{i=1}^{l} \zeta_i \tag{4}$$

$$Subject\ to\ y_i[(x_i, y_i) + b] \geq 1 - \zeta_i \tag{5}$$

In the above formula: ζ_i represents the non-negative slack variable introduced when solving the linear indivisible condition, $C > 0$ represents the custom penalty coefficient, which can maintain the balance between the maximum classification interval and the classification error, and w represents the image feature coefficient.

The optimization problem of this constraint can be solved by formula (6). The specific formula is as follows:

$$L = \frac{1}{2}\|w\|^2 + C\sum_{i=1}^{l} \zeta_i - \sum_{i=1}^{l} a_i[y_i(x_i \bullet w) - 1 + \zeta_i] - \sum_{i=1}^{l} \beta_i \zeta_i \tag{6}$$

In the above formula: $a_i \geq 0$, $\beta_i \geq 0$ are the coefficients of Lagrange, the optimal solution of its constraint is determined by the saddle point of the Lagrange function [9], this function minimizes w and b but maximizes a_i.

Use formula (6) to find partial differentials for w and b, make it equal to 0, then we can convert the optimal problem formulas (4) and (5) into simpler dual problems,the formula is as follows:

$$Minimize\ \phi(a) = \sum_{i=1}^{l} a_i - \frac{1}{2} + \sum_{i=1}^{l}\sum_{j=1}^{l} a_i a_j y_i y_j K(x_i, x_j) \tag{7}$$

$$Subject\ to\ \sum_{j=1}^{l} a_i y_i = 0(0 \leq a_i \leq C, i = 1, 2, \cdots, l) \tag{8}$$

In the above formula: $K(x_i, x_j) = (\phi(x_i), \phi(x_j))$ can satisfy the kernel theorem function of Mercer. Let a^* be the best solution of formula (6), to satisfy the formula:

$$a_i^*\{[(x_i \bullet w) + b^*] - 1 + \zeta_i^*\} = 0 \tag{9}$$

In the above formula: non-zero corresponding vector subsets are called support vectors.

In the normal sample space, a large part of the input data cannot be classified linearly or approximately, so it is necessary to map the sample space to the high-dimensional feature space through nonlinear mapping. Problems that cannot be solved in the low-dimensional space can be used Kernel function conversion can be solved in high-dimensional space. Therefore, kernel function is the main key to support vector machines to solve nonlinear problems [10].

2.2.2 Support Vector Machine Regression

According to the principle of support vector machine, support vector machine can be divided into support vector machine classification and support vector machine regression, and the regression idea of support vector function is follows:

Given training sample points: $\{(x_1, y_1), (x_2, y_2), \cdots, (x_n, y_n)\} \subset X \times R$, Use support vector machine regression to train the function. Through this function, the target value corresponding to the output value of all input samples and the input value is calculated. The value cannot exceed ε, and the regression function should be kept as smooth as possible.

For the linear case, assume that the function form is: $f(x) = w \bullet x + b, w \in x, b \in R$. If you want to make the regression function to minimize the smoothing value, you must calculate a smaller one. The above problem is described as an optimization problem, and the formula is:

$$min \frac{1}{2}\|w\|^2 s.t. y_i - w \bullet x_i - b \le \varepsilon \quad i = 1, 2, \cdots, nw \bullet x_i + b - y_i \le \varepsilon \quad (10)$$

In the presence of fitting errors, the relaxation factors ζ_i^*, ζ_i are introduced, so the above formula can be written in the following form:

$$min \frac{1}{2}\|w\|^2 + C \sum_{i=1}^{n} \frac{(\zeta_i^* + \zeta_i)s.t. y_i}{-w \bullet x_i - b \le \varepsilon +} \zeta_i$$
$$w \bullet x_i + b - y_i \le \varepsilon + \zeta_i^* \quad i = 1, 2, \cdots, n\zeta_i^*, \zeta_i \ge 0 \quad (11)$$

Using the same optimization method, the dual problem can be obtained, the formula is:

$$f(x) = (w \bullet x) + b = \sum_{i}^{n} (a_i^* - a_i)(x_i - x) + b^* \quad (12)$$

In the above formula: a_i^* represents the Laguange factor, which is the same as the support vector machine method used in pattern recognition, only a small part of a^*, a_i is not 0, and the corresponding sample is the support vector. According to the above analysis, the kernel function can be used to replace the inner product operation above to complete the nonlinear fitting [11].

2.2.3 Support Vector Machine Regression Representation and Image Edge Detection

According to the results of nonlinear fitting, the two-dimensional gray image is regarded as a continuous function: $y = f(x) : R^2 \to R^1$, the output x is a two-dimensional vector, it can represent the coordinates of pixel columns and rows, and the output y is a scalar, representing the gray value corresponding to the output vector x [12, 13]. Take each pixel in an image as a training sample, and train it through support vector machine regression. The two-dimensional image is only expressed by the support vector obtained by training and the corresponding Lagrangian function, which can be expressed as a linear combination of the kernel function, the specific formula is:

$$f(x, y) = \sum_{i=1}^{L} a_i K(x_i, x) + b \quad (13)$$

The Lagrange must meet the following two restrictions:

$$\sum_{i=1}^{L} a_i = 0, -c \le a_i \le c \quad (14)$$

The sample points in the image, after the support vector machine regression training, each training sample point can correspond to a Lagrangian, but only the SVM Lagrang is a non-zero value, the image can rely on the SVM position and the corresponding Lagrange is described, and the image can also be converted from the previous gray domain to the support vector machine regression domain, so that the image processing can be carried out in the support vector machine regression domain.

In the actual processing of the two-dimensional gray image, it must first be converted to the PGM format, which can store the gray values of all pixels in the image, and can generate a gray matrix from the pixels, which is beneficial to support vector machines Samples used in regression training [14].

After the image samples are extracted, the support vector machine can be used for regression training. After the training is completed, the image support vector and the corresponding Lagrange a_i set and deviation b can be obtained to construct the image regression function $f(x, y)$. After analyzing the support vector coordinates, a large part of the support vectors of the image can be found, focusing on the positions where the gray value of the image changes more strongly. Because support vector machine regression is used to represent the image, the image finally represents a linear combination of kernel functions, which is actually a scalar function. It is necessary to extract samples from the image to be detected and obtain function $f(x, y)$ after training. Then, in the image of support vector machine regression, use the zero-cross method to complete the detection of image edges.

In the method of zero-cross detection, the second derivative is usually realized by using Laps operator. Because the Laplacian is more sensitive to noise in the image, in order to reduce the influence of noise, Gaussian smoothing should be used before the Laplacian transformation [16]. The Gaussian smoothing filter can convolve the original image with the Gaussian function, so as to suppress noise and smooth the image. Assuming the original image is $F(x, y)$, then the image after Gaussian smooth filtering is $F'(x, y)$, the specific formula is:

$$F'(x, y) = f(x, y) \otimes \frac{1}{2\pi\sigma} exp\left(-\frac{x^2 + y^2}{2\sigma^2}\right) \tag{15}$$

In the above formula: $\otimes$ stands for convolution and σ stands for Gaussian function variance.

In an image expressed by support vector machine regression, Gaussian smoothing filter can be seen as both the support vector machine regression function and the Gaussian function of the image, when convolution in two-dimensional space, when training the image, using Gaussian RBF kernel function, we can train image support vector machine regression function, that is, linear combination of kernel function of Gaussian function RBF, this kernel function and Gaussian smoothing filter function are calculated by convolution, and the obtained is still a Gaussian function, then after the regression image of support vector machine is filtered by Gaussian smoothing filter, a new Gaussian function can be obtained [17], and its convolution result is:

$$F(x) = \frac{\sigma_f^2}{\sigma_f^2 + \sigma_g^2}\left[\sum a_i \, exp\left(-\frac{\|x - x_i\|^2}{2\sigma_f^2 + 2\sigma_g^2}\right) + b\right] \tag{16}$$

It can be seen from the above analysis, after the support vector machine regression image represented by Gaussian RBF kernel function adopts Gaussian filtering, the support vector machine regression is not changed, the image $F(x, y)$ obtained after Gaussian smoothing filtering is adopted, and the zero-crossing edge is used for detection. In other words, after the Laplace transform is detected in the regression image of support vector machine, all the pixels are replaced by the corresponding $M(x, y)$. Because the characteristics of the image are different from the actual error, the value of $M(x, y)$ is usually taken as the edge point within a fixed threshold to obtain the image edge detection result.

3 Experimental Simulation

In order to confirm the validity of the detection results of the proposed supervised machine learning algorithm image edge detection system, experiments were carried out.

3.1 Image Edge Detection Performance Index

The performance of image edge detection can be achieved through the accuracy of edge position, edge continuity and edge width, the objective criteria for edge detection performance are defined as follows:

$$P = max \frac{1}{(I_b, I_L)} \sum_{i=1}^{I_n} \frac{1}{1 + aI_i} \tag{17}$$

In the above formula: I_n represents the distance between the edge pixels of the detected image and the closest ideal edge pixels, I_b and I_L represent the number of edge pixels actually detected and the number of ideal edge pixels respectively, a represents the penalty factor, the value is a positive number between 0 and 1. The edge features of the image selected for the experiment are known and introduce different kinds of noise to the test image (Signal to noise ratio SNR $= 10 \lg p_1 / p_2$, p_1 represents the initial image signal power, p_2 represents noise power), using different calculation methods to extract the edge features of the noise image, and then compare it with the known edge features, that is, to obtain the edge detection performance index P, so as to obtain the quality of edge detection calculation method. According to Eq. (17), we can know that it is equal to or less than 1. The larger the value, the better the detection method.

3.2 The Optimal Parameter Selection and Performance Comparison of the System in This Paper

In this paper, the system will choose different kernel functions for image edge extraction. First of all, we must determine the difference of the parameters, the σ^2 in the Gaussian kernel function and the d in the polynomial kernel, as well as the convolution kernel and the threshold size, are closely related to the performance of edge detection, for the choice of convolution kernel size, this paper compares the influence of the commonly used convolution kernels of size $3 * 3$, $5 * 5$ and $7 * 7$ on the edge detection performance. The size of the best image convolution kernel can be determined. On this basis, the genetic algorithm is used to find the best quality of σ^2, d and threshold, and the optimal values of all parameters are obtained.

In order to analyze the detection performance of the convolution kernel affecting the edge at low signal-to-noise ratio, add 5 db Gaussian noise to the image, according to the gradient value and the statistical characteristics of the second derivative, it can be determined that the threshold T_1 is 0.8 and the threshold T_2 is 0.6, choose Gaussian kernel parameter σ^2 and polynomial order parameter d, the value of both is 1–20, for different convolution kernel experiments, the results are shown below:

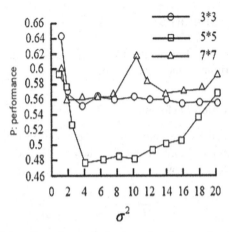

Fig. 3. σ^2 and the effect of convolution kernel on image edge detection index

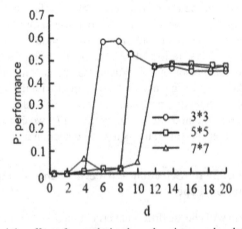

Fig. 4. d and the effect of convolution kernel on image edge detection index

It can be seen from Fig. 3 above, for the selection of Gaussian kernel function, this method has the best performance when extracting the convolution kernel function of according to Fig. 4, for the choice of polynomial, for the selection of polynomials, the method of this paper has the best performance when extracting the convolution kernel

a.   Initial image

a.   System 1

a.   System 2

a.   Text system

Fig. 5. Comparison of edge detection results of different systems

function of $3 * 3$, when the method of Gaussian kernel function is used to extract the polynomials of the convolution kernel size of $7 * 7$ and the convolution kernel size of $3 * 3$, the gap between the edge points and non-edge points is relatively large, and the extraction effect is better.

In order to verify the effectiveness of the system in this paper, the system is compared with the traditional UV imager-based UV-visible image overlay accuracy test system (System 1) and the DSP-based two-frame differential and improved semi-causal weak target detection research (System 2). The edge of the image is extracted, and the detection effects of different systems are compared. The specific results are as follows (Fig. 5):

We can see from the above picture, the edges extracted by the system in this paper are more accurate than the traditional system. The specific edges do not have obvious fluctuations, there are fewer false edges, while the details of the image edges of the traditional system are blurred, this shows that the detection system of this paper is better than the traditional system. Because the system in this paper uses a polynomial kernel function to detect the edge of the image when the signal-to-noise ratio is high, it can get better edge performance, and when the signal-to-noise ratio is low, it needs to use a Gaussian kernel function, that is, it can get Better edge feature performance.

Through the above experiments, we can see that the image detection system constructed in this paper can detect the image edges well, the edges are clear,and the detection effect is good.

4   Conclusion

In order to solve the problem that the detection result of the image shows obscure details in operation of traditional system, an image edge detection system based on supervised machine learning algorithms is designed. The hardware processing and execution speed of the system is fast, and it can be programmed on-site, so it has good adaptability. The software implementation process processes the image by way of support vector machine to complete the nonlinear fitting. Then through the zero-crossing detection method, the edge of the image can be detected. Finally, the experiment proved that the system can detect the edge of the image well. Compared with the traditional system, the edge details are more obvious and there is no loss.

Acknowledgments. This study was supported by science and technology plan of Qinghai province Key Research &Development and conversion plan, Qinghai Province, Qinghai (No. 2019-GX-170).

References

1. Ma, H., Yang, W., Zhang, X.: Segmentation and location algorithm for infrared image of roller on conveyor belt. J. Xi'an Univ. Sci. Technol. **37**(6), 892–898 (2017)
2. Wang, X., Lu, H., Ma, X., et al.: No-reference image quality assessment method for different ambient illumination. Opt. Tech. **44**(5), 569–575 (2018)
3. Gu, Y., Lv, Y., Yang, F., et al.: Testing System for UV Imager Superposition Accuracy. Infrared Technol. **41**(08), 695–698 (2019)

4. Li, T., Xu, S., Yao, Z., et al.: Dim and small target detection based on two frame difference and modified semi-causal with DSP. Laser Infrared **47**(10), 1316–1320 (2017)
5. Kong, D., Cui, Y., Kong, L., et al.: Spectroscopy and spectral analysis **39**(11), 3407–3413 (2019)
6. Cai, H., Zhang, W., Chen, X., et al.: Image processing method for ophthalmic optical coherence tomography. Chin. Opt. **12**(04), 731–740 (2019)
7. Xu, Y., Yu, M., Chen, K., et al.: Stereoscopic high dynamic range image synthesis using virtual exposure images. J. Optoelectron.·Laser **30**(07), 768–778 (2019)
8. Li, F., Zhao, Y., Xiang, W., et al.: Infrared image mixed noise removal method based on improved NL-means. Infrared Laser Eng. **48**(1), 169–179 (2019)
9. Yang, B., Wang, X.: Boosting quality of pansharpened images using deep residual denoising network. Laser Optoelectron. Progess **56**(16), 88–97 (2019)
10. Wang, Y., Yi, S., Lv, Z.: Underwater image restoration with adaptive background Lightest imation and non-local prior. Opt. Precis. Eng. **27**(02), 499–510 (2019)
11. Li, H., Yun, L., Gao, Y.: fog image enhancement algorithm based on boundary-limited weighted least squares filtering. Chin. J. Lasers **46**(03), 255–263 (2019)
12. Ma, H., Ma, S., Xu, Y., et al.: Low-light image enhancement based on deep convolutional neural network. Acta Opt. Sin. **39**(02), 99–108 (2019)
13. Chen, W., Liu, S., Chi, K., et al.: Development of digital image transmission device based on visible light communication. Visible Light Commun. **42**(11), 13–17 (2018)
14. Pei, H., Yang, X., Hou, L.: Infrared image detection of double circuit UHV transmission lines on the same tower. J. CAEIT **14**(02), 212–217 (2019)
15. Le, J., Zhou, X., Sun, A., et al.: Experimental study about improving the quality of in-focus image by means of optical scanning holography. Laser Technol. **41**(03), 332–336 (2017)
16. Tan, J., Huang, J., Wang, K., et al.: Grading detecting method for obervation images of geosynchronous earth orbit debris. Acta Photonic Sin. **46**(02), 96–104 (2017)
17. Li, X., Guo, J., Peng, F., et al.: Improved-algorithm of road detection based on Hough transform. J. Appl. Opt. **37**(02), 229–234 (2016)

On the Upper Bound of the Forwarding Index of Strong Product Networks

Shijie Duan[1,2(✉)] and Feng Li[1]

[1] College of Computer Science, Qinghai Normal University, Xining, China
[2] Key Laboratory of Tibetan Information Processing, Ministry of Education, Xining, China

Abstract. The pros and cons of routing is one of the most important factors that affect the effectiveness of network communication performance. In very large-scale integration and parallel computer systems, it is inevitable that some components and lines will fail, which will directly affect the route selection. Vertex forwarding index is an important parameter to measure the quality of routing. The strong product method can be used to construct a large-scale network through several smaller-scale networks. This paper analyzes the topological structure parameters such as the vertex forwarding index and order of the factor network to determine an upper bound of the Vertex forwarding index of strong product networks.

Keywords: Strong product networks · Topological structure · Routing · Vertex-forwarding index

1 Introduction

Interconnection network of a multiprocessor system is essentially the connection mode of the components in the system, and the topology of the interconnection network essentially describes the structural characteristics of the system. By a graph G we mean an ordered binary $(V(G), E(G))$, where $V(G)$ is the non-empty vertex set of G, it can be used to represent the components in the system. $E(G) \subseteq V(G) \times V(G)$ is the edge set of G, the edges in the collection elements represent the physical connections between the components [1]. Hence, in the following content we will use "graph" instead of "network."

Let G be an n-order connected undirected graph or strongly connected directed graph, x and y are two different vertices in G, and we use $P(G; x, y)$ to represent all $n(n-1)$ sets of (x, y) paths in G. That is,

$$R = \{(x, y) | x, y \in V(G), x \neq y\},$$
$$P(G) = \bigcup_{x,y \in V(G)} P(G; x, y).$$

Then the routing of G is defined as the following mapping:

$$\rho : R \to G$$
$$(x, y) \mapsto \rho(x, y).$$

X. Wang et al. (Eds.): AICON 2021, LNICST 397, pp. 268–274, 2021.
https://doi.org/10.1007/978-3-030-90199-8_25

The mapping $\rho : R \mapsto P(G)$ specifies the set of paths between all $n(n-1)$ ordered vertex pairs (x, y) in the graph G. The path $\rho(x, y)$ determined by ρ represents the transmission of data from its source x to its destination y, if $(x, y) \notin E(G)$, then we stipulate that the intermediate vertices of path (x, y) has a forwarding function. Therefore, if the path determined by ρ passes through a certain vertex too many times, then the load of this vertex is likely to be too large and cause the capacity of the vertex to be exceeded, which leads to paralysis of the entire network and ultimately affects the efficiency of data transmission. Literature [2] first proposed the concept of vertex forwarding index.

Let G be a strongly connected directed graph or a connected undirected graph, ρ is its routing, denoted as (G, ρ), v is a vertex in G, the forwarding index of v to routing ρ is defined as the number of paths determined by ρ through v, denoted as $\tau_x(G, \rho)$, the parameter

$$\tau(G, \rho) = \max\{\tau_x(G, \rho) : x \in V(G)\}$$

is called the forwarding index of (G, ρ); The parameters

$$\tau(G) = \min\{\tau(G, \rho) : \forall \rho\}, \ \tau_m(G) = \min\{\tau(G, \rho_m) : \forall \rho_m\}.$$

represent the forwarding index and minimum routing forwarding index of G, respectively. Since the forwarding index contains the minimum routing forwarding index, we can easily get $\tau(G) \le \tau_m(G)$.

Let G be a definite network, and the order of G is v. The constant m is the data transmission rate of the path determined by ρ. In this context, the total transmission rate of each vertex as the sending and receiving point of data, the total transmission rate of the vertex is the sum of all transmission rates from this vertex to other vertices is $2(n-1)m$, so the total transmission rate between all vertices in the entire network is $n(n-1)m$. Since the capacity C_v of the vertex limits the maximum amount of data forwarding of the vertex, so

$$C_v \ge 2m(n-1) + \tau_v m,$$

where $\tau_v = \tau_v(G, \rho)$. Assuming that the maximum capacity of all vertices in the network is C, then

$$2m(n-1) + \tau_v m \le C_v \le C.$$

From the above formula, we can conclude that the transmission rate m of the vertex must satisfy

$$m \le \frac{C}{2(n-1) + \tau}$$

where $\tau = \tau(G, \rho)$, so the total transmission rate of each vertices must satisfy

$$2(n-1)m \le \frac{2(n-1)C}{\tau + 2(n-1)},$$

the above formula defines the capacity of the vertex, so the corresponding total network data transmission rate can define the capacity of the entire network, that is,

$$mn(n-1) \leq \frac{n(n-1)C}{\tau + 2(n-1)},$$

since m, n, C in the above formula are all constants, when the number of network vertices, network data transmission rate and vertex capacity are determined, the forwarding index τ of the network is inversely proportional to the capacity $mn(n-1)$ of the network. The problem of maximizing network capacity is transformed into a problem of minimizing the network forwarding index, therefore, it makes sense to determine the upper bound of the vertex forwarding index of some special networks. In 1989, Heydemann et al. described the upper bound of the forwarding index of the Cartesian product graph [3]. Recently, Li gave the upper bound of the forwarding index of lexicographic product graph for the first time [4]. For more results about the forwarding index, please refer to [5, 6]. Sabidussi first proposed the concept of strong product of graphs in 1959 in [7]. The strong product of two graphs G and H is denoted as $G \otimes H$, with vertex set.

$$V(G \otimes H) = V(G) \times V(H) = \{(g, h) | g \in V(G), h \in V(H)\}.$$

Two vertices (g, h) and (g', h') (where $g, g' \in V(G)$, $h, h' \in V(H)$) are adjacent if and only if $g = g'$ and $(h, h') \in V(H)$ or $h = h'$ and $(g, g') \in V(G)$ or $(h, h') \in V(H)$ and $(g, g') \in V(G)$. The graphs G and H are called the factor graphs of the strong product graph $G \otimes H$. Strong product is a method of constructing a large graph from some small graphs, and many properties of the large graph, such as super-connectivity, symmetry, embeddability, etc., can be described by the properties of factor graphs, further content about product graphs refer to [8–10].

This paper gives an upper bound of the vertex forwarding index of strong product graphs. Since strong product graph $G \otimes H$ are constructed by factor graphs G and H, the vertex forwarding index of factor graphs G and H must affect the vertex forwarding index of strong product graphs $G \otimes H$, so we characterize the vertex forwarding index of strong product graphs by the vertex forwarding index and the order of factor graphs.

2   Proof of Main Results

The vertex forwarding index is used to measure the load of the vertices in the determined routing in a network, and it is an important index to measure the advantages and disadvantages of the routing. First, we give a rough upper bound of the vertex forwarding index, which is suitable for all simple connected undirected graphs and also for strong product graphs.

Let G_i be a simple connected undirected graph of order n_i. For any routing ρ of strong product graph $G_1 \otimes G_2 \otimes \cdots \otimes G_k$, The number of paths determined by ρ passing through each vertex $(v_1, v_2 \ldots, v_k)$ is less than or equal to the total number of paths of the entire strong product graph minus the number of paths with vertex $(v_1, v_2 \ldots, v_k)$ as the endpoint, so the upper bound of the vertex forwarding index is:

$$n_1 \times n_2 \times \cdots \times n_k \times (n_1 \times n_2 \times \cdots \times n_k - 1) - 2n_1 \times n_2 \times \cdots \times n_k,$$

that is

$$(n_1 \times n_2 \times \cdots \times n_k - 1) \times (n_1 \times n_2 \times \cdots \times n_k - 2).$$

According to the above formula, when a factor graph of a strong product graph $G_i(1 \leq i \leq k)$ is a star graph $K_{1, n_1 \times n_2 \times \cdots n_k(n_1 \times n_2 \times \cdots n_k - 1)}$, and the other $n - 1$ factor graphs are all K_1, the vertex forwarding index of $G_1 \otimes G_2 \otimes \cdots \otimes G_k$ can reach this upper bound.

In order to proof our results, we introduce the distance between any two vertices of strong product graph:

Lemma 2.1 [9] . *Let* $g, g' \in V(G), h, h' \in V(H)$ *then the distance between any two vertices* $(g, h), (g', h')$ *in* $G \otimes H$ *is:*

$$d_{G \otimes H}((g, h)(g', h')) = \max\{d_G(g, g'), d_H(h, h')\}.$$

Combined with the properties of strong product graphs, we give the main results and proofs.

Theorem 2.2. *Let* G *and* H *be two nontrivial connected graphs or strongly connected directed graphs with orders* n_1 *and* n_2, *then*

$$\tau(G \otimes H) \leq \max\{2n_1\tau(H) + n_2\tau(G), 2n_2\tau(G) + n_1\tau(H)\}, .$$

Proof: Let ρ_G and ρ_H be the routing in G and H, such that

$$\tau(G) = \tau(G, \rho_G), \tau(H) = \tau(H, \rho_H).$$

Suppose $(g, g') \in E(G), (h, h') \in E(H)$ and set ρ to be the route selection in $G \otimes H$, where the definition of the path $P((g, h), (g', h')) \in G \otimes H$ can be divided into the following three situations:

Situation 1: If both vertices (g, h) and (g', h') are in $gH(g \in V(G))$, combing with $\tau(G) \leq \tau_m(G)$ and the properties of strong product, we can define $P((g, h)(g', h'))$ as $\rho_H(h, h')$. When the paths determined by the routing ρ only satisfies the situation 1, the path $P((g, h)(g', h'))$ is isomorphic to the path $\rho_H(h, h')$ in H. By $\tau_H = \tau(H, \rho_H)$ and the properties of factor graph G, there are at most n_1 groups of such paths in the strong product graph $G \otimes H$, so in situation 1 the upper bound of the vertex forwarding index of the strong product is:

$$\tau(G \otimes H) \leq n_1\tau(H).$$

Situation 2: If both vertices (g, h) and (g', h') are in $Gh(h \in V(H))$, combing with $\tau(G) \leq \tau_m(G)$ and the definition of strong product, we can define $P((g, h)(g', h'))$ as $\rho_G(g, g')$. When the paths determined by the routing ρ only satisfies the situation 2, the path $P((g, h)(g', h'))$ is isomorphic to the path $\rho_G(g, g')$ in G. By $\tau_H = \tau(H, \rho_H)$ and the properties of factor graph H, there are at most n_2 groups of such paths in the strong product graph $G \otimes H$, so in situation 2 the upper bound of the vertex forwarding index of the strong product is:

$$\tau(G \otimes H) \leq n_2\tau(G).$$

Situation 3: If (g, h) and (g', h') are in $gH(g \in V(G))$ and $Gh(h \in V(H))$ respectively, by $\tau(G) \leq \tau_m(G)$ and the distance formula of the strong product graphs (Lemma 2.1), we can define the path $P((g, h)(g', h'))$ as the following form:

$$P((g, h)(g', h')) = \max\{\rho_G(g, g'), \rho_H(h, h')\}.$$

When the paths determined by the routing ρ only satisfies the situation 3, due to

$$\tau(G) = \tau(G, \rho_G), \tau(H) = \tau(H, \rho_H).$$

Obviously, in situation 3, the upper bound of the vertex forwarding index of the strong product does not exceed the larger one in situations 1 and 2, i.e.

$$\tau(G \otimes H) \leq \max\{n_1 \tau(H), n_2 \tau(G)\}.$$

Combining the above three situations, when a path determined by the routing ρ of the strong product graph $G \otimes H$ satisfies the above three conditions at the same time, that is, one of the paths determined by the routing ρ when a certain vertex forwards the data transmitted by the above three situations at the same time, the vertex forwarding index of the strong product graph $G \otimes H$ reaches an upper bound:

$$\tau(G \otimes H) \leq n_1 \tau(H) + n_2 \tau(G) + \max\{n_1 \tau(H), n_2 \tau(G)\}$$
$$\leq \max\{2n_1 \tau(H) + n_2 \tau(G), 2n_2 \tau(G) + n_1 \tau(H)\}.$$

$\square$

Through the above method, we extend the result of the strong product of the two factor graphs of Theorem 2.2 to the strong product of $k(k \geq 2)$ factor graphs, and the results are as follows:

Theorem 2.3. *Suppose that $G_1, G_2, \ldots G_k$ are non-trivial connected graphs or strongly connected directed graph, with orders of $n_1, n_2, \ldots n_k$, where $u_i, v_i, w_i \in G_i$ then*

$$\tau(G_1 \otimes G_2 \otimes \cdots \otimes G_k) \leq \sum_{i=1}^{k} n_1 n_2 \cdots n_{i-1} \tau_i n_{i+1} \cdots n_k + max$$

where

$$max = \max\{n_1 n_2 \cdots n_{r-1} \tau_r n_{r+1} \cdots n_k, n_1 n_2 \cdots n_{s-1} \tau_s n_{s+1} \cdots n_k\},$$

r and s in the above formula represents the two endpoints of the path in ρ in

$$w_1 w_2 \cdots w_{r-1} G_r w_{r+1} \cdots w_k$$

and

$$w_1 w_2 \cdots w_{s-1} G_s w_{s+1} \cdots w_k,$$

respectively.

Proof: For the convenience of narration, let

$$D = G_1 \otimes G_2 \otimes \cdots \otimes G_k.$$

We can divide the routing of D into the following two situations:

Situation 1: If the vertices $(u_1, u_2, \ldots, u_k)$ and $(v_1, v_2, \ldots, v_k)$ are both in a certain

$$w_1 w_2 \ldots w_{i-1} G_i w_{i+1} \ldots w_k$$

the upper bound of the vertex forwarding index of the strong product graph D under this condition is:

$$\tau(D) \leq \sum_{i=1}^{k} n_1 n_2 \cdots n_{i-1} \tau_i n_{i+1} \cdots n_k.$$

Situation 2: If the vertices $(u_1, u_2, \ldots, u_k)$ and $(v_1, v_2, \ldots, v_k)$ are in different

$$w_1 w_2 \ldots w_{r-1} G_r w_{r+1} \ldots w_k$$

and

$$w_1 w_2 \ldots w_{s-1} G_s w_{s+1} \ldots w_k.$$

Hence, from the distance formula and definition of strong product, the upper bound of vertex forwarding index of strong product graph D in this situation is:

$$\tau(D) \leq \max\{n_1 n_2 \cdots n_{r-1} \tau_r n_{r+1} \cdots n_k, n_1 n_2 \cdots n_{s-1} \tau_s n_{s+1} \cdots n_k\}.$$

Through the above two situations, when a certain routing in the strong product graph $G_1 \otimes G_2 \otimes \cdots \otimes G_k$ satisfies the above two situations at the same time, the upper bound of the vertex forwarding index of the strong product graph $G_1 \otimes G_2 \otimes \cdots \otimes G_k$ is:

$$\tau(G_1 \otimes G_2 \otimes \cdots \otimes G_k) \leq \sum_{i=1}^{k} n_1 n_2 \cdots n_{i-1} \tau_i n_{i+1} \cdots n_k + max$$

where

$$max = \max\{n_1 n_2 \cdots n_{r-1} \tau_r n_{r+1} \cdots n_k, n_1 n_2 \cdots n_{s-1} \tau_s n_{s+1} \cdots n_k\}.$$

$\square$

3   Conclusion

As one of the classical methods of interconnection networks design, strong product can build large-scale network through some small-scale networks, and large-scale network retain some "good" properties of small networks. This paper researches the construction properties of strong product graphs, and gives an upper bound of vertex forwarding index of strong product graphs.

Acknowledgments. The authors acknowledge the financial support of the National Natural Science Foundation of China (Grant. 11551002), and the Natural Science Foundation of Qinghai Province (Grant. 2019-ZJ-7093).

References

1. Xu, J.M.: Combinatorial Theory in Networks. Science Press, Inc., Beijing (2007)
2. Chung, F., Coffman, E., Reiman, M., Simon, B.: The forwarding index of communication networks. IEEE Trans. Inf. Theory **33**(2), 224–232 (1987)
3. Heydemann, M.C., Meyer, J.C., Sotteau, D.: On forwarding indices of networks. Discrete Appl. Math. **23**(2), 103–123 (1989)
4. Xu, Z.B., Li, F., Zhao, H.X.: Vertex forwarding indices of the lexicographic product of graphs. Sci. Sin. Inform. **44**(4), 482–497 (2014). in Chinese
5. Parthiban, N., Rajasingh, I., Sundara, R.R.: Improved bounds on forwarding index of networks. Procedia Comput. Sci. **57**, 592–595 (2015)
6. Hamid, M.: Cube-connected circulants: bisection width, Wiener and forwarding indices. Discrete Appl. Math. **272**, 48–68 (2020)
7. Sabidussi, G.: Graph multiplication. Math. Z. **72**, 446–457 (1959). https://doi.org/10.1007/BF01162967
8. Hammack, R.: Handbook of Product Graphs, 2nd edn. CRC Press Inc., Boca Raton (2016)
9. Yang, C., Xu, J.M.: Connectivity and edge-connectivity of strong product graphs. J. Univ. Sci. Technol. China **38**(5), 449–455 (2008)
10. Li, F., Wang, W., Xu, Z.B., Zhao, H.X.: Some results on the lexicographic product of vertex-transitive graphs. Appl. Math. Lett. **24**(11), 1924–1926 (2011)

A Forecasting Method for Rainfall Distribution at Four Rainfall Stations in Xining Area Based on BP Neural Network

Zhuang Xiong[1,4], Jun Ma[1,2(✉)], Bingrong Zhou[3], Lingfei Zhang[1], Bohang Chen[1], and Haiming Lan[1]

[1] The Computer College, Qinghai Normal University, Xining 810008, Qinghai, China
[2] Academy of Plateau Science and Sustainability, Xining 810016, Qinghai, People's Republic of China
[3] Institute of Meteorological Science of Qinghai Province, Xining 810001, China
[4] College of XiNing Urban Vocational and Technical Xining, Xining 810000, Qinghai, China

Abstract. The recent years have witnessed increasing precipitation in Xining area. This makes the statistics of rainfall particularly important since crucial reference can be provided for mudslides, landslides, and urban waterlogging. The mathematical models constructed based on the improvement or reorganization of neural network algorithms are mainly used to predict rainfall intensity and analyze rainfall data, and there are few studies on the changes in rainfall characteristics and rainfall distribution. This study made full use of 4380 data on rainfall collected from the four stations in Xining area in 2017, 2018, and 2019, analyzed the rainfall distribution at each station; 4380 data were used as the dataset, which was reorganized and divided into two parts: the training set and the test set, and a prediction method for rainfall distribution at four stations in Xining area based on the BP neural network was proposed. This forecasting method uses an improved model algorithm for the number of iterations of rainfall data adjustment and neuron nodes in the hidden layer. Through MATLAB programming and debugging, and data comparison and analysis, a stable and reliable identification and classification algorithm model was obtained. The model algorithm can be used to compare and analyze the data of daily rainfall of different regions, latitudes, longitudes, and altitudes in Xining area in the future.

Keywords: BP neural network algorithm · Daily rainfall · MATLAB · Neuron node · Mathematical model

1 Introduction

Xining is located in the eastern part of Qinghai Province in northwestern China. It has a plateau alpine cold temperate climate [1] with an altitude of 2261 m and an average annual precipitation of 360 mm. In recent years, the precipitation in Xining area has shown an obvious upward trend [2]. This makes the statistics on precipitation particularly important since the data provide important reference for mudslides, landslides, and urban waterlogging [3]; the precipitation in Xining area is mainly concentrated from May to October each year, and promotes the formation of atmospheric moist convection and cloud [4], which has a huge impact on solar radiation and vegetation growth. Through the analysis and research of the four precipitation stations in Xining area, the distribution, frequency and the characteristics of precipitation at the four stations were calculated.

In reference [5], based on the daily precipitation in the Yangtze River Basin from March to November from 1998 to 2000, artificial neural network algorithm was used to establish a forecasting model for heavy rainfall levels in six major river basins. Reference [6] used the genetic algorithm to optimize the initial weight of the network. The genetic algorithm (GA) was appropriately combined with the feedforward error back propagation (BP) algorithm, and the GA-BP neural network model has achieved significantly higher accuracy than other traditional methods in terms of the prediction for the precipitation in the next 6 h in the basin. Reference [7] solved the problem of unstable forecasting of secondary rainfall runoff in the basin with uneven distribution of precipitation stations. The BP network used the secondary rainstorm and the preceding affected precipitation as the input, and the total runoff of the secondary rainstorm as the output. The results showed the relative prediction error is 9.2% lower than that of the runoff yielding mode under saturated condition. In reference [8], artificial neural network model and two-dimensional interpolation model were constructed, and the accuracy of the two rainfall forecasting methods were qualitatively and quantitatively evaluated. In reference [9], to overcome the problems such as the structure or system error in the rainfall collection, the failure to measure small precipitation in real time, and the interception error in the accuracy [10], the hardware structure of the rain gauge was designed based on the working principle of the infrared diffuse reflection system, and combined with the fully connected neural network algorithm. The 20-dimensional data of the input frequency were input as neurons, the hidden layer was designed with 20 neurons, and the output conforms to a parameter of the actual rainfall intensity. In this way, a neuron data model was built; STM32F103c8t6 single-chip microcomputer was used as the micro-control chip to collect the captured pulse signal of light reflection, which was converted into frequency parameters and substituted into the algorithm program to reverse the rainfall intensity. Reference [11] used the method of "noise elimination" to process the data to obtain the target data, and then adopted the L-M optimization algorithm to simulate each observation station, so as to obtain the predicted value of 91 observation stations and calculate the cumulative error between the predicted values and measured values. The mathematical models constructed based on improved or reorganized neural network algorithm are mainly used to predict rainfall intensity, and there are few studies on rainfall data analysis, the changes in rainfall characteristics and rainfall distribution. This study made full use of 4380 rainfall data collected from four stations in Xining area from 2017 to 2019, analyzed the rainfall distribution at each station, and observed whether the rainfall frequency is consistent with the precipitation distribution in the rainy season in Xining area; 4380 data were used as the dataset, which was reorganized and divided into two parts based on the recognition and classification of the BP neural network algorithm: the training set and test set. After the network training, the mathematical model was established and the accuracy of the mathematical model was tested. According to the error rate after recognition and classification, the characteristics of the rainfall distribution at different stations and the difference in rainfall distribution were derived. The data of rainfall characteristics in different regions provide a basis for future automatic identification and classification of the data on rainfall [12], and the study of rainfall in different regions and spaces.

2 Data Processing

The data come from the Qinghai Provincial Institute of Meteorological Sciences. The precipitation was calculated according to the cumulative statistics on daily precipitation in 24 h from 20-20 o'clock; the data were collected from four stations in Xining area from 2017 to 2019, including the Meteorological Station of Xining City (52866, 36°44′N, 101°45′E, altitude: 2295.2 m), the Meteorological Station of Datong County (52862, 36°58′N, 101°40′E, altitude: 2470.5 m), the Meteorological Station of Huangyuan County (52855, 36°41′N, 101°15′E, altitude: 2675.0 m), and the Meteorological Station of Huangzhong County (52869, 36°30′N, 101°35′E, altitude: 2667.5 m). According to different data sources and different time periods, the data were stored as data1, data2, data3, and data4 based on the MATLAB variable working area, where data1 means the data on daily precipitation at the Xining Station in 2017, 2018, and 2019, with a total of (365 × 3) 1095 data. In order to facilitate the identification of the data on rainfall at different stations, code "1" was used to identify Xining Station. Similarly, data2 refers to the 3-year data of Datong Station, "2" is Datong Station, data3 indicates the 3-year data of Huangyuan Station, "3" represents the Huangyuan Station, data4 means the 3-year data of Huangzhong Station, and "4" denotes Huangzhong Station.

Data1 is a 91 × 12 double matrix, in which the first row is the identifier of stations, for example, Xining Station is represented by "1". Rows 2–91 display the data on daily rainfall in each month of 2017, 2018, and 2019 (30 days per month); 12 rows indicate that there are 12 months per year, and 12 sets of 91-dimensional daily rainfall arrays constitute a 91 × 12 matrix.

Figure 1 shows the data of daily precipitation in the same month in 2017, 2018, and 2019. It can be seen from Fig. 1 that the data of total daily precipitation at the four stations are roughly the same. In the daily rainfall map of Xining Station in Fig. 1, it can be found that the heavy rainfall was mainly concentrated in 2017 and 2019. Large daily rainfall at Datong Station and Huangyuan Station is significantly lower than that at Xining Station and Huangzhong Station, and daily rainfall at Datong Station in 2019 was the highest in the three years, approaching 50 mm. Due to the small difference in the latitude, longitude, altitude, and straight-line distance of the stations, obvious difference cannot be clearly seen from the figure.

According to the data of daily rainfall at 4 stations in three years, the rainy season in Xining area is mainly concentrated from May to September. The most abundant precipitation appears in June, July, and August, when the moderate and heavy rains significantly increase. The data of daily rainfall at four different stations in 90 days in July of 2017, 2018 and 2019 were analyzed respectively, as shown in Fig. 2. On the horizontal axis, 0–30 indicates the data of daily rainfall in July of 2017, 30–60 means the daily rainfall data in July of 2018, and 60–90 represents the daily rainfall data in July of 2019. Taking the daily rainfall map in July at Xining Station as an example,

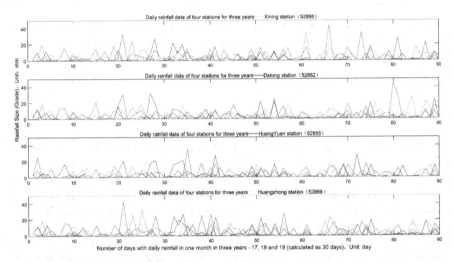

Fig. 1. The data of daily rainfall at the stations in 3 years

the distribution of daily rainfall shows large daily rainfall in July of 2017, indicating 2018 saw the most frequent rainfall, followed by 2019. The Qinghai-Tibet Plateau is the upper reaches of the Yangtze River. In 2018, floods occurred along the Yangtze River nationwide, confirming that there is a certain relationship between floods and rainfall.

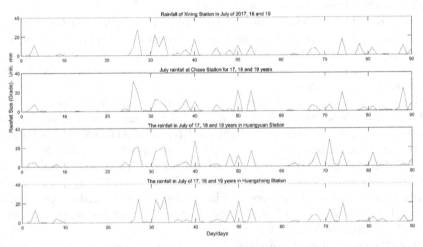

Fig. 2. The data of daily rainfall at the four stations in July of 2017, 2018, and 2019

Based on the data of the four existing stations, a 48 × 91 double matrix was synthesized, and 4368 data were stored in the data variable working area, of which 48 data are the identifiers of four stations and 4320 data are data inputs. In order to better verify the reliability of the algorithm, the data were sorted from small to large and randomly shuffled according to index number [12]. The command in Fig. 3 was input into the matlab script file, and the data were randomly sorted from 1–48. Rand is a uniformly distributed random number. The first command returns the matrix at the 1th row and 28th column. Sort means to sort the array elements, describing the arrangement of the "yufen" element in m along the sorted latitude, and n is the index of the new array.

```
yuefen=rand(1, 48);
[m, n]=sort(yuefen);
```

Fig. 3. Matlab sorting command and the method of array rearrangement

The input data was made correspond to the output data in the dataset. The input data is the daily rainfall in 3 years (2017, 2018, 2019), and the data in the first column is the sum of the data of daily rainfall in the first month (30 days) of 2017, 2018 and 2019, with a total of 90 characteristic rainfall data. The rest can be derived in the same manner. The input data is composed of a 12 × 90 double matrix. The data in the first row represent the identifiers of stations. Classification rules were established to change the output from 1-dimensional to 4-dimensional unit vector. For example, Xining station—"1" was converted into Xining station—[1 0 0 0], and Datong station—"2" was converted into Datong station—[0 1 0 0] through the classification algorithm. Figure 4 shows the data of classification and identification corresponding to each station after the establishment of classification rule [13].

The training set and test set were extracted from the input data [14]. The training set uses 1–36 sets of data in n-indexed mode, that is, a 36 × 90 double matrix was used as the training dataset, and 37–48 sets of data, namely a 12 × 90 double matrix was used as the test set.

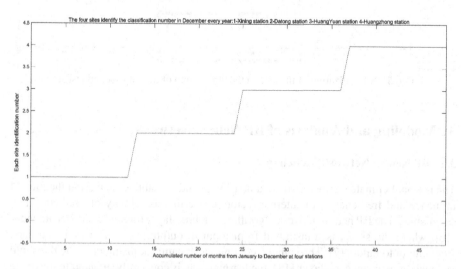

Fig. 4. Corresponding data of 4-dimensional output of four stations

The data were normalized to eliminate inconsistencies in units and orders of magnitude in different datasets, so as to avoid large accidental excessive errors caused by the inconsistencies in order of magnitude and units, and ensure data accuracy [15]. Generally, there are two methods for data normalization, the maximum and minimum method, and the mean variance method.

$$x_k = (x_k - x_{\min})/(x_{\max} - x_{\min}) \tag{1}$$

$$x_k = (x_k - x_{mean})/x_{var} \tag{2}$$

Where $x_{\min}$ and $x_{\max}$ are the minimum and maximum in the data; x_{mean} is the mean of data, and x_{var} is the data variance. The training set and test set in the dataset were normalized, and the data in the 9th column of each dataset was used as a reference, as shown in Fig. 5.

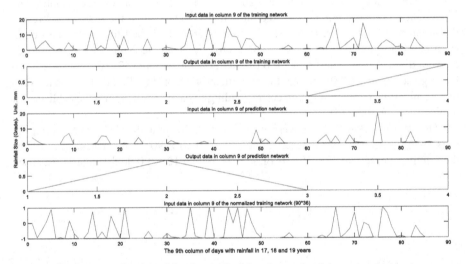

Fig. 5. Normalization of the data in the 9th column of training set and test set

3   Modeling and Analysis of BP Neural Network

3.1   BP Neural Network Modeling

The regional climate characteristic is a non-linear and unstable system, and the mutual influence and free change of internal factors cause the complexity of prediction and calculation. The BP neural network algorithm is a three-layer forward feedback network [16], where the signal is transmitted from input to output, and the error is fed back from output to input [17]. Through the continuous dynamic adjustment of the threshold and weight between each layer [18], the learning rate is constantly updated to make the error approach the minimum after several iterations [19], so that the output continuously approaches the expected value.

The modeling of the prediction algorithm for rainfall distribution at four stations in Xining area based on BP neutral network mainly includes three modules: the construction, training, and identification and classification of BP neural network. Figure 6 shows the detailed process of the system modeling algorithm.

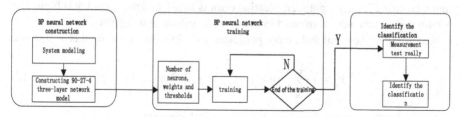

Fig. 6. Flow chart of the modeling algorithm

3.2 BP Neural Network Analysis

The established BP neural network is a bidirectional 3-layer neural network with forward data and backward error [20], as shown in Fig. 7.

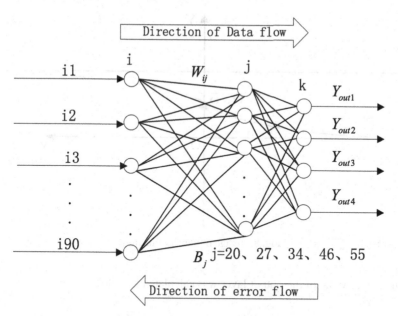

Fig. 7. Neural network topology

According to the characteristics of the data of rainfall, the number of neurons in the input layer was determined to be i = 90 [21], and the output corresponds to four stations k = 4. The hidden layer can be dynamically adjusted by combining with the network algorithm, as shown in Fig. 5. The number of neurons in the hidden layer was adjusted to 20, 27, 34, 46, 55 according to the structure, and when the number of nodes in the hidden layer is 27, the output identification error is small, and the accuracy is high. The specific parameters were compared in detail in the subsequent chapters.

According to the input and output parameters, the hidden layer output is as follows:

$$F_j = f(\sum_{i=1}^{n} w_{ij} - a_j) \quad j = 1, 2, 3 \ldots \ldots m \tag{3}$$

Where f is the transfer function [22] and w_{ij} is the weight.

$$f(x) = \frac{1}{1 + e^{-x}} \tag{4}$$

The transfer function f mainly converts the range of the independent variable from $(-\infty, +\infty)$ to the range (0, 1). The specific image of the transfer function is as follows, as shown in Fig. 8.:

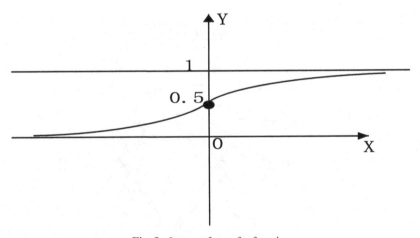

Fig. 8. Image of transfer function

The output value of the output layer was calculated as follows:

$$O_k = \sum_{j=1}^{m} F_j w_{ij} - b_k \quad k = 1, 2, 3 \ldots \ldots m1 \tag{5}$$

Where b_k is the threshold.
The error was calculated by

$$E_k = Y_k - O_k \quad k = 1, 2, 3 \ldots \ldots m \tag{6}$$

Where E_k is the prediction error of the network.
Weight replacement:

$$w_{ij} = w_{ij} + \eta F_j(1 - F_j)x(i)\sum_{k=1}^{m} w_{jk}e_k \quad j = 1, 2, 3 \ldots n \quad k = 1, 2, 3 \ldots m \quad (7)$$

Where η is the learning rate, generally between [0–1].
Threshold replacement:

$$a_j = a_j + \eta F_j(1 - F_j)\sum_{k=1}^{m} w_{ij}e_k \quad j = 1, 2, 3 \ldots \ldots m \quad (8)$$

$$b_k = b_k + e_k \quad k = 1, 2, 3 \ldots m \quad (9)$$

3.3 Mathematical Modeling Based on MATLAB

The number of nodes in the input layer of the network was determined according to the data characteristics of daily rainfall at the four stations in three years, that is, the number of neurons is 90; the output is the four stations after classification and identification [23], that is, the number of output neurons is 4; according to program compilation and debugging, the number of nodes in hidden layer has a great impact on the output accuracy. If there are few nodes, the number of iterations [24] needs to be increased to reduce the accuracy. Too many nodes will decrease the network learning results and affect the network accuracy. The optimal number of nodes in the hidden layer was estimated through program debugging, trial and error.

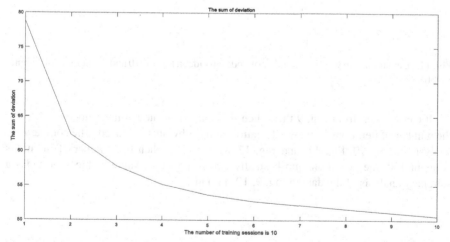

Fig. 9. Deviation sum when the number of nodes in hidden layer is 10 and the number of training is 10

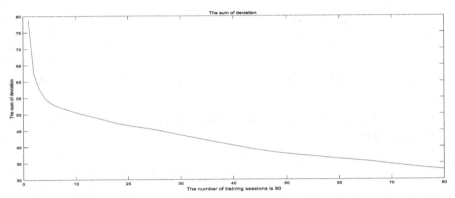

Fig. 10. Deviation sum when the number of nodes in hidden layer is 10 and the number of training is 80

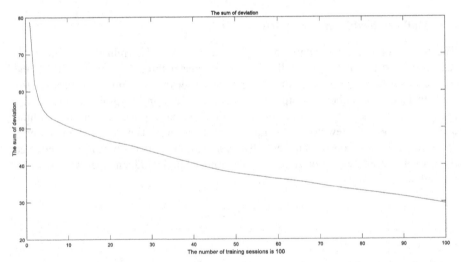

Fig. 11. Deviation sum when the number of nodes in hidden layer is 10 and the number of training is 100

It can be seen from Fig. 9 that when the number of hidden layer nodes is 10, and the number of iterations is 10, the deviation sum is obviously reduced. The comparative analysis of Fig. 10, Fig. 11, and Fig. 12 showed that when the number of iterations is about 130, the deviation sum basically tends to a stable value. Table 1 provides a summary analysis of the data in Fig. 9, 10, 11 and 12.

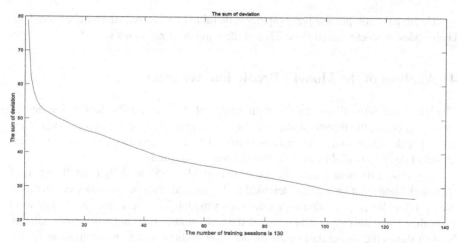

Fig. 12. Deviation sum when the number of nodes in hidden layer is 10 and the number of training is 130

Table 1. The influence of the number of iterations on the error

Number of hidden layer nodes	The number of iterations	The sum of the deviations from the estimates
10	10	36
	80	33
	100	30
	130	28

When the number of nodes in the hidden layer was adjusted to 27, minimum deviation sum was obtained. The number of nodes in hidden layer was fixed and the number of iterations was adjusted, as shown in Table 2.

Table 2. Determination of the number of iterations

Number of hidden layer nodes	The number of iterations	The sum of the deviations from the estimates
27	55	21
	66	30
	89	33
	100	37

Through the comprehensive comparison of Table 1 and Table 2, the number of hidden layer nodes was determined to be 27, and the number of iterations was 55.

4 Analysis of the Model's Prediction Accuracy

The BP neural network was trained with 36 sets of 90 data of daily rainfall. During the training process, the threshold and weight of the network were adjusted through back error. The deviation sum was minimized through repeated iterations and a mathematical model of daily rainfall data of four stations was established.

The trained BP neural network was used to predict [25] the daily rainfall signals of the four stations that have been identified and classified. The output data were stored in the 4×1 double F_{OUT} variable matrix defined by matlab. The data of the test module were normalized, and the output data stored in the F_{OUT} matrix were not reverse-normalized. Table 3 shows the output data of the output layer without reverse normalization.

In Table 3, each row represents the information of station, and each column is the probability that the data of rainfall belongs to the station. The largest absolute value of the data was used to identify as which station the rainfall information is classified. For example, the data in the second row and the first column is 0.9943381, which is the largest, and it can be considered that the rainfall information in the first column of the test belongs to the second station, that is, the Datong station.

Through reverse normalization [26], that is:

for i = 1:12

FOUTPUT(i) = find(Fout(:,i) = = max(Fout(:,i)));

end

The matlab program traverses the data from the first column to the 12th column to find the maximum in each column, and outputs the corresponding index number through the find command, that is, the corresponding information of the identified and classified station.

What are stored in F_{OUTPUT} are the data subject to reverse normalization, that is, the corresponding four-dimensional information of stations. Table 4 displays the reverse-normalized information of stations. Figure 13 describes the classification of F_{OUT} and F_{OUTPUT}, and the randomly sampled 3rd-9th groups.

By calculating the accuracy of classification and identification of rainfall information of four stations, the reliability and accuracy of the mathematical model for the daily rainfall information system based on BP neural network were verified. Two variables error_M and sum_M were defined based on the matlab program, and used to store the number of incorrect stations and the sum of the identified stations respectively, so that the identification and classification rate of each station can be obtained. Table 5 shows the statistics on incorrect stations.

In Table 5, one classification error occurs on Xining station and Datong station respectively, two classification errors occur on Huangyuan station, and there is no classification error on Huangzhong station. The rainfall information of Huangzhong has its own characteristics compared with that of the other three stations, and the rainfall distribution is quite different from the other three stations.

Table 6 shows the data of each station.

Table 3. F_{OUT} output data without reverse normalization

	1	2	3	4	5	6	7	8	9	10	11	12
1	0.032474	0.106569	-0.23009	0.056859	-0.29417	0.705917	0.184111	0.364406	2.751824	0.609499	-0.0498	0.261297
2	0.994381	0.377006	1.078399	0.250777	1.661047	2.190163	0.512899	0.432535	2.12624	0.130108	0.996518	0.158031
3	0.079328	-0.25847	0.154902	0.458619	-0.85696	0.194148	0.109911	-0.04784	-0.50089	0.633056	0.088736	0.147738
4	-0.23872	0.60025	0.157861	0.103908	0.845363	1.802186	0.333733	-0.5803	0.821823	1.353207	-0.0668	0.050633

Table 4. Output data after reverse normalization

	One group	Two group	Three group	Four group	Five group	Six group	Seven group	Eight group	Nine group	Ten group	Eleven group	Twelve group
Stand no.	2	4	2	3	2	2	2	2	1	4	2	1

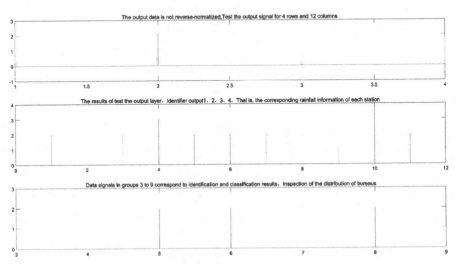

Fig. 13. Classification of F_{OUT} and F_{OUTPUT} and sampled signal data

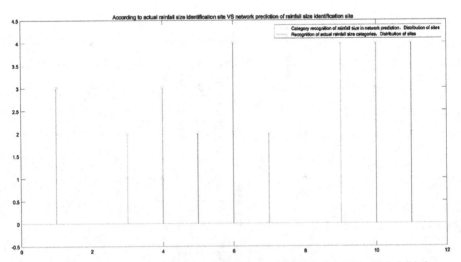

Fig. 14. Comparison of the actual number of identified and classified stations of rainfall information and the number of identified and classified stations of rainfall information predicted by the network

Table 5. Statistics on incorrect stations

	Xining station	Datong station	Huangyuan station	Huangzhong station
Wrong number	1	1	2	0

Table 6. Statistics on rainfal

	Xining station	Datong station	Huangyuan station	Huangzhong station
The sum of classified individual	2	5	3	2

Through data comparison and analysis, the number of test samples of Xining Station is 2, and the number of error station is 1, thus the sample accuracy rate is 50%. A total of 5 random samples of Datong Station were tested, and one error station was found. The model calculation showed the accuracy rate is 80%. The number of test samples of Huangyuan Station is 3, and there are 2 error stations, hence the accuracy rate is 33.3%. There are 2 test samples of Huangzhong Station, of which there is 0 error station, and the accuracy rate is 100%.

Figure 14 compares the number of stations corresponding to the actual rainfall characteristic signals and the number of stations of rainfall information predicted by the network.

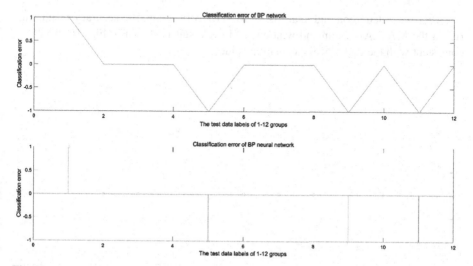

Fig. 15. The linear graph and the discrete graph of the identification and classification error of the numerical comparison

According to the predicted value of rainfall, the difference between the number of classified stations and the actual number of classified stations was obtained. The error value was calculated, and the numerical index analysis was performed. The analysis was conducted according to formula 1–9.

error = output_predict-output_initial(n(37:48))';

Substitute into MATLAB to compile and debug, and the error value corresponding to each station was calculated. Table 7 shows the corresponding error value.

Table 7. Errors in identified and classified stations

	One group	Two group	Three group	Four group	Five group	Six group	Seven group	Eight group	Nine group	The group	Eleven group	Twelve group
Difference	1	0	0	0	−1	0	0	0	−1	0	−1	0

The current map and the discrete map of the identification and classification errors corresponding to the numerical comparison are shown in Fig. 15.

Fig. 16. The accuracy results of rainfall identification and classification of the four stations are run in MATLAB

After the calculation and analysis by MATLAB program, the accuracy result was run in the MATLAB command window, and the result is shown in Fig. 16, which is consistent with the theoretical calculation value.

5   Conclusion

A prediction method for rainfall information distribution at four stations in Xining area based on BP neural network was proposed. The BP neural network algorithm was briefly introduced, and an improved model algorithm for the number of iterations of rainfall data adjustment and hidden layer neurons was presented. Through comparative analysis, a stable and reliable identification and classification algorithm model was obtained. Finally, the test data were input into the improved trained BP neural network algorithm model. The results revealed the predicted values are not much different from the actual values, and the accuracy rate is high, indicating that the model can accurately identify and classify the stations of rainfall information. The model algorithm can be used to analyze the data on daily rainfall of different regions, latitudes, longitudes, and altitudes in the Xining area in the future. Through the errors of identification and classification, the characteristics and differences of the rainfall distribution at different stations can be derived. The characteristic data of rainfall in different regions provide a realistic basis for the automatic identification and classification of rainfall data and the study of rainfall in different areas and spaces in the future.

Acknowledgments. The authors acknowledge the financial support of the Major Scientific and Technological Project of Qinghai Province (2019-ZJ-A10).

References

1. Xin, Q., Li, X., Zhu, B.: Characteristics analysis of a heavy rainfall process in Xining in 2016. Sci. Technol. Qinghai Agric. For. (03), 33–37 (2017)
2. Zhang, C., Nie, Y., Hao, X.: Analysis of the climatic characteristics of extreme precipitation and precipitation of different levels in the flood season in Xining area. J. Agric. Catastrophology **10**(03), 74–78 (2020)
3. Zhang, H., Zhao, B., Li, Y.: Application of rainfall monitoring and alarm system in Qinghai meteorology. China Sci. Technol. Inf. (Z2), 42–43 (2014)
4. Liu, Y., Ma, Y., Yang, Y.: Analysis on the temporal and spatial variation characteristics of day and night rainfall in Qinghai Plateau from 1961 to 2018. J. Glaciol. Geocryol. **42**(03), 996–1006 (2020)
5. Chen, R., Liu, J.: The area rainfall prediction of up-river valleys in Yangtze River based on artificial neural network modes. Sci. Meteorol. Sin. **24**(04), 483–487 (2004)
6. Gu, X., Wang, C., Yuan, S.: GA-BP ANN model for river catchment precipitation forecast. J. Trop. Meteorol. **22**(03), 248–252 (2006)
7. Wang, S., Feng, G., Song, S.: Artificial neural network model of rainfall-runoff forecasting for rain gauge unevenly distributed watersheds. J. Northwest Sci-Tech Univ. Agric. For. (Nat. Sci. Ed.) (05), 81–84 (2002)
8. Zhou, X., Li, Y., Zhang, J.: Evaluation model of rainfall forecast method based on man-made nerve network and two-dimensional interpolation. J. Lanzhou Petrochemical Coll. Technol. (04), 38–41 (2005)
9. Lang, Y., Xing, H.: Design of infrared diffuse reflection optical automatic rain gauge based on fully connected neural network. Chin. J. Sens. Actuators **32**(03), 476–480 (2019)
10. Chen, K., Fang, H., Shen, Y.: Measuring principle and error analysis of tipping bucket and piezoelectric rain gauges. Sci. Technol. Innov. (30), 10–11 (2020)

11. Huang, J., Chen, Z.: Artificial nerve net model of short-term raining forecast. J. Nanhua Univ. (Sci. Technol.) (03), 83–87 (2006)
12. Yi, Z.: BP neural network algorithms and application and MATLAB programs. https://sho p108509999.taobao.com. Accessed 27 Jan 2019
13. Zhu, F., Guo, J., Cao, L.: Hierarchical identification of multi-label features in data based on classification rule mining. Comput. Simul. 38(04), 310–314 (2021)
14. Shi, Y.: Research on Spatial Parameter Optimization Based on BP Neural Network and Multi-objective Optimization Algorithm. Tianjin University (2019)
15. Yuan, Q.: Research on Training Optimization Method of Deep Neural Network. South China University of Technology (2020)
16. Xin, J., Jing, G. E., Zhu, S.: Research on iterative repair method of dam safety monitoring data missing based on partial least squares regression. Water Resour. Plann. Des. (11), 100–104 (2021)
17. Zhang, J., Yang, Y., Qian, F.: Research on GNSS/INS error feedback correction based on Kalman filter-neural network prediction. Electron. Des. Eng. 23(10), 103–105 (2015)
18. Zhao, F., Jiang, S.: GA-BP based on optimization and its application in wine quality prediction. J. Harbin Univ. Commer. (Nat. Sci. Ed.) 37(03), 307–313 (2021)
19. Hu, H., Zhao, S., Liu, Q., Wang, Q., Wang, T.: BP neural network PID parameter tuning algorithm based on momentum factor to optimize learning rate. J. Jilin Univ. (Nat. Sci. Ed.) 58(06), 1415–1420 (2020)
20. Liu, K., Li, J., Shen, J., Ma, J.: Research on road network selection based on BP neural network and topological parameters. J. Surv. Mapp. Sci. Technol. 33(03), 325–330 (2016)
21. Wenlong, L., Hu, L., Yan, D.: Influence of input mode on annual runoff prediction of BP model. Water Saving Irrig. (10), 58–61 (2014)
22. Lin, X.: Research on Damage Detection Method of Steel Structure Based on BP Neural Network and Transmittance Function Fusion. Zhejiang University of Technology (2020)
23. Wang, Y.: Behavior recognition algorithm based on deep neural network. Comput. Knowl. Technol. 17(03), 17–18 (2021)
24. Hu, H.: Research on parallel iterative optimization based on BP neural network and genetic algorithm. Mach. Electron. 37(01), 26–32 (2019)
25. Li, X.: Air quality forecasting based on GAB and fuzzy BP neural network. J. Huazhong Univ. Sci. Technol. (Nat. Sci. Ed.) 41(S1), 63–65 (2013)
26. Wang, Y., Wu, X.: Normalization algorithm suitable for small batches in deep neural network training. Comput. Sci. 46(S2), 273–276 (2019)

The 3-Set Tree Connectivity
of the Folded Petersen Cube Networks

Huifen Ge[1], Shumin Zhang[2,3(✉)], He Li[1], and Chengfu Ye[2,3]

[1] School of Computer, Qinghai Normal University, Xining 810008, China
[2] School of Mathematics and Statistics, Qinghai Normal University,
Xining 810008, China
[3] Academy of Plateau Science and Sustainability, People's Government
of Qinghai Province, Beijing Normal University, Xining, China
{zhangshumin,yechf}@qhnu.edu.cn

Abstract. The layout of the processors and links are represented a network structure in a distributed computer system. A graph is regarded as the topological structure of an interconnection network as usual, vertices and edges stand for processors and links between them, respectively. The internally disjoint Steiner trees of graphs are used in information engineering design and telecommunication networks. The ℓ-set tree connectivity (also is called generalized ℓ-connectivity), as an extension of the traditional connectivity, can provide for measuring the capability of connection arbitrary ℓ vertices in a network. The folded Petersen cube networks $FPQ_{n,k}$ have good properties and can be modeled the topological structure of a massively parallel processing system. This article shows the 3-set tree connectivity of $FPQ_{n,k}$ is $n + 3k - 1$.

Keywords: Interconnection network · 3-set tree connectivity · Folded Petersen cube networks · Cartesian product

1 Introduction

Nowadays, Big data and Internet of Things are flourishing in computer information era. The prevailing of social networks, cloud computing and enormous amount of data are emerging in high speed because of the promulgation of mobile devices which are in a position to collect a wide range of data. So, it is significant to develop Big Data in the parallel and distributed system.

An undirected graph is a model of an interconnection network, the vertices and the edges correspond to the processors and the links between them, respectively. Connectivity of a graph can measure the fault tolerance which is a major concern to design and analyze a computer network. In general, the stronger reliability depends on the larger connectivity of a graph. Although the traditional connectivity can express the fault tolerance of a network systems, it just

Supported by the Science Found of Qinghai Province (Nos. 2019-ZJ-921).

X. Wang et al. (Eds.): AICON 2021, LNICST 397, pp. 293–304, 2021.
https://doi.org/10.1007/978-3-030-90199-8_27

reflects the connectivity between any two processors. It means that the traditional connectivity is circumscribed and imprecise in estimating the toughness of an interconnection network. At this time, the ℓ-set tree connectivity provides a more accurate way to overcome the shortcoming and it is useful for weighing up the fault tolerance in a network system.

In networks, the system allows at most $\kappa(G) - 1$ nodes to make mistakes simultaneously, and the information can still be transmitted efficiently between any two nodes of the remaining network within the specified time. The traditional connectivity $\kappa(G)$ of a graph G is defined as $\min\{|X|\}$ such that G delete X has at least two connected components or a trivial component. A graph G is said to be ℓ-connected if $\kappa(G) \geq \ell$. An equivalent definition of $\kappa(G)$ was provided by Whitney [27] with the form of a theorem: for any vertices subset S with $|S| = 2$, say $S = \{x, y\}$, the maximum quantity of internally disjoint (x, y)-paths in G are denoted by $\kappa(S)$, if S goes through all 2-subsets of $V(G)$, then $\kappa(G)$ is minimum value of $\kappa(S)$.

Chartrand et al. [3] brought in the definition of the ℓ-set tree connectivity of a graph G in 1984, which is an extension of the traditional connectivity. For $S \subseteq V(G)$ and $|S| \geq 3$, if $V(T)$ contains S, then a tree T is called S-Steiner tree. The Steiner tree is vulgarly applied in the physical design of VLSI circuits, see [10,11,26]. Moreover, internally disjoint S-trees mean that the intersection of their edges are empty set and of their vertices are S. The maximum quantity of the internally disjoint S-trees in G are denoted by $\kappa(S)$. Let $\kappa_\ell(G)$ be the ℓ-set tree connectivity of G and $\kappa_\ell(G) = \min\{\kappa(S)|S \subseteq V(G), |S| = \ell\}$ for $2 \leq \ell \leq |V(G)|$. Clearly, $\kappa_2(G) = \kappa(G)$. Over the past few years, the ℓ-set tree connectivity has been investigated widely and yielded a great deal of results, more details see [2–5,9,13,14,16,18–21,23,28]. We study the $\kappa_3(G)$ when G is the folded Petersen cube networks $FPQ_{n,k}$, and obtain $\kappa_3(FPQ_{n,k}) = n+3k-1$ in this paper.

2   Preliminaries

This part shows some basic notations and results that will be available throughout the paper.

2.1   Basic Notions and Lemmas

We tend to be the reader to [1] for the notations and terminology not described here. All graphs mentioned are connected, simple, finite and undirected.

Let $G = (V, E)$ be a graph, we use $V(G)$ and $E(G)$ to denote vertex set and edge set of G, respectively. Two vertices v_1 and v_2 are adjacent if $v_1 v_2 \in E(G)$, also v_1 and v_2 are neighbors each other, the neighborhood of v is a set of all neighbors of v in G, denoted by $N_G(v)$. The cardinality $|N_G(v)|$ represents the degree of v, denoted by $d_G(v)$. The minimum degree (resp. maximum degree) of G are denoted by $\delta(G)$ (resp. $\Delta(G)$). If every vertex of G has degree r, then G is

r-regular. For any $x, y \in V(G)$, an (x, y)-path is denoted by P_{xy} and the length of a shortest (x, y)-path is called the distance from x to y, denoted by $d_G(x, y)$.

A subgraph of G is a graph $H = (V', E')$ such that V' is contained V and E' is contained E. If $V' = V$, then H is a spanning subgraph of G. Using $G[V']$ to denote the subgraph of G induced by V'.

Lemma 1 [17]. *If G is a connected graph, then $\kappa_3(G) \leq \delta(G)$. In particular, if there are two adjacent vertices of degree $\delta(G)$, then $\kappa_3(G) \leq \delta(G) - 1$.*

Lemma 2 *(Fan Lemma [1]). Let G be a ℓ-connected graph and $u \in V(G)$, let U be a subset of $V(G) - \{u\}$ with $|U| \geq \ell$. Then there exists a family of ℓ internally disjoint (u, U)-paths whose terminal vertices are distinct in U, also is called a ℓ-fan in G from u to U.*

Lemma 3 [17]. *Let n be order of a connected graph G. For every two integers ℓ and r with $\ell \geq 0$ and $r \in \{0, 1, 2, 3\}$, if $\kappa(G) = 4\ell + r$, then $\kappa_3(G) \geq 3\ell + \lceil \frac{r}{2} \rceil$. Moreover, the lower bound is sharp.*

Lemma 4 [1]. *$\kappa(Q_n) = n$ for $n \geq 1$.*

Lemma 5 [20]. *$\kappa_3(Q_n) = n - 1$ for $n \geq 2$.*

2.2   The Folded Petersen Cube Networks

To construct a bigger network, the Cartesian product of graphs is one of the most momentous method and plays a key role in networks.

Remember the definition of Cartesian product. Let $G \square H$ be Cartesian product of two graphs G and H, which is a graph with vertex set $\{(g, h) | g \in V(G), h \in V(H)\}$ such that $((g, h), (g', h')) \in E(G \square H)$ if and only if either $g = g'$ and $hh' \in E(H)$, or $h = h'$ and $gg' \in E(G)$. For a fixed vertex g of G, let $H(g)$ be the induced subgraph by vertices $\{(g, h)\}$ with h traversal $V(H)$, clearly, $H(g)$ is isomorphic to H. For a vertex V' of $V(G)$, let $H(V')$ denote the subgraph of $G \square H$ induced by the vertices $\{(g, h) | g \in V', h \in V(H)\}$. We can define similarly $G(h)$ and $G(U')$ for $h \in V(H)$ and $U' \subseteq V(H)$.

Meanwhile, the Cartesian product of graphs possesses many excellent characters.

Proposition 1. *Let G, H and L are three connected graphs, for their Cartesian product the following properties hold:*

(i) *[15] (commutative) $G \square H = H \square G$.*
(ii) *[15] (associative) $(G \square H) \square L = G \square (H \square L)$.*
(iii) *[12] The distance between (g_1, h_1) and (g_2, h_2) in $G \square H$ is equal to the distance $d_G(g_1, g_2) + d_H(h_1, h_2)$.*

Lemma 6 [24]. *For two connected graphs G and H. We have*

$$\kappa(G \square H) \geq \kappa(G) + \kappa(H).$$

Lemma 7 [20]. *For a graph G and a path P_m with m vertices.*

$$\kappa_3(G\square P_m) \geq \begin{cases} \kappa_3(G), & \text{if } \kappa_3(G) = \kappa(G) \geq 1; \\ \kappa_3(G) + 1, & \text{if } 1 \leq \kappa_3(G) < \kappa(G). \end{cases}$$

Moreover, the bounds are sharp.

Lemma 8 [20]. *For two connected graphs G and H satisfy $\kappa_3(G) \geq \kappa_3(H)$.*

$$\kappa_3(G\square H) \geq \begin{cases} \kappa_3(G) + \kappa_3(H), & \text{if } \kappa(G) > \kappa_3(G); \\ \kappa_3(G) + \kappa_3(H) - 1, & \text{if } \kappa(G) = \kappa_3(G). \end{cases}$$

Moreover, the bounds are sharp.

Hypercube Q_n and folded Petersen graph FP_k compose the folded Petersen cube networks through Cartesian product.

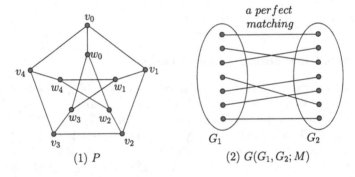

(1) P (2) $G(G_1, G_2; M)$

Fig. 1. The Petersen graph P and $G(G_1, G_2; M)$.

Let G and ℓ be a graph and a positive integer, respectively, we use G^ℓ to denote the ℓ-th iteration of Cartesian product on graph G, namely $G^k = G^{\ell-1}\square G$ if $\ell \geq 2$. In particular, $G^\ell = G$ when $\ell = 1$. A n-dimensional hypercube $Q_n = Q_{n-1}\square Q_1$ for any positive integer n. Specially, $Q_1 \cong P_2$, where P_2 is a path with two vertices. In fact, $Q_n = P_2^n$. The Petersen graph P has 10 vertices and an outer 5-cycle and an inner 5-cycle, they are joined with five spokes, see Fig. 1(1). The k-dimensional folded Petersen graph FP_k is made up of the k-th iteration of Cartesian product on Petersen graph P. The FP_k possesses some good topology qualities for network systems, for example, it is symmetric and accommodates 10^k vertices, $3k$-regular graph with diameter $2k$ [8].

Öhring and Das [22] gave out the notion of the folded Petersen cube networks $FPQ_{n,k}$ and we can embedded many normative topology structures into it, like linear arrays, rings, meshes, hypercubes and so on. The folded Petersen cube network $FPQ_{n,k}$ is a generalization of the FP_k, defined as $Q_n\square FP_k$ with $2^n \times 10^k$

vertices. In particular, $FPQ_{0,k} = FP_k = P^k$ and $FPQ_{n,0} = Q_n$. Over the years, some results [7,22,25] about the folded Petersen cube networks were put out.

A perfect matching of a graph G is a set of edges such that every vertex is incident with exactly one edge of this set. Let G_1, G_2 be two graphs with same vertices number and M be an arbitrary perfect matching between the vertices of G_1 and G_2, then $G(G_1, G_2; M)$ be the graph with the vertex set $V(G_1) \cup V(G_2)$ and the edge set $E(G_1) \cup E(G_2) \cup M$ (see Fig. 1(2)), thus the Petersen graph P can be regarded as $G(C_5, C_5; M)$ for some perfect matching M. Furthermore, $P \Box C_5$ can be regarded as $G(C_5 \Box C_5, C_5 \Box C_5; M)$ for some perfect matching M, P^k can be regarded as $G(P^{k-1} \Box C_5, P^{k-1} \Box C_5; M)$, where $k \geq 2$.

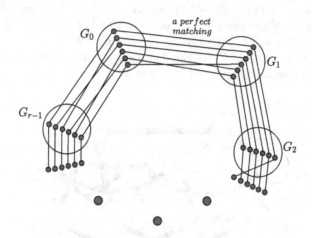

Fig. 2. The graph $G(G_0, G_1, \cdots, G_{r-1}; \mathcal{M})$.

Chen et al. [6] amplified their scheme to another construction. Let r and t be positive integers, where $r \geq 3, t \geq 1$ and $G_0, G_1, \cdots, G_{r-1}$ are the graphs with $|V(G_i)| = t$ for $0 \leq i \leq r - 1$. We define $H = G(G_0, G_1, \cdots, G_{r-1}; \mathcal{M})$, where $V(H) = \bigcup_{i=0}^{r-1} V(G_i)$, $E(H) = \mathcal{M} \cup \bigcup_{i=0}^{r-1} E(G_i)$ and $\mathcal{M} = \bigcup_{i=0}^{r-1} M_{i,i+1(mod\ r)}$, note that $M_{i,i+1(mod\ r)}$ is an arbitrary perfect matching between $V(G_i)$ and $V(G_{i+1(mod\ r)})$, see Fig. 2. Thus $P^{k-1} \Box C_5$ can be viewed as $G(P^{k-1}, P^{k-1}, P^{k-1}, P^{k-1}, P^{k-1}, \mathcal{M})$.

3   Main Results

In this part, we show that the 3-set tree connectivity of the folded Petersen cube network. The following results are useful to prove the main result.

Lemma 9. $\kappa(FP_k) = 3k$ for any $k \geq 1$.

Proof. It is a well-known result that $\kappa(G) \leq \delta(G)$, then $\kappa(FP_k) = \kappa(P^k) \leq 3k$. By $\kappa(P) = 3$ and Lemma 6, we know $\kappa(FP_k) \geq k\kappa(P) = 3k$.

Lemma 10. $\kappa(FPQ_{n,k}) = n + 3k$ *for* $n, k \geq 1$.

Proof. Since the folded Petersen cube network $FPQ_{n,k}$ is $(n + 3k)$-regular, it is easy to see that $\kappa(FPQ_{n,k}) \leq n + 3k$. Moreover, according to the Lemma 4, Lemma 6 and Lemma 9, we obtain $\kappa(FPQ_{n,k}) \geq \kappa(Q_n) + \kappa(FP_k) = n + 3k$.

Theorem 1. $\kappa_3(FP_k) = 3k - 1$ *for* $k \geq 1$.

Proof. Since FP_k is a 3k-regular graph, $\kappa_3(FP_k) \leq \delta(FP_k) - 1 = 3k - 1$. We will prove that $\kappa_3(FP_k) \geq 3k - 1$. It suffices to show that there exist $3k - 1$ internally disjoint S-trees in FP_k for any $S \subseteq V(FP_k)$ with $|S| = 3$.

Recall that $FP_k = P^k$. We prove by induction on k.

For $k = 1$, obviously, P^1 is the Petersen graph P, thus $\kappa(P) = 3$. By Lemma 3, we know that $\kappa_3(P) \geq \lceil \frac{3}{2} \rceil = 2 = 3k - 1$.

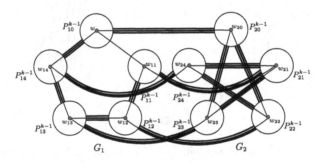

Fig. 3. The graph P^k.

Now suppose that $k \geq 2$. As P^k can be regarded as $G(P^{k-1}\square C_5, P^{k-1}\square C_5; M)$, we denote the first $P^{k-1}\square C_5$ by G_1, the second $P^{k-1}\square C_5$ by G_2 and ten copies of P^{k-1} by $P_{i0}^{k-1}, P_{i1}^{k-1}, P_{i2}^{k-1}, P_{i3}^{k-1}, P_{i4}^{k-1}$ for $i = 1, 2$, respectively. Let w be an arbitrary vertex of P_{10}^{k-1}, then there are the nine vertices $w_{11}, w_{12}, w_{13}, w_{14}, w_{20}, w_{21}, w_{22}, w_{23}, w_{24}$ mutual corresponding to w in P^k and exactly three neighbors w_{11}, w_{14} and w_{20} in $P_{11}^{k-1}, P_{14}^{k-1}$ and P_{20}^{k-1}, respectively. Note that $ww_{11}w_{12}w_{13}w_{14}w$ be a C_5 in G_1 and $\{w_{20}, w_{21}, w_{22}, w_{23}, w_{24}\}$ induces a C_5 of G_2. See Fig. 3.

Without loss of generality, let $S = \{x, y, z\}$ and $|S \cap V(G_1)| \geq |S \cap V(G_2)|$. We distinguish two cases.

Case 1. $|S \cap V(G_1)| = 3$.

Case 1.1. x, y and z belong to one copy.

Without loss of generality, let $x, y, z \in P_{10}^{k-1}$, see Fig. 4. By the inductive hypothesis, $\kappa_3(P_{10}^{k-1}) \geq 3k - 4$. That is to say, there are at least $3k - 4$ internally disjoint S-trees $T_1, T_2, \cdots, T_{3k-4}$ in P_{10}^{k-1}. Clearly, each of x, y, z has a unique

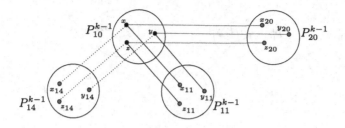

Fig. 4. The illustration of Case 1.1

neighbor in P_{11}^{k-1}, P_{14}^{k-1} and P_{20}^{k-1}, denoted by $\{x_{11}, x_{14}, x_{20}\}$, $\{y_{11}, y_{14}, y_{20}\}$ and $\{z_{11}, z_{14}, z_{20}\}$, respectively. Choose a $\{x_{11}, y_{11}, z_{11}\}$-tree $\widehat{T}_{3k-3}$ in P_{11}^{k-1}, a $\{x_{14}, y_{14}, z_{14}\}$-tree $\widehat{T}_{3k-2}$ in P_{14}^{k-1} and a $\{x_{20}, y_{20}, z_{20}\}$-tree $\widehat{T}_{3k-1}$ in P_{20}^{k-1}. Let $T_{3k-3} = \widehat{T}_{3k-3} + \{xx_{11}, yy_{11}, zz_{11}\}$, $T_{3k-2} = \widehat{T}_{3k-2} + \{xx_{14}, yy_{14}, zz_{14}\}$ and $T_{3k-1} = \widehat{T}_{3k-1} + \{xx_{20}, yy_{20}, zz_{20}\}$, then $T_1, T_2, \cdots, T_{3k-1}$ are $3k - 1$ internally disjoint S-trees.

Case 1.2. Exact two of x, y, z belong to one copy.

Without loss of generality, suppose that $x, y \in P_{10}^{k-1}$ and $z \in P_{11}^{k-1}$. By Lemma 9, we have $\kappa(P^{k-1}) = 3k - 3$, hence there are $3k - 3$ internally disjoint (x, y)-paths $P_1, P_2, \cdots, P_{3k-3}$ in P_{10}^{k-1}. Pick up $3k - 3$ distinct vertices $x_1, x_2, \cdots, x_{3k-3}$ from the paths such that $x_i \in V(P_i)$ and $xx_i \in E(P_i)$, $i = 1, 2, \cdots, 3k - 3$. Notice that at most one of these paths, say P_1, has length 1, if so $x_1 = y$. Let z_{10} be the corresponding vertex of z in P_{10}^{k-1}. We discuss the following two subcases.

subcase 1.2.1. $z_{10} \in \{x, y\}$.

Without loss of generality, suppose that $z_{10} = x$, see Fig. 5. If x_i' is the corresponding vertex of x_i in P_{11}^{k-1}, then $x_i'z \in E(G_1)$. Let $T_i = P_i + \{x_ix_i', x_i'z\}$, $i = 1, 2, \cdots, 3k - 3$. Since P_{14}^{k-1}, P_{20}^{k-1} are connected, we can choose a path $P_{x_{14}y_{14}}$ connecting x_{14} and y_{14} in P_{14}^{k-1} and a path $P_{x_{20}y_{20}}$ connecting x_{20} and y_{20} in P_{20}^{k-1}.

Notice that x_{14}, x, z are mutual corresponding in G_1 and they are in a C_5, Choose a path $P_{x_{14}z}$ containing x. Since x_{20}, z_{21} are in a C_5 of G_2, we choose a (x_{20}, z_{21})-path $P_{x_{20}z_{21}}$. Let $T_{3k-2} = P_{x_{14}z} + P_{x_{14}y_{14}} + \{yy_{14}\}$, $T_{3k-1} = P_{x_{20}y_{20}} + P_{x_{20}z_{21}} + \{xx_{20}, yy_{20}, zz_{21}\}$, then $T_1, T_2, \cdots, T_{3k-1}$ are $3k - 1$ internally disjoint S-trees.

subcase 1.2.2. $z_{10} \notin \{x, y\}$.

If $z_{10} \notin \bigcup_{i=1}^{3k-3} V(P_i)$. Choose $3k - 3$ vertices $x_1', x_2', \cdots, x_{3k-3}'$ from P_{11}^{k-1}, where x_i' is the corresponding vertex of x_i, $i = 1, 2, \cdots, 3k - 3$. Let $X = \{x_1', x_2', \cdots, x_{3k-3}'\}$, by Lemma 2, there are $3k - 3$ internally disjoint paths $P_1', P_2', \cdots, P_{3k-3}'$ from z to X in P_{11}^{k-1}. We can get $3k - 3$ internally disjoint trees $T_i = P_i + \{x_ix_i'\} + P_i'$, $i = 1, 2, \cdots, 3k - 3$.

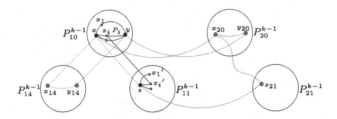

Fig. 5. The illustration of Case 1.2.1

Notice that x, z, z_{14} are mutual corresponding in G_1 and they are in a C_5, hence there are two internally disjoint paths $P_{zz_{14}}$ connecting z and z_{14}. Choose one of the two paths no containing x and a $\{x_{14}, y_{14}, z_{14}\}$-tree $\widehat{T}_{3k-2}$ in P_{14}^{k-1}, let $T_{3k-2} = \widehat{T}_{3k-2} + \{xx_{14}, yy_{14}\} + P_{zz_{14}}$. Since x_{20}, y_{20} be two corresponding vertices of x, y in P_{20}^{k-1}, respectively, there exists a path (z_{21}, z_{20})-path $P_{z_{21}z_{20}}$ in G_2. Choose a $\{x_{20}, y_{20}, z_{20}\}$-tree $\widehat{T}_{3k-1}$ in P_{20}^{k-1}, and let $T_{3k-1} = \widehat{T}_{3k-1} + \{xx_{20}, yy_{20}\} + P_{z_{20}z_{21}} + \{z_{21}z\}$. Then $T_1, T_2, \cdots, T_{3k-1}$ are $3k-1$ internally disjoint S-trees.

If $z_{10} \in \bigcup_{i=1}^{3k-3} V(P_i)$ and z_{10} is not the end vertex. Without loss of generality, suppose that $z_{10} \in V(P_{3k-3})$. Choose $3k-3$ vertices $x_{11}, y_1{}', y_2{}', \cdots, y_{3k-4}{}'$ from P_{11}^{k-1} such that x_{11} is the corresponding vertex of x and $y_i{}'$ is the corresponding vertex of y_i, $i = 1, 2, \cdots, 3k-4$, where y_i is an inner vertex of P_i. Let $Y = x_{11} \cup \bigcup_{i=1}^{3k-4} y_i$. By Lemma 2, there are $3k-3$ internally disjoint paths $Q_1{}', Q_2{}', \cdots, Q_{3k-3}{}'$ from z to Y in P_{11}^{k-1}. We can get $3k-3$ internally disjoint S-trees $T_i = P_i + \{y_i y_i{}'\} + Q_i$, $i = 1, 2, \cdots, 3k-4$ and $T_{3k-3} = P_{3k-3} + \{zz_{10}\}$.

Now we choose a (x_{14}, y_{14})-path $P_{x_{14}y_{14}}$ containing z_{14} in P_{14}^{k-1} and a (z, z_{14})-path $P_{zz_{14}}$ no containing x, and let $T_{3k-2} = P_{x_{14}y_{14}} + \{xx_{14}, yy_{14}\} + P_{zz_{14}}$. Moreover, choose a (x_{20}, y_{20})-path $P_{x_{20}y_{20}}$ containing z_{20} in P_{20}^{k-1} and a (z_{20}, z_{21})-path $P_{z_{20}z_{21}}$ in G_2, let $T_{3k-1} = P_{x_{20}y_{20}} + \{xx_{20}, yy_{20}\} + P_{z_{20}z_{21}} + \{zz_{21}\}$. Then $T_1, T_2, \cdots, T_{3k-1}$ are $3k-1$ internally disjoint S-trees.

If $z_{10} \in \bigcup_{i=1}^{3k-3} V(P_i)$ and z_{10} is the end vertex. The proof is similar to Case 1.2.1.

Case 1.3. x, y and z belong to the three distinct copies.

Without loss of generality, assume that $x \in P_{10}^{k-1}$, $y \in P_{11}^{k-1}$, and $z \in P_{12}^{k-1}$.

subcase 1.3.1. Three of x, y, z are mutual corresponding.

Let x_i, y_i, z_i be the neighbors of x, y, z in $P_{10}^{k-1}, P_{11}^{k-1}, P_{12}^{k-1}$, $i = 1, 2, \cdots, 3k-3$, respectively, then there exists a path P_i in C_5 connecting x_i, y_i and z_i for every i. We can get $3k-2$ internally disjoint S-trees, $T_i = P_i + \{xx_i, yy_i, zz_i\}$, $i = 1, 2, \cdots, 3k-3$ and $T_{3k-2} = \{xy, yz\}$. Furthermore, we can obtain $T_{3k-1} = P_{x_{20}y_{21}} + P_{y_{21}z_{22}} + \{xx_{20}, yy_{21}, zz_{22}\}$. Then $T_1, T_2, \cdots, T_{3k-1}$ are $3k-1$ internally disjoint S-trees.

subcase 1.3.2. Two of x, y, z are mutual corresponding.

Without loss of generality, let x is corresponding vertex of y.

Let $X = \{x_1, x_2, \cdots, x_{3k-3}\}$ be the neighborhood of x in P_{10}^{k-1}, $Y = \{y_1, y_2, \cdots, y_{3k-3}\}$ be the neighborhood of y in P_{11}^{k-1} and z_{10} is the corresponding vertex of z in P_{10}^{k-1}.

If $z_{10} \notin X$. Choose $3k - 3$ vertices $z_1, z_2, \cdots, z_{3k-3}$ distinct z from P_{12}^{k-1} such that z_i is the corresponding vertex of x_i in P_{12}^{k-1}, $i = 1, 2, \cdots, 3k - 3$. Let $Z = \{z_1, z_2, \cdots, z_{3k-3}\}$. By Lemma 2, there are $3k - 3$ internally disjoint paths $P_1, P_2, \cdots, P_{3k-3}$ from z to Z in P_{12}^{k-1}. We can find out $3k - 3$ internally disjoint S-trees $T_i = P_i + \{x_i y_i, y_i z_i, x x_i, y y_i\}$, $i = 1, 2, \cdots, 3k - 3$. Choose a (x_{14}, z_{14})-path $P_{x_{14} z_{14}}$ in P_{14}^{k-1} and a (z, z_{14})-path $P_{z z_{14}}$ containing z_{13}, let $T_{3k-2} = P_{x_{14} z_{14}} + P_{z z_{14}} + \{xy, x x_{14}\}$. Similarly, there are a path $P_{x_{22} z_{22}}$ in P_{22}^{k-1} and a path $P_{x_{20} x_{22}}$ containing y_{21} in G_2, let $T_{3k-1} = P_{x_{20} x_{22}} + P_{x_{22} z_{22}} + \{x x_{20}, y y_{21}, z z_{22}\}$. Then $T_1, T_2, \cdots, T_{3k-1}$ are $3k - 1$ internally disjoint S-trees.

If $z_{10} \in X$. Without loss of generality, assume that $z_{10} = x_1$. Choose $3k - 3$ vertices $z_1, z_2, \cdots, z_{3k-3}$ from P_{12}^{k-1} such that $z_1 = x_{12}, z_i \neq z$, where x_{12} is the corresponding vertex of x and z_i is the corresponding vertex of x_i in P_{12}^{k-1}, $i = 2, 3, \cdots, 3k - 3$. Let $Z = \{z_1, z_2, \cdots, z_{3k-3}\}$, by Lemma 2, there are $3k - 3$ internally disjoint paths $P_1, P_2, \cdots, P_{3k-3}$ from z to Z in P_{12}^{k-1}. Note that $P_1 = z x_{12}$ and x_i, y_i, z_i be mutual corresponding, $i = 2, 3, \cdots, 3k - 3$. Let $T_1 = \{x x_1, x_1 y_1, y_1 y\}$, $T_i = P_i + \{x x_i, x_i y_i, y_i z_i, y_i y\}$, $i = 2, \cdots, 3k - 3$ and $T_{3k-2} = P_1 + \{xy, x_{12}y\}$. Clearly, there are a path $P_{x_{20} x_{22}}$ containing y_{21} in G_2 and a path $P_{x_{22} z_{22}}$ in P_{22}^{k-1}. Let $T_{3k-1} = P_{x_{20} x_{22}} + P_{x_{22} z_{22}} + \{x x_{20}, y y_{21}, z z_{22}\}$. Then $T_1, T_2, \cdots, T_{3k-1}$ are $3k - 1$ internally disjoint S-trees.

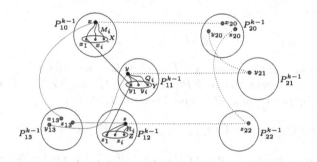

Fig. 6. The illustration of Case 1.3.3

subcase 1.3.3. None of x, y, z is mutual corresponding.

Without loss of generality, assume that $x \in P_{10}^{k-1}$, $y \in P_{11}^{k-1}$ and $z \in P_{12}^{k-1}$.

Let u, v, w be any three vertices in P^{k-1}. Since $10^{k-1} - 3 > 3k - 3$ for $k \geq 2$, there exists a vertex set $U \subseteq V(P^{k-1})$ with $|U| = 3k - 3$ such that $U \cap \{u, v, w\} = \emptyset$. It means that we can find the vertex sets $X = \{x_1, x_2, \cdots, x_{3k-3}\}$, $Y = \{y_1, y_2, \cdots, y_{3k-3}\}$ and $Z = \{z_1, z_2, \cdots, z_{3k-3}\}$ such that there are a (x, X)-fan, a (y, Y)-fan and a (z, Z)-fan in each $P_{10}^{k-1}, P_{11}^{k-1}, P_{12}^{k-1}$, and denoted M_i, Q_i, R_i by (x, x_i)-path, (y, y_i)-path and (z, z_i)-path, respectively, see Fig. 6. We can get $3k - 3$ internally disjoint S-trees $T_i = M_i + \{x_i y_i\} + Q_i + \{y_i z_i\} + R_i$, $i = 1, 2, \cdots, 3k - 3$.

Since x_{13}, y_{13}, z_{13} are the corresponding vertices of x, y, z in P_{13}^{k-1}, and x_{20}, y_{20}, z_{20} are the corresponding vertices of x, y, z in P_{20}^{k-1}. Choose a $\{x_{13}, y_{13}, z_{13}\}$-tree $\widehat{T}_{3k-2}$ in P_{13}^{k-1} and a $\{x_{20}, y_{20}, z_{20}\}$-tree $\widehat{T}_{3k-1}$ in P_{20}^{k-1}, let $T_{3k-2} = \widehat{T}_{3k-2} + P_{xx_{13}} + P_{yy_{13}} + \{zz_{13}\}$ and $T_{3k-1} = \widehat{T}_{3k-1} + P_{y_{20}y_{21}} + P_{z_{20}z_{22}} + \{xx_{20}, yy_{21}, zz_{22}\}$. Then $T_1, T_2, \cdots, T_{3k-1}$ are $3k-1$ internally disjoint S-trees.

Case 2. $|S \cap V(G_1)| = 2$.

Actually, there always exists a tree that relies on the corresponding vertices of x, y, z in G_2 by the discussion of Case 1. So we can gain symmetrically $3k-1$ internally disjoint S-trees in Case 2. The proof is similar to Case 1, and is omitted.

According to above discussions, there are always $3k-1$ internally disjoint S-trees for any $S \subseteq V(FP_k)$ with $|S| = 3$, that is, $\kappa_3(FP_k) \geq 3k-1$.

The proof is complete.

By the Lemma 8(i), we receive a lower bound of the 3-set tree connectivity on folded Petersen cube network directly.

Corollary 1. $\kappa_3(FPQ_{n,k}) \geq n + 3k - 2$ for $n, k \geq 1$.

In fact, by the Lemma 7(ii), we get the following result.

Theorem 2. $\kappa_3(FPQ_{n,k}) = n + 3k - 1$ for $n, k \geq 1$.

Proof. Since $\kappa(FP_k) = 3k > 3k - 1 = \kappa_3(FP_k)$, by the Lemma 7($ii$) and Theorem 1, we have

$$\kappa_3(FPQ_{1,k}) = \kappa_3(FP_k \square Q_1) \geq \kappa_3(FP_k) + 1 = 3k.$$

And the Lemma 1 implies that $\kappa_3(FPQ_{1,k}) \leq 3k$, then $\kappa_3(FPQ_{1,k}) = 3k$.

Similarly, we observe that $\kappa(FPQ_{1,k}) \geq \kappa(FP_k) + \kappa(Q_1) = 3k + 1 > 3k = \kappa_3(FPQ_{1,k})$, by the Lemma 7($ii$) and Theorem 1, we have

$$\kappa_3(FPQ_{2,k}) = \kappa_3(FPQ_{1,k} \square Q_1) \geq \kappa_3(FPQ_{1,k}) + 1 = 3k + 1.$$

And the Lemma 1 implies that $\kappa_3(FPQ_{2,k}) \leq 3k+1$, then $\kappa_3(FPQ_{2,k}) = 3k+1$. Successively, we can get $\kappa_3(FPQ_{n,k}) = n + 3k - 1$.

4   Conclusion

The ℓ-set tree connectivity is an essential consequence of the traditional connectivity and it provides a way to measure the fault tolerance capability of a network. We studied the 3-set tree connectivity of $FPQ_{n,k}$ and displayed that $\kappa_3(FPQ_{n,k}) = n + 3k - 1$. In the next work, we feel like learning the ℓ-set tree connectivity of $FPQ_{n,k}$ for $\ell \geq 4$.

References

1. Bondy, J.A., Murty, U.S.R.: Graph Theory. GTM, vol. 244. Springer, London (2008)
2. Chang, N.W., Tsai, C.Y., Hsieh, S.Y.: On 3-extra connectivity and 3-extra edge connectivity of folded hypercubes. IEEE Trans. Comput. **6**(63), 1594–1600 (2014)
3. Chartrand, G., Kapoor, S.F., Lesniak, L., Lick, D.R.: Generalized connectivity in graphs. Bombay Math. **2**, 1–6 (1984)
4. Chartrand, G., Okamoto, F., Zhang, P.: Rainbow trees in graphs and generalized connectivity. Networks **55**(4), 360–367 (2010)
5. Cheng, E., Lipman, M.J.: Increasing the connectivity of the star graphs. Networks **40**, 165–169 (2002)
6. Chen, Y.C., Hsu, L.H., Tan, J.M.: A recursively construction scheme for super fault tolerant Hamiltonian graphs. Appl. Math. Comput. **177**, 465–481 (2006)
7. Das, S.K., Öhring, S., Banejee, A.K.: Embeddings into hyper Petersen networks: yet another hypercube-like interconnection topology. J. VLSl Des. **2**, 335–351 (1995)
8. Efe, K., Blackwell, P.K., Slough, W., Shiau, T.: Topological properties of the crossed cube architecture. Parallel Comput. **20**, 1763–1775 (1994)
9. Esfahanian, A.H.: Generalized measures of fault tolerance with application to n-cube networks. IEEE Trans. Comput. **38**, 1586–1591 (1989)
10. Grötschel, M., Martin, A., Weismantel, R.: The Steiner tree packing problem in VLSI design. Math. Program. **78**, 265–281 (1997). https://doi.org/10.1007/BF02614374
11. Grötschel, M., Martin, A., Weismantel, R.: Packing Steiner trees: a cutting plane algorithm and computational results. Math. Program. **72**, 125–145 (1996). https://doi.org/10.1007/BF02592086
12. Hammack, R., Imrich, W., Klavžar, S.: Handbook of Product Graphs, 2nd edn. CRC Press, Boca Raton (2001)
13. Hsieh, S.-Y., Chang, Y.-H.: Extraconnectivity of k-ary n-cube networks. Theoret. Comput. Sci. **443**, 63–69 (2012)
14. Hsu, H.-C., Lin, C.-K., Hung, H.-M., Hsu, L.-H.: The spanning connectivity of the (n, k)-star graphs. Int. J. Found. Comput. Sci. **17**(2), 415–434 (2006)
15. Imrich, W., Klavžar, S.: Product Graphs Structure and Recongnition. Wiley, New York (2000)
16. Latifi, S.: Combinatorial analysis of the fault-diameter of n-cube. IEEE Trans. Comput. **42**, 27–33 (1993)
17. Li, S.S., Li, X.L., Zhou, W.L.: Sharp bounds for the generalized connectivity $\kappa_3(G)$. Discrete Math. **310**, 2147–2165 (2010)
18. Li, S.S.: Some topics on generalized connectivity of graphs. Ph.D. thesis, Nankai University (2012)
19. Li, S.S., Li, W., Li, X.: The generalized connectivity of complete bipartite graphs. Ars Comb. **104**, 65–79 (2012)
20. Li, H.Z., Li, X.L., Sun, Y.F.: The generalized 3-connectivity of Cartesian product graphs. Discrete Math. Theor. Comput. Sci. **14**, 43–54 (2012)
21. Li, S.S., Tu, J.H., Yu, C.Y.: The generalized 3-connectivity of star graphs and bubble-sort graphs. Appl. Math. Comput. **274**, 41–46 (2016)
22. Öhring, S.R., Das, S.K.: Folded Petersen cube networks: new competitors for the hypercubes. IEEE Trans. Parallel Distrib. Syst. **7**, 151–168 (1996)

23. Roskind, J., Tarjan, R.E.: A note on finding minimum-cost edge-disjoint spanning trees. Math. Oper. Res. **10**, 701–708 (1985)
24. Sabidussi, G.: Graphs with given group and given graph theoretical properties. Can. J. Math. **9**, 515–525 (1957)
25. Saxena, P.C., Gupta, S., Rai, J.: A delay optimal coterie on the k-dimensional folded Petersen graph. J. Parallel Distrib. Comput. **63**, 1026–1035 (2003)
26. Sherwani, N.: Algorithms for VLSI Physical Design Automation, 3rd edn. Kluwer Academic Publishers, London (1999)
27. Whitney, H.: Congruent graphs and connectivity of graphs. J. Am. Math. Soc. **54**, 150–168 (1932)
28. Yang, W.H., Li, H.: On reliability of the folded hypercubes in terms of the extra edge-connectivity. Inform. Sci. **272**, 238–243 (2014)

DFT Channel Estimation Algorithm Based on Dynamic Threshold Filtering in OFDM System

Lingfei Zhang[1], Tingting Xiang[2], Chen Liu[2(✉)], Yiting Zhao[1], and Cheng Xiong[1]

[1] College of Physics and Electronic Information Engineering, Qinghai Nationalities University, Xining 810007, China

[2] The Institute of Electronic CAD, Xidian University, Xi'an 710071, China
liuc@xidian.edu.cn

Abstract. With the increasing development of digital communications, it is necessary to use a larger transmission bandwidth to achieve a higher data transmission rate. Orthogonal Frequency Division Multiplexing (OFDM), as a multi-carrier transmission technology to increase the data transmission rate, has important research value. The accuracy of channel estimation in OFDM systems directly affects the quality of data transmission. How to improve the accuracy of channel estimation algorithms under low complexity has always been the focus of research in OFDM systems. This paper proposes an improved DFT channel estimation algorithm based on dynamic threshold filtering. Based on the traditional DFT channel estimation algorithm, two long training sequences (LTF) among the OFDM preamble sequences are used for least squares (LS) channel estimation, and the channel frequency responses of the two LTF sequences are summed and averaged to reduces the influence of Gaussian white noise in the wireless channel on the accuracy of the estimation result, and determines the sample points whose channel time domain impulse response after inverse fast Fourier transform (IFFT) is greater than the length of the cyclic prefix (CP) Training samples and extracting the noise characteristics of the noise training samples, using the noise characteristics to set a dynamic threshold to threshold filter the sample points within the cyclic prefix length, reducing the noise within the cyclic prefix length, and improving channel estimation performance 4 dB.

Keywords: Channel estimation · DFT · Threshold filtering · OFDM

1 Channel Estimation in OFDM Systems

1.1 OFDM System Model

OFDM is a widely used multi-carrier transmission technology. Compared with single-carrier transmission, multi-carrier transmission can carry out data transmission at a high rate, and multi-carrier system does not need complex equalization technology. The realization steps of modulation and demodulation in OFDM system are as follows.

X. Wang et al. (Eds.): AICON 2021, LNICST 397, pp. 305–314, 2021.
https://doi.org/10.1007/978-3-030-90199-8_28

The sending end inputs bit data, then carries out channel coding and interleaving on serial bit data, and then uses digital modulation to carry out constellation mapping on the interleaved bit stream, and converts the bit data stream into complex signals in frequency domain [1]. The frequency domain complex signals are inserted with pilot and virtual subcarriers, and N serial complex signals are converted into parallel symbols. Each complex signal in the parallel symbols is modulated by different subcarriers, and the transmitting end of OFDM system is modulated in the way of IFFT [2].

A Cyclic Prefix (CP) is added between the modulated symbols, the content of the cyclic prefix is a part of the data at the tail end of the current OFDM symbol, which is extracted and spliced to the head end of the current OFDM symbol [3]. After passing through IFFT, the data at the sending end is expressed as $x(t)$, which reaches the receiving end through the wireless channel. The impulse response of the channel is $h_l(t)$, and the lth OFDM symbol received by the receiving end is $y_l(t) = x_l(t) \otimes h_l(t) + z_l(t)$, where $\otimes$ represents circular convolution and $z_l(t)$ represents Gaussian white noise. The sampling interval t_s is used to sample y_l, and the sampled received signal can be expressed as Eq. (1).

$$y_l(n) = x_l(n) * h_l(n) + z_l = \sum_{m=0}^{\infty} h_l(m)x_l(n-m) + z_l(m) \qquad (1)$$

The common principle of adding cyclic prefixes is to convert linear convolution into cyclic convolution, which ensures the continuity of OFDM symbols in time domain. The orthogonality of different subcarriers in the same path and different subcarriers in different paths can be maintained. After the packet at the initiating terminal passes through a path with a delay time of t_0, the orthogonality relation of different subcarriers at the receiving end can be expressed as Eq. (2).

$$\frac{1}{T_{sym}} \int_0^{T_{sym}} e^{i2\pi f_i(t-t_0)} e^{-j2\pi f_j(t-t_0)} dt = 0 \ i \neq j \qquad (2)$$

For the subcarrier f_i in the received data with a delay time of t_0, the mutual orthogonal relation between it and the subcarrier with a delay time of $t_0 + t_s$ can be expressed as Eq. (3).

$$\frac{1}{T_{sym}} \int_0^{T_{sym}} e^{i2\pi f_i(t-t_0)} e^{-j2\pi f_j(t-t_0-t_s)} dt = 0 \ i \neq j \qquad (3)$$

Equation (1) and Eq. (2) show that the cyclic prefix can guarantee orthogonality between subcarriers. According to the above analysis, during the construction of the data at the sending end, the length of CP, L_{CP}, will be set to be greater than the length of the maximum path delay, L_h. Since there is no path loss in the first path, the energy intensity of the first path is also the largest. As the delay time increases, the energy intensity of the first path generally decreases exponentially, and most of the energy is concentrated in the first few paths [4]. The energy intensity value of time-domain impulse response of the channel decreases gradually, and the amplitude value of channel frequency also fluctuates with the increase of delay time, indicating that the frequency selectivity in the channel is obvious, and signals of different frequencies will undergo different fading through the channel. Therefore, according to this characteristic of multi-path channel, the multi-path with strong energy can be extracted.

1.2 Channel Modeling

Modeling of wireless communication channels mainly includes modeling of two aspects, one is the multipath delay, and the other is the time variation caused by Doppler frequency offset. The schematic diagram of its modelling (see Fig. 1). The fading simulator emulates the time variability caused by Doppler frequency offset, the parameters a_i and τ_i in the figure simulate the multipath effect, where a_i represents the amplitude value of the i path and τ_i represents its corresponding delay [5]. Common wireless channel models include JAKE model, Clarkes/Gans model, IEEE 802.11 model and AR model.

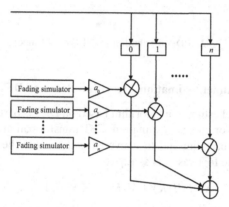

Fig. 1. Schematic diagram of wireless channel modeling.

In outdoor channel modeling, due to the rapid movement of mobile terminals, it will bring. Doppler shift, while in indoor channel modeling, the moving speed of terminal is slow or static. Generally, only the influence of multipath effect on the wireless channel is considered. IEEE802.11 channel model is a typical indoor channel model. The average power of each path in the channel model follows exponential distribution, and can be modeled as a tap of a FIR. The taps corresponding to each path satisfy the Gaussian random distribution in amplitude. Then the average power of each path in the channel can be expressed as Eq. (4).

$$P(l) = \frac{1}{\tau_d}e^{-\frac{lT_s}{\tau_d}} \ l = 0, 1, \cdots, l_{\max} \tag{4}$$

Maximum delay of multipath is $\tau_m = 10\tau_d$ and τ_d is RMS delay extension, $l_{\max} = [10\tau_d/T_s]$, $l_{\max}$ represents the time label of the path corresponding to the maxi-mum path delay and T_s is the sampling period. Through normalizing energy of Eq. (4), the average power of each path after normalization can be obtained as follows Eq. (5).

$$P(l) = P(0)e^{-lT_s/\tau_d} \tag{5}$$

where, $P(0) = 1/P_{ada}\tau_d$, P_{ada} is the sum of energy of all paths. The PDP for each tap o-f the IEEE 802.11 channel model is shown as follows (see Fig. 2).

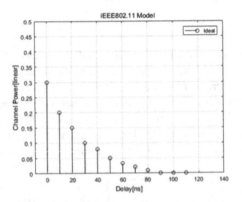

Fig. 2. PDP distribution of IEEE802.11 model

1.3 Traditional Channel Estimation Algorithm Based on DFT

The traditional channel estimation algorithm based on DFT is based on the LS channel estimation algorithm for channel estimation. FFT transformation is carried out on the received data at the receiving end to convert the data from the time domain to the frequency domain. The FFT result is as Eq. (6).

$$Y(K) = X(K)H(K) + V(K) \quad K = 0, 1, \ldots\ldots, N-1 \tag{6}$$

N in Eq. (4) represents the length of an OFDM symbol, which can be specified by the non-VHT signal domain. Assuming that each subcarrier at the receiving end is orthogonal to each other, $Y(K)$ can be expressed as follow Eq. (7).

$$
\begin{bmatrix} Y(0) \\ Y(1) \\ Y(2) \\ . \\ . \\ . \\ Y(N-1) \end{bmatrix} = \begin{bmatrix} X(0) & 0 & 0 & \cdots & 0 \\ 0 & X(1) & 0 & \cdots & 0 \\ 0 & 0 & X(2) & \cdots & 0 \\ 0 & 0 & 0 & \cdots & 0 \\ 0 & 0 & 0 & \cdots & 0 \\ 0 & 0 & 0 & \cdots & 0 \\ 0 & 0 & 0 & \cdots & X(N-1) \end{bmatrix} \begin{bmatrix} H(0) \\ H(1) \\ H(2) \\ . \\ . \\ . \\ H(N-1) \end{bmatrix} + \begin{bmatrix} V(0) \\ V(1) \\ V(2) \\ . \\ . \\ . \\ V(N-1) \end{bmatrix}
$$

$$\tag{7}$$

The cost function of LS estimation method can be expressed as $C = ||\overline{Y} - X\overline{H}||^2$, when the cost function gets the minimum value, we can get Eq. (8).

$$\hat{H}_{LS} = \overline{X}^{-1}(\overline{X}^H)^{-1}\overline{X}^H\overline{Y} = \overline{X}^{-1}\overline{Y} \tag{8}$$

In the traditional channel estimation algorithm based on DFT, the noise beyond the length of the loop prefix is set to zero in order to suppress the noise beyond the length

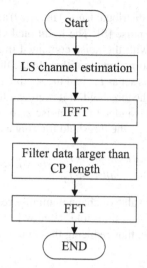

Fig. 3. PDP distribution of IEEE802.11 model

of the loop prefix [7]. The flow diagram of the channel estimation as shown as follows (see Fig. 3).

The implementation steps are as follows.

Step 1. The LS channel estimation method is used to estimate the channel frequency domain response as Eq. (9).

$$H_{ls}(k) = Y_{ls}(k)/X_{ls}(k) = H(k) + Z_l(k) \quad k = 0, 1, \cdots N - 1 \tag{9}$$

Step 2. IFFT is performed on $H_{ls}(k)$ to obtain the channel time-domain impulse response as Eq. (10).

$$h_l(n) = \sum_{k=0}^{N-1} H_{ls}(k)e^{-j2\pi kn} \quad k = 0, 1, \cdots N - 1 \tag{10}$$

Step 3. According to the relationship between the multipath channel and the cyclic prefix, the time-domain impulse response is filtered and de-noised to preserve the multipath with strong energy. The time-domain impulse response sample points larger than the length of the cyclic prefix are set to zero, and the time-domain impulse response sample points smaller than the length of the cyclic prefix are retained, and the following results can be obtained Eq. (11).

$$h(n) = \begin{cases} h_l(n) & 0 \le n \le L_{cp} - 1 \\ 0 & n > L_{cp} \end{cases} \tag{11}$$

Step 4. The $h(n)$ in Eq. (12) is FFT to obtain the channel frequency domain response after get rid of the noise.

$$H(K) = \sum_{n=0}^{N-1} h(n)e^{-j2\pi kn} \quad n = 0, 1, \cdots N-1 \tag{12}$$

Since the noise is randomly distributed, $h_l(n)$ in Eq. (9) actually contains the real time-domain channel response and noise [8]. The traditional channel estimation algorithm based on DFT does not deal with the noise contained in it, so it can be improved on the traditional DFT channel estimation algorithm. In the threshold filtering with a fixed threshold, the threshold value is set as L_p, and the sample point within the length of the cycle prefix is compared with the threshold. If it is greater than the threshold, the sample point is retained, otherwise, it is judged to be noise zero [9], then the channel impulse response in the time domain after the threshold filtering as Eq. (13).

$$h(n) = \begin{cases} h_l(n) & h_l(n) > L_p \\ 0 & h_l(n) < L_p \end{cases} \quad 0 \le n \le L_{cp} - 1 \tag{13}$$

However, when the energy value of channel impulse response in time domain is less than the threshold value, the fixed threshold value will misjudge the channel impulse response sample value as noise, thus reducing the accuracy of the judgment result.

2 Improved DFT Channel Estimation Algorithm Based on Time-Domain Threshold Filtering

2.1 OFDM System Model

The improved DFT channel estimation algorithm proposed in this paper carries out threshold filtering on the sample points within the length of the circular prefix. Aiming at the shortcomings of the traditional DFT algorithm and DFT algorithm based on fixed threshold decision, the time-domain threshold filtering proposed in this paper sets a dynamic threshold. The sample points whose channel impulse response after IFFT is larger than the length of the cyclic prefix (CP) are judged as the noise training samples. The noise characteristics of the noise training samples are extracted, and the dynamic threshold is set by the noise characteristics to carry out threshold filtering on the sample points within the length of the cyclic prefix, so as to reduce the noise within the length of the cyclic prefix. The flow chart of the improved time-domain threshold filtering DFT channel estimation algorithm is given (see Fig. 4).

This algorithm reduces the probability that the data point is determined as noise by the fixed threshold value. The receiving end receives the time domain signal sent by the sending end, then carries out AD conversion and serial-parallel conversion, and then converts the CP removed signal into frequency domain signal by FFT. The specific implementation steps are as follows.

Step 1. First we need to do an initial LS estimate for the channel. The LS estimation algorithm adopted in this paper uses the leading sequence in OFDM data frame to estimate the channel frequency domain response. The leading sequence is the known data inserted at the initial position of the data frame, and the receiver can use these known leading sequences to construct local sequences to synchronize or estimate the channel of the data at the receiver. Using the two long training sequences of the receiving end after FFT transformation and the local long training sequence of the sending end, the LS channel estimation is carried out respectively, then H_{1LS} and H_{2LS} are obtained. Assuming that the channel frequency response is basically unchanged in the two LTF

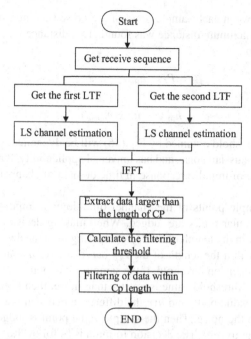

Fig. 4. Improved flow chart of time-domain threshold DFT channel estimation algorithm

lengths, the sum and average of H_{1LS} and H_{2LS} can reduce the influence of Gaussian white noise on the estimation performance. The estimated result is $H_{LS12} = (H_{1LS} + H_{2LS})/2$.

Step 2. IFFT is performed on H_{2LS} to obtain the channel's time-domain impulse response as Eq. (14).

$$h(n) = \frac{1}{N} \sum_{k=0}^{N} H_{LS12}(k)e^{j2\pi kn/N} \quad 0 \le n \le N - 1 \tag{14}$$

Step 3. Calculate the filtering threshold. According to the traditional channel estimation algorithm, the sample point of channel impulse response within the loop prefix length contains both signal and noise, while the sample point outside the loop prefix contains only noise. The length of the cycle prefix is defined as L_{CP}. According to the theoretical knowledge of discrimination and classification, the data in the time domain impulse response can be divided into two categories: one is the data containing only noise greater than L_{CP} length, and the other is the data less than L_{CP} length. The data greater than the length of L_{CP} is used as the noise training sample $h_{noise} = \{h_{cp+1}, h_{cp}, \ldots, h_k, \ldots, h_N\}$, in this way, noise characteristics extracted from noise training samples can be used to discriminate and extract the noise within the circular prefix. The mean value of the noise training sample is calculated to obtain the center of gravity ave of Gaussian white noise as Eq. (15).

$$ave = \frac{1}{N - L_{CP}} \sum_{k=CP}^{N-1} h_k \tag{15}$$

The distance between each sample point of the noise training sample and *ave* was calculated, and the maximum distance was found. This distance was taken as the noise judgment threshold p_l.

$$P_l = h_{max} - ave \tag{16}$$

$$h_{max} = \max(h_{noise}) \tag{17}$$

The judgment threshold obtained by Eq. (16) will be dynamically adjusted with the amplitude of white Gaussian noise, and has universal applicability. It avoids the problem that the energy value of impulse response in time domain of channel is too high and is misjudged as noise.

Step 4. The sample points of the channel time-domain impulse response within the length of the circular prefix are judged. When making decision, this paper is not directly the data within the length of the L_{cp} comparing with the decision threshold, but the sample values within the length of the L_{cp} barycenter of *ave* and noise difference comparing with the decision threshold, if the sample value point and *ave* the difference between the decision threshold value is greater than noise, then keep the sample value point, if the sample value point and *ave* the difference between the decision threshold value is greater than the noise, Then the sample value point is judged as noise and its amplitude value is set to zero. The decision formula is as follow Eq. (18).

$$h_f(r) = \begin{cases} h(n) & if \ |h(n) - ave| > P_l \\ 0 & otherwise \end{cases} \quad 0 \leq n \leq L_{cp} - 1 \tag{18}$$

Step 5. The $h_{f(r)}$ after the decision obtained in the fourth step is FFT to obtain the channel frequency response $H(k)$.

3 Simulation Analysis

In order to compare the performance of the improved DFT channel estimation algorithm based on time-domain threshold filtering with the traditional DFT channel estimation algorithm, the SNR value range of the constructed OFDM system is 0 dB–25 dB, and the value interval of the SNR is 1 dB. 50 packets are constructed at the sending end and sent to the receiving end in a circular manner. The channel between the sending and receiving terminals is modeled by using IEEE802.11 model. Its simulation parameters are shown in Table 1. Based on channel estimation algorithm of DFT and the improved dynamic threshold channel estimation algorithm in this paper, the classical frequency domain LS channel estimation algorithm and MMSE channel estimation algorithm are respectively used to estimate the channel frequency domain response and conduct channel equalization at the receiving end. Demodulation and decoding of the equalized frequency domain data can be carried out to calculate the bit error rate corresponding to different channel estimation algorithms (see Fig. 5).

As can be seen from the Fig. 5, when BER is 10^{-4}, the SNR required by the channel estimation algorithm of the improved dynamic threshold filter is 4 dB lower than that o-f

Table 1. System simulation parameters.

Modulation scheme	16QAM
Multi-path delay	120 ns
Number of carriers	64
Circular prefix (CP) length	16
Pilot position	$-21, -7, 7, 21$
Channel model	IEE802.11 model

the traditional LS channel estimation algorithm, and 3dB lower than that of the traditional DFT channel estimation algorithm, which is basically consistent with the SNR required by the MMSE channel estimation algorithm. However, due to the need to invert the matrix in the MMSE channel estimation algorithm, its hardware implementation is difficult, and the improved threshold filtering channel estimation algorithm proposed in this paper has low implementation complexity and good practical application value.

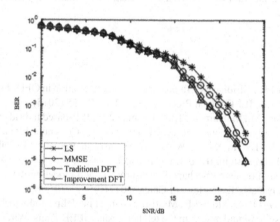

Fig. 5. Performance simulation diagram of different channel estimation algorithms

Different modulation modes will also affect the BER of the system. BPSK, QPSK and 16QAM are respectively selected to carry out bit mapping on the transmitted data at the sending end of OFDM, and a packet with a length of 10 is constructed, and each packet contains 200 OFDM symbols. The corresponding modulation mode is demodulated at the receiving end. The improved DFT channel estimation algorithm is adopted to estimate and equalize the channel, and the SNR_BER comparison diagram of algorithm performance under different modulation modes can be obtained (see Fig. 6).

As can be seen from Fig. 6, in the case of the same SNR for the three modulation modes of BPSK, QPSK and 16QAM, the system BER of the improved DFT channel estimation algorithm is all lower than that of the unimproved DFT channel estimation algorithm. It is shown that the performance of the improved DFT channel estimation algorithm is better than that of the traditional DFT channel estimation algorithm under different modulation modes.

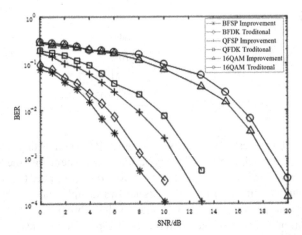

Fig. 6. Performance diagram of improved DFT channel estimation algorithm under different modulation modes

References

1. Raghavendra, M.R., Giridhar, K.: Improving channel estimation in OFDM systems for sparse multipath channels. IEEE Signal Process. Lett. **12**(1), 52–55 (2015)
2. Takano, Y., Juntti, M., Matsumoto, T.: $\ell 1$ LS and $\ell 2$ MMSE-based hybrid channel estimation for intermittent wireless connections. IEEE Trans. Wirel. Commun. **15**(1), 314–328 (2016)
3. Liu, G., Zeng, L., Li, H., Xu, L., Wang, Z.: Adaptive interpolation for pilot-aided channel estimator in OFDM system. IEEE Trans. Broadcast. **60**(3), 486–498 (2014)
4. Tang, Y.: Research on wireless channel measurement and modeling methods. University of Electronic Science and Technology of China (2017)
5. Han, C., Bicen, A.O., Akyildiz, I.F.: Multi-ray channel modeling and wideband characterization for wireless communications in the terahertz band. IEEE Trans. Wirel. Commun. **14**(5), 2402–2412 (2015)
6. Zhang, Y., Gelfand, S.B., Fitz, M.P.: Soft-output demodulation on frequency-selective Rayleigh fading channels using AR channel models. IEEE Trans. Commun. **55**(10), 1929–1939 (2007)
7. Fan, R., Mu, F., Su, M.: Improved DFT channel estimation algorithm based on pilot frequency for OFDM systems. J. Nanjing Univ. Posts Telecommunications (Nat. Sci. Ed.) **35**(02), 79–83 (2015)
8. Xiong, X., Jiang, B., Gao, X., You, X.: DFT-based channel estimator for OFDM systems with leakage estimation. IEEE Commun. Lett. **17**(8), 1592–1595 (2013)
9. Ma, C., Xiao, C., Zhu, J., Lai, Y., Chen, Y.: Improved threshold filtering algorithm based on DFT transform channel estimation. Acta Scientiarum Naturalium Universitatis Nankaiensis **47**(06), 11–14 (2014)
10. You, S.D.: Channel estimation with iterative discrete Fourier transform-based smoothing for orthogonal frequency-division multiplexing systems with non-uniformly spaced pilots in channels with long delay spread. IET Commun. **8**(17), 2984–2992 (2014)

Author Index

Printed in the United States
by Baker & Taylor Publisher Services

Printed in the United States
by Baker & Taylor Publisher Services